INSIDE THE ARK

NEW EDITION

INSIDE THE ARK

*The Hutterites in Canada
and the United States*

YOSSI KATZ & JOHN LEHR

University of Regina Press

Printed and bound in Canada at Friesens.
The text of this book is printed on 100% post-consumer recycled paper with earth-friendly vegetable-based inks.

Index prepared by Judy Dunlop.

Cover image: "Lambing Shed, Surprise Creek Colony" by Julie Melton, juliemeltonphotography.com. Used by permission.

Library and Archives Canada Cataloguing in Publication
Kats, Yosef, author
Inside the ark : the Hutterites in Canada and the United States / Yossi Katz & John Lehr.—New edition.

Revision of Inside the ark, originally published under the title Be-emunatam yiḥeyu. Includes bibliographical references and index.
Issued in print and electronic formats.
ISBN 978-0-88977-358-5 (pbk.).—ISBN 978-0-88977360-8 (pdf).—ISBN 978-0-88977-359-2 (html)

1. Hutterian Brethren—Canada—History. 2. Hutterian Brethren—United States—History. I. Lehr, John, author II. Title.

BX8129.H8K3813 2014   289.7'3   C2014-906067-X   C2014-906068-8

10 9 8 7 6 5 4 3 2 1

University of Regina Press, University of Regina
Regina, Saskatchewan, Canada, s4s 0A2
TEL: (306) 585-4758 FAX: (306) 585-4699
WEB: www.uofrpress.ca

U OF R PRESS

The University of Regina Press acknowledges the support of the Creative Industry Growth and Sustainability program, made possible through funding provided to the Saskatchewan Arts Board by the Government of Saskatchewan through the Ministry of Parks, Culture, and Sport. We also acknowledge the financial support of the Government of Canada through the Canada Book Fund for our publishing activities. We acknowledge the support of the Canada Council for the Arts for our publishing program.

This book has been published with the help of a grant from the Canadian Federation for the Humanities and Social Sciences, through the Awards to Scholarly Publications Program, using funds provided by the Social Sciences and Humanities Research Council of Canada.

Contents

Acknowledgements

THIS BOOK HAS BEEN PUBLISHED WITH THE HELP OF A grant from the Canadian Federation for the Humanities and Social Sciences, through the Awards to Scholarly Publications Program, using funds provided by the Social Sciences and Humanities Research Council of Canada.

The Chair of German-Canadian Studies at the University of Winnipeg provided a grant to partially fund the translation of the *Ordnungen und Konferenz Briefen* [sic] from the original German.

The D.F. Plett Historical Research Foundation, at the University of Winnipeg, provided a grant to assist with the reproduction of maps and photographs for this volume.

The authors gratefully acknowledge the financial assistance received from these organizations.

PREFACE

to the New Edition (2014)

SINCE THE FIRST EDITION OF *Inside the Ark* WENT TO press some three years ago Hutterite society has continued to evolve and scholarship examining the Hutterites has continued to appear. This new edition affords us an opportunity to incorporate this new scholarship into our work, correct the seemingly inevitable errors of spelling and syntax, and update population figures and appendices 1, 4, and 5.

During the last few years a number of events have shocked Hutterite society. The *National Geographic* television reality series set in the Dariusleut Kings Ranch Colony in Montana scandalized all the leute, who rejected it as a sensationalized, contrived, and inaccurate portrayal of colony life. This was followed shortly afterwards by the release of an inflammatory book by nine young former Hutterites, rationalizing their decision to leave their communities and join an evangelical church. For the first time, individuals from within the Hutterite community responded publicly through social media. Blogs and tweets from the colonies repudiating the contentions of "the nine" showed the extent to which the digital revolution has begun to transform the relationship between the colonies and the outside world. We welcome the opportunity to comment, albeit briefly, upon these developments.

Outside of the Prairies and Great Plains, where Hutterites are not generally known to the population at large, documentary programs, such as the one filmed by the BBC at Maple Grove Colony in Manitoba and broadcast in the United Kingdom, tend to focus on the deficiencies of the Hutterite way as identified by those who choose to leave and make their way in the outside world. The concern of the liberal democracies with individual rights rather than with individual responsibilities and community rights, together with the increasing secularization of society, has meant many popular appraisals of Hutterite society are somewhat jaundiced, if not hostile. It is easy to find fault with any social organization, less easy to analyze it from a dispassionate standpoint. We hope that this book will help toward the understanding of a remarkably complex and often misunderstood community.

Shortly after the appearance of the first edition of *Inside the Ark* some sharp-eyed readers spotted omissions and errors and were kind enough to notify us about them. In this regard we would particularly like to thank Tighe McMannus and Dr. Alvin Kienetz of Winnipeg. Dr. Kienetz also ensured any German terms in the book were used in a grammatically correct fashion. We also want to thank Dan Katz for agreeing to write an account of his return visit to James Valley Colony, this time as a married man in his twenties. This new account serves as a counterpoint to his earlier impressions of the colony as a teenager (Appendix 4).

John Hofer, the First Minister of James Valley Colony, kindly provided the 2009–2012 *Ordnungen und Konferenz Briefen* of the Group Two Schmiedeleut, which enables us to provide a complete record of the ordinances and conference letter from 1772 to the present day. They were translated from the German by David Fuss. Cartographer Weldon Hiebert at the Department of Geography, University of Winnipeg, used information provided by Patrick Murphy from James Valley Colony to update the map showing the distribution of colonies in 2014. We thank them all.

Since the publication of the first edition of *Inside the Ark* the authors have continued to visit their Hutterite friends and have been privileged to visit and attend social events at James Valley and other colonies. We extend our thanks for their friendship and unfailingly generous hospitality.

—John Lehr, Winnipeg, Canada.
—Yossi Katz, K'far Tavor, Israel.

PREFACE

to the First Edition (2012)

VISIONS OF COMMUNAL LIFE, WITH TRUE EQUALITY BE-
tween all members of society, have inspired generations of
idealists. Communal living appears to be a simple concept
but it is one that has been frustratingly difficult to attain;
indeed, history is littered with the wreckage of attempts to create
egalitarian societies based on the principles of shared wealth and
subscription to common ideals. The Soviet Kolkoz in Russia and
the Kholhosp in Ukraine are no more; Chinese collective farms
have disappeared and, in the Americas, the Mormons' Orderville
and other 19th and early 20th century utopian experiments in
communal life have largely faded from the landscape. Worldwide,
scholars from a wide variety of disciplines have pondered why
some communal societies flourished and others failed. In Israel,
especially, the academic community has devoted considerable attention to the study of communal society, an interest that is far
from surprising given that Israel is the home of the kibbutz, one
of the best-known examples of communal living and the largest
surviving system of communal life. Since the collapse of the Soviet
Union and China's embrace of capitalism during the last decade
of the 20th century, there are only two communal agricultural
systems of any significance in the world today: the kibbutzim and
the colonies of the Hutterian Brethren in North America. Even

before the decline of political communism, the kibbutz and the Hutterite colonies were rare examples of voluntary collectivism. Since both institutions are driven by ideology and religious conviction, each has long been fascinated by the workings of the other.

Communal life is an idealistic concept whose implementation is fraught with difficulties. The kibbutz and the colony thus share many common concerns. The greatest challenge is to overcome the natural tendency to place one's loyalty to family before that of the community at large, and to sacrifice self-interest in favour of the needs of the community. The challenges of governance in a communal society are many, not least the difficulty of maintaining the political or religious fervour necessary to retain deep commitment to the ideology of communal life.

Since the kibbutz system ranked among the better-known and more open systems of communal life, it is not surprising that there is a rich literature dealing with the kibbutzim. The pioneer of the kibbutz research, Zigfried Landshut, devoted a major part of his book, *The Kvuza* (published in Hebrew in 1944) to the discussion of collective communities in the world, before he began his discussion of the kibbutz itself.[1] It is only natural that kibbutz members have always been especially interested in other communes, and the kibbutz was the home of the researchers who wrote essays on communes in Hebrew. Some of them, for example, are David Knaani, member of Kibbutz Merchavia, who wrote the book, *Batei Midot: the Communes and their Consequences* (1960);[2] Shalom Worm, member of Kibbutz Ramat Yochanan, whose book of essays on the communes, *Communes and Their Way of Life*, was published in 1968;[3] Professor Yaacov Oved, a member of Kibbutz Palmachim, and one of the most renowned researchers who has been studying the subject for decades, wrote *Two Hundred Years of American Communes*, and *Testimony of the Brothers: The Communes of the Bruderhof*, and, more recently, in Hebrew, *Communes and Intentional Communities in Second Half of the 20th Century*.[4] Menachem Shadmi, a member of Kibbutz Maabrot, authored *Communes in the World and the Kibbutz*;[5] Shlomo Shalmon, from Kibbutz Gesher, wrote *The Niderkaufungen Community*, 1996;[6] and Dr. Shlomo Shealtiel who wrote an essay, "The Zadaroga and the circumstances of its disintegration," were all veterans of communal life.[7] During their trips abroad, many kibbutz members were eager to visit Hutterite colonies in order to get to know their "distant brothers." Their enthusiastic impressions were expressed in the kibbutz movement papers such as *Niv Hakvuza, Mibifnim, Alonim,* and *Amudim.* Some of these impressions were published in Yaacov Oved's essay, *Distant Brothers: The History of Relations Between the Bruderhof and the Kibbutz.*[8] It was Yaacov Oved who, in 1985, established the "section for the study of the communes' history" in the Institute for Research and Teaching in Yad Tabenkin, and Mordechai Bentov, member of Kibbutz Mishmar HaEmek, in 1981 initiated the "International Communes Desk" which operates in Yad Tabenkin. Both sections promote studies and publications on the subject of communes throughout the world.

After the Israeli kibbutz, the Hutterite community is considered the largest communal-agricultural community in the world. Today [2012], there are about 40,000 Hutterites in 480 colonies, most of which are located in western Canada. Unlike the kibbutzim, which are mostly secular and socialist, the communal life in the Hutterite community is based on Christian religious beliefs and principles. An underlying tenet of the Hutterites is that in order to maintain their religious integrity and express it through the practise of communal life they must isolate themselves from the outside world. The rural colony system is thus integral and vital to the practise of their faith.

It is not surprising that the Hutterites have fascinated scholars from a variety of disciplines in Israel, North America and Europe who have described their colony system from a variety of perspectives.[9] Best known are Victor Peters' *All Things Common*; John A. Hostetler's books, *The Hutterites in North America, Hutterite Life,* and *Hutterite Society*; John W. Bennett's *Hutterian Brethren: The Agricultural Economy and Social Organization of a Communal People*; and John Hofer's more recent, *The History of the Hutterites,* all of which give an account of the Hutterites' history of migration and explain the bases of Hutterite belief and their social organization.[10] John Ryan examined the economic geography of Hutterite agriculture in Manitoba in some detail and also provided a general introductory overview of Hutterites in Canada from a geographical perspective in a short 1985 article.[11] Various aspects of Hutterite life have been the subjects of numerous articles that have ranged from studies of those who have left the colony, to the genetics of the Hutterites as a religious/ethnic group. Matters that are normally internal concerns of the group continue to fascinate scholars from a range of disciplines when they intersect with the interests of the outside world. Karl Peter examined the dynamics of

Hutterite society in the mid-1980s and pointed out that statistical data alone are not reliable indicators of the state of the Hutterite community. He emphasized that participant observation and case studies are of value only if obtained from "inside the wall of secrecy, that is to say, under conditions of trust."[12] Geographers Simon Evans and John Everitt have respectively discussed the spatial implications of nativism on Hutterite colony expansion and on the Hutterite perception of their world.[13] Hutterite migrations are mapped in William Schroeder's *Hutterite Migrations in Europe*, while colony diffusion in North America from 1874 until 2004 has also been mapped by geographers.[14]

Scholars from other disciplines have studied particular aspects of Hutterite life, such as child-rearing practices, often comparing the Hutterites with the Woodcrest Bruderhof.[15] Events leading to the schism in the Schmiedeleut are well covered by Preston and Samuel Hofer.[16] In 2004, Law Professor Alvin Esau from the University of Manitoba provided a detailed account of the intra-group tensions that erupted into a complex legal battle fought in the Manitoba courts and which triggered the split in the Schmiedeleut.[17]

Hutterite and secular worlds most commonly collide when a colony member decides to leave the group and reside away from the colony in "the world." Former Hutterite colony members have recently published two books. Samuel Hofer's *The Hutterites: Lives and Images of a Communal People* is remarkable for its excellent photographic images of everyday Hutterite life and its succinct but insightful explanation of the recent split in the Schmiedeleut.[18] Mary-Ann Kirkby spent her early years as a Hutterite but left with her parents when she was 10 tears old. In *I Am Hutterite*, she paints a fond portrait of her life as a child on a Hutterite colony but her account of her parents' decision to leave seems to be based largely on her parents' version of events.[19] Her rather harsh indictment of some aspects of colony life and colony governance is rather one-sided. Many familiar with her former colony, people well acquainted with the principal actors involved in her family's decision to leave the colony, are sceptical of the version of events given in her book.

While there is a fairly extensive literature describing various facets of the Hutterite history and theology, it is not easy to gain personal insights into the Hutterite way of life because their colonies are essentially closed communities. While hundreds, if not thousands, of people in Canada and the United States have visited a Hutterite colony, most do so as members of an organized group that is escorted around the colony, having access only to public and semi-public spaces such as the colony kitchen, dining hall, school and church. It is not easy to penetrate more deeply into Hutterite colonies, for strangers are not always welcome guests. A rare exception is Michael Holzach's *The Forgotten People: A Year Among the Hutterites*, which gives an intimate account of a year spent on an Alberta Dariusleut colony.[20]

Hutterites have themselves explained the basic tenets of their philosophy and religious beliefs in a number of publications, most of which enjoyed only limited circulation. John Hofer's *The History of the Hutterites* is well known and informative as is Paul Gross' book, *The Hutterite Way*.[21] Histories and descriptions of individual colonies are rare.[22]

While an outsider may paste together a picture of Hutterite life from a colony tour supplemented by a reading of such published materials, the dated, fragmentary, and biased nature of the literature complicates the issue. Nevertheless, while one may piece together a picture of daily life upon a colony, it would be impossible to find any study that addresses threats to the Hutterite way of life posed by the intrusion of modern communications technology. The advent of computers, the Internet, cell-phones and so forth, have diminished the insularity and isolation of the Hutterites from the outside world. Improvements in roads and vehicles have had a similar effect. Here we attempt to evaluate the effects of these technological intrusions, the strategies employed by the Hutterite leaders to manage the penetration of the outside world into the colony, and consider the future of the Hutterite colony system as arks on the prairies.

This book has a long genesis. In 1975, the late Larry Anderson, Professor of Geography at Mankato State University in Minnesota, introduced Professor John Lehr to the Reverend John Hofer, minister of James Valley Colony. Over the years Professor Lehr visited the Reverend Hofer's colony at James Valley on an occasional basis, both with Professor Anderson and his students, and also escorting his own students and visiting groups on field trips to the colony. During a sabbatical leave that I (Yossi Katz) spent in Canada in 1998–1999, Professor Lehr and Professor John Everett of Bandon University were anxious for me to visit a Hutterite colony, knowing of my interest in communal life as expressed in the Israeli kibbutz, and the obvious parallels that could be drawn between them. Subsequent visits to James Valley and Decker Colonies in Manitoba sparked my interest in this remarkable group whose members live by their faith and, indeed, express their faith everyday through their commitment to their communal lifestyle. In both kibbutz and colony, members lead a full communal life and are bound to the concept of communal living by deep ideological commitments: to socialist principles by the kibbutzim and to Christian beliefs by the Hutterites.

During the 1990s, the authors visited (together or individually) Decker Colony in Manitoba, Forest River and Maple River colonies in North Dakota and, many times, James Valley Colony near Winnipeg, Manitoba. We both became welcome guests in James Valley and good friends with the minister of the colony, John Hofer. The minister in each colony is the leader of the colony, and is the most important religious authority in the colony, its spiritual leader, a preacher, and also the president of its economic organization. Reverend Hofer is one of the most influential members of the Schmiedeleut, one of the three *leute,* or groups, that comprise the Hutterite church. The other two leute are the Dariusleut and the Lehrerleut. The Schmiedeleut themselves split into two factions in the early 1990s after a complex dispute concerning Church governance and procedures.

The Hutterites' decision to isolate themselves is based upon deep theological grounds, and is one of the reasons to their cautious attitude to visits from strangers. I (Yossi Katz) was lucky that my first appointments with the Hutterites were with the Schmiedeleut, which are considered more open to the outside world. The other two leute guard their privacy more zealously, and were it not for the help of friends from the Schmiedeleut colonies, it would not have been possible to later visit the Lehrerleut colonies. However, an attempt during the summer of 2005 to visit one of the Dariusleut colonies without making prior arrangements was unsuccessful.

Research during the early 1990s into the history of the religious kibbutz movement and its settlement, summarized in my book, *The Religious Kibbutz*, published in 1996, raised my curiosity and heightened my interest in the Hutterites.[23] It seemed to me then that, in many ways, the Hutterites most of all resemble the religious kibbutzim. And indeed, in the late 1990s, Professor Lehr and I started comparative research into the two movements. At the same time, I invited the Reverend John Hofer from James Valley to present a lecture on the Hutterites at an international research conference on the religious kibbutzim that I organized in late 1999 at Bar Ilan University, on the occasion of the 65th anniversary of the religious kibbutz movement. Since the conference took place just before the new millennium, Minister Hofer asked to bring along two other ministers: Minister David Maendel, then minister of the Sturgeon Creek Colony in Manitoba, and Minister Mike Hofer, head of the Sommerfeld Colony in Manitoba. These two colonies, like those mentioned above, belong to the Schmiedeleut.[24]

The three distinguished ministers stayed in our home in Efrat, Israel, for more then a week, accompanied by my friend, Professor Lehr. Together we visited many of the holy places in Israel, places about which our guests knew a great deal from their intimate knowledge of both the Old and New Testaments of the Holy Bible. The time spent in Israel together with three Hutterite leaders, and our many open and honest conversations, furnished a rare opportunity for us to learn about the Hutterite community, both in the past and the present. The special relationship that was built between us during their stay in Israel was also very important. The Hutterites greatly appreciated the opportunity to visit the Holy Land and the stay in the Katz home with members of my family, and they did their utmost to convey to us that their homes are also open to us any time we want to visit. As a gift from the Hutterites we received a series of research, theology and history books which all deal with Hutterites and Anabaptism.

The ministers' visit to Israel was followed by a regular correspondence and also by trans-Atlantic phone calls from time to time. In the spring of 2003, I visited James Valley again during a short visit to Canada which was part of planning my sabbatical leave which began six months later. This time I received valuable archival documents including protocols, and summaries of discussions and regulations, which were issued by the leaders of the Schmiedeleut from 1874 until the end of the 1990s. Later, at the end of summer 2005, we received the protocols, summaries of discussions and regulations relating to the early 2000s through 2004. In 2010, Professor Lehr received these updated to 2009. These documents are all in German and, as far as we know, no previous studies have drawn upon them. I would like to emphasize that similar documents relating to similar issues within the Lehrerleut and the Dariusleut are considered by their leaders to be strictly confidential, and the ministers and leaders of these leute are responsible for their safekeeping.

I spent the 2003–04 academic year on leave in Canada. For part of this year I continued to research the Hutterites, concentrating especially on the Schmiedeleut, whose colonies are located mainly in Manitoba. Besides collecting library materials, during the months of May and August 2004 I stayed (for about a month altogether) in Hutterite colonies, mainly in James Valley and Bloomfield, Manitoba. Other colonies I visited in Manitoba that year were Deerboine, Norquay, Rock Lake, Sommerfeld, Starlite, and Sturgeon Creek. My wife Ruthie and my son Dan accompanied me in May, and Dan's impressions of the life and attitudes of youth in the colonies gave new insights into the realities of colony life.

In September 2005, my wife and I spent another week in the colonies of James Valley and Bloomfield, and we also visited for the first time the Lehrerleut colony of Castor, Alberta, and the Dariusleut colony of Leedale, Alberta. In 2006, Professor Lehr together with John and Johnny Hofer from James Valley Colony and Ken and Sara Gross from Bloomfield Colony were my guests in Israel, where they visited some of the Christian and Jewish holy sites and had the opportunity to visit Israeli settlements, both Moshavim and Kibbutzim. At Kibbutz Migdal Oz, for example, my Hutterite guests addressed a public meeting and had the opportunity to compare the communal life as practiced in a Jewish religious kibbutz with that practiced in the Christian Hutterite colony. They also addressed a fascinated audience of academic experts on communal life in Israel and Kibbutz members at Yad Tabenkin during a one-day workshop on communal settlement. During the several days we spent together in Israel the conversation revolved around issues of communal life in the kibbutz and the colony, interpretation of the scriptures, and their impressions of Israel, as well as more personal issues concerning our family and mutual friends.

During the time that we were conducting field research in Canada our hosts in the various colonies knew that we had been the Israeli hosts of three distinguished and well-known ministers of the Schmiedeleut colonies. They were also aware of the special relationship we had with the James Valley Colony and with its minister, Reverend John Hofer. They did their utmost to make our stay enjoyable; they answered sincerely and in detail every question we had; they permitted us to take part in community rituals; they introduced us to officials of the community; they toured the colonies and their agricultural lands with us; they let us follow closely everyday life in the colonies; they let us take part in the colony chores; they supplied us with written sources; and, what was extremely important to the observant Katz family, they supplied their Jewish guests with strictly kosher food.

This work is, therefore, the result of my and Professor Lehr's long interest in the Hutterite community and the summation of the research that we conducted during the last several years. Its objective is to tell the story of the Hutterites—especially since their arrival in North America at the end of the 19th century—as a religious-communal-agricultural community which cherishes its isolation; a community which has come from the Old World to confront in the New World new political, cultural and legal circumstances. We analyze their ideological-religious conceptions and see how they are expressed in the principles of colony governance, the way colonies function, and the ways in which they bear upon the role of the individual and the family in the colony. We examine differences between the colonies and the changes that the colonies underwent over the years—especially in the last decades, following global developments and other changes; we also offer an evaluation of the Hutterite community's odds of survival. At the summation of our work, we suggest some steps the Hutterites might consider taking in order to prevent the weakening of the colony system and the erosion of their system of communal life.

While writing this work, it was difficult not to point out the similarity and the differences between the Hutterites and the kibbutzim, and also between the Hutterites and the Jewish Religious Orthodox community, but this work is not intended to be a comparative study of the three communities. Its focus is squarely on the Hutterites in North America.

Unlike the classical studies dealing with the Hutterites in North America which were conducted in the past, like those of Robert Friedmann,[25] Victor Peters,[26] John Hostetler[27] and John Horsch,[28] which regard the Hutterites as a monolithic body ("you have seen one colony—you have seen them all"), our work shows that today, especially, one cannot view the Hutterite colonies as a monolithic entity, just as in Israel, the kibbutzim or the Orthodox Jewish communities cannot be so viewed. Differences exist within the colonies, between the colonies in each leut and between the leute. We would like to emphasize that visits were made to, and the interviews were conducted in, the more conservative colonies of the Schmiedeleut in Canada, and from them we also received the preliminary texts on which this study is based. As mentioned before, at the beginning of the 1990s the Schmiedeleut split into two sections: one, which can be called "conservative" (Group Two), and another, which can be called "reform" (Group One). Therefore, with all caution we must limit part of the findings and most of our conclusions—especially those referring to Hutterites today—to the conservative section of the Schmiedeleut, although readers may extend our reasoning to draw their own conclusions that will apply to the "reform" Group One colonies.

The research that spawned this book drew upon primary and secondary sources, a number of interviews and some years of intermittent first-hand observation of colony life. The secondary sources include the classical works mentioned above and books and articles written more recently. Peter Riedemann's *Confession of Faith*,[29] which was written in the first half of the 16th century, was invaluable. His work contains many references to the Bible and the New Testament, and it is considered the basic religious-philosophic text of the Hutterites. It sets the rules for Hutterite behaviour in most areas of life. Without being acquainted with it, it is impossible to understand the rationale behind the Hutterites' past or the present conduct.

All Hutterite colonies and their three (four) branches have many common elements, but we must re-emphasize that today there are significant distinctions between the three church branches and between the two groups of the Schmiedeleut. There are also differences between the colonies of the same branch in the way that each colony negotiates its relationship with the outside world. For example, colonies determine the level of technology employed, their level of adherence to conservative commandments, (such as the prohibition to have one's picture taken), the details of clothing, the openness of the women, the extent to which computers are used, accessibility to the Internet, and so forth. Colony decisions in this regard are a reflection of the minister's zeal and/or conservatism and the colony's economic success. Nevertheless, on the scale of religious-social orthodoxy, the Lehrerleut colonies are generally considered to be the most "orthodox," the Schmiedeleut colonies are more "liberal," and the Dariusleut are somewhere between but are usually defined as "conservative."[30] Similarly, although the Hutterite Church is essentially a totally communal society, the three leute differ in their level of communal life: the Lehrerleut are the most communal, the Schmiedeleut are on the other side of the scale, and the Dariusleut occupy the middle ground. As to the use of advanced technology and their economic status: the Schmiedeleut are the most advanced, the Dariusleut follow them and the Lehrerleut are the least advanced. Differences can also be found in clothing and uniformity of colony patterns. As mentioned above, this book focuses on the Schmiedeleut, but also refers to the other branches of the Hutterite community.

The book is divided into two parts. The first part has 12 chapters. Chapter 1 deals with the beginning of the Hutterite community in the 16th century and with the foundations of its religious belief; Chapter 2 describes the history of the community until its arrival in North America in the last quarter of the 19th century; Chapter 3 deals with the organizational-legal structure of the community and its institutions since its arrival into the New World. This chapter also deals with central legal issues and precedents which the community faced in the second half of the 20th century; Chapter 4 deals with the spatial organization of the Hutterite colonies; Chapter 5 considers economic activity; Chapter 6 focuses on the education system; Chapter 7 deals with leisure time in and outside the colony; Chapter 8 describes everyday religious practice; Chapter 9 analyzes the relationship between the Hutterites, their neighbours, and the Canadian establishment; Chapter 10 discusses the position and role of women in the colonies; Chapter 11 deals with the reasons for leaving the colonies and the status of those who leave; and Chapter 12 describes the changes which the Hutterites encountered throughout the years in face of the external influences and internal processes. The epilogue emphasizes the unique nature of Hutterites as a community, the chances of their survival and the measures they must take in order to prevent disintegration in face of their accelerated exposure to the outside world.

The second part of the book contains the discussions and annual decisions of the Schmiedeleut council and regulations since their arrival in North America in 1874 (Appendix 5). The *Ordnungen und Konferenz Briefen*[31] have been lightly edited to remove material that identified specific individuals, dealt with the specifics of colony financial concerns, or that dealt with other sensitive personal material that would be inappropriate to publish. These *Ordnungen und Konferenz Briefen* offer a rare glimpse into the concerns faced by the Hutterite leadership in managing the interaction of the colonies with the world that surrounds them. The other appendices shed some additional light on issues raised in the book, and they include statistical data and analyses and also a report of a visit to the colonies by a religious Israeli teenager who gained insights of colony life denied to adult visitors.

We owe thanks, first and foremost, to Minister John Hofer from James Valley Colony for the time he devoted to us, for the important sources he shared with us, for opening to us the doors to many other colonies and for the warm hospitality he offered us on many occasions, particularly during our long stay in his home in 2004. We also thank his wife Sara, his daughter Sara Gross, his son Johnny and his son-in-law, Kenny Gross, for their warm welcome into their home on many occasions. Linda Maendel from Elm River Colony graciously responded to numerous email enquiries, read the manuscript and offered her insightful and frank opinions. She provided invaluable Schmiedeleut Group One colony perspectives. Minister John Hofer and Sara Gross also read the manuscript and corrected errors of fact. We thank cartographer Lev Karnibad from Bar Ilan University, Israel, for graphing the results of the statistical analysis; cartographer Weldon Hiebert and Brian MacGregor from the Department of Geography at the University of Winnipeg who produced the maps of colony diffusion. We also acknowledge the helpful comments of the anonymous readers of the original Hebrew manuscript, and those of two anonymous Canadian referees.

Robyn Sneath and Adrian Vannahme translated the *Ordnungen und Koferenz Briefen* from the original German. Reverend John Hofer, other members of James Valley Colony, and Linda Maendel, graciously assisted with the translation of uncommon and specialized words and those words in the Hutterite lexicon that are not of German origin. Our thanks go also to the Chair for the Kakal Studies at Bar Ilan University and to the Israeli Association for Canadian Studies for their help in publishing the initial version of this book in Hebrew. Henia Columbus provided the draft translation of the Hebrew manuscript into English, which is the basis for this revised and expanded English-language version. We offer her our sincere thanks.

Last but not least, we are grateful to Ruthie and Dan Katz—without them, the research could not have been carried out—and to Kay Lehr, who over the last 30 years accompanied the second author on numerous visits to colonies in Manitoba and North Dakota.

—Yossi Katz and John C. Lehr

Notes

1. Zigfried Landshut, *The Kvuza*, a facsimile edition of the book published in 1944 (Ramat Efal: Yad Tabenkin, 2000).
2. David Knaani, *Batei Midot: the Communes and their Consequences* (Tel Aviv: Betei Midot, 1960).
3. Shalom Worm, *Communes and Their Way of Life* (Tel Aviv: 1968).
4. Yaacov Oved, *Two Hundred Years of American Communes* (Tel Aviv: Yad Tabenkin and Hakibbutz Hameuchad Publishing House, 1986) [in Hebrew]/*Two Hundred Years of American Communes* (New Brunswick, NJ: Transaction Books, 1988) [English language version]; Yaacov Oved, *Witness of the Brothers: A History of the Bruderhof* (New Brunswick, NJ: Transaction Books, 1996); and *Communes and Intentional Communities in Second Half of the 20th Century* (Ramat Efal: Yad Tabenkin, 2009).
5. Menachem Shadmi, *Communes in the World and the Kibbutz* (Tel Aviv: Sifriat Poalim, 1985).
6. Shlomo Shalman, *The Niderkaufungen Community* (Ramat Efal: Yad Tabenkin, 1996).
7. Shlomo Shealtiel, "The Zadaroga and the Circumstances of Its Disintegration," *Shorashim* (1997): 106–21.
8. Yaacov Oved, *Distant Brothers: The History of Relations Between the Bruderhof and the Kibbutz* (Ramat Efal: Yad Tabenkin, 1993).
9. See, for example, Ran Aharonson, "The Hutterite Communes in North America: A Personal View of an Israeli Geographer," *Mifneh* 49 (December 2005): 46–52.
10. Victor Peters, *All Things Common: The Hutterian Way of Life* (Minneapolis: University of Minnesota Press, 1965); John A. Hostelter, *Hutterite Society* (Baltimore and London: Johns Hopkins University Press, 1974); John W. Bennett, *Hutterian Brethren: The Agricultural Economy and Social Organization of a Communal People* (Stanford, CA: Stanford University Press, 1967); John Hofer, *The History of the Hutterites* (Elie, MB: James Valley Book Centre, 2004).
11. John Ryan, *The Agricultural Economy of Manitoba Hutterite Colonies* (Toronto, ON: McClelland and Stewart, 1977) and "Hutterites," *Horizon Canada* 2, no. 21 (1985): 494–99.
12. Karl Peter, Edward D. Boldt, Ian Whitaker and Lance W. Roberts, "The Dynamics of Religious Defection among Hutterites," *Journal for the Scientific Study of Religion* 21, no. 4 (1982): 327–37.
13. Simon Evans, "Spatial Bias in the Incidence of Nativism-Opposition to Hutterite Expansion in Alberta," *Canadian Ethnic Studies* 6 (1974): 1–16; John Everitt, "Social Space and Group Life-styles in Rural Manitoba," *Canadian Geographer* 24 (1980): 237–54.
14. William Schroeder, *Hutterite Migrations in Europe* (Winnipeg: the author, 2001); J. Lehr, B. McGregor and W. Hiebert. "Mapping Hutterite Colony Diffusion in North America," *Manitoba History* 53 (2006): 29–31.
15. For example, Ruth Bar-Lembach, *A Member of the Community: Childhood and Adolescence in a Hutterite Colony and a Bruderhof Settlement in North America* (Ramat Efal: Yad Tabenkin, 1992).
16. B. Preston, "Jacob's Ladder," *Saturday Night* 107, no. 3 (April 1, 1992): 30–38, 78–80; Samuel Hofer, *The Hutterites: Lives and Images of Communal People* (Saskatoon, SK: Hofer Publishers, 1998), 131–40.
17. Alvin J. Esau, *The Courts and the Colonies: The Litigation of Hutterite Church Disputes* (Vancouver: UBC Press, 2004).
18. Samuel Hofer, *The Hutterites*.
19. Mary-Ann Kirkby, *I am Hutterite* (Saskatoon, SK: Polka Dot Press, 2007).
20. Michael Holzach, *The Forgotten People: A Year Among the Hutterites* (Sioux Falls, SD: Ex Machina Books, 1993).
21. John Hofer, *The History of the Hutterites*, note 10; Paul Gross, *The Hutterite Way: The Inside Story of the Life, Customs, Religion and Traditions of the Hutterites*

(Saskatoon, SK: Freeman Publishing Company, 1965); See also Peter Hofer, *The Hutterian Brethren and Their Beliefs* (Starbuck: The Hutterian Brethren of Manitoba, 1973); Arnold M. Hofer and Norman Hofer, *Hutterite Roots* (Saskatoon: Freeman Publishing Company, 1985).

22. There are exceptions. See, for example, Solomon Stahl, *The History of Bonne Homme Colony, Manitoba* (Fordville: Forest River Bookbindery, 2001); R. Ward, J. Lehr and B. McGregor, "Graven Images of a Closed Society: The Huron Hutterite Colony, 1920s," *Manitoba History* 54 (2007): 45–50.

23. Yossi Katz, *The Religious Kibbutz during the Mandate Period* (Ramat Gan: Bar Ilan University Press, 1996).

24. It quickly became clear that it was not a simple matter for Hutterites to travel overseas, even though their trip was to be to the Holy Land. In the Lehrerleut and the Dariusleut, overseas trips are unacceptable, and a trip to Israel would be virtually impossible. Even the Schmiedeleut, which are considered by the Hutterites to be more open- and broad-minded, would sanction this trip only after it was defined as a "mission." This mission's purpose was for the ministers to have a spiritual experience, and to enable them to better interpret Bible stories to other colony members on their return. Interviews by Yossi Katz with Eida Waldner in Castor Colony on September 14, 2005; Minister John Hofer in James Valley Colony on September 26, 2005; and Minister David Maendel in James Valley Colony on September 26, 2005.

25. Robert Friedmann, *Hutterite Studies* (Goshen, Indiana: Mennonite Historical Society, 1961).

26. Victor Peters, *All Things Common*, note 9.

27. John Hostetler, *Hutterite Society* (Baltimore and London: Johns Hopkins University Press, 1974), note 9.

28. John Horsch, *The Hutterian Brethren 1528–1931* (Cayley: Macmillan Colony, 1985).

29. Peter Riedemann, *Confession of Faith* [originally published in 1545 as *Rechenschaft unserer Religion*] (Rifton, New York: Plough Publishers, 1970).

30. As an illustration of the distinctions existing not only between the three branches, but also among colonies of the same branch is the attitude toward photography. Within the Schmiedeleut, usually regarded as the most liberal leut, some individuals obtained exemption from having their photographs on their driver's licences yet some in the Lehrerleut, usually far more conservative, were quite happy to be photographed.

31. Although many German speakers would use *Briefe* as the form of this word, the Hutterites use *Briefen*, and this is the form we have used throughout the text when we are referring to *Ordnungen und Konferenz Briefen*.

Chapter 1

IN THE FOOTSTEPS OF JESUS
AND ANCIENT CHRISTIANITY:

The Beginning of the Hutterite Community
and the Origins of Its Religious Belief

THE HUTTERITE COMMUNITY ("THE HUTTERIAN BRETH-
ren") was formed in 1528 in the town of Nikolsburg in
south Moravia (Czech Republic), close to the Austrian
border. It began as one of the many radical Anabaptist
communities that sprang up during the Reformation, refusing
to accept the authority of either the Catholic or the Protestant
churches. In 1533 the community accepted the leadership of Jacob
Hutter from Innsbruck, in Tyrol.[1] Hutter was an ardent follower
of the radical left wing of the Reformation, an Anabaptist who
had lived in Moravia since 1529. He brought together the various
groups that constituted the community, molded its first theological
ideas, and was the first leader of the community until his impris-
onment and subsequent martyrdom at the beginning of 1536. His
successor, Peter Riedemann, who was theologically well educated,
formulated the principles of the Hutterite belief based on both
the Old and the New Testaments of the Holy Bible. These were
published in German in 1545 in an essay called "Rechenschaft unserer Religion, Lehr und Glaubens," later translated into English,[2]

then published under the title, "Confession of Faith: Account of our Religion, Doctrine and Faith."[3]

At the beginning of the 16th century, the Christian Reformation Movement spawned Christian denominations that challenged the authority of the established Roman Catholic and Greek Orthodox churches to function as the principal intermediary between man and God. These dissidents protested against the use of Latin in worship rather than the vernacular tongue of the people, the lack of morality, and corruption in the established churches, and were hence known as "Protestants." All Protestant churches believe in the direct connection of the believer to God and the Holy Scriptures, which constitute the only source for the knowledge of the religious truth. Although most Protestant churches initially rejected the ritual and the priestly hierarchy of the Catholic and Orthodox churches and placed their faith in a lay clergy, over the years it became accepted that some of the congregation were called upon to teach God's word to the others, and thus fulfill the role of clergy. Supreme importance was—and is—applied to belief in God—rather than to deeds—since this means that the believer is assured of God's mercy and of the redemptive act of Jesus Christ, who took upon himself the sins of all mankind while dying on the cross.

The Anabaptist Christians, whose movement expanded throughout central Europe at the beginning of the 1520s, somewhat later in other parts of the world, went even farther. According to their belief, the principles of the Reformation dictate that the Holy Scripture alone, and not the institutes of the Catholic Church, should be regarded as a source of redemption for man, and that the understanding of the scriptures is possible without the mediation and intervention of the Church. This conviction led the Anabaptists to the conclusion that baptism cannot be a formal and external ritual administered to those who are unaware of its symbolism and incapable of making a real decision to commit their lives to a new path. Mental preparation is necessary for acceptance of God's kingdom as well as for spiritual purification and revival. This concept was based on the words of the New Testament: "He who believes and is baptized will be saved; but he who does not believe will be condemned" (Mark 16, 16).[4] Therefore, they objected to baptism of children (hence their name, Anabaptists), and postponed baptism to an age of maturity, when the believer has a deep consciousness of his or her belief and a commitment to it.

The issue of baptism was only one element of the Anabaptist faith, but was characteristic of the entire faith, which was, in fact, a logical conclusion of the Reformation movement. The Anabaptists preached that other religious rituals should also manifest the connection of the believer to the underlying principles of the rituals. At the basis of their faith was the will to rebuild God's kingdom on earth, in the form of man's love to God and to his fellow men, keeping away from hate and war, looking for peace and serenity, and adopting the way of life of Jesus Christ. All of these principles were commanded by Christ in the New Testament, and, according to the Anabaptists, were ignored for hundreds of years:

> Then one of the scribes came, and having heard them reasoning together, perceiving that He had answered them well, asked Him, Which is the first commandment of all? Jesus answered him, The first of all the commandments is: Hear, O Israel, the LORD our God, the LORD is one. And you shall love the LORD your God with all your heart, with all your soul, with all your mind, and with all your strength.' This is the first commandment. And the second, like it, is this: 'You shall love your neighbor as yourself. There is no other commandment greater than these. So the scribe said to Him, Well said, Teacher. You have spoken the truth, for there is one God, and there is no other but He. And to love Him with all the heart, with all the understanding, with all the soul, and with all the strength, and to love one's neighbor as oneself, is more than all the whole burnt offerings and sacrifices. Now when Jesus saw that he answered wisely, He said to him, You are not far from the Kingdom of God. But after that no one dared question Him. (Mark 12, 28–34)

According to the Anabaptists, the individual's voice of conscience and power of belief are to guide the relationship between man and society and the institutions of the state. On the basis of their religious principles and in accordance with the spirit of the first Christian commune, they demanded complete social equality; they opposed any religious or secular rule that refused to consider the voice of inner justice of the individual based on his heart's belief. They denied the assumption that Jesus was flesh and blood, emphasized his godly essence and generally tended to the symbolization of concepts and events in the Bible and the New Testament. The

Anabaptists forbade their fellows to turn to courts of law, religious or secular, outside the Anabaptist circles, they did not permit the use of weapons, frowned upon compulsory acts, forbade serving as clerks for the existing authorities, and so forth. Their pacifist zeal had a great influence on their history and their wanderings throughout Europe, and later, from Europe to the New World.[5] The Hutterites were only one of many Anabaptist communities, such as the Mennonites and Amish, that shared similar histories of persecution and migration in Europe and North America.[6]

The principles of the Hutterite theological doctrine were based squarely on Anabaptist principles: the *Holy Bible*, both Old and New Testaments, and the wish to resemble early Christianity—the Christianity of the Apostles described in the New Testament. They wished to obey the Holy Scriptures word for word and to adopt completely the model of the First Church. As do other Anabaptists, they consider the Catholics and the other less radical Protestant groups to be false prophets, but they believe that God guards the Jews because "they were the Chosen People until they rejected God's saving grace through Jesus Christ and his disciples, with Peter and Paul opening the way of salvation for them."[7] The worship of God according to the Old Testament and the New Testament, which they believe completes it, is the central mission in Hutterite life; in every act one should ask what God desires. According to their belief, the designation of this world is war against evil and against evil inclination—Ammalek—and constant preparation towards the eternal life in the world to come. Without fighting the evil inclination and evil in general, one cannot assure the world to come. A summary of the Hutterite theology after its formation in the 16th century can be found in Riedemann's book.[8]

One of the main principles of the Hutterian theology, which now differentiates it from other Anabaptist communities, is the demand for total communal life, to achieve full community of goods, and waive any personal property in favour of the community. The full sharing of property lies in the centre of the being and existence of the Hutterite community. The organization and management of the community throughout the years was designed to guarantee this. The Hutterite community believes strongly in the motto "from each according to his ability, to each according to his needs."

The full sharing of goods in the Hutterite community is purely a theological concept. It is not related to economic doctrine, nor is it the product of adaptation to adverse economic circumstances, such as the difficult economic situation the Hutterites experienced when they first formed their Church and community. It is not influenced by any social—or class—secular conception, nor can it be identified with the beginnings of socialism. Now, as in the past, a Hutterite community cannot exist without the sharing of goods and community life. Abandoning community life implies the rejection of a central tenet of Hutterite theological doctrine. Thus individuals, families, or groups, who leave the community, can no longer properly be called Hutterites.

The origins of the communal idea in the Hutterite theology lie in the Holy Bible's Old Testament, which records the Commandments, and the New Testament, which reveals the teachings of Jesus and the Apostles and describes early Christianity. The creation of Adam and Eve is for the Hutterites the earliest source for the idea of community and sharing. The Garden of Eden, according to their belief, was the first colony.[9] The bread from heaven given to the People of Israel during their traveling in the desert was another source. The Bible tells us: "And Moses said to them, This is the bread which the LORD has given you to eat. This is the thing which the LORD has commanded: Let every man gather it according to each one's need, one omer for each person, according to the number of persons; let every man take for those who are in his tent. Then the children of Israel did so and gathered, some more, some less. So when they measured it by omers, he who gathered much had nothing left over, and he who gathered little had no lack. Every man had gathered according to each one's need" (Exodus 16, 15–18). According to the Hutterite commentary on this episode, a commentary based on the New Testament, the commandment of God demands that food be divided equally according to needs, and it forbids that one person have plenty and the other shall lack food. The New Testament tells us: "For you know the grace of our Lord Jesus Christ, that though He was rich, yet for your sakes He became poor, that you through His poverty might become rich. For I do not mean that others should be eased and you burdened; but by an equality, that now at this time your abundance may supply their lack, that their abundance also may supply your lack—that there may be equality. As it is written, 'He who gathered much had nothing left over, and he who gathered little had no lack'" (II Corinthians 16, 9–15).

A third Biblical source is the Jubilee (Yovel) which is destined to create equality and which Jesus regarded as an eternal reality. The Lord's commandment to care for the poor, as is commanded in Deuteronomy (15, 7–11), was yet another Biblical source for the doctrine of community of goods. Moreover, the need to help the poor and the imperative to the rich to waive their earthly assets in favour of the poor as a precondition for achieving wholeness, were emphasized by Jesus: "Now behold, one came and said to Him, Good Teacher, what good thing shall I do that I may have eternal life? ... Jesus said to him, 'If you want to be perfect, go, sell what you have and give to the poor, and you will have treasure in heaven...' Then Jesus said to His disciples, Assuredly, I say to you that it is hard for a rich man to enter the kingdom of heaven... And everyone who has left houses or brothers or sisters or father or mother or wife or children or lands, for My name's sake, shall receive a hundredfold, and inherit eternal life" (Matthew 19, 16–29). The prophecy of Isaiah, "The wolf also shall dwell with the lamb," also alludes, according to the Hutterites, to the idea of community of property, and peaceful co-existence.[10]

The compilers of the Hutterite theology used The Acts of the Apostles in the New Testament as the clearest source for establishing the Christians' duty to adopt a communal way of life and waive every form of personal ownership of goods. Within the New Testament there are many allusions to the desirability of the new Christian community embracing an egalitarian philosophy, sharing wealth and ensuring that all were treated equally. For example: "Now all who believed were together, and had all things in common, and sold their possessions and goods, and divided them among all, as anyone had need. So continuing daily with one accord in the temple..." (Acts 2, 44–46); "Now the multitude of those who believed were of one heart and one soul; neither did anyone say that any of the things he possessed was his own, but they had all things in common... Nor was there anyone among them who lacked; for all who were possessors of lands or houses sold them, and brought the proceeds of the things that were sold, and laid them at the apostles' feet; and they distributed to each as anyone had need. And Joseph... having land, sold it, and brought the money and laid it at the apostles' feet" (Acts 4, 32–37). Furthermore, Philippians (2, 3–4) says: "Let nothing be done through selfish ambition or conceit, but in lowliness of mind let each esteem others better than himself. Let each of you look out not only for his own interests, but also for the interests of others."[11]

During the 16th century and afterwards, the compilers of Hutterite theology presented more evidence and arguments supporting the need to adopt a communal way of life; all were derived from their conception of true Christianity and the life Jesus ordered his disciples to follow. They argued that each believer should adopt this way of life as a testament to their faith. To live individually was to fail to truly practice Christianity; it was a stain on the Church. To argue that communal life was lived in Jerusalem only, and that this way of life is irrelevant in modern times, was not acceptable to the Hutterites.

The core of Hutterite belief in the importance of communal life in the practice of true Christianity revolved around the following arguments:

God created the world not for one man only, but for all human beings together.

Things man cannot accumulate, such as the sun, the day and the air, prove that all creation is intended for all men communally.

The fact that man can take with him nothing after his death shows that property should not be accumulated.

Accumulation of property by men caused them to move away from God and made Mammon a worshipped idol. The Hutterites used – and still do – the word "Mammon" (in Hebrew) in order to describe the idol of materialism. They believe that one should do everything to remove it from man; if man is to be revived in the image of God, he must reject anything that keeps him away from God, he must obey God, subordinate his will to God's will and ask nothing for himself. He must do only what is requested of him, even if that leads to suffering and torture. True following of God means, "Not my will shall be done but yours." Moreover, complete devotion to God, which is needed in order to reach salvation, requires one to give in completely, surrender even his "self" (Gelassenheit), even if it means death. What follows from this is the need to renounce all private property and to live a full communal life.

From Mammon and private materialism stems greed, which is forbidden in the Bible. He who refuses to live communally tolerates greed and cannot enter the kingdom of heaven. Only in this sense can the teachings of Jesus (Luke 16, 9) be understood: "make to yourselves friends of the mammon." [12]

Only he who frees himself of the material world can grasp the true and divine. When that happens, it becomes the property of all children of God. And as the saints share their spiritual assets, material assets should also be shared, and even more so.

The Hutterite community is one family, where brotherly love, mutual sharing and giving should exist. And since in the family all material assets are shared as a matter of fact, so must it be in the community as a whole. Indeed, the principle of love—a basic principle in Christianity—is emphasized in the Hutterite writings: "Love is the tie of perfection... Where she dwelleth she does not work partial but complete communion. It means having everything in common out of sheer love for the neighbor... Where Christian love of the neighbor does not produce community in things temporal, there the blood of Christ does not cleanse from sin... Private property is the greatest enemy of Christian love." [13]

Sharing and the practice of communal life are prerequisites for redemption, salvation, and fighting the weaknesses and sins of the community. [14]

All gifts of God—spiritual as well as material—are given to man to share with all his brothers, rather than keep them to himself or use them alone. [15]

Equality in the community finds its actual expression in the rule "from each according to his ability, to each according to his needs." However, even among the Hutterites, total equality cannot exist. First of all, women have no voting rights, and because work is strictly gendered the number of the tasks they are allowed to perform is limited. Secondly, the rights and duties of the individual depend on age, and on status according to the Hutterite theology (e.g., someone who was baptized vs. someone who was not yet baptized). Thirdly, in each colony there are people who have leading jobs and responsibilities in the colony, and who serve as the leaders of the community. Full community is therefore expressed not in social or occupational terms but in full ownership of the colony of all its assets, the lack of private property, full mutual responsibility and commitment and extensive communal activity in all areas of life.

The principle of the "two worlds" still dictates the spatial seclusion of the Hutterite colonies and their cultural disengagement from the non-Hutterite society. For the Hutterites there are two diametrically opposed worlds. One is the world of the Hutterite colony, which can be compared to Noah's Ark or to Jerusalem within the walls; the other world, the external world, is the world that surrounds the Hutterite community. [16] According to Hutterite theology, which is strongly rooted in Anabaptist theology, the Hutterites are responsible for the establishment of the new Kingdom of God, which is separated from the existing World Order governed by Satan. The Hutterites believe that the fact that the mainstream churches—Catholic, Orthodox, and Protestant—as well as the secular forces of the State, are antagonistic to the true Church—the Hutterite Church. This is further evidence of the evil of the existing world order. The old Church has failed to combine the two worlds; therefore, the new Church (the Hutterite Church) must be established here and now, not in the eternal world, in Heaven, but in a new world—God's kingdom—which is theologically and physically separated from the surrounding world—the kingdom of darkness. Strict adherence to use of their specific language throughout the generations, as well as today, is part of the Hutterite conception that they should isolate themselves from the outside world.

The existing Kingdom of God is the only one obeying unconditionally God's commandments according to Jesus. This theological conception was the cause for the persecution of the Anabaptists in general and, together with their communal theology, of the Hutterites in particular. In Hutterite doctrine suffering is a necessary element for the establishment of God's kingdom. Thus, enduring persecution, and persecution itself, is a price they pay willingly in their quest to establish the Kingdom of God.

The concept of God's kingdom commands a new set of values, or more precisely, the revival of old fundamental values, such as: love, forgiveness, self-submission, and the prohibition to hate even your own persecutors. All these show purity of spirit as opposed to the pragmatic and amoral secular judgments of the outside world. Those who dwell in God's kingdom accept the leadership of Jesus Christ and his doctrine, their heart is connected to God and Jesus, and thus they receive strength from above to do good and eschew evil. They deliberately isolate themselves from the outside world so that they participate as little as possible in the affairs of the outside world, which in their view consists of powers opposed to the Kingdom of God; powers which are secular and destructive, powers of evil and darkness. Culture also stands in contradiction to God's kingdom, since it originates from a Greek-Roman concept and from the Renaissance, and is not a Christian concept. Culture is suspected as containing the origins of destruction, despair and an inability to reach salvation, and as lacking the vital elements of Jesus' teachings.[17]

The colony itself is perceived as "Jerusalem," and as according to Hutterite sermons, Jerusalem belonged totally to God, so the colony and everything within it is essentially a Hutterite Church belonging to God. Therefore, when one chooses to leave the colony, nothing can be taken because everything belongs to the colony, to the Church, and to God and has been donated by the members. As nothing can be taken from God and given to the individual, so can nothing be taken from the colony and given to someone who is no longer part of it.[18]

The Hutterites' initial specialization in agriculture, and various arts and crafts (nowadays also in manufacturing), also originates from their religious belief, which totally prohibited engagement in commerce because it was regarded as a sinful occupation. Basing his words on the New Testament (Paul's Epistle to the Ephesians 4, 28), Riedemann said:

> It is almost impossible for a merchant and trader to keep himself from sin. And as a nail sticketh fast between door and hinge; so doth sin stick close between buying and selling. Therefore do we allow no one to buy to sell again, as merchants and traders do. But to buy what is necessary for the needs of one's house or craft, to use it and then to sell what one by means of his craft hath made therefrom, we consider to be right and not wrong. This only we regard as wrong: when one buyeth a ware and selleth the same again even as he bought it, taking to himself profit, making the ware dearer thereby for the poor, taking bread from their very mouths and thus making the poor man nothing but the bondman of the rich. Thus, it was prohibited to deal with selling liquors since it may lead to lack of chastity, sin and weakening of the spirit.[19]

Another reason for the dominance of agriculture in the life of the Hutterites is that it enables them to live together in a rural environment as a discrete community and to be spatially segregated, functioning as a religious unit, away from the disturbing influence of city life.

According to Hutterite doctrine, the Hutterite colony and the Hutterite Church are one and the same. Wherever there is a Hutterite colony, there is a Hutterite Church, and vice versa. In a legal decision Canadian Chief Justice Samuel Freedman quoted Dickson when he wrote that

The Hutterite Church is the Colony, and the Colony is the Church. These terms are interchangeable... the Colony exists only as a part of the total... When you are a Hutterian, the whole life is a Church. It is totalistic. Every aspect of the work is religiously sanctioned. The Hutterian Colony is a segment of the Hutterian Church... Each Bruderhof of 80 to 200 people is an agricultural family, like an Israeli Kibbutz or a Chinese commune; but it is not only or mainly an economic organism. It is a Church, which has chosen this organism as a means to realize religious beliefs and a religious way of life... A colony of the Hutterian Brethren [is] a local expression of the Hutterian Church engaged in full unanimity of faith, life and work.[20]

As mentioned above, in 1545 Riedemann had identified the principles of Hutterite doctrine. In addition to the subjects previously mentioned, Riedemann also dealt with various issues that have established the Hutterite way of live. For example, he mentioned prayer,[21] baptism, marriage, the inferior status of women, prohibition of divorce and bigamy,[22] sins, repentance and punishments, including excommunication and expulsion,[23] reacceptance, singing hymns and the prohibition to sing secular songs,[24] educating the children in separate Hutterite schools where the children are taught to know God and believe in him, and the prohibition to send the children to general schools where they teach only the arts and the customs and wisdoms of this world,[25] the prohibition to sue someone in court or to serve there ("Now therefore, it is already an utter failure for you that you go to law against one another. Why do you not rather accept wrong? Why do you not rather let yourselves be cheated?" [II Corinthians 6, 7]).[26] He also mentioned the prohibition to carry weapons and fighting in wars, and the need to keep apart from other churches. Riedemann also dealt with Hutterite clothes that, he noted, should not express pride and magnificence. For example, it is forbidden to use ornate fabrics, patterns of flowers and embroidery. All this is intended to keep a clear conscience toward God and serve Him in faith. Wearing jewelry and other forms of adornment was forbidden from the same reason.[27]

As early as the 16th century the principles of the Hutterite religious faith became transformed into regulations which bound the Hutterite community in all aspects of life: religious-spiritual as well as practical. In later centuries, dozens of collections of regulations have been compiled. These are extremely detailed. They emphasize the status and authority of the ministers and leaders as the ones who carry the word of God. In many ways the regulations remind us of the regulations of medieval monasteries or guilds, although their strong and clear Christian emphasis distinguishes them from those of the secular guilds.

The prominent message of the regulations is the duty of community members to adhere to a strict lifestyle, to overcome temptations, and never to stray from the path of righteousness. The regulations are intended to combat selfishness, individualism, greed and the will to earn more. These constitute a guide for believers to steer them through a life devoted to total communalism, modesty, puritan simplicity, and to some degree, a life of mortification.[28] Educating the young should also be strict and unforgiving, for the young ones need to be educated to endure hard times and suffering.[29] All handicrafts and labour should be done industriously, without waste; one should pay attention to the tiniest detail; all luxuries are forbidden, as well as private property of all kinds. Even personal inheritance is to be shared with the community.[30]

Despite the strict nature of the regulations, which characterized the Hutterite community as a "church of rules," they were rules that were willingly accepted by all members of the community. The regulations express a spirit of brotherly love and determination to follow the way, which the Hutterites regard as the true form of Christian adherence.[31]

Notes

1. Hutter's last name is unknown. He is called Hutter because of his occupation as a hatter (in German "hutter"), and the community is therefore called "the Hutterian Brethren." In English its members are referred to as "Hutterites."
2. Peter Riedemann, *Confession of Faith* (Rifton, NY: Plough Publishers, 1970).
3. Yaacov Oved, *Two Hundred Years of American Communes* (Tel Aviv: Yad Tabenkin and Hakibbutz Hameuchad Publishing House, 1986) [in Hebrew], 385–88; Robert Friedmann, *Hutterite Studies* (Goshen, IN: Mennonite Historical Society, 1961), 76ff.; John A. Hostetler, *Hutterite Society* (Baltimore and London: Johns Hopkins University Press, 1974), 5–25; *The Chronicle of the Hutterian Brethren*, Vol. 1 (Elie, MB: Hutterian Education Committee, 2003), 83–86.
4. All quotations from the Holy Bible were taken from the new King James version, http://www.biblegateway.com/versions/index.php?action=getVersionInfo&vid=50.
5. Hostelter, *Hutterite Society*, 5–25; Friedmann, *Hutterite Studies*, 76ff.; Leonard Gross, *The Golden Years of the Hutterites* (Kitchener, ON: Pandora Press, 1998), 20–24; "Christianity," *The Hebrew Encyclopedia* (Jerusalem and Tel Aviv, 1974),

Vol. 25: 350–354; "Anabaptists," *The Hebrew Encyclopedia* (Jerusalem and Tel Aviv, 1968), Vol. 4: 298–299.

6. See, for example, Yossi Katz and John C. Lehr, *The Last Best West: Essays on the Historical Geography of the Canadian Prairies* (Jerusalem, Israel: Magnes Press, 1999), 17–43; Gross, *Golden Years of the Hutterites*, 179. For a detailed description of the Anabaptist communities, see Kraybill and Bowman, *On the Backroad to Heaven: Old Order Hutterites, Mennonites, Amish and Brethren* (Baltimore and London: Johns Hopkins University Press, 2001).

7. John Hofer, interview by John Lehr, James Valley Colony, June 7, 2008.

8. Gross, *Golden Years of the Hutterites*, 210–14; Oved, *Two Hundred Years*, 392; Friedmann, *Hutterite Studies*; John Hofer, interview by Yossi Katz, James Valley Colony, May 15, 2004.

9. John Hofer, interview by Yossi Katz, James Valley Colony, July 26, 2004.

10. Ibid.

11. Riedemann, *Confession of Faith*, 88–91.

12. John Hofer, interview by John Lehr, James Valley Colony, June 7, 2008.

13. Friedmann, *Hutterite Studies*, 83.

14. Ibid., 76. See also Gross, *The Hutterite Way: The Inside Story of the Life, Customs, Religion and Traditions of the Hutterites* (Saskatoon, SK: Freeman Publishing Company, 1965), 178–79; Donald E. Pitzer, *America's Communal Utopias* (Chapel Hill: University of North Carolina Press, 1997), 332–33.

15. James Valley Colony Archive. Judge Dickson's verdict in the lawsuit of Benjamin Hofer et al., against Zacharias Hofer et al., May 6, 1966.

16. Friedmann, *Hutterite Studies*, 92ff.

17. Ibid.

18. Kenny Gross, interview by Yossi Katz, Bloomfield Colony, August 2004. John Hofer, interview by John Lehr, James Valley Colony, June 7, 2008.

19. Riedemann, *Confession of Faith*, 126–28.

20. Samuel Freedman and Cameron Harvey, *Chief Justice Samuel Freedman: A Great Canadian Judge: A Collection of the Reasons for Judgment of the Honourable Samuel Freedman, Justice of the Court of Queen's Bench of Manitoba (1952-60), Justice of the Court of Appeal of Manitoba (1960-83), and Chief Justice of Manitoba (1971-83)*, (Winnipeg: Law Society of Manitoba, 1983), 25.

21. Riedemann, *Confession of Faith*, 121.

22. Ibid., 97.

23. Ibid., 101, 131.

24. Ibid., 123.

25. Ibid., 130.

26. Ibid., 112.

27. Ibid., 112, 133.

28. Friedmann, *Hutterite Studies*, 107–110.

29. Ibid. See also Hostetler, *Hutterite Society*, 321–28, regarding discipline regulations in schools compiled in 1568.

30. Friedmann, *Hutterite Studies*, 107–10.

31. Ibid., 107ff.

Chapter 2

FROM MORAVIA TO AMERICA:

The Hutterites in the Old World until Their Establishment in North America

HUTTERITES FIRST ESTABLISHED COMMUNAL SETTLE-ments—*Bruderhofe*—in Moravia and Slovakia in the first half of the 16th century.[1] These were then modern farms, with buildings arranged around a square or public area of the village. The ground floors of buildings were used for communal living, and contained a dining hall, kitchen, kindergarten, school, laundry, spinning mill, and weaving and sewing rooms. The upper floors were used for residences. Each of these settlements was independent, had fields and agricultural lands (which were owned by the noblemen and rented by their Hutterite tenants), and various workshops: a carpenter's shop, blacksmith, brewery, and so forth. According to one source, in 1605 there were more than 70 such settlements, each one numbering a few hundred people (including children). The prosperity of the settlements, resulting from communal living and from Hutterite frugality and diligence, was a cause of much envy from their neighbours, who agitated against them demanding that the authorities prevent the Hutterites from expanding further in Moravia.

The Hutterite communal settlements functioned (and still do, as will be shown later) as a beehive, where everyone knows their duty in the broad community system. The organizational framework of the Hutterite Bruderhof has not changed much since the 16th century; in fact, it remains much the same today as when it was first established. Then, as now, three elected and authorized managers led each settlement: one, the Minister, was the spiritual leader of the settlement responsible for preserving the principles of the Hutterite community but also devoting part of his time to farming matters. The second official, the Steward, *Haushalter* (later, in North America, called the Boss or Secretary), was responsible for running the economy of the Bruderhof and supplying all the material needs of the brethren. (The Farm Boss/*Weinzedel* was responsible for allocating work and field management, monitoring the performance of Bruderhof members and ensuring that all were employed in some capacity. The Steward/Haushalter also had to disburse the profits and to ensure that every member received a fair allocation, in accordance with the principle of frugality, as was appropriate in a strictly disciplined Christian community. He was in charge of all purchases and sales—in fact, of all economic aspects in the settlement. There were also officials in charge of the workshops; the buyer responsible for dealing with the outside world, who was enjoined to be careful with all his purchases, and "not fall into the tricks of the traders, butchers, and Jews," and farming managers who were in charge of the fields, plantations, warehouses and so on.[2]

The historical literature of the Hutterites, such as *The Chronicle of the Hutterian Brethren*,[3] Vol. 1, which refers to the years 1517–1665, and the books by John Horsch,[4] Robert Friedmann[5] and Leonard Gross,[6] describe with some degree of pride the condition of Hutterite settlements in Moravia in the 16th century and the beginning of the 17th century, a period which is known as the "golden era" of the Hutterites.

The Hutterites in Moravia at this time were described as a pious and hard-working community:

> The Christian community of goods was practiced according to the teachings of Christ and his practice with the disciples as well as the usage of the apostolic church. All shared alike in one common treasury, one common house, and one common table, there being, of course, special provisions for

the sick and the children... Everyone was his fellowman's brother and all lived together in harmony as a peaceful people who did not give any assistance to the bloody business of war. They were subject to the authorities and obedient in all good works that are not contrary to God, the faith and conscience... There was no singing of shameful songs ... but [only] Christian and spiritual songs... There was no usury nor taking of interest, and no buying or selling for gain. There was only that which had been obtained through honest labour, through daily work of various descriptions, including all kinds of agricultural and horticultural work. There were quite a few carpenters and masons who built many substantial dwellings for noblemen, citizenry and others especially in Moravia but also in Austria, Hungary and Bohemia... Numerous mills were rented from the owners at their request and operated by brethren as millers. In short no one went idle. Each did what was required of him and what he was able to do, whether he had been poor or rich, noble or commoner before [before he joined the brethren] It was a perfect body, where each member served and was served by every other member.[7]

Others compared the Hutterite communities to beehives where some of the bees make the honey, some make the wax, some supply the water, and the rest take care of everything else, so that eventually they produce enough honey to supply their own needs and the needs of many other people. Friedmann concluded that the economic and social enterprises of the Hutterites at that time were extremely successful. Diligence and efficiency, combined with limited consumption of goods, prohibition of luxury, frugality and thrift, made for a prosperous community. The principles of diligence, caring, honesty, thrift, stability in work and reliability, unselfishness, and caring for the other were also transferred to the younger generation who participated in the work force at quite an early age.[8]

In contrast to the situation today, Hutterite economic activity was then divided into two parts: activities within the settlements, and activity beyond the settlements—work undertaken on the estates of the aristocracy or in distant cities. Today, working outside the colonies is rare. Within the settlements activities exploited the economies of scale, taking advantage of many workers specializing in various crafts:

> Nothing was wasted everything was used. For example, hides were transferred from the abattoir to the leather factory, and from there—to the rein makers and leather workers; wool was sent to the women so that they should spin it, and then to the weavers or the fabric makers and from them to the tailors... cooking was done for the whole settlement, and thus they could manage a careful economy. In the settlements themselves, the brethren made unique articles, which were not common in their environment and in other places, such as various pottery objects, clocks and wagons [translated from Hebrew].[9]

Working outside the settlements was driven by the need for liquid capital and a desire to demonstrate that the Hutterites were an economic asset to the nobility. They hoped to win the favour of the nobles as protection from the government and clergy. Thus, the Hutterites served as managers of farms, flourmills and saw mills, as well as practitioners of the various medical professions. Their excellent training, moral qualities, and diligence made them the nobility's trusted employees.

The economic success and prosperity of Hutterites in Moravia generated envy and promoted hatred within the surrounding population. Persecution of Hutterites by the Roman Catholic clergy, orders received from the government in Vienna, the Ottoman invasion of Moravia, and the outbreak of the Thirty Years War between the Catholics and the Protestants, all combined to lead to the destruction of Hutterite settlements. The Hutterite community in Moravia declined until, in 1622, all remaining Hutterites, some 7,000 people, were expelled when they refused to convert to Catholicism.[10]

From Moravia most of the Hutterites moved on to Upper Hungary (Slovakia) where a few Hutterite settlements had existed since the first half of the 16th century. A few Hutterites from Moravia (about 200 people), were transported against their will by the local aristocracy to establish colonies in Alwinz, Transylvania. In Slovakia the Hutterites suffered from raids during the Thirty Years War, as well as from theft by their impoverished and often starving neighbours. By 1631, the number of the Hutterites in Hungary had declined to 1,000, and their ability to retain their religious life weakened. In the following years, their economic position improved, as did their spiritual state, thanks to the charismatic leadership of Andreas Ehrenpreis, who also did much to strengthen the framework of communal life. However, the Catholic victory in the Thirty Years War resulted in increased persecution of Hutterites and revived attempts to convert them to Catholicism. They were forced to abandon communal life and to baptize infants. Hutterites resisted and did everything they could to retain other elements of their Anabaptist faith, rebaptizing their children in adulthood.

During the second half of the 17th century and the first half of the 18th century, persecution of the Hutterites intensified. Among other things, Catholics tried to destroy the theological and historical literature of the Hutterites and thus disconnect them from their origins. Children were taken from their parents, Hutterite assembly halls were sealed, and Hutterites were forced to attend Catholic Church services and ceremonies. In 1781, most Hutterites were forcibly converted to Roman Catholicism, and the remaining Hutterites went to Transylvania to join a tiny Hutterite community there.

The Hutterite community in Transylvania was established in the first half of the 17th century when 200 people arrived in Alwinz from Moravia. At first they enjoyed good living conditions but during the second half of the 17th century conditions deteriorated because of the war between the Turks and the Habsburg monarchy. Hutterite numbers in Transylvania decreased to a few dozen by the beginning of the 18th century, and they were unable to maintain communal life, though they still adhered to other tenets of Hutterite theology. In 1755, the remaining Hutterites were joined by a group of 220 Lutheran refugees, who accepted Hutterite principles of faith and embraced their traditions, including the revival of communal living. Unfortunately, this renaissance did not last. Catholic persecution followed the Hutterites into Transylvania, where their leaders were arrested and exiled to Wallachia (Romania), which then was under the rule of the Ottomans. Moslems were more tolerant of the Hutterites than were their Catholic Christian brothers. Furthermore, the nobles in Wallachia were prepared to grant Hutterites lands for settlement. The remaining Hutterite community, then numbering no more than 67 people, was thus convinced to leave Transylvania and move to Wallachia, and in 1767 they settled near Bucharest. Peace and serenity still eluded the Hutterites. The war between Russia and the Ottoman Empire, which broke out in 1769, found the Hutterites in the midst of conflict, subject to looting and violence. Their settlement was destroyed.

In 1770, the Russians conquered the area, and suggested that the Hutterites move to Russia. In the spring of that year, about 60 Hutterites began their migration to Russia. On the basis of settlement policy established at the time of Catherine the Great, they were promised an opportunity to settle in Vishenka, near Kyiv, Ukraine, on the estate of the nobleman Alexandrovich Rumiantsev, who had participated in the conquest of Wallachia.

Hutterites first settled in Vishenka, where they received from Rumiantsev rights to freedom of worship, exemption from military service and also exemption from the need to stand before civil courts. They were able to establish a settlement similar to the one they had established in Moravia in the 16th century. In Vishenka, conservative elements, determined to strictly follow their forefathers' traditions and keep the community's regulations, became stronger.

After some 30 years in Vishenka, in 1802, the Hutterites, now numbering about 200 people, moved to nearby Radichev. In their new place they were able to establish their settlement under better conditions, but economic progress was accompanied by spiritual decline. Disagreements deepened between the younger generation who were demanding change, including changes to the communal tradition, and the older, more conservative, leadership who opposed it. Spiritual decline affected the settlement's economic status. After a fire burned down most of the settlement's buildings, the Hutterites abandoned communal living, establishing themselves on individual private farms, like their Mennonite neighbours. Mennonites strongly resembled the Hutterites in their Anabaptist religious tenets and practices and use of German as their *lingua franca* but did not practice communal living. Nevertheless, they practiced community cooperation, and held a strong belief in the provision of mutual aid, which both involved a level of collectivism.

Shortage of land for expansion on to private farms compelled the Hutterites to request and receive (in 1842) state lands in Molotschna, in southern Ukraine near Crimea. Mennonites had been settled in this area for several decades. Five Hutterite settlements that closely resembled those of their Mennonite neighbours were established there. From the Mennonites, especially Johann Cornies, the Hutterites obtained advice on farming on the steppes, advice and experience that would stand them in good stead when they moved to the grasslands of North America 30 years later.

Hostetler, Peters, Von Schlacta,[11] and Oved concur that this was a crucial formative period in Hutterite history and credit the revival of the Hutterite tradition and the return to full communal living to Mennonite influence:

> The main effect of their settlement near the Mennonites was the urging of the revival process of the communal heritage. Living alongside people of a sect close to them ideologically, enhanced the process of assimilation of those elements among the Hutterites whose ties to their ancestors' tradition weakened, but on the other hand encouraged among the faithful Hutterites the inclination to retain their uniqueness. The Hutterite preachers, who continued to read chapters from the Holy Scriptures at their gatherings, did not skip the chapters that pointed to the full community of assets that existed in their community in the past, and also emphasized the difference between this form of sharing and the partial sharing practiced by the Mennonites. Desire for a return to the golden era and the tradition of their forefathers grew among the Hutterites.[12] [Translated from Hebrew]

This cultural and religious upsurge within the community resulted in the organization in 1859–60 of two discrete Hutterite groups that adopted full communal life consistent with the basic principles of Hutterite faith. The first group was organized under the leadership of Michael Waldner, who was told in a dream to assemble his flock in a fully communal lifestyle. Waldner was a blacksmith, in German a *Schmied*, and therefore his group was called the *Schmiedeleut*. The second group assembled under the leadership of Darius Walter became known as the *Dariusleut* or Darius's group. Twenty-five years later, in 1875, a third group was formed in Russia, inspired by the teacher Jakob Wipf, a teacher, in German a *Lehrer*, and his group were known as the *Lehrerleut*.

As the Hutterite community was undergoing a process of revival, the Russian government enacted a law regarding compulsory military service, imposed government supervision of the schools, and introduced an obligation to study the Russian language. The Hutterites and Mennonites perceived these innovations as a real threat to their religious practices and community ideology. After the government officials made it clear that they would receive no special status regarding compulsory military service and supervision of their education system, they started to consider the possibility of immigrating to the "New World" of North America. A Hutterite delegation that visited the United States in 1873 managed to receive from the President of the United States an assurance the Hutterites would not be subject to conscription. This, combined with religious freedom and the great potential for agricultural settlement in the United States, convinced the Hutterites to emigrate from Russia to North America. During the years 1874–79, all Hutterites in Russia, some 1,265 people, immigrated into the United States. Most of them had never practiced communal living, and they soon found their place among those Mennonites who immigrated to America for the same reasons and who settled in South Dakota. These Hutterites became known as the *Prairieleut*.[13] By the close of the 1870s, the United States' Hutterite community in communal settlements numbered less than 450 people. As in Russia, it was divided into three groups.

In 1874, the Schmiedeleut established the colony Bon Homme in South Dakota. This was the first Hutterite colony in North America. Not far from Bon Homme, the Dariusleut established their first colony a year later at Wolf Creek, also in South Dakota. In 1877, the Lehrerleut established their first colony, Old Elm Spring, again in South Dakota. New colonies branched from these colonies, as the Hutterites, for reasons discussed later, did not let their colonies in North America exceed 100–120 people, a principle they still adhere to. After their arrival in North America, Hutterites continued to use High German in their prayers and religious services but their *lingua franca* remained a dialect from the province of Carinthia, Austria, known as Carinthian German (*Kärntner Deutsch*), but fondly called *Hutterisch* by Hutterites. They learned English, but in keeping with their policy of isolating themselves from the secular world, used it only for communication with outsiders.

In 1917, there were 19 Hutterite colonies in the United States, with a total of 2,000 people. Except for two colonies established in Montana, all colonies were in South Dakota. An attempt to establish a colony in Pennsylvania was unsuccessful. The year 1917 marked the end of a period of serenity and prosperity during which they developed their farms and economy by adopting the most advanced agricultural machinery and techniques. In contrast, in their daily domestic life they strove to prevent modernity from intruding into their community, fearing that it carried the seeds of communal decay that would threaten their extremely conservative culture. Although they never hesitated to adopt the most advanced agricultural technology and production methods, they strictly controlled access to goods from the outside world, especially those items that they felt would introduce secular influences and attitudes alien to the Hutterite way of life. This attitude has been a hallmark of Hutterite strategy from their earliest days in North America. Thus, today Hutterites install satellite-positioning systems to guide their combine harvesters but generally refrain from installing radios or Compact Disc players, as they do not want to encourage combine operators to listen to recorded music or radio broadcasts. Nevertheless, cD players and radios are now found on most Schmiedeleut colonies.

When the United States entered the First World War, Hutterites, as committed pacifists, refused conscription. Their refusal to serve in the United States military, combined with their German identity, and their reluctance to contribute to the war effort by purchasing war bonds, brought persecution in its train. Dozens of young Hutterite men who refused to enlist were arrested, imprisoned, abused, and tortured. Two died in a military prison in Alcatraz from brutal treatment. Acts of violence were directed at their settlements, their property was seized, and access to markets denied to them.

This was not entirely unexpected. In 1898, with the outbreak of the Spanish-American War, Hutterites had feared the introduction of conscription. This led them to approach the federal government of Canada and the provincial government of Manitoba, with a request for admission to Canada with special privileges, namely exemption from military service. The governments of the day were anxious to secure settlers with agricultural expertise and capital and indicated to the Hutterites that they would be granted conscientious objector status, have the chance to live in communal settlements, and the right to maintain an independent education system. Similar rights had been granted earlier to the Mennonites. As a precautionary measure, in 1898 the Dariusleut established a colony near Dominion City in southern Manitoba as a Canadian bridgehead lest conditions in the United States deteriorate and they were pressured to serve in the United States military. After the war's end the threat of conscription disappeared and in 1903 the Hutterites in Manitoba sold their land holdings and returned to the United States.

For the Hutterites the experience of forced conscription was traumatic, and was not easily forgotten. Enquiries conducted by the Hutterites in Canada in 1918 revealed that the government still held out its special proposals regarding Hutterite settlement in Canada. They liquidated their settlements in the United States in 1918, purchased land in Manitoba and Alberta, and began the move north in the same year. Although hostilities ceased in Europe on November 11, 1918, in the United States anti-German sentiment still ran high for some years, especially in areas colonized by Hutterites; the move was already underway and there was no guarantee that, pending the signing of a peace agreement between the allies and Germany, hostilities would not be resumed. By 1922 there were already 15 colonies in Manitoba and Alberta; only one colony remained in South Dakota.

Hutterite settlement in South Dakota was renewed only in the 1930s. Despite their earlier unpleasant experience in the United States, the option of purchasing vast areas in South Dakota for relatively low prices was an attractive one. Furthermore, American farmers in South Dakota knew the value of the Hutterite settlements and their contribution to the agricultural activity, and attitudes towards the German-speaking population had changed for the better. After the Hutterites were promised similar rights to those enjoyed in Canada, they began to resettle in the United States. However, since 1918, most Hutterite settlements have been established in Canada's three Prairie Provinces.

By 1950 there were 60 colonies in western Canada and 26 colonies in the United States, in South Dakota and Montana.[14] Appendix 1, which is based on books by Hostetler,[15] Hofer,[16] Ryan,[17] Kraybill and Bowman,[18] and Janzen and Stanton,[19] on the 2014 *Hutterite Directory*,[20] and on demographic information collected by Patrick Murphy of James Valley Colony, Manitoba,[21] presents detailed data on the increase in the number of colonies since the arrival of the Hutterites in North America, showing the province/state, the parent colony, the year of establishment, leut, and, for the Schmiedeleut, the group with which they are affiliated.

It is not uncommon to find a variety of establishment dates for a colony, depending on which source is consulted. This results from the difficulty of determining exactly when a new colony comes into existence. Colony branching is a process rather than an event; several years can elapse between the time of the initial purchase of land and the date when the new colony is fully independent and operates as a discrete economic and social unit. For example, in 2014 James Valley Colony in Manitoba, having reached a population of 160, purchased land to establish a new daughter colony. It will be at least a year before they begin to work the land and longer before they begin to build dwellings there. It may take up to ten years before the new colony (as yet unnamed) becomes fully operational and independent,[22] although the colony will be listed in the *Hutterite Directory* when there is a Hutterite presence on the land, well before branching is formally complete.[23]

There are a few Christian communal communities loosely affiliated with the Hutterite community whose status as Hutterite colonies is debatable. Some colonies that are not formally part of the Hutterite Church (such as Elmendorf Colony in Minnesota or Rainbow Colony in Manitoba), but which practice community of goods, speak Hutterisch, have family names traditionally associated with Hutterite society, or are listed in the 2014 *Hutterite Directory*, we consider to be a part of the Hutterite community. Other colonies located overseas do not figure in our estimates of the Hutterite population: Owa Colony in Japan (now with only nine members) is composed of Japanese Christians who founded

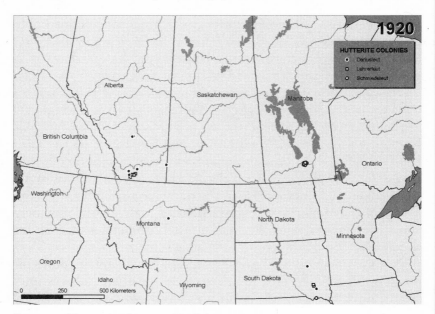

Figure 2.1 Hutterite colonies in North America, 1920.

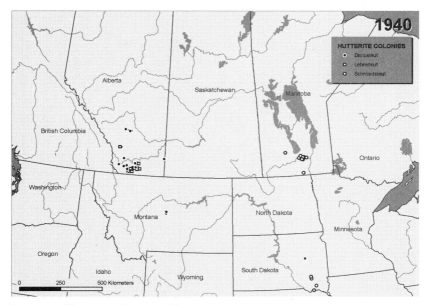

Figure 2.2 Hutterite colonies in North America, 1940.

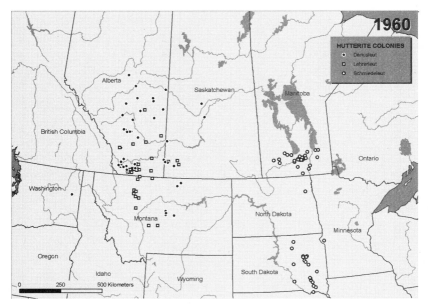

Figure 2.3 Hutterite colonies in North America, 1960.

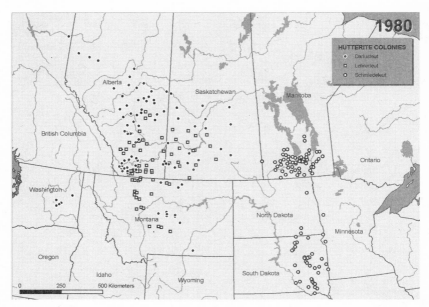

Figure 2.4 Hutterite colonies in North America, 1980.

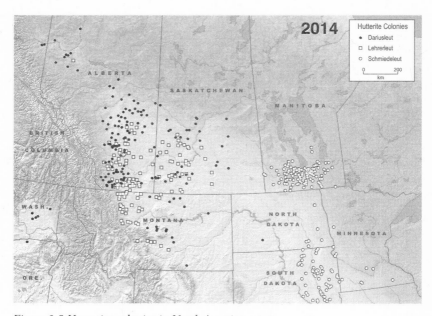

Figure 2.5 Hutterite colonies in North America, 2014.

the colony in 1972 to practice community of goods and a Christian lifestyle;[24] Rocky Cape Christian Community in Tasmania, Australia, is modelled on the Hutterite colony; and Palmgrove Colony in Nigeria, now with 190 members, was established in 1989.[25] In our calculations of the Hutterite population only colonies located in North America were considered.

The Hutterite population has increased significantly, fueled by one of the highest birth rates of any society in the western world. In the twenty years from 1947, when there were about 7,000 people living in 58 colonies, to 1967, the population more than doubled to 15,000 people.[26] Growth rates remained high. By 1974, there were 21,000 Hutterites in 229 colonies;[27] less than ten years later, in 1981, the population had grown to an estimated 24,000 people, living in 275 colonies.[28] By 1994, there were some 36,000 Hutterites in 400 colonies.[29] Kraybill and Bowman put the number of colonies in 2001 at 424.[30] Max Stanton's estimate of a Hutterite population of about 49,000 people in 2005 was perhaps a little high.[31] Today, the Hutterite population in North America is about 48,500 people.

In 2014 there are 507 colonies in North America, though some are embryonic. About 29 percent of this North American Hutterite population belong to the Lehrerleut, 33 percent to the Dariusleut and 38 percent to the Schmiedeleut. The latter are divided roughly 32/64 percent between the Group One and Group Two factions. Most colonies, about 73 percent, are located in Canada. Almost all the Canadian colonies are located in the three Prairie Provinces; just two are found in British Columbia, both in the Peace River district. The remainder are in the United States, mostly in South Dakota and Montana, with a few in Minnesota, North Dakota and Washington (see Appendix 1). Two colonies were recently established in Oregon and Missouri.[32] Figures 2.1–2.6 show the spread of Hutterite colonies in North America from 1920 to 2014.

Colonies range in size from 11 people in some embryonic colonies to over 170 people in colonies that are beginning the branching process. Most have a population of between 90 and 115 people. In recent years the growth rate has steadily declined as a result of apostasy and desertion, as well as a more lenient attitude to the employment of birth control when mandated for medical reasons. Thus, although in the past this prohibition against artificial birth control was strictly observed and the average number of children was ten or more, over the last 70 years this injunction has not been enforced so rigorously. The number of children in Hutterite

families has now decreased to between three and five.[33] In recent
years the number of people leaving the colonies has exceeded the
number of births, although many who leave later return. Even
though the defection rate is currently about 15 percent, the rate
of population growth in the colonies is still about twice the average in Canada and the United States.[34] Today there are about 21
or 22 families in a typical colony, most of whom are interrelated.
This is reflected in the limited number of family names found on
any one colony.[35]

Notes

1. At the end of the 19th century, when the Hutterites began their settlement in North America, these settlements were called "colonies."
2. Robert Friedmann, *Hutterite Studies* (Goshen, IN: Mennonite Historical Society, 1961), 111–14. All unacknowledged citations are from there.
3. *The Chronicle of the Hutterian Brethren*, Vol. 1.
4. John Horsch, *The Hutterian Brethren 1528–1931* (Cayley: Macmillan Colony, 1985).
5. Friedmann, *Hutterite Studies*.
6. Leonard Gross, *The Golden Years of the Hutterites* (Kitchener, ON: Pandora Press, 1998).
7. *Geschichte Buch* cited in Yaacov Oved, *Two Hundred Years of American Communes* (Tel Aviv: Yad Tabenkin and Hakibbutz Publishing House, 1986) [in Hebrew], 340.
8. Ibid., 341–42.
9. Ibid., 392–93.
10. Oved, *Two Hundred Years of American Communes* (New Brunswick, NJ: Transaction Books 1988), 103–6, 115–22.
11. Victor Peters, *All Things Common: The Hutterian Way of Life* (Minneapolis: University of Minnesota Press, 1965); Astrid Von Schlacta, "Struggle for Identity and Confession. The Hutterian Brethren in the Molochna Colony, South Russia, 1842–74," *Preservings*, No. 24, December (2004): 38–40.
12. Oved, *Two Hundred Years of American Communes*, 401–2.
13. For an account of the settlement of the Prairieleut in North America, see Rod A. Janzen, *The Prairie People: Forgotten Anabaptists* (Hanover, NH: University Press of New England, 1999).
14. On the history of the Hutterites until their arrival to North America, see John Hofer, *The History of the Hutterites* (Elie, MB: James Valley Book Centre, 2004), 24–69, and 92–100; Oved, *Two Hundred Years of American Communes*, 403–16; ibid., 33–350; John A. Hostetler, *Hutterite Society* (Baltimore and London: Johns Hopkins University Press, 1974), 91–136; John Ryan, *The Agricultural Economy of Manitoba Hutterite Colonies* (Toronto, ON: McClelland and Stewart, 1977), 33–45, and "Hutterites," *Horizon Canada* 2, no. 21 (1985). For a diagram illustrating the colonies' branching process in North America see Appendix 2.
15. Hostetler, *Hutterite Society*, 359–66.
16. Hofer, *History of the Hutterites*, 58–69.
17. Ryan, *Agricultural Economy*, 275.
18. Donald B. Kraybill and Carl F. Bowman, *On the Backroad to Heaven: Old Order Hutterites, Mennonites, Amish and Brethren* (Baltimore and London: Johns Hopkins University Press, 2001), 23.
19. Rod Janzen and Max Stanton, *The Hutterites in North America* (Baltimore: The Johns Hopkins University Press, 2010), 307–319.

20. 2014 *Hutterite Directory* (Elie, MB: James Valley Book Centre).

21. Patrick Murphy produces the annual *Hutterite Directory*. As a part of his information-gathering in 2014, he requested population numbers from every colony. He received an 84 percent response rate.

22. John Hofer, interview by John Lehr, James Valley Colony, July 17, 2014.

23. Patrick Murphy, James Valley Colony, telephone conversation with John Lehr, July 24, 2014.

24. John C. Lehr, "Owa: a Dariusleut Hutterite Colony in Japan," *Prairie Perspectives: Geographical Essays*, Vol. 13 (2010), 30–38.

25. *Hutterite Directory*, 49.

26. Aharon Meged, "A Christian Commune in Canada," *Mibifnim* (1947): 543–53; James Valley Colony Archive, Judge Dickson's verdict in the lawsuit of Benjamin Hofer et al. against Zacharias Hofer et al., May 6, 1966.

27. Edward D. Boldt, "Structural Tightness, Autonomy, and Observability: An Analysis of Hutterite Conformity and Orderliness," *Canadian Journal of Sociology* 3, no. 3 (1978): 350–51.

28. Edward D. Boldt, "The Hutterites: Current Developments and Future Prospects," in James S. Frideres (ed.), *Multiculturalism and Intergroup Relations* (New York and London: n.p., 1989), 60–61.

29. Donald E. Pitzer, *America's Communal Utopias* (Chapel Hill, NC: University of North Carolina Press, 1997), 332–33.

30. Kraybill and Bowman, *On the Backroad to Heaven*, 22–23, 48–49.

31. Prof. Max Stanton at the ICSA conference, October 2005.

32. Tammy Huffman, "First Hutterite Colony in Missouri Moves Here," *The North Missourian*, January 22, 2014; 2014 *Hutterite Directory*; and Jeaninne Koranda, "Part of Ritzville Hutterite Group Is Moving to Oregon," *Seattle Times*, March 8, 2003.

33. John Hofer, interview by Yossi Katz, James Valley Colony, May 2004 and September 26, 2005; Sara Gross, interview by Yossi Katz, Bloomfield Colony, August 2004; data presented by Prof. Max Stanton at ICSA conference, October 2005. Janzen and Stanton, *Hutterites in North America*, note that the number of children born per woman has declined from 10.4 in 1940 to 4.8 in 1990 (p. 235). See also Appendix 3.

34. Janzen and Stanton, *Hutterites in North America*, 301.

35. John Hofer, interview by Yossi Katz, James Valley Colony, September 26, 2005; Appendix 3. See also the 2014 *Hutterite Directory*.

Chapter 3

ORGANIZATION AND LAW
IN THE NEW WORLD:

The Organizational and Legal Frameworks
of the Hutterite Church and its Leute in North America

ROM THE TIME OF THEIR ARRIVAL IN NORTH AMERICA
the three Hutterite leute have been interrelated, though
not in a formal or legal sense. It was only in the summer
of 1950, after the provinces of Alberta and Manitoba
imposed restrictions on land purchase by Hutterite colonies, that
the relationship became formal.

In August 1950, the leaders of all the 60 colonies in Canada
at the time assembled in order to formulate a constitution for all
Hutterites: the Constitution of the Hutterian Brethren Church. The
purpose of the association was to represent the Hutterite Church
(namely, the Hutterite colonies) whenever common issues, such
as restrictions on land purchase, challenged the community as
a whole.[1] The general constitution was the basis for the Articles
of Association of each colony, and for legislation enacted by the
Canadian Parliament in 1951.

According to the constitution, the Hutterian Church is comprised of the members of the colonies whose elders assembled
to sign the constitution, as well as from all future colonies that

accept the constitution.[2] The constitution specifies that the Hutterite Church is divided into three leute: the Schmiedeleut colonies, the Dariusleut colonies, and the Lehrerleut colonies. A Board of nine members—three from each leut—who serve on a voluntary basis, head the Church. This board should meet at least once a year in order to determine the principles by which the Church will conduct itself, and to approve the acceptance to the Church of communities of appropriate faith that are willing to join the Hutterite Church. The decisions of the board of managers are valid only when the three leute accept and approve them beforehand. The board of managers elects a president, a vice-president and a secretary-treasurer to head the committee for a period of three years. They make decisions according to majority vote, but the president is entitled to a decisive vote in the event of an equally split decision, or the board may decide to resolve an issue by drawing lots.

According to the constitution, the supreme goal of the Church is to help its members in any possible way to establish colonies in the spirit of Jesus, the Apostles, the Early Church of Jerusalem and the early Hutterian community—established by Jacob Hutter—colonies whose members will "achieve one entire spiritual unit in complete community of goods (whether production or consumption) in perfect purity in mutual relationships, absolute truthfulness and a real attitude of peace, confessing and testifying by word and deed that Love, Justice, Truth and Peace is God's will for all men on earth."[3] To fulfill this goal members of the colonies must devote themselves completely to their work, but "no colony shall be liable for the debts, liabilities, or any financial obligation whatsoever of any other colony or the Church."[4]

Each of the three leute is headed by a board of managers, comprised of two representatives from each colony. The boards of managers "shall have charge of all matters pertaining to the Church and the Hutterian Brethren within its Conference, and shall have power to take such action as it deems appropriate in respect to matters affecting or pertaining to the Church and the Hutterian Brethren of that Conference."[5] In addition, the leut may accept new colonies. The board of managers has a chairman, vice-chairman and secretary, who are elected from the members of the board for a period of two years.[6]

A significant part of the constitution deals with the principles of organization and function of the colonies:

1. The colonies will be comprised of all persons whose membership has been approved by a majority vote of the male members of the colony at the annual meeting or special meeting.

2. The colony's capital will be used for social work, helping the poor, the weak and the sickly people, purchase of lands, stock, other means of production and inventory, in order to maintain the members of the colony and carry out the purposes of the Hutterite Church.

3. The members of the colony will have no rights whatsoever to the colonies' assets, including those of their own colony.

4. The members must transfer to the colony all the assets they had before they joined the colony. This obligation includes the assets they might receive from outside sources after they join the colony.

5. All the colony's property will serve all members of the colony, for the colony's purposes only.

6. No property can be removed from the colony, and if a certain member will cease to be part of the colony or will be expelled, he will have no right to its property.

7. The death of a member will not grant his heirs any rights to the colony's property.

8. All the colony's members must devote all their time and energies to the benefit of the colony and its purposes, without expecting any compensation.

9. The members of the colony and their families who are not members thereof, are entitled to be supported by the colony as long as they obey its rules and live by them.

10. Relatives of members of the colony will be entitled to remain in the colony after the death of the members and enjoy the support of the colony as long as they live by the colony's rules and devote all their time and energies to it.

11. A colony will not be dismantled without the consent of all its members.

12. Each member of the colony may be expelled from it because of his deeds or his refusal to accept and obey the colony's rules, upon a majority vote in favour of his expulsion.

13. The officers of the colony may buy, sell, mortgage, and lease the real and personal property of the colony for any purpose whatsoever, upon the consent of the majority of the male members of the colony.[7]

Each colony compiled Articles of Association based on the Constitution of the Hutterian Brethren. These articles, signed by all the members of the colony, comprise the legal document for the communal association of the colony, determining its organization and the rights and duties of its members.

The Articles of Association are similar in all the colonies. We have, for example, the Articles of Association of the colonies of James Valley and Interlake, both belonging to the Schmiedeleut.[8] James Valley is one of the oldest colonies in North America. It was originally established in South Dakota, moving in 1918 to Manitoba. It is still considered one of the Hutterites' most successful colonies, both religiously and economically. It is located in eastern Manitoba, Canada, not far from Winnipeg, the provincial capital.

The Hutterites, not surprisingly, define the religious purpose as the main goal of association: "to promote, engage in and carry on the Christian Religion, Christian worship, and religious education and teachings, and to worship God according to the religious belief of the Hutterian Brethren Church."[9] The economic organization and communal way of life of the Hutterites is a part of their religious purpose.

The colony is defined as a Mutual Corporation, quite similar to the legal definition of the Israeli kibbutz or communal association. Its institutions are the general meeting and the board of managers. The general meeting is comprised of the colony's members, who sign the Articles of Association, and they must be above the age of 17, confirmed as members by a majority of the male members at the general meeting of the colony, and members of the Hutterian Church. The general meeting is supposed to assemble at least once a year, in the middle of January. At the meeting the board of managers presents issues for discussion and decision. The general meeting meets for the same purpose on dates appointed by the board of managers, following the announcement of the president at the end of the Sunday prayer service.

Except for instructions regarding the election of officials, the Articles of Association of the Schmiedeleut are quite vague regarding issues that should be discussed during the general meeting and it seems that the board of managers determines which issues are brought forward for discussion.

Only the male members of the colony who are married and baptized bachelors above the age of 25 have the right to vote at the general meeting.[10] The right to vote is also conditional on keeping the customs and rules that the board of managers of the Schmiedeleut decides upon from time to time (see the decisions and regulations in Appendix 5). A member who chooses not to participate in the vote is subject to discipline from the colony or the board of managers.

The board of managers is responsible for managing the colony's business and assets. According to the rules, the board is comprised of three to seven members, including the president, who is also the minister of the colony— the highest religious authority in the colony and the person who leads the prayers and the rituals. The president is also one of the two authorized signatories in the colony. The other official is the secretary-treasurer, *Haushalter*, who is in fact the general manager of the colony. He is called the "Boss" and is the second authorized signatory. Two other officials are the manager of the farm—the Farm Boss, *Weinzedel*—and the vice president, who is usually the second minister. The president, the Boss and the vice president are usually elected for life, unless they are punished, or they resign and the general meeting of the colony approves their resignation. The rest of the members of the board of managers are elected for a period of two years as is legally required, although they may serve for longer. The general meeting of the colony elects all officials except for the president.

The election system is unique. Except for the position of the president, there are no candidates for any position. The election process involves each male colony member writing on a slip of paper the name of the individual who, from all the male members of the colony, he believes is best suited for the position under discussion. The person who receives the most nominations is declared elected to the position (in the Lehrerleut colonies, the members of the branching colonies also participate in the election of officials, and vice versa). However, the process does not rule out collusion and the formation of tacit agreements to assure the election of a certain member for a certain position. Unless they do so for health reasons, colony members have no right to refuse the position to which they were elected.

Theoretically, the Hutterian Brethren Church elects each colony president, and he is the head of the board of managers, of the colony general assembly, and of the colony. Placing the president—the most senior religious figure—as the head of the elders running the colony is yet another expression of its being first and foremost a Christian religious entity. This presents a straightforward approach to the worship of God.

The decisions of the board of managers are made according to majority of votes. However, in case of tied votes, decisions are made by casting lots, rather than by awarding the president the power to break ties. The recourse to casting lots is a theological expression of handing decisions to God when it is "hinted from heaven" that a human being cannot handle them. Electing the minister (the president of the colony) is similar, since it is seen as a combination of human choice and divine selection. A colony where the position of the minister is vacant chooses a few candidates and at the same time notifies the Elder or Bishop of the leut that it needs a new minister. The minister notifies the rest of the colonies in the leut. At a predetermined date, the Elder or Bishop, accompanied by one or two members from each colony in the leut, visits the colony, and they, together with the members of the colony electing a minister, pass in front of the Bishop of the leut and name their preferred minister. The names of all the candidates who received five or more votes are recorded on a slip of paper, and the Bishop of the leut elects the new minister by drawing a name at random.[11]

Every morning, the officials (the minister, the second minister, the Boss/Haushalter and the Farm Boss/Weinzedel) meet to make their decisions regarding current issues. In the case of disagreement and tied votes, the rest of the members of the board are called upon to participate in the discussion and take part in the decision-making process. If disagreement makes it impossible to reach a consensus in this forum, drawing lots decides the issue.

In accordance with the Articles of Association, the colony's lands and assets are in the name of a private holding company, which holds the assets in trust for the colony. Liquidation of the colony is possible only with the assent of all its members and by written confirmation of the leut. Assets remaining after payment of the colony's debts go to the Hutterite Church.

The Constitution of the Hutterian Brethren states explicitly that there are no mutual obligations between colonies. The Articles of Association do not deny this statement, but under certain conditions, they enable mutual obligation. According to the Articles of Association, "The Board of Directors of the said Colony may, by and with the consent of a majority of the voting members of the Colony, guarantee or become surety for the payment of any debts or liabilities or the performance of any obligations of any one or more Hutterian Organizations, and may, for that purpose, execute any bonds, pledges or undertakings whatsoever."[12] It seems that this clause was introduced on the basis that the greater benefit of the colonies calls for mutuality under certain conditions, as opposed to the implication in the wording of the Constitution of the Hutterian Brethren. We shall see that there is a high degree of cooperation and provision of mutual aid between colonies, and colonies within a leut generally maintain close relationships.

The Articles of Association expand on the rights and duties of the individual in the colony, the obligation for complete community of goods (assets), the rejection of private property and the retention of expulsion as a punishment. Besides this elaboration, there is some repetition of clauses specified in the Constitution of the Hutterian Brethren. The Articles of Association state:

1. All the colony's property, either real or personal, which was received from any source whatsoever, will be permanently kept by the colony and will be used for its purposes.

2. All property, both real and personal, that each member of the colony was entitled to at the time he joined the colony, and any property that a member of the colony owns or is entitled to after he joined the colony, will become the property of the colony. The act of joining the colony and signing the Articles of Association will be considered as the release of the property and passing it to the colony, whether it is real or personal property owned by the member at the time he joined the colony, or property acquired by him or received as an inheritance at any time after that.[13] This property

will be held by the colony and will be used for the benefit of all members.

3. No property of the colony, real or personal, will be ever taken away from the colony, or given, sold or transferred from the colony, unless it is by the order of the Board of Directors. If a member will be expelled from the colony or cease to be a member thereof, he will not be entitled to take, withdraw, sell or transfer any property of the colony and will have no right or interest at the property. If a member of the colony dies, is expelled or ceases to be a member thereof, he or his representatives, heirs or creditors, or any other person, will not be entitled to any share in the property, whether the deceased had a share in the property at the time he joined the colony or not.

4. Each member will devote all his time, labour, services and profits to the colony and its purposes out of his own free will, without any compensation, except that which is detailed hereafter.

5. Colony members will have the right to have their spouse and children, who are not colony members, live with them. These family members will be supported, maintained and educated by the colony, in accordance with the rules, regulations and requirements of the Hutterite Church, the colony, the Christian religion, Christian worship and Christian education, and the beliefs carried on by the colony, as long as they obey the rules of the colony.

6. When a member of the colony shall die, his spouse and children, who are not members thereof, will have the right to remain in the colony and be supported, instructed and educated by it, as long as they live there and devote all their time and energies to the colony.

7. Husbands, wives and children of all colony members, who are not members thereof, will devote all their time and energies to the benefit of the colony and its purposes out of their own free will and without any compensation beside the one detailed here, and will

obey all the rules of the colony and the Church, as long as they live in the colony.

8. Each member of the colony may be expelled from it upon the decision of a general meeting or special meeting which will be assembled in response to his departure.[14] Expulsion may follow refusal to obey the rules of the Church or the colony; refusal to devote all his time, labour and services to the colony; refusal to perform any task or job required of him; or refusal to participate in general meetings or prayer services in the colony.[15]

9. In the case where a group of members leaves the colony and ceases to reside there in order to establish an independent Hutterite colony, upon the consent of the colony or without it, the members who continue to live in the colony may discontinue the membership of those who leave.[16]

It should be emphasized that the obligation to waive private property is declared not only by signing the Articles of Association. Members of the colony announce it at two more events: at the ritual of Baptism (which is done, as mentioned above, at adulthood), and the ceremony of marriage. At the ritual of Baptism, the minister says: "This we plainly state to everyone beforehand, so that we may be under no obligations to return anything to anyone afterwards. Therefore, if anyone should undertake to join us and later feel it impossible to remain and wish to have anything returned, let him now remain away, keep his own, and leave us in peace. We are not anxious for money and possessions, but desire Godly hearts." [17]

Current Management and the Decision-making Process

EVERY MORNING, THE Boss/Haushalter, the Farm Boss/Weinzedel and the second minister meet at the house of the minister and determine the day's agenda for the colony. They decide which members may leave the colony that day, where they will go, and for what purposes; which vehicles will be driven off the colony, etc. They have also to approve or reject requests of members to go to town for a doctor's appointment or for other personal and special needs, for example, to visit another colony and so on. Requests for leaving the colony (for personal matters) need to be presented to the minister at the evening before the intended absence. Similarly, requests for trips regarding colony business have to be presented to the Boss. In any case, members cannot leave the colony without prior approval from these people. If a request to leave the colony has been submitted during the day, the minister or the Boss must vet it. Approval for the farm boss and minister to both be absent at the same time must be obtained during the morning meeting. It is considered inappropriate for one of the elders to leave the colony without informing the other elders and receiving their approval.

The minister, second minister, Boss and Farm Boss are authorized to make decisions regarding expenses below a specified limit. In Bloomfield Colony, for example, the upper limit for such discretionary spending is between one and two thousand dollars. This amount applies to purchases of such items as tools, or sundry materials. Things that are required on a daily basis, such as animal feed, machinery parts, and kitchen supplies may exceed this amount. If there is disagreement among the four overseers, they invite other members of the board of managers to join the discussion and help reach a decision. If consensus cannot be achieved the issue is resolved by ballot or by general meeting.

Decisions made by the board of managers, whether in the small forum or in the expanded format, are final. That is, no man in the colony (including the board of managers) can challenge them about the disputed issue at the general meeting or at any other forum. The board of managers is the only one authorized to decide on the issues for discussion at the general meeting, other than those fixed issues that are mentioned in the Articles of Association. The board also determines the dates of the general meetings. It is therefore obvious that the board of managers and the four officials—the minister, the Boss, the second minister and the Farm Boss—are extremely powerful. Four members, often related through family ties, therefore decide most of the issues in the colony. It is not rare to find two or more brothers among these four officials. Some Schmiedeleut colony members expressed reservations about this situation: "Indeed, everything is communal, but there is no democracy, we are blessed with 'intrigues,' partly because substantial decisions may be made by one family."

The members of the general meeting who have full rights are all the male members of the colony that have been baptized and are married. Those who have been baptized but are still not married may participate and vote at the general meetings discussing financial issues only, but not at other general meetings. Under certain conditions, a bachelor may also take part in all general meetings and vote, provided he grows a beard, is baptized and 25 years of age or older.

At the Schmiedeleut colonies with which we are familiar, the general meeting discusses expenses above $2,000, confirms the annual financial report, the budget and the annual balance sheet. It also decides on the date of colony branching, members' trips abroad (including those undertaken for medical reasons), purchase of lands, and the building of new houses. With the consent of the church Elder, it also determines whether or not charity grants should be made to members who have left the colony, and determines the amount of such grants. The general meetings, except for the one that takes place at the beginning of each year, take place on Sunday after the morning service. Attendance is obligatory. Those who fail to attend without good cause may be questioned as to the reason for their absence.

The Assets of Expelled and Defecting Members

THE COLONY'S RIGHT to expel any of its members on account of exceptional acts, and its full ownership of communal assets even at the time of expulsion or defection, was put to a legal precedent-setting test in the 1960s, and received extensive journalistic coverage.[18] Some members of the Schmiedeleut Interlake Colony, Manitoba, demanded their full share of the colony's assets after they were expelled for religious causes (joining the evangelical Church of God). The first court rejected their claim that the expulsion was illegal and their demand to receive their share of the colony's assets. The court's decision was in accordance with the Articles of Association and the Constitution of the Hutterian Brethren Church. This verdict was adopted by the High Court of Appeals of the Province of Manitoba and by the Supreme Court of Canada in Ottawa.[19] The assets of the Hutterite colony are therefore communal assets that cannot be divided (in fact, as we shall see, they are the assets of the colony's church).[20] Interlake Colony was established at the end of 1961 as a daughter colony of Rock Lake Colony. Not long after that it turned out that two of its members were proselytes of the Church of God, which they became acquainted with from frequent reading of *The Plain Truth* magazine, the magazine of the *Radio Church of God*. In the spring of 1963, the Schmiedeleut president demanded that the apostates discontinue their subscription to the magazine. He threatened that if they did not do so he would forbid them to celebrate Easter with the colony, but the two refused to do so. Moreover, they zealously observed the Sabbath, refrained from eating pork and even demanded that the seniors of the Hutterite ministry order the Hutterian community to observe the festivals mentioned in the Bible: Passover, Pentecost, Day of Atonement, and Succoth.

A year later, when it was clear that the two had no intention of obeying the minister's ruling, despite all the efforts at persuasion by 20 ministers from Schmiedeleut colonies who visited the Interlake Colony specifically for that purpose, disciplinary measures were taken. At first they were expelled from church services but to no avail. Another year passed, and once again 24 Schmiedeleut ministers visited the colony. They held long conversations with the two apostates to little effect. It was then decided to inflict upon them the punishment of temporary excommunication (*Unfrieden*). "When a member is in *Unfrieden* he is not to associate with any other member, including his wife, nor eat in the public dining room; he is required to sleep alone; he must not leave the farm on business or on visiting trips; he is expected to attend church but to sit by the door and not with the congregation; he is expected to work. It is assumed that if the offender is a brother in spirit the initiative will be taken by him and that he will ask for his penalty and, having served it (which in the case of the shunning experienced in *Unfrieden* may continue for two or three weeks), he will return to the fold."[21] But the apostates refused to accept the punishment and did not waver in their convictions. In March 1964 they were disciplined more severely, when in addition to temporal excommunication, they were obliged to repeat the ritual of Baptism at the end of the excommunication period, namely, to be reaccepted to the Church (*Ausschluss*). However, even the declaration of this punishment, as well as the warnings and implorations by the senior ministers of the Schmiedeleut, were of no avail, and the seniors had no choice but to decide, in June 1964, to inflict the most severe punishment: expel the apostates and their families from the colony and discontinue their membership in the Hutterian Church as *abgefallen*. It was announced in Interlake that Benjamin Hofer and David Hofer and their wives had broken off from the Schmiedeleut in certain religious articles of faith, principally by their insistence that the Sabbath be observed on Saturday not Sunday and that the old Jewish law not to eat pork be observed. In other words, they broke away from the Church on principles of religious doctrine.

Shortly afterwards, two more members of the Interlake Colony followed their former brethren and joined the Church of God. As before, the efforts of persuasion of the senior ministers of the Schmiedeleut were to no avail, and at the beginning of 1965 they too were expelled from the colony. In the decision to do so, the president of the Schmiedeleut wrote:

> It was decided to expel these Members... from the membership of the Colony, and cease to be members thereof... because of differences of Faith and belief not being of the same faith in worship as the Hutterian Brethren Faith and Belief... We did not deal with the expulsion until they in reality practiced, and stopped going to our Church and stopped working on Saturdays.

Later, all four members were baptized into the Church of God, and removed all signs of Hutterite appearance, such as growing a beard and wearing suspenders, black pants and plain black jackets, from their person.

The four expelled members appealed to the court in Manitoba and challenged the decision to expel them as well as the colony's refusal to give them their share in the colony's property. Moreover, they demanded that the colony be liquidated and that each member receive his share of the colony's assets.

The judge at the first court, Judge J. Dickson, ruled against the two and justified both the colony's and the senior Hutterian ministry's decision to expel them and reject their demand for any share of colony assets. He declared that the two decisions of the colony and the seniors were well grounded in the Constitution of the Hutterian Brethren Church as well as in the Articles of Association. In a detailed verdict written on May 6, 1966, the judge asserted that people whose faith is opposed to that of the Hutterites cannot live together with the Hutterites, since they harm the unity of faith and custom that is so fundamental to the Hutterite community, and thus they endanger the existence of the community:

The Radio Church of God takes the position that the Fourth Commandment—Remember the Sabbath Day and keep it holy—is of continuing and perpetual validity and that therefore, Saturday, should be observed as the Lord's Day. From their very beginning the Hutterites have never had the Sabbath on a Saturday. They have always, pursuant to the teaching or Riedemann and in common with most of Christendom, had their Sabbath on a Sunday... A person who propagandizes that Saturday is more proper as a Holy Day, as opposed to Sunday, would be departing from standard Christian doctrine; the Fourth Commandment merely has historical significance because the Sabbath of the Old Israel was displaced or replaced for Christians by the Resurrection day. I accept the evidence of Reverend Decker that the Hutterian Brethren Church takes Sunday as the day of rest and considers it the Lord's Day; and the evidence of Reverend Jacob Kleinsasser that Sunday is a day of rest when the Hutterian Brethren worship and re-inspire themselves in the word of God—and that it is also the resurrection day of Jesus Christ and for the Brethren a resurrection day, that they shall rise too... The argument of Saturday observance as opposed to Sunday observance has been long and bitter. It is not the function of the Court to say which day should be observed as a holy day. For present purposes it is sufficient that the Hutterian Brethren for four hundred years have observed Sunday as the weekly day of rest for study of the word of God. Plaintiffs insisted that the other Hutterians were theologically in error and that Saturday should be observed. It is not surprising that the leaders of the Hutterian Brethren Church regarded such doctrinal departure as fundamental and serious in a community, the existence of which rests upon a unity of religious belief and practice...The Hutterian Brethren Church believes that the laws of the Old Covenant were abrogated by the fulfillment which took place in Christ and therefore pork may be eaten... when a member of a Hutterian Colony refuses to eat meat for religious reasons the Hutterians consider this destructive in a community where unity is needed... The evidence of Reverend Blake Wood, which I accept, is that a Christian who professed that the only true religious celebrations are Passover, Feast of the Tabernacles and Day of Atonement would be departing from the teachings and beliefs of the Hutterian Brethren, to whom these festivals have historical significance only; that Christianity celebrates Christmas because the birth of Christ has tremendous doctrinal significance but the Church of God does not celebrate this day... The significant and only relevant consideration is that the Hutterian Brethren Church, rightly or wrongly, holds, and for over four hundred years has held, certain clearly defined doctrinal convictions respecting Sunday observance, unclean meat, and festivals, which are in direct conflict with those held by adherents of the Church of God.

The judge then ruled that he found:

... the teachings and beliefs of the Church of God and those of the Hutterian Brethren cannot co-exist within one religious organization because fundamentally they are entirely different brands of religion. In some churches, members holding different beliefs achieve peaceful co-existence. That is out of the question here. The doctrines of the Church of God are aggressively hostile to, and critical of, the faith and practices of the Hutterian Brethren... Those in authority in the Hutterian Brethren were justified in concluding that plaintiffs as at the dates of their respective expulsions had not only endorsed another faith but were also guilty of persistent breach of discipline. This was not simply a discussion of metaphysical subtleties but a denunciation by plaintiffs of the doctrines of their Church. To quote Prof. Pickering: "...the basis of the Colony is religion... therefore if there is divergence over religion, the very foundation of the community collapses, because it is here that the centre of the community is to be found." Plaintiffs, as members of a community in which the totality of religion permeates all life and uniform doctrinal belief is essential to survival, chose to endorse foreign doctrines. The disruptive force of such behavior in a closely-knit community is obvious. By adopting divergent religious views, they had, even before the meetings at which they were formally expelled, excluded themselves from the spiritual community of which they had previously been a part. There had ceased to be that full unanimity of faith, life and work essential to communal living... It is no longer possible for the plaintiffs and Defendants to live as one religious community. Obviously, two groups professing conflicting religious doctrines cannot co-exist within a colony of the Hutterian Brethren. Plaintiffs, in failing to adhere to the doctrines upon which the congregation was originally established, and in severing their religious connection with the Hutterian Brethren Church, have become heretical and schismatic from the viewpoint of the Hutterian Brethren... The plaintiffs [could have been] reinstated in Church and Colony, if [they] had been prepared to return to Hutterian faith and practice. They chose not to do so... I find that their expulsion from the Hutterian Brethren Church was warranted... The right of expulsion for good cause is not only necessary for the preservation of harmony and good order but is expressly reserved in the articles.

The plaintiffs' demand to receive their share of the colony's property was also rejected, as it contradicted the Constitution of the Hutterian Brethren Church and some specific clauses in the Articles of Association, which the expelled members signed at the time of their Baptism. As Judge Dickson emphasized:

Nothing contained in the Articles of Association gives plaintiffs any claim to any part of the assets of the Colony. On the contrary, there is a repeated negation of such right. Paragraph 30 says that all the property of the Colony shall forever be owned by the Colony for the purposes of the Colony. The purposes of the Colony (paragraph 2) include "to worship God according to the religious beliefs of the members," i.e., according to the beliefs of the Hutterian Brethren Church. Paragraph 31 dedicates to the Colony, for the common use of all members, all property which a member owns on joining the Colony, and all property which he obtains after becoming a member of the colony. Paragraph 32 specifically provides that none of the property of the Colony shall ever be withdrawn from the Colony and paragraph 38 operates as a grant to the Colony of all property owned by any person at the time of becoming a member or acquired at any time subsequent thereto.

Moreover, the judge cited the words of the founders of the Hutterian Church:

> Also through Jesus Christ, we should give up earthly possessions, then we will be before God as purified gold and He will receive us as a burnt offering... God from the beginning ordained naught private for man, but all things to be common.

He also mentioned a similar demand that was rejected by the Hutterian Church in 1921:

> When they joined the church they did so upon the distinct understanding that they would have no individual interest in the property, which was common to them and all other members of it. They knew and they agreed that so long as they lived and remained members of the church they and their families would be fed and clothed and cared for in sickness and otherwise provided for to the extent of their actual needs and that upon their death those whom they left behind would be similarly cared for, but they also knew that no property in the community holdings would ever vest in them and that if they left the church they would go out empty handed. This was a solemn compact between them and those who in like spirit and under the same pledge formed with them the church.

Therefore, Judge Dickson found it plain that:

> Nothing could be more opposed to the terms and manifest intent of the Articles than to hold, that any one of the subscribers, upon affixing his signature thereto, acquired a proportionate share in the property then belonging to the Society, which was subject to withdrawal by him from the common fund on his voluntary retirement, and transmissible upon his decease to his heirs at law... The donation is not to each other, in the nature of a community of goods among individuals, but as members of the Society. Their proprietorship of the usufruct continues so long only as they continue as members. When they cease to be members, they cease to be proprietors... It is clear that where a portion of a church congregation refuses to adhere to the distinctive tenets imposed upon members of

the congregation, and secedes and adopts new tenets or a new belief it forfeits its rights in the church property.

Judge Dickson totally rejected the claim of the plaintiffs that the colony is analogous to a commercial partnership, and when one partner is forced to leave the partnership, he is entitled to his share. According to the judge, the colony is a church, and its property is the property of the church, granted by it so that it would be used communally for the purposes of the colony. It is by no means the property of business partners. Therefore, the plaintiffs have no ownership interest in this property. In Dickson's words:

> I cannot accept this view. The Articles must not be construed in a vacuum but rather in the light of Hutterianism. What is being dealt with here is a Church, not a business enterprise. This is clear from the Articles and from the entire evidence. The signatories are not partners. There are no partnership assets, only church assets. It is these church assets which Plaintiffs are seeking to obtain, assets impressed with the trust expressed in the Articles of Association that they will be held and enjoyed in common for the purposes of the Interlake Colony of Hutterian Brethren... Even if the Interlake Colony of Hutterian Brethren had acquired corporate status, and a majority of its members, officers and directors did as plaintiffs have done here, the minority adhering and submitting to the regular order of the Hutterian Church would be the true corporation.

The judge based his assertion on precedence from 1920 regarding branching and association of other churches, in which it was determined that the church's property is mortgaged for the purposes described in the church's constitution or rules, and even the majority of the community cannot divert the use of property to other purposes against the protest of the minority:

> In church organizations those who adhere and submit to the regular order of the church, local and general, though a minority, are the true congregation and corporation, if incorporated... The title to the church property of a divided congregation is in that part of it which is acting in harmony with its own law, and the ecclesiastical laws, usages, customs and principles which were accepted among them before the

dispute began, are the standards for determining which party is right... The guarantee of religious freedom has nothing to do with the property. It does not guarantee freedom to steal churches... It does not confer upon them the right of taking the property consecrated to other uses by those who may now be sleeping in their graves... Those who adhere to the principles of the founders of the congregation are entitled to the use of the church built by the founders.

Therefore, the judge forced the plaintiffs to evacuate the lands they were holding in Interlake and to return to the colony all the property held by them which belonged to the colony, including their personal property, which, too, belonged in fact to the colony. [22]

The expelled dissidents did not agree. They appealed to the Supreme Court of Appeals of the Province of Manitoba in Winnipeg. Judge Samuel Freedman sat in judgment. Freedman adopted Judge Dickson's ruling and added that although the plaintiffs' claim evokes some sympathy, for they must leave the colony with no rights to the property, this outcome, however, in spite of its severity, is a direct outcome of their own free-will actions:

As Hutterites, they committed themselves by specific covenants to abide by the property arrangements characteristic of Hutterianism. Knowing that membership in the Hutterian Brethren Church was an indispensable condition of membership in the Colony they deliberately embraced doctrines in conflict with those of their Church. Later they formally joined the Church of God. Their own acts made it impossible for them to remain with the colony and enjoy its property in common with their brethren... In my view the judgment should be affirmed and the appeal dismissed...

Some time later the Supreme Court of Canada approved this lower court ruling. [23]

In principle, even today a defector or expelled member is not entitled to any part of the colony's property, whether liquid assets, movable property or real estate. Some colonies strictly interpret this rule but others are more charitable and act beyond the letter of the law to provide members who wish to leave with means of livelihood for up to a month. Other colonies let them take the contents of their house. However, there was a problem of stealing property by defectors, or those who had been expelled, just before they physically left the colony: Once you decided to leave, you steal things from the colony and move them somewhere else, for example, building materials needed for building your house in another place. You steal, and prepare to leave.

In the case of the death of a spouse, the house contents remain with the survivor. Similarly, when parents die, the household furniture remains for the children who live there to use. If the children have already left the house, the remaining property is divided among the children. The colony does not demand to receive the property. However, a colony member inheriting property from his parents who are not part of the Hutterian community must pass the inheritance to the colony.[24]

Notes

1. James Valley Colony Archive, Judge Dickson's verdict in the lawsuit of Benjamin Hofer et al. against Zacharias Hofer et al., May 6, 1966.
2. James Valley Colony Archive, Constitution of the Hutterian Brethren Church and Rules as to Community of Property, 1993.
3. Constitution of 1993, Article 3(a).
4. Constitution of 1993, Article 33.
5. Constitution of 1993, Article 22.
6. The board of the Schmiedeleut assembles once a year and, at the end of its discussions, it publishes its decisions and the new regulations it approved. These regulations bind all the brethren of the Schmiedeleut; however, not everybody obeys them. Appendix 5 presents an edited selection of the decisions and annual regulations of the Schmiedeleut since the second half of the 18th century until today.
7. James Valley Colony Archive, Constitution of the Hutterian Brethren Church and Rules as to Community of Property, 1950. [paraphrased] The constitution is published also in Victor Peters, *All Things Common: The Hutterian Way of Life* (Minneapolis: University of Minnesota Press, 1965), 193–201. As we shall see later, it seems that there are differences between the leute regarding the extent of adherence to the decisions of the board. Thus, the Lehrerleut colonies adhere more closely and consistently to the decisions of their board of managers than do the Schmiedeleut colonies. Ken Gross, interview by Yossi Katz, Bloomfield Colony, Manitoba, August 2004.
8. See, for example, James Valley Colony Archive, Articles of Association of the James Valley Colony of Hutterian Brethren of the Post Office of Elie, Manitoba, Canada; Note 1 above, Articles of Association of the Interlake Colony.
9. James Valley Colony, Articles of Association, 2.
10. John Hofer, interview by John Lehr, James Valley Colony, September 3, 2008.
11. James Valley Colony Archive, Judge Dickson's verdict in the lawsuit of Benjamin Hofer et al. against Zacharias Hofer et al., May 6, 1966.
12. James Valley Colony, Articles of Association, 41.
13. Robert Friedmann mentions that according to the Hutterite regulations of the 16th and 17th centuries, when a Hutterite dies, everything he used must be returned to the community, including his books. Today, books are almost the only "property" which the Hutterite may bequeath to his children. See Robert Friedmann, *Hutterite Studies* (Goshen, IN: Mennonite Historical Society, 1961), 108.

14. The Hutterite term is *Weg-gelofen* (runaways) for those who leave voluntarily and *Ausgeschlossen* for those who are expelled from the Church. The term "defection" is used by Hostetler but Samuel Hofer, *The Hutterites: Lives and Images of Communal People* (Saskatoon, sk: Hofer Publishers, 1998), 159, says that this is an unfortunate term. We have used the more neutral term "departure."

15. Articles of Association of the James Valley Colony.

16. Ibid.

17. Samuel Freedman and Cameron Harvey, *Chief Justice Samuel Freedman: A Great Canadian Judge: A Collection of the Reasons for Judgment of the Honourable Samuel Freedman, Justice of the Court of Queen's Bench of Manitoba (1952-60), Justice of the Court of Appeal of Manitoba (1960-83), and Chief Justice of Manitoba (1971-83)*, (Winnipeg: Law Society of Manitoba, 1983), 23–25.

18. On the media coverage of this affair see, for example: "Hutterite Expulsion Without Property Legal, Says Judge," *Winnipeg Free Press*, November 17, 1966; "Colony Expulsion Recalled in Court," *Winnipeg Free Press*, March 31, 1966; "Hutterites Ordered to Practice What They Preach," *The Globe and Mail*, May 4, 1966.

19. Freedman, *Chief Justice Samuel Freedman*, 23–25.

20. There is an interesting contrast to be made with the status of lands in Israel which are defined as Mushaa, for these can be divided with the assent of the partners. For example, communal lands in Israel that are defined as Mushaa can be divided with the assent of the partners. However, Hutterite properties, including land, have a similar status to that of Israeli kibbutz assets, which even today cannot be divided, and a member who leaves the kibbutz or is expelled from it is not entitled to a share of these assets.

21. There are a series of sanctions that are used to maintain order and discipline within the colony. In order of severity they are: 1. *Brüder*, an apology to the brothers (the baptized male members of the colony); 2. *Gebert*, an apology to all at the evening service; 3. *Lehr*, an apology to all at the Sunday morning service; 4. *Unfrieden* (not in peace), exclusion from colony communal affairs and social shunning; 5. *Ausschluss*, temporary expulsion from the colony and Church. The most severe sanction is applied only to those who break their marriage vows, fall away from the faith and leave the colony, or steal large amounts of colony money. John Hofer, James Valley Colony, interview by J. Lehr, September 4, 2010.

22. See Note 1. All citations are from there. Compare this to the Chapter 1 section regarding the basic Hutterite conception that the whole colony belongs to God. Therefore, no part of its property might be given to those who do not belong in the colony.

23. See Freedman, *Chief Justice Samuel Freedman*, 23–31. On the discussion in the Supreme Court of Canada, see Janzen, *Limits to Liberty: The Experience of Mennonite, Hutterite and Doukhobor Communities in Canada* (Toronto: University of Toronto Press, 1990), 63–67. See also Hostetler, *Hutterite Society* (Baltimore and London: Johns Hopkins University Press, 1974), 276–78. During the 1980s, two brothers of the Hofer family left the James Valley Colony. They, too, filed a suit and demanded their share in the colony's assets. On the basis of the precedent set by the Supreme Court of Canada, their suit was rejected. The Supreme Court's resolution has also been used recently in a case of members of a certain synagogue in Saskatoon, Canada, who have discontinued their membership in the synagogue and demanded their financial share of its assets. The leaders of the synagogue used the Hutterian precedent to defend themselves. S.R. Wolchock, Schmiedeleut colonies' lawyer, who represented the Hutterian colonies since the 1960s. Interview by Yossi Katz and John Lehr, Winnipeg, August 22, 2004.

24. Schmiedeleut colony member, interview by Yossi Katz, August 2004.

Chapter 4

ISOLATION IN SPACE
AND SOCIAL CONVERGENCE:

The Spatial Organization
of the Colony in the New World

Planning and Physical Structure

THE COMMON BASIS OF THE SPATIAL AND LEGAL ORGA-
nization of the Hutterite communities in Canada and the
United States creates many similarities between them.
However, the colonies are by no means identical, as Sara
Gross from Bloomfield Colony remarked: "Since God did not create us equal, there is no uniform pattern of a colony among the
Schmiedeleut. However, the Lehrerleut colonies [as opposed to
the Schmiedeleut and the Dariusleut], because of their Orthodox-
communal orientation, share an almost identical pattern." Thus,
there are certain differences between the older Schmiedeleut colonies and the more recently established ones. The circular layout of
residences in Starlite and Norquay colonies, established in 1991 and
1993 respectively, intends to provide colony members with equally
easy access to the central dining hall and it also facilitates equal
access to each house by motor vehicles. James Valley Colony near
Elie, Manitoba, is presently adopting a new plan as it replaces older

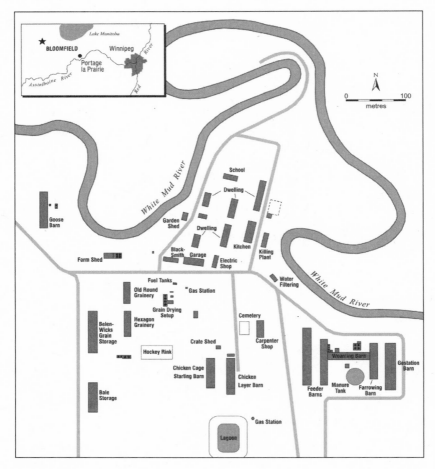

Figure 4.1 Bloomfield Colony.

buildings first erected in the 1920s (Figs. 4.1–4.6 show examples of colony layouts). The colony will eventually convert from the rectangular to circular arrangement of houses. It should be noted that the plan is made by the colony's board of managers, together with technical craftsmen in the colony, e.g. the carpenter, and the governmental-regional planning authorities must approve it.

Except for considering the availability of land for purchase or lease, the choice of colony location is usually dependent on three main variables: firstly, the availability of extensive lands for agriculture, for the colonies' economy is based first and foremost on cereal agriculture. Secondly, proximity to a reliable water supply is important to assure a regular supply of water for stock, the main

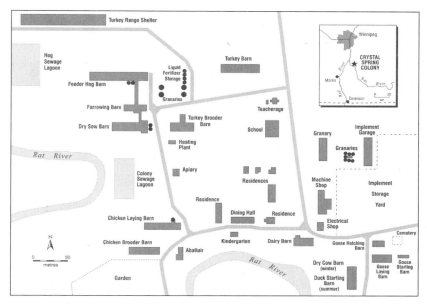

Figure 4.2 Crystal Spring Colony.

source of income. In the southern Manitoba rural municipality of Cartier, which has the highest density of Hutterite colonies in Canada, all colonies are located adjacent to the Assiniboine River or along intermittent surface streams that follow paleo-channels of the Assiniboine. Thirdly, it is considered advantageous to maintain some distance from urban settlements and major transportation routes, so that colonies are isolated from the secular world and its negative influences. Generally, colonies are located away from major roads and may be accessible only by unpaved roads.

Hutterite colonies are marked (as clusters of buildings) but not named on official Canadian topographic maps because they are not considered to be settlements but private business enterprises. For the same reason, provincial highway signs do not indicate their presence. Those signs that point the way to a colony are erected by the colonies themselves and are placed on privately owned land alongside provincial roads. During the period when governments were trying to restrict their expansion (see below) the Hutterites thought it judicious to maintain a low profile so colonies seldom advertised their presence. Today, signs posted by the Hutterites near their colonies are the only indication of their existence, and a casual traveler will be unlikely to stumble across a colony if he or she sticks to the major routes. Even the Hutterites themselves

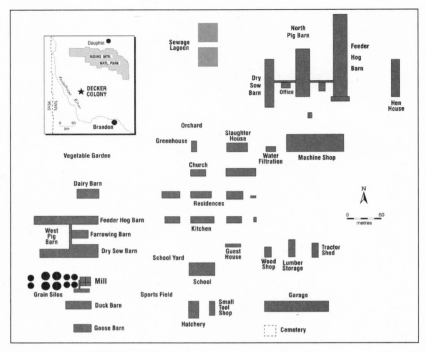

Figure 4.3 Decker Colony.

often find it difficult to locate unfamiliar colonies, as the postal address of a colony may be many miles away from its actual location. In at least one instance, a colony has a postal address in a province different from its actual location!

The settlement itself is divided into two areas: the residential area and the farm area. The residential area usually includes houses, dining hall and kitchen, church, school, and kindergarten.[1] Since the circular arrangement appears to be a fairly recent innovation first introduced in the 1980s, houses and some of these buildings are more commonly arranged in a rectangle, at the centre of which there is an open space consisting of a lawn and access paths. The houses are usually built in a row—a few buildings, each containing two, three or four apartments, and a passage between every two buildings. The proximity of the houses to each other facilitates interaction and mutual supervision of the residents. The entrance facades of the apartments face inwards to the central yard's lawn, crisscrossed by walkways. Thus, a visitor approaching a colony sees the backs of the apartments rather than the facades. In the new colonies, a back entrance to the apartments leads to a small

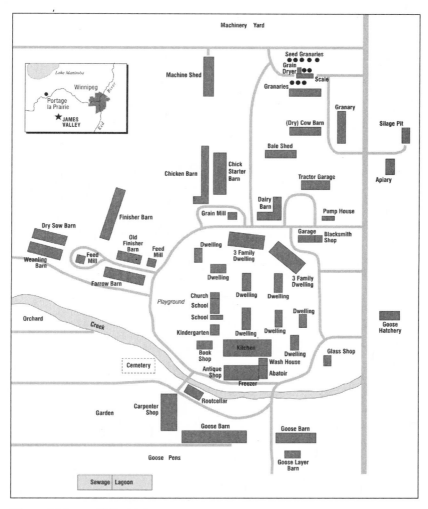

Figure 4.4 James Valley Colony.

yard, where one can find a small, well-kept flower garden and a clothes-drying rack.

Another form of arrangement has the residential area comprised of three rows of buildings. The two external rows consist of residences; the middle row includes the kitchen, dining hall, school, kindergarten, and church. These public buildings have two entrances, and thus, the people who live on either side are at the same distance from them—a fact that is supposed to express equality.[2] This model, for example, can be found in Castor Colony, Alberta, a Lehrerleut colony.

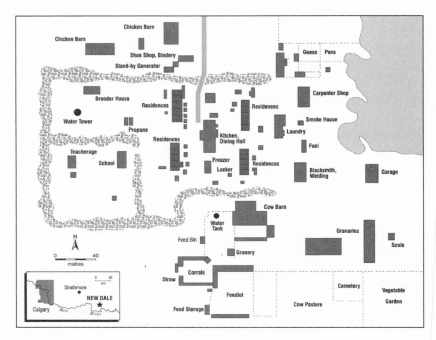

Figure 4.5 Newdale Colony.

In some of the colonies, the apartments are large and include six, or even more, spacious rooms. The church, the school, the dining hall and the kindergarten are also big and spacious, not only those which were built lately but also the older ones. However, it should be noted that the apartments in the Lehrerleut colonies are smaller than those of the Schmiedeleut, owing to the differences in the average income of the Schmiedeleut colonies as compared to that of the Lehrerleut colonies.

Apartments often include a basement, and sometimes an upper floor (in addition to the ground floor), and many storage areas. The size and space of the apartments does not seem to correspond with the otherwise modest and frugal way of life of the Hutterites.[3] The relative economy of construction by colony members rather than outside contractors does not fully explain this. Hutterites usually have large families and need several bedrooms in addition to workrooms for the women and offices for the men, and rooms for hosting visitors. Hutterites frequently visit back and forth between colonies and are accustomed to offering hospitality to other Hutterites, especially to close relatives from other colonies. The size of the Hutterite families, the branching of the colonies and

Figure 4.6 Starlite Colony.

the fact that there are few non-Hutterite recruits to the colonies explains why every Hutterite has many relatives in other colonies. In addition, there are many visits of relatives and acquaintances due to family events (happy and sad ones) and visits for mutual aid, all of which are quite common. All these compel them to build additional rooms for hosting visitors, and to build the church and dining hall bigger than needed for the colony's usual population. It seems that the North American external environment has some effect—lately, at least—on the size of the buildings, for the colony wants to retain a standard of living comparable to the outside world so as to minimize the material temptations facing colony members there.

Rooms are conspicuously simple. Floors are usually covered with linoleum and almost all houses have handmade rugs on the floors. The walls are bare except for some landscape pictures and handicrafts such as needlepoint embroidery that usually have a religious motif. Pictures featuring people, including family portraits, usually are not found in a Hutterite home, because of the prohibition to have one's picture taken: "You shall not make for yourself a graven image." If photographs are present, most likely they will be of children, and they will be displayed only in the most private area, the bedroom, but the chances are they are in an album shown only to close friends and family members. Non-religious books are very rare in a Hutterite home (see below for the reasons), and therefore there are seldom any open bookshelves in the rooms. Books are stored in cupboards. In contrast, storage areas in the house are spacious, meant mainly for storing clothes and raw materials for the women's crafts and handiwork. In each house, a modest kitchen has a refrigerator, a countertop hotplate, and sets of dishes. An ordinance in 1972 stated that refrigerators were not allowed other than in certain instances such as for the elderly and senior ministers who did not, or could not, take their meals communally.[4] This has never been recinded but today most families have a refrigerator. Microwave ovens, for reheating food and preparing snacks are increasingly common, although almost all baking and cooking is communal, undertaken in the colony kitchen adjacent to the dining hall, not in the house. In some of the Lehrerleut colonies, there is no refrigerator in the home kitchens; ice blocks keep foodstuffs cool.

The colony's church, which the community visits at least once each day for the evening service (at about 18:00) and on Sundays and holidays, like the churches of other Anabaptist groups, stands out in its Spartan simplicity. The building largely resembles the other buildings of the colony; it carries no external symbolism. According to the theological principles of Anabaptistism, no crosses, icons, pictures or statues will be found inside the church. Two separate sets of benches—one for women (with girls sitting on the front benches) and the other for men (with boys sitting on the front benches)—occupy about three quarters of the church's space. The entrance and exit are separate in some cases, depending on the whim of the builder.[5] The worshippers face the front of the church and the bench where the colony's elders (the minister and the board of managers) sit.

The dining hall, where the adults dine at least three times a day, together with the church, is the centre of the colony. The dining hall, too, looks very simple. Men and women never sit together in the dining hall but rather sit at separate tables, men on one side of the room, women on the other. Every person has his or her assigned place and the younger members sit at a table with the most senior members of the colony. Children under 15 years of age do not eat together with the adults, but rather in an adjacent but separate room where an adult, usually the German teacher, supervises them. The children's mealtime is before the adults'. The kitchen, attached to the dining room, is large and usually spotless. It is equipped with modern cooking equipment, dishwashers and automatic gadgets such as an automatic bread slicer, toaster, and a commercial-sized deep fryer. Walk-in cold storage and freezers are common. Often a separate room is designated for baking bread and pastries. Only women work in the kitchen or bakery as cooks and dishwashers. The dining hall basement provides storage, especially for preserved, refrigerated and frozen food. A small notice board, located in the basement, usually for the women, announces the scheduled times for work in the vegetable garden.

Each colony has a school and kindergarten of its own, regardless of the number of children. Since their arrival in North America, as a part of their concept of isolation from the outside world, Hutterites have not sent their children to local public schools. The colony places the family and education (as opposed to higher education) at the top of its priorities, and this means keeping the children near the family and colony at all times. During the morning and afternoon breaks each family gathers at home for a drink and snack. Also, the difficulties of transportation in rural areas during the winter made it impossible for the Hutterites to establish joint schools for a few colonies. Even in cases where colonies are physically very close, as with the Westroc and Bloomfield colonies in Manitoba, each colony maintains its own school. As we shall see, the Hutterites reached agreements with the governments according to which the school will "come" to the colony and not vice versa; in other words, the children do not attend public schools—teachers employed by the government arrive daily at the schools in each colony, which are designated for the colony's children only.

In addition, after the official school day is over, from October to May the colony's German teacher (who is a member of the colony, but is not necessarily an accredited teacher) teaches High German for two hours a day. High German is used in prayers and rituals. The German Carinthian dialect, Hutterisch, is used in everyday life, religious studies and Hutterite history and tradition. The school may have only one room with multiple grades, with the older children sitting in the back rows and the younger children in the front rows. The kindergarten is usually in a separate building. The kindergarten is an important element in education. Children learn basic concepts of communal life and acquire basic social skills there. In addition to its educational function, the kindergarten enables mothers to work in the colony instead of staying at home and taking care of the children. Not all schools are small; in Bloomfield, the colony school is a modern multi-room building (completed in 2007) complete with large gymnasium: a multi-grade school that is not dissimilar to any modern school in a small community outside the colony.[6]

The residential/domestic area is therefore the heart of the colony. Surrounding it, and not far from it, is the agricultural/economic area. It encompasses animal operations, which may include turkey, chicken, geese, hog and cattle barns, milk storage tanks, grain silos and elevators, a carpenter's workshop, a locksmith's workshop and lathe shop, a garage for fixing and maintaining colony vehicles, agricultural machinery sheds (some of the machines are stored for the whole winter), a garage for a fire truck, a control building for all the electric, cooling and heating systems in the colony, buildings for refrigerated storage of agricultural produce, etc. All these buildings are insulated, making year-round operation possible even in the harsh prairie winter when temperatures regularly fall to -30°C or lower.

The colony cemetery is located on the periphery of the agricultural buildings' area not far from the dwelling area. The graves, gravestones and the inscription on them are uniform and equal, and resemble military cemeteries in their conformity with the principle of community and equality of the Hutterian colony. However, not every colony adheres strictly to these principles in cemeteries. Today, each colony's cemetery reflects its level of orthodoxy and the degree to which egalitarian principles are currently applied.

Between the agricultural-economic area and the fields surrounding the colony there is a large vegetable garden of some 10 to 20 acres or more. In James Valley, for example, garden crops include corn, a wide range of vegetables—beets, squash, beans, peas, cabbage, onions, carrots, parsnips, and so forth—as well as tomatoes, raspberries, and strawberries. Some colonies keep bees. The garden requires intensive labour, mainly provided by the colony women and German teacher with younger boys aged 5 to 13, as only so much can be done using mechanical aids. Fields comprise the external circle of the colony; they may encompass several thousand acres of owned or rented land.[7]

Colony Branching

When a colony approaches a population of 120–150 (including children) its members begin to plan for its division and the creation of a daughter colony. Large colonies do not function well in the Hutterite model. Colonies with populations in excess of 100–120 people face employment problems, although with colonies becoming more diversified by manufacturing a wide variety of things, including furniture, fans, hog equipment, rafter and floor joists, all kinds of stainless steel equipment, fire trucks and grain truck boxes, more people can be employed, so colonies tend to get bigger before branching out. In a highly efficient "high tech" agricultural operation that is the typical Hutterite colony, there are a limited number of jobs where the incumbent has a measure of responsibility and the opportunity to exercise independent judgment. For the Hutterites it is important to provide work for everybody: "When the brothers or sisters are not busy at work, Satan finds a way to employ them, and it is quite easy to imagine the negative implications of such employment." The difficulty of providing work is a major barrier to integrating new male members into a colony for the newcomer would occupy a position earmarked for, or occupied by, an existing colony member, generating resentment and complicating intra-colony relationships.[8] Thus when a Hutterite couple marry the bride moves to the groom's colony, never the groom to the bride's colony.

Other reasons for branching are the wish to retain the community's intimacy and the interpersonal and communal relationship, and to enable mutual support and maintain the elders' authority. For data regarding branching of the colonies, see Appendices 2 and 3.

The branching process lasts three to eight years (in the Schmiedeleut colonies up to eight years, and in the Lehrerleut colonies up to four years). It is not an easy process, organizationally or socially, although branching has long been part of the Hutterian life and the way that colonies increase in numbers. It is not unusual to find a colony that has branched more than twice. For example, Bon Homme Colony, established in Manitoba in 1918, has already branched five times.[9]

The branching process is arranged so as to achieve parity in the division of all assets between the parent colony and the daughter colony. This includes provision of equal lands, buildings, capital, vehicles, agricultural equipment, machinery, and food stocks. Branching is carried out only after the new colony has been built and parity has been achieved. Drawing lots, or colony members volunteering, determines who stays in the parent colony and who moves to the new daughter colony. However, it is almost impossible to achieve true parity in assets, for the buildings in the daughter colony are new and the parent colony has older buildings, sometimes dozens of years old, and there may be some tension between the two.

Branching does not split nuclear families, but extended families are affected. Sometimes the decision regarding who stays and who moves is done voluntarily, by mutual agreement before lots are drawn. The plan is to divide the extended families in a way that will make the colonies more heterogeneous, so "the chance of intrigues will be smaller." Members of the parent colony plan and build the new colony. At this stage, nobody knows whether he or she will live in the new colony or will stay in his or her original home.

Hutterites prefer that the daughter colony be established as close as possible to the parent colony, for this carries numerous advantages: the long acquaintance between the members of the two colonies and the potential of cooperation will ameliorate the major difficulties involved in branching. Thus, for example, in 1959, Bon Homme Colony in Manitoba established its daughter colony, Grand Colony, less than five kilometres away.[10] In the same year, New Rosedale, Manitoba, established its daughter colony, Fairholme, less than 10 kilometres away. Westroc, the daughter colony of Bloomfield, was built only four kilometres away. Starlite, established in 1991, is only 10 kilometres from James Valley, its parent colony.

Over the past twenty years James Valley's population has increased to 160 people, of which close to half are under fifteen. Faced with further, and rapid, growth, the colony is searching for land to establish another daughter colony. The decision as to where to purchase land is complex. Land in their immediate vicinity, although first class agricultural land, is very expensive. Initially land in southern Manitoba was considered but a tract of land in eastern Saskatchewan was available at about a third of the price and was seriously considered as an option. Some colony members opposed the purchase and women were generally unenthusiastic about the prospect of moving so far away from friends and relatives. Neither purchase was pursued.[11]

The preferred strategy of locating daughter colonies close to parent colonies has never been easy to execute. It has always been difficult for parent colonies to purchase extensive tracts of land nearby for their daughter colonies at reasonable prices. The establishment of the parent colony itself brings a rise in the prices of land surrounding it, since the neighbouring farmers know that the colonies need reserves of land for expansion. Also, some neighbouring farmers resent expansion of Hutterite holdings in the immediate district. In the past, many feared Hutterites would come to control entire districts; they claimed that local service centres patronized only by non-Hutterites would slowly disappear when Hutterite colonies made bulk purchases in distant towns. They also considered Hutterites to be an alien and strange element that refused to have any economic or social relationship with them. During the Second World War xenophobia and resentment against all pacifist groups contributed to anti-Hutterite feelings, particularly in anglophone districts. Opponents of Hutterite expansion did whatever they could to convince provincial governments to place restrictions on land purchase, in order to prevent them from becoming the predominant element in any district. In 1957, Hutterites in Manitoba were pressured to reach a so-called "Gentlemen's Agreement" with the provincial government whereby the area of each new colony was limited to 5,120 acres. The Hutterites undertook to build no more than two colonies in any Manitoba municipality, and the minimum distance between two colonies would be 16 kilometres. As a result, while this agreement was in force, many daughter colonies were located far from their parent colonies. For example, in 1957, Waldheim built its daughter colony, Rose Valley, some 72 kilometres away. In 1956, Spring Valley, Manitoba, was built 160 kilometres from its parent colony of James Valley. Not all Hutterites considered this to be a necessarily bad thing. Greater dispersal of colonies restricted inter-colony visiting by young people, thus reducing interference with colony daily life. Greater dispersal of colonies also reduced competition for the new lands needed for colony branching, and prevented the price of land around colonies from rising too sharply.[12]

The socio-economic equation that determined Hutterite decision-making in land purchases to establish new colonies has changed radically over the last forty years. As Simon Evans points out in a recent analysis of the factors affecting the diffusion of Hutterite colonies in Alberta, the rural-urban population balance has shifted radically.[13] Rural communities across the prairies and plains have lost population and influence while urban communities have expanded, gaining political clout and imposing their liberal social values on the political agenda. Within North American society there is increasing recognition of human rights and greater tolerance of diversity and difference. Furthermore, as Evans argues, Hutterites are seen by urban populations as "a link to the mythic rural past from which urbanites have become increasingly disconnected," and urbanites are more inclined than formerly to defend the rights of a rural minority group.[14] Urban voters and their representatives are more likely to be concerned with rural ecological issues than rural social matters so would likely oppose any regulation that impinged on Hutterite rights.

Furthermore, Hutterites have changed over the years, as has the rural environment in which they live; improvements in rural roads and highways have given them greater mobility so they are now much more visible, and are commonly seen in farmers' markets and even in urban stores and supermarkets. In Winnipeg, for example, they are often seen in Costco (a members-only wholesale discount store), Dollarama, Superstore, Value Village, and various second-hand stores. Despite an ordinance condemning it they are sometimes present at hockey, baseball and football games. They are also visibly involved in charity work with the city's underprivileged. Perhaps most important is the increasing presence of Hutterites on the Internet. A cursory search of the term "Hutterite" will identify dozens of sites dealing with the topic, including some social media sites and blogs run by colony members.[15] Increasing visibility and involvement, increasing awareness of other minority groups similarly identified by distinctive clothing, and the policy of inclusion promoted by multiculturalism—these all help to de-mystify the group and establish them as an integral part of Canadian society in the popular mind.

Land acquisition is no longer a primary barrier to branching. Colonies with a strong manufacturing component do not require the same amount of land as those purely reliant on agriculture. For colonies intent on establishing a mixed agricultural economy, a more serious obstacle is the difficulty of purchasing much sought after provincial marketing quotas for eggs, milk, cheese, and so forth.

Notes

1. This description of colonies is based on visits made independently by both authors to colonies in Manitoba, North Dakota, Saskatchewan, and Alberta.
2. Based on a tour of Castor Colony by Yossi Katz on September 13–14, 2005. Castor is located between Edmonton and Calgary, about an hour's drive from each. It is located close to the town of the same name. It numbers 120 people.
3. John Ryan, *The Agricultural Economy of Manitoba Hutterite Colonies* (Toronto, ON: McClelland and Stewart, 1977), 32.
4. *Ordnungen und Konferenz Briefen,* 1972 Ordinance 2 (See Appendix 5).
5. Patrick Murphy, James Valley Colony, email message to John Lehr, April 12, 2010.
6. Group One Schmiedeleut colonies often employ their own members who have qualified as teachers. It is less common with the more conservative Group Two Schmiedeleut, and the Dariusleut and Lehrerleut only have non-Hutterite teachers in their schools.
7. See Ryan, *The Agricultural Economy of Manitoba Hutterite Colonies.*
8. Patrick Murphy, interview by John Lehr, James Valley Colony, September 27, 2007.
9. On the branching chain, see John Hofer, *The History of the Hutterites* (Elie, MB: James Valley Book Centre, 2004), and also Appendix 2.
10. Ryan, *The Agricultural Economy of Manitoba Hutterite Colonies,* 32–47.
11. Members of James Valley Colony, conversations with John Lehr, James Valley Colony, 2009–2013.
12. Information in August 2004 from the German teacher in Bloomfield Colony whose daughter colony, West Roc, established in 1992, was built within four kilometres of the parent colony. See Appendix 3 for a statistical analysis of the distances between the colonies.
13. Simon M. Evans, "Some factors shaping the expansion of Hutterite colonies in Alberta since the repeal of the Communal Properties Act in 1973," *Canadian Ethnic Studies,* 45 / 1-2 (2013), 203–236.
14. Ibid., 218.
15. See, for example, a blog run by Lydia Wollman from a Saskatchewan colony http://offthewollman.blogspot.ca/2013/10/my-thoughts-on-hutterites-nine-our.html (accessed 10 December 2013). Some Group One colony members have active and accessible Twitter accounts.

Chapter 5

RELIGION AND TRADITION
IN DAILY LIFE:

Clothes, Prayers, Rituals, Procreation, Sin,
Discipline and Repentance

H UTTERITES ARE MEMBERS OF A GOD-FEARING CHRIS-
tian community, and regard their daily life as a form of
worship, expressing through practice the fundamental
values of Christianity. Hutterites must thus regulate
daily life so that the will of God is done. They are anxious to
maintain their traditional ways and literally practice what they
preach. Nevertheless, while all aspects of life and the daily round
are governed by regulations that are intended to maintain the tenets of the faith, much is left to individuals to behave according to
their conscience and their understanding of their faith. Infractions
and small incremental changes that might seem insignificant to
outsiders are carefully monitored by the elders of the three leute,
who attempt to ameliorate the impact of change through advice
and rulings intended to protect the principles of the faith and to
ensure the continuity of communal life.

Clothing

HUTTERITE CLOTHING IS unique and, within each leut, almost uniform. It has changed little for hundreds of years. The members of the community have to wear their uniform clothing in the colony as well as outside of it—even when they travel abroad. Their clothing is simple and modest, and the rules forbid any adornment or dressing up. Within the overarching framework of "simplicity and modesty," there are minor stylistic differences between the three leute and between the colonies of each leut. These express differences in tradition and the level of orthodoxy. The greatest variation in clothing colours and patterns is seen in the less traditional and more liberal colonies. The fabric shades are not necessarily dark, and sometimes they bear floral patterns.[1]

Men must wear plain black shoes and black trousers without back "ass" pockets (since they do not ordinarily carry money), suspenders (belts were originally frowned upon as a symbol of the military), solid-coloured or lightly patterned shirts, and a short black working jacket. Some would like to wear belts "but I tell them don't wear them, otherwise there will be nothing left of tradition."[2] A solid black jacket and a white shirt are generally worn on Sunday and for special events. Black hats are worn in the winter; some wear straw hats in the summer. In the Lehrerleut colonies one must wear a hat at all times but in the Schmiedeleut and Dariusleut it is not obligatory. Baseball caps are often seen on Schmiedeleut colonies, most often worn by those who maintain machinery, where the traditional hat is not practical. Traditional hats worn by men in each leut differ slightly in style. Whereas the Schmiedeleut hat has a narrow brim and is somewhat reminiscent of a trilby style, Dariusleut and Lehrerleut hats have the high crown and wide brim of western hats popular in the ranching country of the western plains.

All married Hutterite men must grow a beard, which is kept neatly trimmed. Moustaches without a beard are not permitted in any leut. Schmiedeleut and Dariusleut men's beards incorporate a moustache but the Lehrerleut keep their upper lip cleanly shaven. In the past, moustaches without a beard were associated with soldiers and became seen as a symbol of military values. Avoidance of moustaches is thus a symbolic affirmation of their pacifist values.

Women wear black shoes or sandals with short socks, a dark two-piece outfit with a small, solid pattern: a skirt and vest made from the same fabric. They are not allowed to wear a one-piece outfit. The outfits may be multi-coloured; however, the more conservative the colony, the more uniform and sombre the colour. Beneath the vest the women wear a short-sleeved white blouse with a small collar. They also wear a black apron (as do the Dariusleut and Lehrerleut. In some Schmiedeleut colonies the women wear it all day, but in other colonies it is worn only during prayer services and rituals).[3] Women also wear a black plain jacket for work and for going out (today, some of the young generation are not strict about wearing the plain black jacket or black clothes in general), and they replace it with a black traditional jacket at prayers. They wear black triangular kerchiefs on their heads, and in some colonies these are somewhat ornamented. Unmarried women wear plain kerchiefs but married women's have small white dots. The size of the dots varies between colonies and the leut. The younger girls' outfits are a little more colourful. All Hutterite outfits lack buttons—they are closed with zippers and snap-fasteners. Wearing jewelry or any kind of personal adornment such as earrings, rings, necklaces and bracelets, is forbidden. Even wearing a wristwatch is not allowed, as it is regarded as personal adornment rather than a strictly functional item.[4] However, some youngsters are not strict about this and occasionally girls wearing ankle bracelets or with painted toenails may be encountered.

The extreme insistence on simplicity and modesty in clothing, as well as the adherence to wearing the uniform outfits everywhere—in the colony and outside the colony—is deeply rooted in Hutterite theology. It is a visible affirmation of their isolation from the outside world. It reminds them constantly and everywhere that they should separate themselves from the outside world, and that they are under the obligation to follow commandments and decrees, the prohibitions and permissions of a unique way of life.[5] The *Ordnungen und Konferenz Briefen* of the Schmiedeleut pay much attention to minor changes in traditional dress and stress that maintaining traditional clothing styles is vital in order to visibly separate Hutterites from non-Hutterites. Concern about variation in clothing and incorporation of outside fashion is partly generated by concerns for modesty and propriety but the deeper underlying reason is the determination to retain traditional costume as a mark of identity and their separation from the secular world.[6] Astrid Von Schlacta attributes the plethora of Ordinances devoted to the maintenance of distinctive clothing to the Hutterites' time in Molochna when they became closely integrated with Mennonite society. As they re-established their identity, founded new colonies, and resumed community of goods in the 1850s, they sought outward expressions of separateness by visibly emphasising cultural differences from Mennonites.[7] Adoption of non-traditional elements, wearing cowboy hats, western boots, and western shirts, "cries out to the world that we are becoming worldly, and the outsiders will take comfort in the fact that soon we will be the same as them and as the world," and is therefore resisted by the leadership.[8]

All outfits are made in the colonies, but shoes and some women's underwear are now purchased. Due to the differences of the level of orthodoxy between the colonies regarding handling money, the more open colonies provide funds to enable their members to make their own purchases of shoes, etc. In contrast, in some colonies (even among the Schmiedeleut) members are required to tell the shoe man the size of their shoes, so he can make the purchase for them.[9] As for women's clothing, these are bought during a special trip to town of the minister or Boss together with two colony women appointed as *Zeichschneider,* who then buy the material for sewing clothes.[10]

The issue of unique clothing, the need for simplicity and modesty, was elaborated in Riedemann's writings. Also, a significant part of the annual councils of the Schmiedeleut and the decisions and provisions published after these meetings (see Appendix 5), is dedicated to the subject of clothing, and its regulation in order to prevent immorality and deviation from formal group decisions. Riedemann said, among other things:

> What, however, serveth but pride, magnificence and vanity, such as elaborate braiding, floral and embroidery work, we make for no man, that we may keep our conscience unspotted before God...[11] Firstly, we say with Peter that the dress of Christians consisteth not in outward magnificence and ornament such as the wearing of gold chains and fine clothing and such like trappings, but that the hidden man of the heart be adorned with the incorruptibility of a gentle and quiet spirit, which is glorious and greatly prized in the eyes of God; wherewith also the saints who set their hope on God

adorned themselves. Therefore Christians should not strive to please the world by means of outward decoration as the world doeth, in that one lureth another with such outward show or seeketh his own pleasure therein, thereby forgetting God, forsaking the divine adornment and jewel and concerning himself with vanity, until Satan hath them firmly and utterly within his power... Thus is such decoration and zeal for the same not only not an adornment of Christians, but, on the contrary, a proof of the non-Christian; therefore all godly hearts rightly lay it aside, fight shy of, flee from and avoid it, and concern themselves with and use only the true decoration, jewel and adornment of Christians, which, as is said above, is of the inner man. For, since their citizenship is in heaven, they ought to put on heavenly jewels, and learn diligence from the children of the world, who, in whatsoever land they live, strive to dress and adorn themselves to the very uttermost in accordance with the custom of the same land, in order to please him who dwelleth in the world. How much more should Christians give heed to and regard the ways of their land, into which they are led by Christ: that is the divine nature and character; and in accordance with the custom of the same land also adorn themselves to the uttermost to please him who dwelleth in heaven.[12]

In the annual councils of the Schmiedeleut and the *Ordnungen und Koferenz Briefen*, clothing receives frequent and considerable attention. For many years, the leadership specified that women's skirts should be plain and dark. In 1949 it was agreed that "clothing no longer needs to be one colour, there can be small markings, but they should be small, no bigger than a dime, as is fitting for God's people. Also small flowers are allowed in about the same size but not bigger."[13] In the 1970s regulations reiterated that women's skirts must be black, grey, brown or dark blue. Wearing light-coloured or floral-patterned clothing was "totally forbidden."[14] Changes in women's fashions in the outside world clearly influenced Hutterite society, albeit in the growing pressure to use more varied and brighter colours in their dress. Women tended to modify their clothes in minor ways, something the elders did not favour, and warned against constantly. The Ordinances also revealed that:

Sisters and young women going around the yard bare-headed or with caps on is frequently appearing in the colonies. That is wrong. No virtuous, honourable, or God-fearing Sister would allow herself to be seen that way for it is not fitting... Paul says: "And every woman who prays or prophesies with her head uncovered dishonours her head—it is just as though her head were shaved. If a woman does not cover her head, she should have her hair cut off; and if it is a disgrace for a woman to have her hair cut or shaved off, she should cover her head... For this reason, and because of the angels, the woman ought to have a sign of authority on her head... Judge for yourselves: Is it proper for a woman to pray to God with her head uncovered?"[15]

Later, it was concluded that:

Too many floral[16] clothes are being worn by and the same goes for aprons, and this is directly contrary to the ordinance that stipulates that no colours other than black, dark blue, or coffee brown may be worn, and that aprons must be one colour. As far as dresses are concerned, women may wear a print with roses that are no larger than a dime. This is often violated. Therefore we are adding to this ordinance and putting a stop to this garbage. The fabric buyer should not dare to buy the forbidden fabric and thereby to spread arrogance and pride through one's clothing and to enable such things.[17]

Men will also be influenced by the fashions of the outside world. In the 1920s concern over this was manifested in an ordinance specifying exactly how hair should be cut. In the 1970s long hair became fashionable in the outside world and, to the dismay of the elders, Hutterite youth followed the trend. The frequency of ordinances reminding members of the 1921 Ordinance on the subject speaks to the difficulty of maintaining conformity. Hairstyles for men or women were the subject of ordinances in 1957, 1972, 1973, 1988, 1993 and 1997.

The differences in clothing between each leut, although barely noticeable to an outsider, carry considerable meaning to the Hutterites themselves. When, as happens on occasion, members of different leute marry, the woman, who always moves to her husband's colony, adopts the dress style of that colony's leut, sewing a completely new wardrobe in preparation for the move. Some differences in women's dress styles have evolved since the brethren have been in Canada. For example, whereas all Lehrerleut and many Dariusleut women still have narrow raised pleats (French pleats) on their skirts, the Schmiedeleut now use a wider flat pleat. This innovation was introduced to reduce sewing time by women in a southern Manitoba colony, from whence the style diffused.[18]

For men, the most obvious differences in apparel are seen in the style of jacket; the Schmiedeleut jacket has a collar and lapels, whereas those of the Lehrerleut and Dariusleut are collarless. Both the Lehrerleut and Dariusleut men wear broad-brimmed western style hats; the Schmiedeleut hat has a narrow brim. Some members of each leut consider the hats of the other leute to be inappropriate. A Dariusleut minister from a Saskatchewan colony disapproved of the Schmiedeleut narrow-brimmed hat as a style favoured "by cigar smokers and guitar players," a remark for which he later apologized.[19] On the other hand, the Schmeideleut's *Ordnungen und Konferenz Briefen* has a 1975 injunction against wide-brimmed western hats or "big hats," stating: "These types—the tall kind with the long feather—have never been allowed. The Indians and Mexicans wear this kind of hat."

Prayer

AS A RELIGIOUS-CONSERVATIVE community, prayers, rituals, and punishments for those who do not follow the rules play a significant role in the colony's everyday life. Although nearly 500 years have passed since the formation of the Hutterite faith, and in spite of their eager acceptance of modern agricultural technology, they fervently adhere to their beliefs, prayers and rituals, as did their forefathers hundreds of years ago.

Riedemann put great emphasis on prayer, preparations towards it and its significance to the believer. He criticized those who pray without real intention, just as a matter of routine, and he emphasized that no believer should come before his creator without first making peace with his brother ("at the Day of Atonement, man is forgiven only for sins between himself and his creator"). Riedemann argued that prayer:

> must and ought to be from a right heart, that is, in spirit and in truth, if it is to be pleasing to God. Therefore he who would so pray must prepare his heart, firstly, through the laying aside of all that is wrong, since God heareth not sinners; and must strive, as far as it is at all possible, to be at peace

with all men, above all with the believers; as Christ saith, "If thou comest before the altar to lay thy sacrifice thereon, and rememberest at the same moment that thy brother hath something against thee, then go and first be reconciled to him, and then come and sacrifice thy gift." Therefore each one who would offer the fruit of his lips to God—that is, praise and prayer—must first be reconciled to all, so that none of the believers have aught against him. Further, he also must have forgiven if he have aught in his heart against any, as Christ teacheth, saying, "When ye stand and pray, forgive, if ye have aught against any: that your Father also which is in heaven may forgive you your trespasses." And when the heart is thus purified it must then be adorned with true faith and real confidence. Yea, the man must have such trust in God that he surely, firmly and certainly believeth that God, as a father who seeketh always the best for his children, will hear him and grant his prayer; as the words of Christ show and indicate, "If ye, who are evil, can yet give your children good gifts, how much more will your Father in heaven give the Holy Spirit to them that ask him?" Thus, they who pray in faith will receive. And he who prayeth thus in faith ceaseth not to make his request to God, and alloweth no other concern to hinder or delay him; and if there should be delay and it seem as though God will not grant it, he waiteth with all patience in the firm confidence that God will certainly give without delay. He, however, who after he hath prayed turneth his heart to something else and so is drawn away from his request, and ceaseth to pray, and becometh weary of his request and leaveth it, can receive nothing, since he hath not continued in faith; as James saith, "If one would ask aught of God, let him ask in faith, nothing wavering. For he that then doubteth or ceaseth to make his request is an unstable man. Let not that man think that he shall receive anything of God."[20]

The Hutterite daily agenda includes prayers and blessings, all of which are recited in High German. Upon rising in the morning, before leaving their houses, Hutterites recite the Morning Prayer, which has two parts: one is a fixed and formal prayer and the other is personal. In the uniform part of the prayer, which can be the Lord's Prayer, the Hutterite asks God to protect the community during the upcoming day, to show them the way they should follow, to fulfill the believers' wishes, to retain the sanctity of their work, to prevent them from doing wrong and following Mammon, and to strengthen their faith even when faced with evil and difficult events. The content of the personal part of the prayer is for each person to choose. Some read verses from the Old or New Testament, some ask God to fulfill their personal needs, and others pray for the recovery of some sick person or for the fulfillment of any other need.

During the five daily meals (breakfast, mid-morning snack, lunch, mid-afternoon snack, and the evening dinner) grace is said in German both before and after eating. Usually one of the members says the blessing loudly. There is also a short prayer for those traveling, "Mir wean in Guttes Nomen lusfoden" "In the name of God, we are beginning our trip."

There is a long tradition that both ministers eat at the first minister's house—without their wives—not with the other colony members in the dining hall.[21] Those who are ill or infirm may also eat at home. This is a long tradition going back to when times were hard and the members tried to honour the ministers with a little better food, because the Bible says to treat elders with respect and honour (1 Timothy 5:17). Ministers were also more likely to be arrested and imprisoned, so the special treatment was a preparation and acknowledgement of their position. Today they eat the same food as the others. Some ministers eat in the dining hall, though some say that can erode their position.[22]

When a family has non-Hutterite guests they may choose to bring food from the kitchen and dine at home with their guests or bring their guests to the colony's dining hall. Meals in the dining hall are eaten quickly with little conversation and people begin to leave as soon as the short after-meal blessing has been said.[23] The manager, cook, her two assistants, the German schoolteacher, school mother, and the server eat afterwards.[24]

Every evening, or in some colonies a few times a week at around six o'clock, the entire colony population, adults and children, assembles in the colony church hall (*Kirchn*) for worship (*Gebet*).[25] About 15 minutes before the service will begin, a bell (today often an electrical chime piped into the residences) sounds, telling members to prepare to go to church. When a second bell indicates it is time to go to church, members will leave their houses; some people will be in front of the ministers, depending on distances from their house to the church. Colony officials take their places at the front of the church, facing the congregation.

To complete the harvest during good weather the men do not attend evening prayer services, since "Delegates for a religious duty are free from another religious duty." Work itself is considered worship of God, so colony members working in the fields are exempt from prayer. During the harvest, when women and men are in the fields or garden for days at a time, the majority cannot always attend services so there may not be a service on some days. This does not imply any erosion of religious commitment: the Hutterites consider every chore in the colony to be religious work; furthermore, without taking care of the physical needs of the colony, it will not be free to deal with spiritual matters:

> We do not attend the service at harvest time, because the colony depends on the grain seeds for feeding the animals (especially the pigs) and for sale, and if we do not finish the harvest before the rain comes, we will lose a lot of money and the colony will be lost. Then we will not be able to carry out our spiritual work and the prayers. In addition, working the land is part of the spiritual work and the worship of God. Also, throughout the year we pray that the crops will turn out fine, and now it is the time to harvest.[26]

Nevertheless, there is some concern that those who are away from the colony in town on business or are working in the fields at the time of the evening prayer do not make sufficient effort to plan their time so as to permit them to attend the evening service. Some colonies have banned "four o'clock trips," where colony members would leave for town on the pretext of picking up a machine part or needed supplies and would not return until late in the evening, having spent time visiting with Hutterite and non-Hutterite friends or socializing in the local restaurant.[27]

Striving for economic accomplishment is seen as a worship of the Creator in its own way. Although not frowned upon, in the eyes of some Hutterites this attitude can affect the pure worship of God through a formal church service:

> We are now much more business and economically oriented, and we devote less time to God. Satan is clever. He keeps you busier, and then you do not have time to worship God.

Indeed, many ministers, when on trips outside the colony, make every effort to arrive to the colony in time for the evening prayer, but there are those who make every effort not to do so; for if you are outside, it is acceptable that you do not attend the prayer. A business-economic inclination forces you to be in the fields, and this keeps you away from the worship of God.[28]

Many feel that economic achievement and prosperity definitely do not go together with spiritual achievement. Economic achievement even leads to a feeling of "My power and the might of my hand have gained me this wealth."[29]

Seating in church is segregated according to age and gender. Men and boys sit to the minister's and the officials' right, and women and girls sit to their left. The prayer is led by the minister, and in his absence—due to illness or being outside the colony—by the second minister. In rare cases, when the two ministers are both absent at the time of the evening prayer, the service is cancelled. Individual prayer is then the rule.[30]

The prayer service, which opens with a hymn, has three parts. In the first part, the minister may speak about the deeper meaning of the hymn, the Old and New Testament and the writings of the forefathers of the Hutterite Church. In the second part, he reads sections from texts by the forefathers, the Old and New Testaments, and traditional Hutterite sermons, written by the ministers in the 1500s and 1600s, which generally explain the deeper spiritual meaning of the Biblical texts. These have been used for hundreds of years. On holy days, the minister reads verses relating to them. The third part of the service is a prayer of thanks to God and a request to protect the colony, its economy, the government, the colony's widows, orphans, the old, and the sick, and to protect the crops from damage; the prayer also requests that God protect the colony from winds, fires, bad weather, accidents, sudden deaths, and concludes with a request to forgive them their sins. After the service, the worshippers leave the church in order, first the congregation, then the officials.

Before going to bed, prayers are said individually while kneeling. God is thanked for helping during the day with each step, for giving protection from enemies and accidents and for heeding their prayers and receiving their thanks. And then, in a justification of the law, adults say: "In case I die during the night, this being your will—I accept it." Children recite a different prayer, which is mainly a request made to God to revere and be obedient to him.[31] On Sundays, the principal prayer service takes place in the morning, between 9:00 to 11:00. It includes prayers and sermons. Special services also take place on Hutterite holidays (some of which are identical to those of other Christian groups), such as New Year's Day, Palm Sunday, Christmas Day, Easter Sunday, Good Friday, and Thanksgiving. Some of these holidays—Christmas, Easter and Pentecost—last three days.

For a significant part of the service the Minister recites a line and the congregation repeats it in song. This recitation and response during services goes back to the writings of Riedemann in the 1540s, who devoted a separate chapter to singing spiritual songs:

Paul saith, "Sing and make melody in your heart to the Lord, with psalms and hymns and spiritual songs." For this reason we say that to sing spiritual songs is good and pleasing to God if we sing in the right way, that is, attentively, in the fear of God and as inspired by the Spirit of Christ.

For it is for this reason that they are called spiritual songs: namely, that they are inspired and made and composed by the urge of the Spirit, and also attract and move men to blessedness. Therefore, since they are composed and made by the inspiration and urge of the Spirit of Christ, they must also be sung as inspired by the same Spirit, if they are to be sung aright and to be of service to men.

Where this is not the case, and one singeth only for carnal joy or for the sweet sound or for some such reason, one misuseth them, changing them into what is carnal and worldly, and singeth not songs of the Spirit, but of the letter. Likewise also, he who enjoyeth listening for the music's sake—he heareth in the letter and not in the Spirit, so with him also is it without fruit; and because they are not used, sung and heard aright, he that so doeth sinneth greatly against God; for he useth his word, which was given for his salvation and as an urge to blessedness, as leading to the lust of the flesh and to sin. Thus, it is changed by him into harm, for though the song in itself is spiritual, yet is it to that man no longer a spiritual song. It is a worldly song, for it is not sung in the Spirit.

He, however, who singeth in the Spirit, considereth diligently every word, how far and whither it goeth, why it hath been used and how it may serve to his betterment. He who doeth this singeth to the Lord's praise, to the betterment of both himself and others and as an instigation to a godly life. This is to sing well; to sing in any other way is in vain. Thus, we allow it not among us that other than spiritual songs are sung.[32]

In some colonies the main services are broadcast to the houses through public address systems. Thus, people who are infirm and unable to attend the church service can still listen to it.

Sundays

SUNDAY ON A Hutterite colony is a day for rest, prayer, for reading the Old and New Testaments, for studying religious writings and spending time with the children. On Sundays, only essential work that livestock operations mandate is performed: feeding and watering stock, collecting eggs and milking cattle. Except during the harvest rush, colony members do not work in the fields or the vegetable garden, and then only after the morning service. On Sunday there is no daily morning session of the colony's elders (the minister, second minister, Boss and Farm Boss). Economic pressures sometimes compromise the sanctity of Sunday, and various non-essential farm chores are undertaken.

Holy Days

HUTTERITES OBSERVE A three-day Christmas with both Boxing Day and December 27 treated as Sundays. On each day there is a morning service and a brief evening service prior to the evening meal. Afternoons are spent relaxing and visiting. The three morning services include specific traditional lessons: "the New Testament story of Jesus' birth from Luke's Gospel on Christmas Day, followed by teaching about the faith and devotion of the Shepherds, Hannah and Simeon. A teaching about the Old Testament prophecies elaborates on the Messiah's effect on people..."[33] In some colonies Christmas Day is marked by the children joining the adults for a candlelight Christmas dinner in the adults' dining room. Christmas dinner is comprised of roast duck or goose often accompanied by a glass of homemade dandelion or chokecherry wine. Sometimes a small glass of schnapps is served.[34]

Gift giving varies among colonies. Children always receive a gift from the colony. Parents are given a small sum according to their child's age group to buy a gift for each child. In some of the more liberal colonies "parents may add to it in order to afford a more expensive gift such as a keyboard or a pair of skates."[35] An ordinance of 1921 warns against having Christmas trees, suggesting that even at that time the practice was creeping in to some colonies. Today it is not uncommon for families in Schmiedeleut Group One colonies to have a Christmas tree in their house during the Christmas holidays.

Easter is celebrated as an important religious occasion. On Good Friday in the *Lehr* church service the minister explains how Christ was betrayed, how he suffered and was crucified to redeem mankind's sins. The scripture is the text from Luke 23. On Easter Sunday there is a morning church service based around the text Exodus 12. In the afternoon at about 2:30 another service is based around 1 Corinthians 10. On Easter Monday the colony has communion (*Obendmol*), recalling the Last Supper, when Jesus and the disciples broke bread and drank wine together. The text is from 1 Corinthians 11. The following day, Christ's triumphant resurrection (*Auferstehung*) is celebrated. (Matthew 28.) Forty days after Auferstehung/Ressurection, Ascension Day (*Christi Himmelfahrt*) is celebrated. Nine days later, Pentecost (*Pfingsten*), when the Holy Ghost came upon the disciples, is observed. For three days the teaching is from Acts 2. This is highly significant for the Hutterites, who base their belief in God's call to communal living in Acts 2: 42–47.[36]

A day within the Easter celebration is much like any given Sunday. No special foods are prepared. In some colonies hot cross buns are may be baked:

> [N]ot that this has any significance with our Easter Days, other than this is something that other people sometimes have for Easter. As Easter is a religious occasion we don't do much, if anything with Easter eggs. Sometimes we'll have bouquets on the dining room tables, which have decorated eggs on towels in them, just for decoration.[37]

Before Easter and other religious holidays the colony choir will practise hymns suited to the occasion. In Elm River Colony, before Easter, the Youth Choir, High School Choir and Children's Choir practice German and English songs such as "The Old Rugged Cross," "The Wood of the Cross was Real," "Fuer mich gingst du nach Golgatha," and "An dem Kreuz," mixing old favourite hymns with newer English ones.[38]

Baptism

BAPTISM IS THE most important ritual performed in the colony, the rite of passage that marks the Hutterite as an adult. By requesting baptism, a Hutterite freely promises to assume the burden of God's kingdom according to the rules of the Hutterite theology, and to make a full commitment to the colony. The ritual symbolizes the end of the period of forgivingness towards juvenile sins. From now on, whenever he or she sins, punishment follows. Now a full member of the colony, with full rights and duties, he or she may get married.[39]

Adult baptism is one of the main and most important principles distinguishing the Hutterite Church from Catholic Christianity and also from many other Protestant Christian groups. As Riedemann emphasized:

> Since children are not born of God after the Christian manner, that is through the preaching of the word, faith and the Holy Spirit, they cannot be baptized in the right way. For baptism is acceptance into the Church of Christ. Now, since all who are born of Adam partake of his fellowship, should they desire to be embodied in the Church of Christ, they must be born of Christ in the Christian way; that they may be accepted in the right way, which was committed to his Church by him.

> The birth of Christ, however, took place as is said above: through the word that was preached or proclaimed. Mary believed the angel, and through faith received the Holy Spirit, who worked together with her faith so that she conceived Christ, who was thus born of her. Whoever now is to be born in Christian wise, must firstly like Mary hear the word and believe the same, that when his faith is sealed with the Holy

Spirit he may be truly accepted into the Church of Christ. In this way also did the apostles.

For which reason we find in no place that the apostles baptized children; on the contrary we find that they kept what had been committed to them and their Master's teaching and say, "Yea, if thou believest with all thine heart, thou mayest indeed be baptized," as though the apostles thereby meant, "If, however, thou believest not, neither mayest thou be baptized."[40]

There are relatively few instances of outsiders joining the Church and proceeding to baptism. Most of the baptized are already members of the community, between the ages of 18 and 25.[41]

Since the middle of the 16th century baptism rituals have changed little. Baptism is always performed on Sunday. In the past, the custom was to gather the candidates for baptism for preparations on the Friday and Saturday preceding baptism. Today, preparations are done during the preceding weeks when the candidates visit the witness brothers, for seven Sunday afternoons, to receive instruction on baptism. During these preparations, the candidates study and memorize issues dealing with the Hutterite Church and its principles, parts of the Bible, differences between the religious way of life and the secular one, based on topics from Riedemann's book (such as "What sin is," "What original sin is," "God punishes those who are disobedient to His word," and so forth). According to Friedmann, candidates for baptism are told clearly that Christians are not baptized to become wretched sinners but to enter a new life. Jesus has always been and will always be for us the mediator, saviour and conciliator:

True faith is nothing but an attachment of the heart to God and Christ. He who believes from the heart is assured and sealed by the Holy Spirit. He receives strength from above to do the good, which he could not do before, and to hate the evil he could not hate before.

Candidates must be aware of what is requested of them. They must regret their former life, repent, and be prepared to enter a new life, one committed life to the Hutterite way.[42] On Friday and Saturday a longer evening service is held on two texts: John 3, 1–8 and Romans 6, 1–8. Confession follows the Saturday evening service. Sunday follows the Mathew 28, 16–20 sermon, which closes with the reading of 20 points concerning "what is the Church of Christ and how one may join it."

Before prayer, candidates for baptism are asked four questions to which they must respond in the affirmative while standing. Six more questions are posed to which the candidate responds positively while kneeling:

1. Do you now acknowledge the doctrines, which have hitherto been taught to you, as being the truth and right foundation to salvation?

2. Do you also believe in and agree with the twelve articles of our Christian faith? [Recite them please]

3. Do you also desire the prayer of intercession of the pious that God may forgive and remit the sins committed by you in ignorance?

4. Do you desire to consecrate, give and sacrifice yourself to the Lord God in the covenant of Christian baptism?

5. Do you now sufficiently understand the word of God and acknowledge it as the only path to life eternal?

6. Do you also truly and heartily repent of the sins, which you have in ignorance committed against God, and do you desire henceforth to fear God, nevermore to sin against God, and rather to suffer death than ever again to sin wilfully against God?

7. Do you also believe that your sins have been forgiven and remitted through Christ and the prayer of intercession of His people?

8. Is it also your desire to accept brotherly punishment and admonition and also to apply the same to others when it is needful?

9. Do you desire thus to consecrate, give and sacrifice yourself with soul and body and all your possessions

to the Lord in heaven, and to be obedient unto Christ and his church?

10. Do you desire thus to establish a covenant with God and all his people and to be baptized upon your confessed belief?[43]

Finally, the minister sprinkles water on the candidates and tells them: "On thy confessed belief I baptize thee, in the name of the Father, the Son, and the Holy Ghost. God Almighty in heaven who has given you grace and mercy through the death of Christ and the prayer of His Saints, may clothe you with fortitude from on high and inscribe your name into the book of eternal life, to preserve thee in piety and faith until death. This is my wish to thee through Jesus Christ. Amen."[44]

Marriage

THE CENTRALITY AND sanctity of marriage in Hutterite life makes the Hutterite marriage ceremony appear to be only slightly less important than the baptism ceremony. Marriage is forever, divorce is forbidden and so is bigamy, and God is a partner to the marriage covenant. Moreover, marriage is part of the principle of complete obedience to God's commandments, for God commanded his chosen people to be fruitful and multiply. Therefore, all his children must accept this commandment and observe it.

Riedemann laid down the Hutterite view of matrimony:

Marriage is the union of two, in which one taketh the other to care for and the second submitteth to obey the first, and thus through their agreement two become one, and are no longer two but one. But if this is to be done in a godly way they must come together not through their own action and choice, but in accordance with God's will and order, and therefore neither leave nor forsake the other but suffer both ill and good together all their day... Thus, we see marriage instructeth and leadeth men to God, for if one regardeth and observeth it aright it teacheth us to know God and to cleave to him. Where, however, it is not regarded and observed rightly it leadeth men away from God and bringeth them to death... Thus to both man and woman is ordained and commanded what is severally theirs, for he willeth thereby to lead us into deeper knowledge, namely, that even as the man should love the woman, care for her and bear rule over her, even so doth the spirit desire to care for, control and rule over the body, and God the spirit. And, on the other hand, as the woman should obey the man, even so should the earthly the heavenly body, that is the spirit; and from now on one should enter upon, do and undertake naught from the carnal or earthly will, but in all things seek, ask and look to the heavenly body and let oneself be ruled thereby. When this hath taken place, then is marriage rightly observed in all its three grades and one is kept close to God. Marriage must not come about through the will of the flesh, whether for the sake of beauty, youth, money, possessions or any other thing that the flesh desireth. For this is not of God, but cometh from the devil... Thus, marriage serveth for destruction to all who enter upon it from carnal desire. Therefore such a thing should not take place, and one should in no case choose from the flesh but await such a gift from God, and with all diligence pray that God in accordance with his divine will might send what he from the beginning hath provided, serving to one's salvation and life. Then after such a prayer one should ask not his flesh but the elders that God might show him through them what he hath appointed for him. This, then, one should take with real gratitude as a gift from God, whether young or old, poor or rich... The man should also be the husband of only one wife, even as Christ is the head of the one Church. For, since marriage is a picture of the same, the likeness and indication must resemble what it indicateth. Therefore must a man have no more than one wife.[45]

The Hutterites sanctify the purity of family life, the marital relationship, and loyalty to one's spouse. The whole family and community are involved in the marriage. In old times, courting was forbidden, the elders made the matches, and soon after that the wedding took place. Today, friendship and even touching before the wedding are allowed. However, pre-marital sex is forbidden, and transgressions are punished severely. The same applies to acts of adultery.[46]

Marriages are most often between members of different colonies although about 25–30 percent are within the colony. Within colonies many families are related, and the Hutterites do not allow marriage between first cousins due to the fear of genetic defects. The marriage initiative must always come from the man.[47] Usually marriage is inside the leut, but inter-leut marriage is permitted, with most of these between the Schmiedeleut and the Dariusleut, and between the Dariusleut and the Lehrerleut. Very rarely do Schmiedeleut marry Lehrerleut. Although there is no specific injunction against this, the difference in the level of orthodoxy of the two leute, and the spatial separation of the colonies of these leute, militate against Schmiedeleut-Lehrerleut unions. Schmiedeleut colonies are concentrated in Manitoba and the Dakotas, while the Lehrerleut are in Alberta, hundreds of kilometres away, restricting opportunities for social interaction between them and, in case of marriage, making it difficult for a couple to retain contact with their families.[48]

The contact that will lead to marriage is created after meetings between people from different colonies while visiting relatives, or during events when one colony helps the other—something that is quite common. The relationship is continued in letters and limited phone calls and also during additional gatherings under the same circumstances.[49] These relationships can last for some years, and when the two decide to get married (usually when in their mid-20s), the marriage cannot take place before they are baptized and before they receive the approval of their parents and of their respective colonies. Each one of these has the right to reject the match, and thus the families and two colonies have control over the marriage.[50]

Until the middle of the 19th century, emotional relationships regarding marriage were forbidden. Marriage was a religious duty. In much of European society, before the industrial era, marriage was also an economic union, but in Hutterite society marriages fulfilled more of an affective and procreative function. It seems somewhat contradictory that, according to Friedmann, even as late as the beginning of the 20th century, courting and romance did not exist and were not acceptable among the Hutterites. In the past, the husband used to call his wife "sister in marriage." According to Riedemann, the elders of the community are those to express God's will regarding marriage, thus they created the custom by which they set up a group of baptized boys beside a group of girls, and each boy was being offered a girl from the group to take as his wife. The wedding took place immediately after the match, so that there was no chance for courting. These strict customs existed until the middle of the 19th century. By then, the young people were given the right to choose their spouses—under the approval of their parents and colony elders, of course.[51]

The Engagement

THE ENGAGEMENT PARTY (*Hulba*) traditionally is held one to four weeks before the wedding.[52] At the Hulba the newly engaged couple is formally and publicly introduced as a couple for the first time. Mostly an occasion for celebration, the Hulba includes a special meeting of the married men of the bride's colony or her relatives, and the father of the boy asks for the girl. The bride's qualities are extolled while her suitor's character and worthiness is scrutinized. The prospective bridegroom is required to rally supporters to speak in his favour, while others raise doubts about his worthiness as a bridegroom.[53] When the parents agree the boy is brought in and personally asks the parents for the girl's hand in marriage. The engagement then follows in church. Alcohol is often served afterwards and the occasion is a festive one, so much so that the *Ordnungen und Konferenz Briefen* frequently commented on the need for restraint and decorum in these celebrations after an ordinance in 1932 first banned the practice. In 1952 the ordinance was affirmed:

> Great sins occur at the Hulba, as everyone should know, and that is why we had to stop them. The enemy finds his way in among the frivolous young people. God is disgraced and driven from among us... . The Hulba is not allowed during any part of the engagement, neither before nor after. Neither is it allowed on any day before or after the wedding, nor during the week. Let us do our best to eliminate the evil which has taken such strong root among us and which has already grown above our ears.[54]

As a product of culture, traditions become deeply ingrained and die hard. Despite official disapproval the Hulba continued. Ordinances in 1960 and 1967 reiterated the ban on Hulbas, while in 1968, presumably to accommodate the need for celebration, an ordinance gave approval for a special meal to be provided on the evening of an engagement and/or the Saturday before a wedding.

Nevertheless, the old tradition still endured on many colonies as further ordinances in 1983, 1991, 1996, and 1997 criticized behaviour at Hulbas. An ordinance of 2002 noted that:

> Celebration of the engagement and Hulba is far too excessive; too many people come together and too many are invited for the engagement. Steps should be taken to ensure that only brothers and brothers-in-law are invited, and not wives or young women, and it should not be announced at prayer. People should be invited to the engagement based on the minister's approval. Dear brothers, let us not die because of high spirits in the matter of drinking and eating and unnecessary get-togethers.

An account of a Hulba on a conservative Dariusleut colony in Alberta noted that the Hulba there had two components. The formal part, where all the colony elders were present, was described by one outside observer as a "sheer tragedy and terrible disappointment" to him, where the congregation [sat] "in the dining hall for hours and [sang] one melancholy song after another." [55] Following this, at about eleven o'clock, the unmarried and unbaptized gathered in a "remote room" to talk and sing popular secular country songs in a relaxed atmosphere without any adult supervision. [56]

The marriage ceremony has two parts: the engagement ceremony taking place in the bride's colony, and the wedding, a few days later, in the groom's colony. The two ceremonies are held in the church, and are performed by the minister. The inherent differences between the sexes in the Hutterite community, which are affirmed in daily life through gender roles, are also embodied in the content of the ceremonies. [57]

During the engagement ceremony, the minister addresses the couple and starts with an introduction: "As the brethren have talked to you individually they have understood that before God each one of you will accept the other as a gift of God in good faith. Neither a resolution nor your final approval have yet been heard." [58] The minister addresses the groom and asks him three questions, which he is supposed to answer with a "yes":

1. Do you desire to accept this sister without complaints and with good will? [59]

2. Do you desire to go before her in such a way that she finds in you a mirror and an example of honesty and will be led to the Lord through you, so that you may live together as Christians, one being of benefit to the other?

3. Marriage has its share of grief and not every day is filled with happiness, but brings suffering, too, as the women are the weaker ones. Thus I ask you, do you desire to have her for good, in health and in sickness, in love and in sorrow, never to leave her, until the Lord separates you through death? And if this is not too difficult, you may answer with a yes.[60]

The minister next addresses the bride and expects to receive from her, too, a positive answer to these questions:

1. You have heard the good intentions of the brother, which will be of comfort to you. Will you also accept him with good will and without complaints?

2. Since God has ordained that the husband is and should be the head of the wife, I ask you: do you wish to obey him in all right and godly things as it is the duty of the wife, so that you can serve each other in godliness?

3. Whether the husband can always enjoy better health than the wife is in God's hands. Will you therefore serve him also in health and sickness, in happiness and in sorrow, and never leave him?

After the series of questions that were answered affirmatively, the minister declares that he wishes to pronounce before the congregation "that with the counsel of your parents you want to come together. You also ask the Lord that His will be done to the glory of His name. For this the congregation will gather once more."

A few weeks later, on Sunday, the two congregations gather in the groom's colony for the marriage ceremony. Once again the bride and groom are asked a series of questions that are intended to assure that the couple is aware of the gravity of their decision, especially of the fact that it is an alliance that is breakable only by death. All questions are to be answered affirmatively. The groom is asked the following questions:

1. Do you still wish to accept this sister that was introduced, in good faith as a gift of the Lord?

2. Are you willing to be a good example for her in honesty and godliness, so that she may be brought closer to the Lord through you?

3. Are you willing to take the introduced sister for good in love and sorrow, in health and sickness, never to leave her until death will part you?

4. If it should happen that one or the other from the congregation should suffer shipwreck of his faith [implying the groom], will you then be satisfied with yourself and not desire that your wife follow you from the right to the wrong and leave behind the community and the church? And would you on behalf of your woman not cause us any trouble with the authorities?

The bride is then asked:

1. You have heard this brother in his good intentions, which will be of comfort to you. Therefore I ask you too, do you desire to accept him in goodwill without complaints?

2. Because it is ordained by God that the husband is the head of his wife, I ask you, do you desire to be obedient in all good things, as a good wife ought to be, so that one can help the other toward godliness?

3. Whether the husband can always enjoy better health than the wife is in God's hands. Will you therefore serve him also in health and in sickness, in happiness and in sorrow, and never leave him, until death will part you?

In closing, I ask you once more, brother and sister, before His church, which is a witness of this honest assembly: Will you in all that pertains to your marriage bond be faithful to each other and to your faith and never leave one another, until death will separate you? For what God has joined together, let no man put asunder. If so, both parties may answer with yes and join hands.

The ceremony ends with endowing the couple with the blessing of the congregation. The minister steps up to the couple and holds their joined hands:

We herewith bear witness that you marry each other as God fearing partners according to the order of God and the example of the forefathers and with the knowledge and counsel of the elders of the whole congregation. May the God of Abraham, Isaac and Jacob bless and keep you, may He lead you Himself together and bless you, that you may live as God-fearing husbands and wives together peacefully and serve God all your lives. This we wish you once again from God through Jesus Christ. Amen.[61]

From now on, the man may vote at the general meeting, and he may elect and be elected to serve various functions in the colony. The wife moves to her husband's colony, where she is granted full rights of a colony member, but, like all women, she has no voting right nor does she have a right to elect to functions in the colony.[62] The couple moves into their new home with the furniture that they received from the colony at the age of 15. They also receive from the colony a double bed, a dining table, chairs and a sofa, all of which were made in the colony. Later, when children are born, the couple will receive a playpen. At the age of about 30, baptized bachelors or spinsters may ask to leave their parents' home and receive a dwelling unit of their own.

Ordination of the Minister

ORDINATION OF THE minister, who serves also as the president of the colony, takes place a few years after his election and he has gained some experience. First, the older minister or one from another colony will ask the Brotherhood if they agree, before a letter concerning the ordination is sent to all colonies. This letter is read to the Brotherhood for their approval. At the initiative of the head of the leut, the colony assembles for the ordination after a Sunday service. The main part of the ceremony consists of the minister's consent to accept upon himself the heavy duties of the office, with devotion and responsibility, until his death. The head of the leut addresses the congregation and reminds them the circumstances that necessitated the election of the new minister (for example, the death of his predecessor), and expresses the thanks of the congregation for the election of the new leader according to the will of God and for his successful trial period in the office. Now, "after he had served for a while, he proved himself so that we and all the elders were well satisfied with him. We know of no obstacle but think that if he also received the support of the congregation, he might be ordered into the service of the Word. For this reason, we will listen to his voice and determine the attitude of the congregation to see whether it also is satisfied with him."[63] The head of the leut moves on to ask the ordained minister, who will be kneeling, some questions for which he expects to receive affirmative answers:

> Firstly, I am asking you, my brother, where do you stand? Do you desire to show your obedience to be given inside and outside the country, wherever needed, in good or evil times as God the Almighty does send it? Secondly, I am asking you, do you desire to exercise discipline and admonition with the right courage and diligence so as to lead this congregation of the Lord that it might further be built and adorned in Him? Thirdly, I am asking you, are you acquainted with the twelve articles of our most holy Christian faith, and do you acknowledge the Confession of Faith of our church as right, and do you desire to keep these, as much as possible until your death? Fourthly, I am asking you, my brother, do you desire to keep all these points to which you have committed yourself before God and this congregation, to continue with these in good faith until death? Now, my brother, while we have all witnessed your answers, agreement and covenant, we want to seal the work of the Lord by appealing to His name for you. I am asking you, my brother, whether you really mean to support those commitments into which you have entered before God and this congregation? Do you desire to serve God and his congregation faithfully unto death, and do you desire to be a faithful witness of the truth?

After presenting the questions and receiving the affirmative answers from the minister, the elder sums up with the three oldest ministers laying their hands on him:

> My brother, since we have given our confidence to you, we lay our hands on your shoulder as evidence, in the name of our Lord Christ and the power of God, that the office and the duty to serve in the word of the Lord will be trusted to you and burdened on you. You shall have the power to serve in this capacity to the redemption and improvement of mankind with us and beside us, to further the work of God with teaching, punishment, exclusion and admittance according to the content of the Gospel and the word of God. We wish that the grace of God may come on you, that God might draw you near to Him, overshadow you and accompany you with His grace and the gift of His holy spirit. This I wish for you from the Almighty God through Jesus Christ. Amen.[64]

Apart from these three main ceremonies, the Hutterites, as a fervent religious community, hold additional ceremonies relating to special occasions. Funerals, for example, last one-and-a-half to two hours, and involve a sermon conducted by the minister.[65]

Procreation and the Prohibition of Birth Control

THE HUTTERITE RELIGION adopted literally God's commandment to Noah: "Go out of the ark, you and your wife, and your sons and your sons' wives with you. Bring out with you every living thing of all flesh that is with you: birds and cattle and every creeping thing that creeps on the earth, so that they may abound on the earth, and be fruitful and multiply on the earth" (Genesis 8, 16–17). Accordingly, it was totally forbidden to use birth control methods; Hutterite women, up to the beginning of the 20th century, bore up to 12 children.

Hutterites approve of contraception only when mandated for medical reasons and even then the colony's minister must approve it. The minister may not always accept the medical opinion, and might demand to be apprised of the reasons for the doctor's recommendation. In spite of this, over the last century there has been a systematic and continuing decline in the number of births. Today, on average, a Hutterite woman will bear three to six children.

This likely reflects a decline in the influence of religious ortho-doxy and—in this matter, at least—of the influence wielded by the minister. Furthermore, there is growing awareness by women (and men, too) of the role that stress plays in their physical and mental health. Women wish to invest more of their time in taking care of and educating their children, and leave some free time to themselves—including some time for worship. It is evident that they are aware of the importance of these values in the "outside world" and they do not see any reason why they should not adopt such values which they do not see as fundamentally incompatible with Hutterite philosophy. Moreover, their mothers, who grew up in very large families and witnessed the physical collapse of their own mothers, encourage them to take care of themselves even if it involves the breach of a religious principle. Also, it turns out that in order to dull the severity of the sin of employing artificial birth control technology women often opt for surgical sterilization or tubal ligation rather than using other external birth control methods.[66]

It seems, however, that the dramatic decline in the number of children per family in the Hutterite community is linked to growing contraceptive use; strictly speaking this is a religious sin. We should emphasize that nearly all our hosts in the Hut-terite colonies, to whom we expressed our wonder regarding the dramatic decline in birth rate, said that this does not prove that the status of religion has weakened, but rather that women today are much weaker physically than women in past generations. For example, one woman from a Lehrerleut colony stated that "today, after a few births [women] suffer from high blood pressure, heart conditions, etc. and thus they receive certificates of approval from the doctors, presented to the ministers, in which they are ordered not to get pregnant any more… In the past, when the doctor used to warn them against giving birth again, they wouldn't listen to him. Today, they do." This is not the complete explanation. Indeed, Johnny Hofer (the minister's son in James Valley), who is the German teacher of the colony, claimed openly that the decline in birth rate is one of the expressions of a weakening of religious adherence in the colonies. He found another proof for this in the fact that, in the past, many members were prepared to undertake the rite of baptism at a relatively early age, while today young people postpone their baptism until their mid-20s.[67] In the past the age of marriage was as low as eighteen, but today few marry before age twenty-five. Interestingly enough, another Hutterite woman also stated that people should bring into the world only the number of children that they are able to support and educate. In her view, since the colonies base their economy on agriculture (in the Lehrerleut colonies—agriculture only), and since today there is a dramatic fall in the income derived from agriculture, the colony might not have the means to support a large population. Additionally, parents will not have enough time to devote to their children and educate them properly. The German teacher in the same colony, also stated that without parents' help he could not achieve his educational goals. Therefore, in cooperation with their husbands, women initiate the restrictions on family size.[68] Use of birth control against the wishes of the leadership does not imply an erosion of Hutterite values. As Peter Laslett has argued, "breaches of social rules do not necessarily weaken those rules, and under certain circumstances can even serve to strengthen them." [69]

Masturbation and premarital sex are forbidden. However, pregnancies before marriage are not uncommon. The Schmiedeleut council felt this to be a sufficiently serious issue to address it in a number of ordinances. Ordinance 1 from July 2, 2002 discusses sexual behaviour and the appropriate response of the Church to certain scenarios. It urges parents to ensure that their children are properly supervised and that boys and girls who are dating are not left alone together. It reaffirms the Conference Ordinance from 4th November 1994 which itself cites an earlier ordinance from 12th July 1990 (#1): on "the matter of young men and women going around together…" It noted that lack of supervision leads to "fornication and children born out of wedlock appear as a result." Such un-Christ like sins occur which the elders considered shameful even to speak of: "in Manitoba, four or five children were born out of wedlock, even 15 and 16 year-old boys and girls are running around and go so far that such mischief occurs." This ordinance also alluded to inappropriate sexual behaviour between unmarried colony members quoting Sirach 42:11: "Keep strict watch over a headstrong daughter, or she may make you a laughingstock to your enemies… and put you to shame in public places." (see statistical analysis in Appendix 3 and the discussions of the Schmiedeleut in the *Ordnungen und Konferenz Briefen* in Appendix 5). Hutterites feel that abortion is morally repugnant. It is forbidden unless medically imperative.[70]

Sins, Discipline and Repentance

ON THE BASIS of the verse "So you shall put away the evil from among you," Riedemann said that it is the duty of each Hutterite to watch his neighbour in order to protect all from backsliding into evil. Transgressions are punished in various ways according to the seriousness of the offence. Punishment ranges from social and religious excommunication to total expulsion from the colony:

> Therefore do we watch over one another, telling each his faults, warning and rebuking with all diligence. But where one will not accept the rebuke, but disregardeth it, the matter is brought before the Church, and if he hear not the Church, then he is excluded and put out.[71]

The Hutterites give warnings to those who overstep the line before they discipline any colony member, but they expect sinners to confess their sins as a first step to redemption, and to sincerely repent before they are received back into the community. However, when dealing with grave sins such as adultery, avarice, the following of other religions, stealing, drunkenness, and anger, the punishment is severe: the transgressor may be excommunicated immediately and without warning. Riedemann based this ruling on the New Testament: "But now I have written to you not to keep company with anyone named a brother, who is sexually immoral, or covetous, or an idolater, or a reviler, or a drunkard, or an extortioner—do not even to eat with such a person" (I Corinthians 5, 11). But even in such cases, the community calls for the culprit to repent and expects compliance, "and where not, that the Church may remain pure and innocent of his sin, and bear not guilt and rebuke from God on his behalf."[72]

The decision to excommunicate, and its various degrees of severity, as an acceptable means of punishment, is based on biblical incident when the prophetess Miriam slandered Zipporah the Cushite [Ethiopian] wife of Moses. For this sin, Miriam was punished with leprosy and excluded for seven days from the camp of the People of Israel in the desert.[73]

Minor offences such incurring fines for traffic infractions, necessitate a public apology to all male colony members. In contrast, the punishment for keeping a radio secretly, or traveling outside the colony without prior approval by an unbaptized boy or girl under

15 years, is to confess in front of the whole congregation during Sunday prayer service and standing up during the whole service as an expression of repentance. More serious offences, such as smoking, swearing, drunkenness and possession of a firearm, may be punished by excommunication of a few days, and the expression of remorse and public repentance. During the period of banishment, the banned member is not allowed to live at home, shake the hands of other members, speak to others—not even his wife—eat at the dining hall or to pray with the rest of the congregation. The punishment is announced in church before the whole community. Theft of large sums of money, selling the colony's property, adultery, pre-marital sex and following other religions are considered to be the most severe offences and carry the greatest punishment: excommunication for two weeks or even permanent expulsion from the colony—unless the sinner will express remorse and repent. As a first step, he is required to acknowledge his grave sin, confess to the minister and ask for punishment. The minister, together with the Brotherhood, has to agree to inflict the punishment. Then, the sinner will be excommunicated for a period of two weeks, at the end of which he will express remorse in front of the congregation and will undergo a process similar to the rite of baptism, except for the sprinkling with water. At the end of the ceremony, the sinner will go from one member to the other, shaking their hands, and they will say to him: "May God be with us and strengthen us." And he will answer: "May God be with us." If the sinner refuses to acknowledge his sin and does not confess, or if he continues to re-offend, he will be expelled from the community, his family will not be allowed to meet with him and he will not be allowed to join other colonies.[74]

A member who consistently re-offends will be placed on probation, where he is deprived of all voting rights. No one is permitted to speak to him, but he will be entitled to food from the colony. It should be emphasized that permanent expulsion from a colony is rare, for today it involves turning to the outside courts.

A member who unintentionally transgresses is also punished, but although he is not liable to excommunication or expulsion, "he is not permitted to use the Lord's greeting, to give or accept 'Peace,' that he may humble himself before God for his sin, and thereafter watch all the more carefully against it."[75]

In general, the Hutterites prefer to handle all legal matters within the colony, or at least within the Church. Problems can arise when transgressions are serious and break not only the colony and Church codes but violate also the laws of the secular world. Colony leaders could theoretically be presented with moral dilemmas when both the perpetrator and victim are colony members since Hutterites have always avoided recourse to outside courts to settle internal matters. However, to fail to notify provincial authorities about a case of child abuse, for example, could lay the minister responsible open to a charge of obstruction of justice or being an accessory after the fact. That this kind of issue was of significant concern is shown by the ordinance of December 2004 that addressed the issue:

> The matter of what to do about men or boys defiling young women who are underage—which is called child abuse or rape by the world—was also discussed. For if a 25-year-old defiles a 15-year-old, even if she was willing, it is seen by the world as rape, which is a very dangerous thing, and which carries with it very serious punishment from the world.

Ultimately the ministers decided to use common sense and exercise their discretion and, whenever possible, "try to mediate through minister's counsel and church discipline." If the matter should go beyond the colony and come to official attention, "then the world may deal with it," as was already decided during the last conference, held July 2, 2002."

Punishing the sinner is not done for the sake of punishment itself. Repentance, not retribution is the objective. Sinners are encouraged to acknowledge their sin, regret it and repent. These purposes are very important in the Hutterite theology. In this regard, Riedemann wrote:

> But he who would truly repent with all his heart must first feel real remorse for his sin... For true remorse followeth the recognition of sin... Now he who is sorry for his sin and regretteth having obeyed it ought and must from henceforth all the more diligently and earnestly guard himself against it, and flee from it as from a serpent... Thus remorse leadeth to true repentance, that is real humiliation and abasement before God because of the transgression... which shame bringeth a real turning point, so that the man runneth with haste, calleth, crieth and prayeth to God for forgiveness and

grace, and beginneth at the same time to bring the flesh into subjection… As David saith, "I lifted up mine eyes unto the hills to see from whence help would come to me, even so cometh my help from the Lord who hath made heaven and earth." Every anxious, troubled, fearful, broken and contrite heart, if it flee to him, will find with him peace and comfort.[76]

The Hutterite community is somewhat tolerant of juvenile transgressions, committed by those who have not yet made a commitment to the faith through baptism. Possession of a camera or radio, for example, for which adults in conservative colonies would be punished, will in the same colonies be met by turning a blind eye if a youngster is involved. The community knows that the human character is materialistic and is inclined towards disobedience; therefore, youngsters must be treated with patience. According to Hutterite concepts, man is not perfect, and he cannot reach perfection without help from his brothers. A youngster who breaks the colony's rules will be disciplined, not because he is "bad," but because a sinner must bear the consequences of his behaviour. Instead of being marked as bad and scarred in the eyes of his peers, he continues to identify with them emotionally. Although he is reprimanded in front of his group, he is never denied food, work or self-respect. Tolerance of minor transgressions by younger colony members relaxes the otherwise tight control of the communal system.[77]

Notes

1. Based on observation during colony visits, especially visits to Deerboine Colony in early May 2004. This is considered a liberal colony. Aharon Meged reported a visit at one of the colonies in 1947, during which his hosts told him of one of the members that went to town and there he exchanged his traditional clothes to regular clothes. When the colony learned of this, they expelled him. See Aharon Meged, "A Christian Commune in Canada," *Mibifnim* (1947).

2. Sara Hofer, interview by Yossi Katz, James Valley Colony, May 2004.

3. The apron was originally intended to cover the closure at the front of the dress, something that does not exist today. Therefore, the apron was given up in most Schmiedeleut colonies. Yet, some of the Schmiedeleut still argue "although the closure is not at the front [of the dress] anymore, it is a matter of tradition which should be followed." Sara Gross, interview by Yossi Katz, Bloomfield Colony, August 2004.

4. Based on visits to various colonies in Canada 2000–2008; James Valley Colony Archive, Decisions and Provisions of the Council of the Schmiedeleut Stream of the Hutterite Church, 1876–2004 (Appendix 5). See also Caroline Hartse, "Social and Religious Change among Contemporary Hutterites," *Folk* 36 (1995): 112–13; Aharon Meged, "A Christian Commune," 548; and Donald B. Kraybill and Carl F. Bowman,

On the Backroad to Heaven: Old Order Hutterites, Mennonites, Amish and Brethren (Baltimore and London: Johns Hopkins University Press), 228–29.

5. Samuel Freedman and Cameron Harvey, *Chief Justice Samuel Freedman: A Great Canadian Judge: A Collection of the Reasons for Judgment of the Honourable Samuel Freedman, Justice of the Court of Queen's Bench of Manitoba (1952-60), Justice of the Court of Appeal of Manitoba (1960-83), and Chief Justice of Manitoba (1971-83),* (Winnipeg: Law Society of Manitoba, 1983), 23–32.

6. *Ordnungen und Konferenz Briefen,* March 12, 1975; June 19–20, 1986.

7. Astrid Von Schlacta, "Struggle for Identity and Confession. The Hutterian Brethren in the Molochna Colony, South Russia, 1842–74," *Preservings,* No. 24, December (2004): 40.

8. *Ordnungen und Konferenz Briefen,* February 16, 1953, Ordinance 8. In the 1970s, the second author met young Hutterite men from Alberta colonies wearing cowboy boots, western-style shirts and western hats. More recently, in 2008 on a Manitoba colony, he encountered a Hutterite teenaged male with painted toenails.

9. According to Michael Holzach, *The Forgotten People: A Year Among the Hutterites* (Sioux Falls, SD: Ex Machina Books, 1993), 49–51, the Wilson Siding Dariusleut colony's cobbler manufactures all the colony's footwear.

10. John Hofer, interview by John Lehr, James Valley Colony, June 7, 2008.

11. Peter Riedemann, *Confession of Faith* (Rifton, New York: Plough Publishers, 1970) [original 1545], 112.

12. Ibid., 133–36.

13. *Ordnungen und Konferenz Briefen,* 1949, Ordinance 1 (see Appendix 5).

14. *Ordnungen und Konferenz Briefen,* 1972, Ordinance 6.

15. Ibid., 1970.

16. In the original German: "rosige." This could mean floral, pink or even bright.

17. *Ordnungen und Konferenz Briefen,* 1963, Ordinance 1.

18. Rhoda Hofer, Lena Hofer, and Sara Hofer, interview by John Lehr, James Valley Colony, November 13, 2013.

19. Minister John Hofer, interview by John Lehr, James Valley Colony, November 13, 2013.

20. Riedemann, *Confession of Faith,* 121–22.

21. Ordinances in 1994 and 1997 emphasized that the minister should eat at home with the second minister.

22. Patrick Murphy, James Valley Colony, email message to John Lehr, April 12, 2010; and Linda Maendel, Elm River Colony, email message to John Lehr, April 4, 2010.

23. Paul Gackle and Sarah Kearney, "A Day on the Colony," *Winnipeg Free Press,* September 14, 2008, B1–3.

24. *Ordnungen und Konferenz Briefen,* 1994.

25. The exact time is set by each colony, though it is usually at 5:30, 5:45 or 6:00. It is always held before the evening meal.

26. Combine operator, interview by Yossi Katz, James Valley Colony, August 23, 2004. This is a common sentiment among members of many colonies.

27. Ken Gross, interview by John Lehr, Bloomfield Colony, June 9, 2007.

28. This respondent did not wish to be identified.

29. Johnny Hofer, interview by Yossi Katz, James Valley Colony, May 2004.

30. In the early years, hands were also laid on the manager so that if the minister was away for some time, perhaps on a mission, the manager could then read from scripture as devotion. John Hofer, interview by John Lehr, James Valley Colony, June 13, 2008.

31. Robert Friedmann, *Hutterite Studies* (Goshen, IN: Mennonite Historical Society, 1961), 184–88, where he discusses extensively the development of Hutterite sermons.

32. Riedemann, *Confession of Faith,* 123–24.

33. Dora Maendel, "Hutterite Christmas Traditions," *Preservings* 26 (2006): 87.

34. Ibid.

35. Ibid., 88.

36. Linda Maendel, Elm River Colony, Manitoba, email message to John Lehr, March 18, 2008.
37. Ibid.
38. Ibid.
39. Hartse, "Social and Religious Change," 112–13.
40. Riedemann, *Confession of Faith*, 68–69.
41. Kraybill and Bowman, *On the Backroad to Heaven: Old Order Hutterites, Mennonites, Amish and Brethren*, 40–41.
42. Friedmann, *Hutterite Studies*, 189–90; John Hostetler, *Hutterite Society* (Baltimore and London: John Hopkins University Press, 1974), 296.
43. Cited in Hostetler, *Hutterite Society*, 337–38.
44. Ibid., 338.
45. Riedemann, *Confession of Faith*, 97–102.
46. Friedmann, *Hutterite Studies*, 123–25. See also Riedemann, *Confession of Faith*, 120–21, stating that "in order to avoid offence and also to give no occasion to the flesh or instigation to sin, let a brother take and embrace a brother in love and a sister a sister that, as is said above, they may thereby show what is in their heart. But brothers and sisters should express this by giving hands and not by embracing, that the teaching of Christ be not thereby brought into disrepute and dishonour."
47. John Hofer, interview by Yossi Katz, James Valley Colony, May 2004; Samuel Hofer, *The Hutterites: Lives and Images of Communal People* (Saskatoon, SK: Hofer Publishers, 1998), 129.
48. Minister Peter Waldner, interview with Yossi Katz, Castor Colony, September 14, 2005.
49. Home phones in some Schmiedeleut colonies are configured in such a way that long-distance calls are cut off after 10 or 15 minutes.
50. Meged, "A Christian Commune," 550; Hartse, "Social and Religious Change," 112–13; Kraybill and Bowman, *On the Backroad to Heaven*, 44–45.
51. Friedmann, *Hutterite Studies*, 123–25. See also Suzanne R. Smith, and Bron B. Ingoldsby, "Courtship and Moral Reasoning of Hutterian Youth," *Communal Societies* 25 (2005), 113–26.
52. The *Hulba* (from the Ukrainian word meaning celebration or get-together) is similar to the *Polterabend,* which is still celebrated in Germany.
53. Mary-Ann Kirkby, *I am Hutterite* (Saskatchewan, SK: Polka Dot Press, 2007), 20–24.
54. *Ordnungen und Konferenz Briefen,* 1956.
55. Holzach, *Forgotten People*, 141.
56. Ibid., 142–43.
57. Kraybill and Bowman, *On the Backroad to Heaven,* 44–45. It should be noted that until recently in the standard wedding vows used in the Anglican and other mainstream Christian Protestant Churches, brides promised to "love, honour and *obey*," their husbands (authors' italics).
58. Hostetler, *Hutterite Society,* 339.
59. A baptised woman is called a sister.
60. Hostetler, *Hutterite Society,* 339–41.
61. Ibid., 339–41.
62. Hartse, "Social and Religious Change," 112–13.
63. Hostetler, *Hutterite Society*, 343.
64. Ibid., 343–44.
65. This is an especially prolonged ceremony, and is attended by relatives from other colonies—even very distant colonies. The ceremony starts in the afternoon and ends with a midnight snack. The first author attended such a ceremony in Deerboine Colony in May 2004.
66. Paul Gross from Bloomfield Colony asserted (May 2005) that a minister who does not respect the doctor's recommendation regarding planned birth, should not be obeyed. See also Kraybill and Bowman, *On the Backroad to Heaven*, 48–51; Edward D. Boldt, "The Hutterites: Current Developments and Future Prospects," in James

S. Frideres (ed.), *Multiculturalism and Intergroup Relations* (New York and London: n.p. 1989), 68–71; Statistics presented by Max Stanton during the ICSA convention, October 2005.

67. Johnny Hofer, interview by Yossi Katz, James Valley Colony, September 26, 2005.

68. Recent research has demonstrated that the fecundity of the rural population in western Canada has declined relative to that of urban populations within the region. There is speculation that this may be due to a higher exposure to agricultural pesticides and herbicides in rural areas. The agricultural economy and rural location of Hutterite colonies would logically lead to higher exposure to such chemicals. The decline in births may thus possibly be due to factors unrelated to religious or economic matters. *The Globe and Mail*, September 20, 2008.

69. Peter Laslett, "Introduction," in *Bastardy and Its Comparative History*, (eds.) Peter Laslett, Karla Osterveen and Richard M. Smith (Cambridge, Mass.: Harvard University Press, 1980).

70. Minister David Maendel, interview by Yossi Katz, Sturgeon Creek Colony, May 2004; Minister Peter Waldner, interview by Yossi Katz, Castor Colony, September 13, 2005. Minister John Hofer stated that he could not recall any such instance. Interview by John Lehr, James Valley Colony, September 3, 2008.

71. Riedemann, *Confession of Faith*, 131–32.

72. Ibid.

73. Minister John Hofer, interview by Yossi Katz, James Valley Colony, May 2004. See the *Holy Bible*, Numbers 12: 1 and 10–14.

74. Hartse, "Social and Religious Change," 120–21; Kraybill and Bowman, *On the Backroad to Heaven*, 51–53; During visits to the colonies in September 2005, we realized that the families of the banned members find it difficult to follow this order, and sometimes they take advantage of going to town on behalf of the colony in order to visit their relative who has been expelled and lives in town.

75. Friedmann, *Hutterite Studies*, 123–25.

76. Riedemann, *Confession of Faith*, 59–61.

77. Hostetler, *Hutterite Society*, 289–90.

Chapter 6

ECONOMIC PROSPERITY:

Economy, Agriculture, Technology, and Work in Hutterite Colonies in the New World

S INCE THE BEGINNING OF THEIR SETTLEMENT IN NORTH America, Hutterites have striven to achieve economic prosperity within an agricultural economy. They have theological objections to commerce and service and wish to live in an isolated rural environment, far removed from the corrupt outside secular world. They assumed too, that they stood no chance of competing against the industrial sector of the North American economy.[1]

Hutterite colonies in North America are generally mixed farming operations, concentrating on grain (wheat, oats, barley and animal feed) and livestock. The colonies vary in their agricultural orientation, but a typical colony today has about 100 cows, a 500–1000 sow hog operation, 50,000–200,000 turkeys, thousands of battery hens, ducks and geese, and cultivates somewhere between 5,000–20,000 acres of owned or rented land. A small part of this, perhaps 20–30 acres or so, is designated as a vegetable garden, an orchard and an apiary, but the great majority of colony land is used for arable farming, principally grains for feedstock. If the colony cannot produce sufficient grain to supply its needs, it will purchase the shortfall from neighbouring farms. For decades Hutterites have used state-of-the-art farm machinery, thus saving on manpower and other expenses while maximizing farm income.

In addition to its farm operation almost every colony also has a modern carpentry shop that fulfills the needs of the colony and may perform jobs for outside clients, an electrical workshop, a modern garage for repair and maintenance of agricultural machinery and colony vehicles, a welding workshop and a variety of technical services. High land prices, the collapse of the hog industry, a general downturn in agricultural prices, and increased difficulty in obtaining production quota licenses have conspired against Hutterite agricultural expansion in recent decades, pushing many colonies away from total reliance on agriculture into manufacturing. A further push came as a result of increasing mechanization of agriculture and the threat of underemployment on the colonies. In the late 1980s some colonies began to introduce manufacturing as a supplemental economic activity, producing hardwood flooring, windows, hog barn equipment, molded plastics, and vinyl. Today, among the Schmiedeleut, involvement in manufacturing is the rule, not the exception. It is estimated that at least half of all Manitoba colonies are involved in a major manufacturing business.[2] Rock Lake, Manitoba, for example, engages in laser cutting of steel, and bending metal components, which provides about half of colony income and employs seventeen colony members on a full-time basis.[3] Green Acres Colony manufactures fire trucks for customers as far away as Vermont and Washington. Homewood Colony manufactures, among other things, overhead door rollers, noodle machines, and feather separators; Clearview produces custom marble and onyx countertops; InterLake Colony produces solid wood cabinet doors; and Whiteshell manufactures patio furniture.[4] Other Manitoba colonies produce kitchen cabinets, metal bike racks, crazy carpets and saucers, pickup truck trailers, gravel truck boxes, tin roofing, and roof trusses.[5]

In the United States similar forces have begun to transform the economics of colonies. Willowbank Colony, North Dakota, has a rafter business and undertakes demolition work, which now furnishes about 20 percent of colony income. Also in North Dakota, Maple River Colony manufactures tin siding and repairs cranes, Fairview Colony manufactures sprayers and, in Minnesota, Spring Prairie makes cement pads for the oil industry.[6]

The move to manufacturing reduces underemployment and facilitates colony branching, as it reduces the need to purchase large tracts of land and negates the need to obtain provincial or state licenses to produce certain agricultural commodities. In Manitoba, for example, production and marketing of poultry, eggs, and milk is strictly regulated to maintain a stable market and uniform prices, so far more than capital and land acquisition is involved when establishing an agricultural operation. In Alberta, Valleyview Colony's new daughter colony, May City, is being set up from the outset with a strong manufacturing component. Plans call for the 3,000-acre colony to have a chicken broiler barn, a chicken layer barn, and a duck and geese barn, but the centre of its economy will be a metal manufacturing business, *May City Roll Forming*, which the mother colony started in 2006.[7] Growth was 10 percent in 2012 and projections are for a 20 percent increase in production in 2013.[8] Harmony, an as yet unaffiliated embryonic colony in Manitoba, has only a section of land and intends to generate most of its income from manufacturing house trailers and exploiting a gravel deposit on its land. Although there will be some agriculture it is intended only for colony consumption.[9]

The move towards manufacturing is no panacea for colony economic difficulties. Airport Colony in Manitoba invested more than a million dollars in a plant to build precast components for hog barns, only to see hog prices plummet and demand for their product shrivel. They lost money on their investment and incurred further debt.[10] There is also intense competition from non-Hutterite businesses and between colonies themselves. Many colonies are reluctant to let other Hutterites visit their manufacturing plants since they are afraid their ideas will be copied and the visitors will eventually compete in the same field. Hutterites do not approve of going to court to protect their intellectual property, so they are very protective of their production details and manufacturing processes. In the opinion of some, the fields in which Hutterites have a presence, such as laser cutting, are now overloaded, so profits are minimal.[11]

When Hutterites rely on manufacturing there is often criticism from competing non-Hutterite businesses who allege unfair competition. A common complaint is that colonies enjoy free labour, since colony members do not receive a wage. Colony labour is far from free, however. The income from colony enterprises must house, clothe and feed all the members, purchase vehicles, pay utility costs, provide capital for expansion, and contribute to the running of the colony school. All colony members over the age of 18 pay income taxes on the proportion of colony income they are deemed to have earned. This generally means they are considered to have an income of "below $35,000 which places individuals in the lowest taxation bracket, where they pay about 25 percent on earnings."[12] Colony companies do not pay employment insurance or pension premiums but they do not access those benefits either.[13] On the other hand, colonies do not have to pay overtime nor provide vacation pay and their workforce has a strong work ethic.

As yet, the move to manufacturing has been with the Schmiedeleut and Dariusleut. The more conservative Lehrerleut colonies still generally base their economy on agriculture.[14]

All the workers are colony members, and they perform all the jobs in the colony. The older people train the young as apprentices: "We believe in on-the-job training. The carpenter trains his assistant and so on."[15] There is little hired help. Women are responsible for tending the vegetable garden and the orchard, and for performing service tasks (see Chapter 10 on women's work in the colony). Men, including young boys, are responsible for all the remaining tasks in the colony, namely, working in the fields, care of livestock, construction, industrial production—if there is any—maintenance of farm machinery, and so forth. Members cannot choose their job. They are assigned to them but talents are considered while determining each member's task. No salary is paid—except for a uniform allowance of $3 a month—and no one is preferred in this regard. The colony takes care of all the needs of the members and their families, including payment of equal board and lodging for those who go to town. The rule of "from each according to his ability, to each according to his needs" is still valid in the colonies. As Aaron Hofer, the Boss of James Valley, said, "There is no pure equality, no such thing ... equality means that each one receives according to his needs, regardless of how much he works and contributes."[16] However, some colonies pay a fixed salary of $40 a month to men, and $20 a month to women, but they do not pay for meals or accommodation when the members stay in town overnight. This system compromises the principle of giving to each one according to needs, for "why pay someone who does not go to town?"[17]

Since no wages are paid, some who leave the colony reason that the colony owes them compensation for their unpaid work while on the colony. In 2008, an ex-Hutterite sued her former colony, Hillside, claiming that she was forced to perform manual labour without adequate compensation, starting at age eight, until she left to join an evangelical sect at age 22. The work involved "carrying heavy baskets of corn, lifting heavy turkeys, and other extremely physically demanding jobs," that allegedly left her with "sore hips, shoulders and hands." The colony's response is that it does not pay wages to any of its members; to do so would affect community life. The case is pending.[18]

Building and equipping the various buildings in the colony, including the dwellings, workshops, hog barns, dairy barns, grain elevators and silos, the kitchen and the modern dining hall, is all done by the members of the colony (after proper training), usually without any help from experts or workers from outside the colony. In this way, the Hutterites husband their capital, which is needed in other projects for employing contractors and expert workers. Since Hutterites produce most of their own food, reliance on their own skills and labour saves a great deal of money and decreases their economic dependency on outside sources. Nevertheless, in the modern world self-sufficiency is an elusive goal. Legal and other specialized services must be purchased and Hutterites, like all others, must purchase an array of products ranging from soft drinks, liquor, candies, spices, personal hygiene products, and cloth, to raw materials, agricultural machinery, telephones, pens, spare parts, gasoline, and so forth.

The Hutterites do not have buying organizations but individual colonies buy from wholesalers and in large quantities. They are well aware of the market prices of agricultural produce, they are experts at comparing prices between the shops, and they bargain (which is unusual in North America). The close ties between the colonies (although there are no economic partnerships or mutual financial commitments) are used, among other things, for mutual trade, transfer of knowledge and experience, transfer of ideas in various areas, such as development and economy, and sharing continuous information regarding feasible deals. Thus, the Hutterites are often able to purchase products for prices far lower than those paid by other consumers. Between the colonies, there is a constant exchange of agricultural and technical knowledge. Colonies trade and barter with each other; they lend equipment to each other and help each other in times of need and during critical times when seeding and harvesting.[19] This greatly contributes to colony efficiency, and leads to an increase in profits, which colonies invest in new equipment, in loans to colonies in need, and in savings accounts. Investments in the stock market are not allowed, for they are considered gambling, which is forbidden according to the Hutterite faith. In the past, the Hutterites used to put aside money in pension funds, but they stopped doing so saying that they should put their trust in God. For that reason, they did not pull out their money from the funds, and today the government is paying them back their investments gradually.[20]

Economic prosperity, maximizing income and minimizing expenses, apart from being vital to sustain the colony's population, is necessary to facilitate colony branching, one of the most important elements in a colony's life. Hutterites fear unemployment or underemployment if the colony's population exceeds 150 or so people. Hidden unemployment (in the outside world, underemployment) they believe, releases negative forces in man and society. A common Hutterite proverb implies that work in itself has a religious value: "When man doesn't work, Satan works." Moreover, "The labor of the believer is a labor of grace, a service which is full of faith, pure charity and love."[21] These can exist when the colony works continuously as a beehive, where all individuals know their duties and carry them out to the best of their ability. Preserving the intimacy of the colony enables close acquaintance between the members, proper community life, mutual supervision, and control over the colony by the elders. Retaining colony size between 100–150 people facilitates this.

Although the Hutterites have not put to test the claim that the colonies find it difficult to function when their population exceeds this number, they consider this limit to be some sort of law, and they strive to branch each colony when its population approaches that number. Some colonies have branched several times, thus, a significant part of each colony's yearly round is devoted to preparations for branching. Since branching is based on complete equality between the parent colony and the daughter colony regarding the number of people, means of production, resources etc., and as branching does not occur before the daughter colony is prepared to accept the people joining it, and since there is a basic desire to maintain the same standard of living in each colony, they must accumulate large resource and capital reserves in order to establish a daughter colony. To achieve this, they must maximize income from work, minimize expenses, save as much as possible and live frugally. It is possible to accomplish this through hard work, diligence, and efficiency, and by letting all members of the colony, including women and young boys, participate in the mutual effort. However, this is not enough. Investment in knowledge, acquisition of skills and advanced machinery is also required. This is the reason why the Hutterites, as opposed to the Amish, are so technologically advanced. As one Schmiedeleut colony member argued, "If we were not advanced in technology, we would have been out of the market, lagging behind. We would have disappeared economically. We must keep a high standard of technology and high income in order to enable branching in a proper manner."

Agricultural machinery in Hutterite colonies is at the forefront of world agricultural technology. The Hutterites watch for every innovation in agricultural technology that might advance their economy. Today, most of the agricultural machinery is computerized, and some is even guided by GPS devices. Combines, ploughs, fertilizers, feeding devices, milking machines, egg-gathering systems, and heating systems, are all automated and computerized. Colonies that developed sophisticated arts and certain industries also use advanced technology. For example, lathes or laser cutters that can cut or engrave are all computerized. Home and office machines are also state-of-the-art: new and updated computers, notebook computers, advanced photocopiers, mobile phones and sophisticated two-way radio communication systems in the combine harvesters out in the fields, and geothermal, computer-controlled heating and cooling systems on the colony are all embraced by the Hutterites. However, there is a downside to this enthusiastic embrace of agricultural efficiency: it reduces the demand for labour and creates unemployment, which the Hutterites fear more than anything and which they try so hard to prevent.

As with most economic activities, the provincial and federal governments closely regulate agriculture. Colonies must comply with production quotas for eggs, milk and other dairy products. Environmental issues also especially affect Hutterite agricultural operations because they tend to be large scale. Disposal of pig manure, for example, is often problematic as it is high in ammonia and phosphorous. If spread as fertilizer on the fields it can raise phosphorous levels and excess manure can wash into ditches and contribute to the pollution of watercourses and lakes. There is always a fear of groundwater and aquifer contamination. The proliferation of large hog-barn operations in Manitoba in the last decade sparked calls for a moratorium on hog-barn expansion in certain areas of the province deemed to be most at risk of environmental damage through disposal of pig manure. In 2008, the province of Manitoba acted to prohibit establishment of new hog barns or expansion of existing capacity in the Red River Valley, southeastern Manitoba and the Interlake region. Starlite Colony, Manitoba, which is in the process of branching, found itself in a very difficult position, as its proposed daughter colony's economy was to have been heavily reliant on hog production. Without a hog operation, its economic viability is in question; branching may be delayed or become economically impractical. For reasons that will become clear this carries grave ramifications for the continued well-being of the colony system.

The ability of Hutterites to self-educate is well known; they are consummate autodidacts. A stranger who visits the colony will find it hard to understand how those responsible for the workshops and the various colony operations, including the operators of the advanced technology, have never studied in universities or technical schools, and usually have not completed more than 10 years of formal education.

Hutterites do not see any contradiction between their inclination for technological advancement, and their efforts to isolate from the outside world, or their religious zealousness and their preaching in favour of modesty and simplicity. A typical attitude is that nothing is too modern if it benefits the colony. Therefore, they clearly distinguish between progress, which brings economic improvement to the colony, and changes that are designated to merely increase personal comfort. Thus, they introduced electricity into the colonies long ago, for its great benefit to the colonies' economy, in spite of the claim of some that "this great power was lit by hell." Similarly, they started using the telephone after they acknowledged its value and importance to the overall efficiency of the colony, although some people objected to it for being a possible bridge to the outside world.

On the other hand, if a technological change seems to be contributing to personal comfort only, the whole community rejects it. Thus, the Hutterites still do not drive cars, but pickup trucks, passenger vans and minibuses only. Cars are considered as instruments for personal comfort and they cannot be used for other purposes. The ministers also preach against modern styles in clothing, accumulation of clothes and objects used for personal comfort. Television, radio and the Internet might be helpful to colony managers for market reports and weather forecasts, but making them available to all colony members for recreational use is seen as detrimental to colony discipline and a threat to the Hutterite way of life. Concern to manage modernity in all of its facets is manifested in the regulations of the *Ordnungen und Konferenz Briefen,* which often caution against the adoption of a particular practice or technological device for a decade or more. Constant reiteration of a prohibition is clear evidence that the instructions of the leadership are not being heeded. When it is clear that further injunctions are pointless, the leadership will accept its adoption, relax the prohibition, and issue an ordinance recognizing and controlling accepted practice.

Economic prosperity is not without its negative effects. In some instances, the abundance has been the reason for postponing colony branching. Prosperity may also entice colony members to seek personal abundance and accumulate property from side work (see below). In general, a very affluent colony becomes a source of envy to neighbouring colonies, with all the problems that this brings in its train.[22]

Working hours in the colony vary according to need and not from a pre-determined work schedule. Thus, in the harvest season, one can see combines in the fields at all hours of the night. Retired members (age 55 and over), both men and women, continue to work as much as they can. Some perform tasks appropriate to their age and health condition, and some nurture the cemetery or perform other less arduous tasks. Since their extended family is in the colony, they are also given the task of taking care of their grandchildren so that the parents will be free to work. Those who hold religious and educational positions, such as the minister, the second minister and the German teacher, work on the farm in addition to fulfilling their duties: being responsible for the vegetable garden and the apiary, marketing agricultural produce, buying goods for the colony or transporting various products from town to the colony and vice versa. A Hutterite never goes to town for a doctor's appointment or for another personal purpose without being asked to carry out some other task, such as bringing spare parts waiting to be picked up from a town dealership. Women work in the kitchen and in the vegetable garden or busy themselves with sewing or other crafts.[23] Vehicles do not leave the colony without being scheduled to transport other members going in the same direction. Working habits, work ethics and diligence are taught to the children from a very early age. There are few toys in some kindergartens; instead, children are encouraged to play and experiment with tools, they go out to the fields and are driven in heavy machines so that they would absorb the "working atmosphere." From age 10, children are given the responsibility for certain chores in the farm: gathering eggs or feeding the animals, freeing adults to perform more complex tasks. Girls over 10 assist with household work and take care of the small children, thus enabling the women to work in the vegetable garden and in the kitchen.[24]

Aharon Meged, who visited one of the colonies in North America in 1947, emphasized the exceptional work ethic of the Hutterites, and the things he said then, quoting his hosts, are equally true today:

> Everybody must work. Work is the economic and moral basis of society. Even those elected for positions in the colony, including the father of the congregation [the minister], must do some physical work. There is no annual vacation, except for the holidays. "We do not feel any need for this. We do not miss town, and we enjoy work." There is one day of rest every week, on Sunday, but it is not considered a sacred day. It has been chosen as the day of rest and spiritual refreshment. All days are equally sacred. The number of the daily working hours is not fixed; usually from dawn until dusk in summer and from eight o'clock until five o'clock in the winter.

The work ethic on Hutterite colonies remains high.[25] The consensus is that

> We believe that if you don't work, Satan will work. We also believe that you must work in order to help the poor and the needy. If you don't work while you are young, when you are old you will tremendously regret it. Sometimes the minister and the Boss tell certain members that they should work more because they are able to. Colony members, who do not have the natural ability to work harder, do not receive any comments. Work is suited to the member's talents; however, if a member wishes to change the kind of work he has been given, it is very hard and complicated, but we are trying to help.[26]

A teacher who has been teaching for many years and has become "burned out" would have his or her request for re-assignment considered sympathetically, as would someone who requested a change because of age or poor health.

Not all colony members have a positive attitude to colony life and work. A group of defectors from Hillside Colony in Manitoba described the colonies as "oppressive corporations that enslave their members and operate under a façade of Christianity."[27] Significantly, these defectors are all now "born-again" evangelical Christians, which suggests that their reasons for leaving the colony may have had less to do with economics than their religious convictions. Some defectors recall life on the colony with some fondness but admit that they would find it difficult to return into a life that from the outside seems more constrained than that to which they had become accustomed. Otherwise, according to Sam Hofer, a defector from Manitoba's Sunnyside Colony, colony life "was like [on] any farm, long hours in summer, shorter hours in winter."[28]

Surprising as it may seem, the Hutterites do not forbid outside work completely. This includes very specific crafts, such as assembling products (usually furniture) produced in the colonies and assembled in the homes of the customers in the towns and farms. Indeed, in some Schmiedeleut colonies that faced unemployment and economic crisis, working outside the colony in rural areas has been allowed. The Hutterites also accept work offers outside the colonies when the neighbouring farmers are looking for construction workers or workers for large-scale agricultural jobs. However, the colonies are not blind to the fact that working outside has in the past entailed a high risk of defection by those workers, and the risk is always present. The Dariusleut colonies are less conservative than they were formerly, and they permit outside work even when there is no unemployment in the colonies. Thus, they allow Hutterite women to place stands in local "farmer's markets" and sell vegetable garden produce. This practice was terminated only recently, when it was felt that the prolonged absence of their mothers from the colony was not in the children's best interest.

In spite of the many efforts invested in the achievement of economic prosperity, some colonies need to take loans in order to prepare for branching. Often, by the time the loans are amortized, the colony again faces another branching. Therefore, in spite of their considerable economic success, it is unwise to generalize and describe the Hutterite colonies as affluent, with money always available.[29] Similarly, introducing machinery and advanced technology into the colonies, which saves on manpower, carries a price in lost jobs, the risk of underemployment that every colony fears, and of damage to the traditional structure of the colony.[30]

Economic prosperity is not only needed for branching; it is also a means for fulfilling the principle of isolation from the outside world. In a closed economy, which supplies its own needs, the colony's members do not have to find their livelihood outside, for most basic needs are supplied from within the colony. Economic prosperity is also supposed to clear some time for religious practice, but this does not necessarily occur, for the efforts to achieve prosperity sometimes come at the expense of the time which could be devoted to it. We have already noted that members often miss church services on account of their work in the fields. As implied before, usually the Hutterites do not see any problem with this, for according to their belief, work in itself means the fulfillment of a religious duty. This is the reason why the minister does not consider it wrong that he and the second minister work full time performing other tasks besides serving as ministers, and similarly there is nothing wrong in cancelling the daily service so that the whole colony may participate in gathering vegetables.[31]

The quest for economic prosperity, if not controlled and balanced, holds within it negative effects. The most obvious of these is the concept of "colonial capitalism" which pervades the behaviour of individuals who seek ways to improve their economic situation. As Aaron Hofer, the Boss of James Valley, said: "The colonies' biggest enemy is individualism."[32] The practice of getting money on the side has long been known in the colonies, namely, those ways through which the individual can obtain money, in addition to the $3 a month that the colony gives, and in addition to the change left from the per diem given when traveling outside the colony. As a rule, elders consider earning side-money a misdemeanor and forbid it but the practice has never been fully rooted out. Ways for getting side-money are quite diverse: boys hunt hares and sell their fur or hunt other animals for sale; women use remainders of cloth, threads and other raw materials to make slippers, socks, pillows, etc. and sell them; food remainders are sold to local people and the proceeds are divided among the kitchen workers; men use wood scraps and off-cuts for making various objects, such as clocks, toys, and chairs for sale. If the annual budget for buying shoes in not fully spent it is sometimes used to buy raw materials to make money on the side.

Introducing industries into the colonies expanded the potential for the side ventures, for more scraps and raw materials are available. Sometimes the offence of making the money is accompanied by another serious offence, for example, when loading produce for marketing, it is agreed between the transporter (who is a non-Hutterite) and the one loading the produce (usually one of the younger Hutterites) that they will load more produce than the amount written in the order. In exchange for the difference in the amounts, the Hutterite who loaded the goods receives money or in-kind benefits, such as a ride to a restaurant or a pub. Others, without permission, perform various tasks for neighbouring farmers for which they receive payment. In order to combat this, the elders raised the per diem given to youngsters traveling to town "so that they will not be tempted to get money and benefits under the table."[33] There is no doubt that illicit work siphons off money and causes real financial losses to the colonies.

Contacts for making money on the side are not difficult to make. Since Hutterites have a reputation for producing high quality goods, there is no shortage of eager customers anxious to contact them. Thus, while we were sitting with our Hutterite friends in a restaurant in Winnipeg in August 2004, one of the diners approached the Hutterite couple and told them that he had read in one of the newspapers that the Hutterites sell high quality linen and requested the Hutterites' phone number in order to obtain Hutterite merchandise through "direct marketing."[34]

Making money on the side is especially common among youngsters before baptism. With side-money they can purchase cameras, cds, television sets and other forbidden products. Some ministers and colonies take a tolerant view of these misdemeanors, for they regard them as adolescent explorations to which adults must turn a blind eye and exercise a degree of forbearance. In any case, these sins are preferable to desertion of the colony in search of the comforts of the outside world.

Adults who are making money on the side justify their behaviour by claiming that firstly, Riedemann, whose writings are the basis for the Hutterian faith, says that people should work in a decent craft so that they have enough money to give to the poor. Therefore, they argue, the money on the side is mainly for "charity work" or giving to the poor. Secondly, there is a need for money on the side in order to furnish and decorate the house, since some colonies give the newlyweds only minimal equipment, to buy presents for the babysitter as well as presents to the children and relatives on holidays, to buy clothes for the youngsters in addition to what they receive from the colony, and so on.

When it comes to generating side-income, women are as active as men. One Hutterite woman argued that:

> We need money on the side because we do not receive everything we need from the colony. In the past especially, we received very little from the colony. Most women make some money on the side... another reason [for making money on the side] is that we want certain things that we cannot receive from the colony, or things that we need and want to give as presents to the children or the babysitter. Where will we get it? We as women know that we should give presents; men do not think that presents are necessary. When someone gets married, the colony does not give everything that they need. Where will we get the rest of the things we need?[35]

This issue is problematic, although those involved are not always aware of this. It creates differences within a population protected from envy, competition, and spiritual deterioration by basic values based on equality and lack of any private property. Indeed, the ministers and the rules continuously preach against individualism and the acquisition of private property and punish those who break the rules. However, it seems that the de facto policy is one of quiet reconciliation, as long as relatively small sums of money are involved and there are no other transgressions, for to eradicate the practice completely would be impossible.

In any event, it is clear that the desire for economic achievement by the colony extends also to the individual, and this brings with it a host of other issues that complicate Hutterite life and colony governance. Colony leaders must tread a fine line if they are to ensure that individuals for their own gain do not use the values that benefit the entire community: an entrepreneurial spirit, initiative and a strong work ethic. When the individual embraces and misapplies group values, spiritual downfall can follow.[36]

Samuel Hofer, a former Hutterite, born in 1962, who left a Dariusleut colony in south Saskatchewan, holds that making big amounts of money on the side is one of the reasons for leaving the colony. According to him, the compulsive activity for getting extra money and looking for ways to invest savings causes the member to lose interest in the colony. He describes the ways that he and his young friends found for making money on the side:

> Aside from making private money by working out occasionally for neighbours, we trapped foxes and coyotes in the fall and winter. While Hutterite boys have always made a bit of money on the side by trapping, our lucrative pastime coincided with extremely high fur prices. A single coyote pelt sent to the Hudson's Bay Fur Auction in Montreal could earn the trapper as much as $380. To send and receive mail, we rented private post office boxes in Moose Jaw. Whereas in the early years in Alberta, some colonies had to trap foxes, coyotes, and badgers, because the animals' sheer numbers were threatening the colonies' chicken and goose stocks, we trapped solely to make money.[37]

Some of Hofer's friends caught up to 50 pelts every year and were far more successful than the generation before them. His generation, he claimed, "took trapping to a new level. The boys divided the colony's and our nearest neighbours' land, each of us claiming an area on a first-come-first-serve basis." As a latecomer to trapping, Hofer had to seek out new territory some five miles from the colony. Competition was intense. He and his fellows read books on trapping, ordered special lures through the mail, and lured their prey with chicken and goose guts. Their business was sufficiently lucrative that some bought bicycles, or motorcycles. Since they were forbidden in the colony, they had to be hidden miles away from the colony.

> After I bought my motorcycle, I expanded my trap-line, traveling fifteen to twenty miles every day. Aside from trapping, I devoted my free time to drawing cartoons and reading books that I bought every time I went to Moose Jaw. Other boys developed more expensive habits. With no experience in handling those amounts of cash, some young people grew restless. Alcohol scared the hell out of me. A few older and already baptized men (who were in a position to be role models) drank too much, and that did nothing to help younger people get a sense of what a good Hutterite

was supposed to be. In any case, too much free time to earn private money and to watch TV, and not having enough responsibilities at a crucial time in our development, distracted many of us from colony affairs.[38]

In the summer of 2005 in Castor (Lehrerleut) colony, Alberta, the minister, Peter Waldner, claimed that the phenomenon of making money on the side did not exist in the colony. Julie Waldner, a colony member, also claimed firmly that members of the colony were not involved is such doings, for "we do not have to do this. We receive everything from the colony. Our allowance is eight dollars a month, and when we go to town for a doctor's appointment or for other things, we receive no money at all. At the evening before, we prepare packaged food for the day and we do not get money for spending outside the colony." The Lehrerleut are extremely strict about making money on the side after baptism, although they are more tolerant of the practice before baptism.[39] One Schmiedeleut woman noted that none of her Lehrerleut friends or acquaintances made money on the side.[40]

According to Hostetler, economic ambition has other undesirable effects. First, the rich colonies become a source of envy for other colonies. Second, branching is delayed. Third, the basic motivation for work is undermined and the religious and spiritual values are neglected. It is the Hutterite custom that on marriage the woman moves to her husband's colony, but because of the differences in the standard of living between the colonies, the young women from a wealthier colony are in no hurry to get married. Hostetler claims they want to enjoy the conveniences of life on an affluent colony and ask: "Why should we get married, we have it so good here?"[41] Delayed marriage has an effect on the birth rate and so affects the survival of the colonies.

Many Hutterites insist that this never happens, and question Hostetler's assumptions that affluence influences marriage behaviour. Several Hutterite women doubted that any girl would delay her marriage simply to enjoy access to some additional creature comforts for a short time. The consensus was that Hostetler's claims are simply wrong.

Lastly, the computer and the Internet, meant for economic use only, are instead a source of entertainment and amusement, which is forbidden according to Hutterite principles.[42] Another Manitoba Hutterite mused that since the colonies are now "much more businesslike and money oriented, we devote less time to God. Satan is clever. He keeps you busier, and then you do not have time to worship God." [43]

Johnny Hofer, the German teacher in James Valley, did not disagree:

> The more we emphasize the economic aspect of the colonies, the lesser will be our spiritual work. We do not have rulebooks like the Jews, therefore the decision whether to leave the fields in order to attend the prayer service is for each one to make. Many will prefer to give up prayer and do whatever they can in order not to attend it. [44]

Hutterites commonly say that a colony's success depends greatly on good leadership (the minister, the Boss and the Farm Boss). Although spiritual leadership is seen as crucial for the religious health of the community, colonies also make every effort to choose leaders who are economically astute and able to balance the need for social stability with the technological demands of modernity.

Notes

1. Aharon Meged (a member of Kibbutz Sdot Yam, who had been an emissary to North America in 1946–48), visited one of the Hutterite colonies in Canada in 1947. Later, he related that during the visit he asked, "why don't you develop industrial branches to a greater extent?" The colony's minister answered that: "Two or three hundred years ago our communes were known throughout Europe for their industrial produce. Our workshops were among the most sophisticated workshops regarding their work organization... but today—the industry in America is so organized that we are unable to compete with them." See Aharon Meged, "A Christian Commune in Canada," *Mibifnim* (1947): 550.
2. Bill Redecopp, "Fire Trucks: Hutterite Style," *Winnipeg Free Press*, January 4, 2009. A6.
3. Sol Gross, Rock Lake Colony, telephone interview by John Lehr, January 15, 2014.
4. 2013 *Hutterite Directory*, Elie, MB: James Valley Book Centre, 2013.
5. Bill Redecopp, "Fire Trucks: Hutterite Style," *Winnipeg Free Press*, January 4, 2009. A6.
6. Tony Waldner, Forest River Colony, telephone interview by John Lehr, January 17, 2014.
7. Drew Penner, "Brand New Colony: Hutterites build on Soaring Metal sales by Planning New Home," *Mountain View Gazette*, May 7, 2013.
8. Ibid.
9. Ken Gross, Harmony Colony, telephone interview by John Lehr, November 13, 2013.
10. Martin Cash, "Hutterites not Afraid of Change," *Winnipeg Free Press*, May 29, 2010.
11. Tony Waldner, Forest River Colony, telephone interview by John Lehr, January 17, 2014.

12. Bill Redecopp, "Fire Trucks: Hutterite Style," *Winnipeg Free Press*, January 4, 2009. A6.

13. Ibid.

14. Peter Waldner, interview by Yossi Katz, Castor Colony, September 14, 2005; Kenny Gross, interviews by Yossi Katz, September 21, 2005, and John Lehr, June 7, 2007, Bloomfield Colony.

15. Sara Gross, interview by John Lehr, Bloomfield Colony, August 2005.

16. Aaron Hofer, interview by Yossi Katz, James Valley Colony, May 2004.

17. See note 14. In the Lehrerleut colonies, the monthly "salary" is $8. Those going to town receive no board and lodging. They take packaged food for the day. Julie Waldner, interview by Yossi Katz, Castor Colony, September 13, 2005.

18. *Winnipeg Free Press*, June 5, 2008; June 14, 2008.

19. James Valley Colony's kitchen and dining hall burned down during the night of December 9, 2005. Colony members related that the next morning scores of vehicles from other colonies "were lined up" down the Colony access road, laden with food, provisions and supplies to help compensate for the loss.

20. Donald B. Kraybill and Carl F. Bowman, *On the Backroad to Heaven: Old Order Hutterites, Mennonites, Amish and Brethren* (Baltimore and London: Johns Hopkins University Press, 2001), 25–38; Donald E. Pitzer, *America's Communal Utopias* (Chapel Hill, NC: University of North Carolina Press, 1997), 337–41; Aharon Meged, "A Christian Commune in Canada," 552; John Ryan, *The Agricultural Economy of Manitoba Hutterite Colonies* (Toronto, ON: McClelland and Stewart, 1977), 13, 29, 81; Johnny Hofer, interview by Yossi Katz, James Valley Colony, May 2004; Aaron Hofer, interview by Yossi Katz, James Valley Colony, May 2004; and conversations with members of various colonies visited between 2000 and 2008.

21. Aharon Meged, "A Christian Commune in Canada," 549.

22. This contention is supported by John A. Hostelter, *Hutterite Society* (Baltimore and London: Johns Hopkins University Press, 1974), 296–302; Ryan, *Agricultural Economy of Manitoba Hutterite Colonies*, 13, 29; Pitzer, *America's Communal Utopias*, 337; and Kraybill and Bowman, *On the Backroad to Heaven*, 25–37.

23. Women who work in the kitchen are exempt from work in the garden.

24. Hostetler, *Hutterite Society*, 177–82; Kraybill and Bowman, *On the Backroad to Heaven*, 9–11, 25–39; Pitzer, *America's Communal Utopias*, 328–29; Edward D. Boldt, "The Hutterites: Current Developments and Future Prospects," in James S. Frideres (ed;), *Multiculturalism and Intergroup Relations* (New York and London, 1989), 60–63; Edward D. Boldt, "Structural Tightness, Autonomy, and Observability: An Analysis of Hutterite Conformity and Orderliness," *Canadian Journal of Sociology* 3, no. 3 (1978): 351–52; Caroline Hartse, "Social and Religious Change among Contemporary Hutterites," *Folk* 36 (1995): 114–15; Ryan, *Agricultural Economy of Manitoba Hutterite Colonies*, 76–83.

25. Michael Holzach, *The Forgotten People: A Year Among the Hutterites* (Sioux Falls, SD: Ex Machina Books, 1993), 120.

26. This statement was made by a Schmiedeleut Colony member in Manitoba but the sentiments were expressed by many Hutterites during visits to colonies from 2000 to 2008.

27. Ian Hitchen, "Ex-members Slam Hutterite Colonies' Rule," *Winnipeg Free Press*, June 14, 2008.

28. Mike McGarry, "Sam Made It—On the Tough Outside," *Winnipeg Tribune*, December 28, 1968.

29. Ryan, *Agricultural Economy of Manitoba Hutterite Colonies*, 14–15, 32–33.

30. Kraybill and Bowman, *On the Backroad to Heaven*, 228–29; Ryan, *Agricultural Economy of Manitoba Hutterite Colonies*, 80–81.

31. John Hofer, interview by Yossi Katz, James Valley Colony, May 2004, and September 23, 2005; Kraybill and Bowman, *On the Backroad to Heaven*, 26–27; Ryan, *Agricultural Economy of Manitoba Hutterite Colonies*, 76–83; Pitzer, *America's Communal Utopias*, 338–39.

32. Aaron Hofer, interview by Yossi Katz, James Valley Colony, May 2004.

33. Member of Sommerfeld Colony, interview by Yossi Katz and John Lehr, Sommerfeld Colony, May 2004.

34. This occurred on August 17, 2004, in the Bathurst Street Market's former "Downstairs Delicatessen" on North Main Street in Winnipeg, in an area that formerly had a high proportion of Jews in the population.

35. During a visit in mid-September in the Lehrerleut colony of Castor, Alberta, the teacher frankly said that "the youngsters, until their baptism, work without permission at the neighbouring farms, where they make money on the side. They work there for about a month, and with the money they buy forbidden things, such as television sets, radios, cameras, etc. Later, they come to the minister to confess, they are punished, and so forth. When the minister asks them whether they have money, they say no, for they have already deposited the money in the bank and have no money in their pocket... the minister and the elders of the colony know that they are not told the whole truth, but they look the other way, otherwise the youngsters will leave the colonies altogether." In a conversation we had with two young people about the age of 20 from the colony, they admitted that this is indeed the situation.

36. We discussed the issue with many Hutterites in Manitoba and Alberta. Few, if any, disagreed with this assessment.

37. Samuel Hofer, *The Hutterites: Lives and Images of a Communal Life* (Saskatoon, SK: Hofer Publishers, 1998), 129.

38. Ibid.

39. Peter Waldner, Julie Waldner, and Tim Croker, interviews by Yossi Katz, Castor Colony, September 13, 2005.

40. This respondent did not wish to be identified. Interview by John Lehr, September 5, 2008.

41. Hostetler, *Hutterite Society,* 268–270.

42. In early May 2004, the authors visited a Schmiedeleut colony in Manitoba. The person in charge of the hog operation had a computer with a connection to the Internet, for work purposes. When they asked the children at home "Where is the internet?," the children immediately connected to the Internet without any problem, although they are not officially allowed to do so. They knew the login password. Other Schmiedeleut [Group Two] colonies consider this colony to be one of the more liberal Group Two Colonies.

43. Interview with Schmiedeleut Colony member, by Yossi Katz, Manitoba, May 2005. We heard similar things from other Hutterites in May 2004: "Today we are much more money oriented. This distances us from God."

44. Johnny Hofer, interview by Yossi Katz, James Valley Colony, May 2004.

Chapter 7
THE EDUCATION SYSTEM AND EDUCATION IN THE NEW WORLD

E DUCATION OF THEIR CHILDREN IS OF UTMOST IMPORtance to Hutterites. Through education Hutterian doctrine is instilled and a significant part of the Hutterian socialization process is achieved. In fact, the whole personality of the Hutterite believer is supposed to develop through his or her education, so that when the time comes, he or she will be able to pass on the Hutterite faith and way of life to the next generation. Education aims to make the individual part of a closed communal religious society, which regards the mundane actions of everyday life as part of religious observance. All the social institutions, the activities and the resources that the individual might need lie within a clearly defined socio-spatial environment. Dependence on other colony members is maximized and interaction with people outside the colony is reduced to a minimum. The child is seen as someone whose materialistic nature needs to be replaced by a spiritual essence, whose personality is basically positive only when personal will is renounced in favour of the colony's will.

The community's early writings state "our children are dear to our heart before God according to truth, and a precious concern, to this God would testify for us on the Day of Judgment." From the beginning of their Church, it was clear to them that the demands that they placed on themselves to meet their religious obligations would not be easy to bear. These duties were some of the gravest liabilities undertaken by any of the Anabaptist groups, and therefore only a systematic and strict religious education could prepare the young generation for a life of faith and commitment. Since every Hutterite male may be elected as a teacher or minister, without any prior requirements or qualifications (such as a ministers' or teachers' seminary education), the importance of proper education for all children is greater than in the outside world. Robert Friedmann, one of the first and most important researchers of the Hutterite community, stated years ago that "Among the various Anabaptist groups of the sixteenth century, perhaps none had so much opportunity for a systematic Christian upbringing of the youth as the Hutterites, who on their large collective Bruderhofs in Moravia could organize and systematically take care of the entire education from the nursery school to kindergarten and through the grades."[1]

The Hutterites' educational principles, established in the 16th century, have been largely retained. They are based on one of the verses in the New Testament, saying: "And you, fathers, do not provoke your children to wrath, but bring them up in the training and admonition of the Lord" (Ephesians 6, 4). On the basis of this verse, Peter Riedemann, in the 16th century, established two principles: firstly, the whole purpose of the Hutterite education system is to know the Lord, follow him and fulfill his commandments; secondly, the Hutterite education system is fully independent, it is separated from the general education system which it does not allow its children to join.

In his *Confession of Faith*, Riedemann described the Hutterite education system in detail:

> For this reason is our education such that we permit them not to carry out their headstrong will and carnal practice. Therefore in such places as in the country of Moravia, where we have many households we have schools in which we bring up our children in the divine discipline, and teach them from the beginning to know God. But we permit them not to go to other schools, since there they teach but the wisdom, art and practices of the world, and are silent about divine things. Our practice is as follows: as soon as the mother hath weaned the child she giveth it to the school. Here there are sisters, appointed by the Church to care for them, who

have been recognized to be competent and diligent therein; and, as soon as they can speak, they lay the word of God's testimony in their mouths and teach them to speak with or from the same, tell them of prayer and such things as children can understand. With them children remain until their fifth or sixth year, that is, until they are able to learn to read and write. When they are thus far they are entrusted to the schoolmaster, who teacheth them the same and thereby instructeth them more and more in the knowledge of God, that they learn to know God and his will and strive to keep the same. He observeth the following order with them: when they all come together in the morning to school he teacheth them to thank the Lord together, and to pray to him. Then he preacheth to them as children for the space of half an hour, telling them how they ought to obey, be subject to and honour their parents, teachers and those set over them, and illustrateth from the Old and New Testaments both the promise to godly and the punishment of disobedient and obstinate children. From such bedienceo to parents he teacheth them obedience to God and the keeping of his will; that they should reverence him as their almighty Father, and love, honour and worship him above all things; and serve and cleave to him alone, as him from whom they have all that is good. Thus we teach our children from babyhood to seek not what is temporal but what is eternal. They remain with the schoolmaster until they reach the stage when they can be taught to work. Then each is set to the work for which he is recognized to be gifted and capable.[2]

It should be noted that Hutterite formal schooling traditionally ended at the end of primary school (at the age of 12-13), although, in North America, these practices were modified by provincial and state educational regulations. According to the forefathers, formal schooling past this age is "nonconducive to the fear of God—the highest goal of all Anabaptist education."[3] And indeed, children older than that were already part of the workforce in the colony.

On the basis of primary sources from the 16th century, including school regulations, in the first half of the 20th century, Friedmann concluded that:

[The Hutterite school in the Old World] was actually more than a mere school, and may be compared to a children's home where they lived and were taken care of practically throughout the year, in conformity with the Hutterite principle of community living... The spirit, which permeates the school regulation of 1578, is that of a free and cheerful discipline in love and the fear of God, peaceful in spirit. To be dutiful and peaceful is conducive to good discipline. One cannot take too much care of the children, and the adults should always be mindful of setting a good example, since the children watch them and learn from their behavior... The use of a rod may sometimes be necessary, but great discretion and discernment should be exercised therein, for often a child can be better trained and corrected by kind words whereas harshness would be altogether in vain... Children should be trained to accept punishment willingly, and care should be taken that they do not become self-willed. But above all they should be trained to love the Lord and to be diligent in prayer... Basically these principles have been preserved fairly unchanged among the Hutterites up to the present day... Bertha W. Clark, who visited the Brethren in South Dakota in 1923, describes the Hutterite system of education in the Bonhomme Bruderhof, showing that in spite of certain necessary adaptations to American ways the spirit of the upbringing of the youth is by and large the same as of old.

Friedmann commented also on the standard of education, saying that "that Hutterite education had a very high standard can still be seen from all their handwritten books," showing "excellent Bible knowledge and often deft arguments—things not so commonly found among people of the sixteenth and seventeenth centuries."[4]

The principle of isolating the Hutterian education system from the state education system, preserved to the present day, created a one-room school system, in which children of various ages study together in the same class. The youngest children sit in the row closest to the teacher, and the oldest sit in the farthest row. Boys and girls study together, but sit apart.

Children's education begins almost at birth, and it has been ever so since the Hutterites arrived in North America. Before and after feeding her baby, the mother will cross its hands and say the blessing with it. In the evening, before bedtime, she prays with her child. At home, the baby acquires the basics of the Hutterite language (Hutterisch), the lingua franca of the colonies that he or she will use everyday to communicate with other Hutterites. Until recently this was a spoken language only, based on an Austrian variant of High German, originally from Tyrol and Carinthia.[5] The Hutterites added words they gathered during their wanderings in Europe until they arrived in North America.[6] Later, during their school years (and even before that, in kindergarten), they learn English and standard German (High German), the language used for prayer services and religious rites. Thus, Hutterites learn three languages at an early age. They distinguish between the German language, their ethnic language, which symbolizes the isolation of the Hutterites from the outside world, and English, the secular language, representing the outside world and used for communication with it.[7]

Proficiency in English continues to increase. In the 1970s it was not unusual to encounter older colony members who were less than fluent; today almost all over the age of seven or eight years can converse easily in English. Increasingly, English terms are integrated into everyday conversation. This is driven in part by the introduction of new technology for which the vocabulary is English, but it also reflects increasing exposure to English through books, newspapers, trade journals, and other communication devices. In liberal Group One colonies, church services are sometimes held in English.[8] Younger Hutterites in more conservative colonies query why only German Bibles are allowed in church when they would prefer to read them in English. A variety of English songs and hymns are performed by Hutterite colony choirs; *Amazing Grace* and other English language songs are heard alongside traditional hymns such as *Keiner wird zu schanden*. At a hulba on James Valley colony attended by John Lehr, the colony's various choirs, quartets, and duos performed spiritual songs in both English and German, sung a cappella, in a range of styles from traditional to country.

Occasionally, hybrid Hutterisch-English phraseology erupts in conversations between colony members, as in: "Ist du busy?" A 2012 ordinance forbade the use of English in church services, suggesting some Group Two ministers were delivering sermons in English. Ministers face a dilemma when some younger members are equally comfortable in either English or German, and some have a better comprehension of English than High German.

English continues to creep into the colonies. Significantly, in the regulations of the 2012 edition of the *Ordnungen und Koferenz Briefen,* a list of items to be given to young people on marriage carried the heading in German, but all item descriptions were in English.

Until the age of two and a half, Hutterite children stay at home. They then join the kindergarten, where they stay until the age of five. The kindergarten enables mothers to go to work, but its hours are not the same in all the colonies. In the Schmiedeleut colonies, the kindergarten is open only during the summer, when the mothers work long hours in the vegetable garden. In the Dariusleut and Lehrerleut colonies, the kindergarten is open throughout the year, and thus it better achieves one of its main goals—educating children for communal life. The women in charge of the kindergarten are usually the eldest in the colony who are still capable of working. Three or four young girls, aged 18-20 who alternate days in the kindergarten, aid them. On Sundays, the school children take over so that the women may attend the prayer services.[9]

In the kindergarten, caregivers help the children memorize prayers and religious songs so that they will know them by heart, but they do not explain their meanings. The children also listen to many Bible stories. Improper behaviour is punished at this early age, and thus the children are taught the principles of discipline. However, there are also positive recompenses for those correcting their ways. Children learn that they are part of a group in which they share everything.[10] Thus, adults hope to minimize the child's natural individualistic inclinations and shape a patient personality, which sees itself as part of a communal society. They invest time and effort to instill the principle in children that in addition to being under the authority of their parents, they are also subject to the authority of the colony and its institutions.

The young child learns to enjoy being with people. In the kindergarten they are somewhat disconnected from their nuclear family and they learn to accept authority. Loneliness is unpleasant, but being with other people is pleasant. During their school years, children move even farther away from their family, they learn more about authority and acquire knowledge about their religion. They acquire the ability to behave positively with their peer group and to respond to its demands. When children are little, their world is unpredictable. However, as they grow up among their peers and take part in colony life, their world becomes increasingly predictable. They learn to diminish self-confidence and accept dependency on the peer group. Each knows clearly who and when to obey.

School age children have only a limited relationship with their parents, and they get very little pampering from them. The emphasis is on building a commitment to the colony rather than to the family, as the development of tight family ties can impede the smooth running of the colony. Children thus learn that their peer group protects them and punishes them. They learn to accept frustration with indifference and to enjoy hard physical work. When children become adults, compensation comes in the form of responsibility, privileges, acknowledgment, and acceptance by their nuclear families. From childhood through adulthood, they experience subordination to the colony; at every stage of their life they learn that objectives are attainable only through the group. They learn not to stick to their own opinions, and are compensated through a meaningful job and awareness that their contributions are really needed.[11]

When they arrived in North America, the Hutterites wished to retain the independence of their education system, as it has been for 400 years. However, under the laws of the state (in both the United States and Canada), they must send their children to school from six until 15 years of age (namely, for 10 years of formal schooling) in district public schools and be educated according to the curriculum set by the province or state. The Hutterites could not accept this, in spite of the great importance they placed on the acquisition of reading and writing skills, arithmetic and other practical fields of knowledge essential for operating machines, management of agriculture and building the colony. Apart from the fact that the public school could not provide a Hutterite education, it could expose the children to the outside world and to undesirable aspects of learning, expose them to non-Hutterite teachers and children, and, in general, to the outside world from which, according to their faith, the Hutterites must isolate themselves. Public schooling has been regarded as a cause of defection, as public schools threatened to undermine the Hutterite faith and the colony's principles of equality, a possible precursor to colony failure.[12] The Hutterites could not send their children to public schools, and found itself in a head-on confrontation with the law.

After a period of tension between the Hutterites and the government, a compromise was reached that the Hutterites accepted as the lesser of two evils. This agreement is still in effect. It was decided that each colony should establish a school exclusively for colony children that would serve two systems of education: the Hutterite system and the public system—namely, "the English school." Unlike the usual public school system, where farm children are sent from their residences to the regional school, teachers come to the colony school from the outside. The same building is used for Hutterite education, when normal "English school" is over for the day. A Hutterite teacher, a resident of the colony who has been elected to this position in a colony general meeting, then teaches religion and German. The school, like the kindergarten, is located in the centre of the colony near the dining hall and the church, and this signifies the great importance that the community places on its "German school." [13]

The Hutterites contributed much to the resolution of this education impasse. Unlike the public schools, which are built and maintained with the help of taxpayer's money, the agreement stated that the colonies are responsible for allocation of land for the school, they must build it at their expense according to government standards, and they are responsible for its maintenance. In the early years in Canada colonies were responsible for supplying dwellings for teachers either on the colony itself or in the immediate vicinity. In an era of improved roads and reliable vehicles, almost all non-Hutterite teachers commute to the colony from their homes in nearby communities. Teachers' salaries and school equipment are the only things financed by the government. [14] However, the Canadian government was never satisfied with this solution, and in the 1960s it decreased the amounts of grants to the Hutterite schools in order to force them to send their children to the regional public schools. The Hutterites knew that this would be a serious blow to the Hutterite way of life, and therefore they were prepared to waive any government funding and take upon themselves all education expenses. [15]

Integration of Hutterite teachers into the public education system for the colonies did not appeal to many conservative Hutterites. Firstly, Hutterites did not have the proper qualifications required by the government to teach in public schools. Although some received permission to acquire a college degree and a teacher's certificate to enable them to teach in the colonies it was feared that exposure to higher education might erode commitment to the faith. Secondly, Hutterian elders did not approve of Hutterian teachers teaching general subjects: "It is better that a teacher from outside will teach in the public school, and thus we will be able to keep the limits strictly." Segregating the secular from the spiritual and having each taught by a person that represented their respective worldview made the distinction between the Hutterite and the secular viewpoint clear to all pupils. Nevertheless, in some Schmiedeleut [mostly Group One] colonies, there are young Hutterite college graduates teaching in colony schools or serving as teaching assistants.[16]

The colony school is called "the English school," and its teachers referred to as "the English teachers." They teach in English, covering general subjects such as English language, mathematics, geography, science, etc. The religious Hutterite school is called "the German school," and the Hutterian teacher is "the German teacher." This role is considered a central role in the process of indoctrination and socialization of Hutterites, and today it is an extremely valued position in the colony. Many of these teachers are later elected as ministers. The German teacher is in fact the educational and supervising role model for school age children and, to some extent, this continues up to the time of their baptism. In one way or another, the German teacher supervises the young people all day long. He or is wife supervise the children in the dining hall during mealtimes. Except for the Group One colonies under the leadership of Minister Jacob Kleinsasser, women cannot be German teachers, but educational aides only.[17]

In spite of the great importance ascribed to the German teacher's position, the Hutterites did not always choose their teachers carefully. In the past the position was not considered at all desirable, and often people who did not have any other job were elected for this position. The method of electing the teacher (until the present day) is similar to the method of election of the Boss and the Farm Boss. At the time of election (on a Sunday after the prayer service), each member in the colony writes the name of someone whom he regards as the most suitable person for the job, and the member whose name has been written most often gets the job. In any case, the person elected cannot refuse the position. The position is for life, unless the German teacher is subsequently elected as minister, although he may stay on as teacher if he chooses. Many do so.

Today many things have changed. Education receives a much more important place in most colonies. Parents stay in contact with the German teacher, and when something in their child's behaviour concerns them, they approach him or the minister directly. The greatest fear among parents is that a teacher might question the Hutterite religion or follow other faiths. The method of electing the German teacher has not changed, but the members know that they should elect only someone who is best qualified for this position. Therefore, the German teacher takes courses, and he purchases and develops teaching materials and teaching aids. There is also a joint education committee of all the Group Two colonies but the committee finds it hard to function because of disagreements between those who would like to go back to the traditional education methods of the past and those who wish to introduce even more liberal education methods.

In order to promote the German school, the minister of James Valley, John Hofer, opened a store for books and teaching aids that sells educational supplies, teaching materials, and historic and theological literature for the German schools. These materials are distributed to many colonies, reaching even the Lehrerleut colonies in Alberta. John Hofer, together with the Hutterite Education Committee, organizes an annual two-day convention of all the German teachers in the Schmiedeleut colonies during which they discuss issues relating to the German school and the German teacher.[18] However, there is no doubt that teaching methods in the German school are old-fashioned, and the prohibition against use of advanced audiovisual methods is a problem for progressive teachers.

Children begin German school when they turn five. In the German school, the children acquire full skills of reading and writing in German, including Old German. They thoroughly study the Bible, memorize hymns and chapters of the Bible, learn faith and religion, Hutterite history, work ethics and good manners, and they acquire an ability to deal with everyday difficulties. From October until May, classes in the German school take place for one hour before English school starts and for one hour after school ends, and on Saturdays. The German teacher supervises the children all day long: during mealtimes, at work and during class time.[19]

When they reach 15 years of age, Hutterite children finish their 10-year formal schooling and join adult society. However, until their baptism at the age of 20-25, they still continue to attend Sunday school, which is in fact an expansion of the German school. The German teacher operates Sunday school on Sunday afternoons and religious holidays. In Sunday school, the students study hymns, sections of prayers and the rituals of Sundays and holidays.[20]

The world of play for Hutterite children is different from that of school children in the outside world. Computer games are forbidden in the colonies; only a few colonies allow war games, such as playing with toy guns (due to Hutterite pacifism). Riding a bicycle is also not allowed in most of the colonies, and thus the children play a lot with classic children toys, scooters, blocks, spinning tops, etc. In the Lehrerleut colonies, unlike the Schmiedeleut colonies, the children do not have a playing yard equipped with toys; they are not allowed any ball games, nor are they allowed to ride bicycles or scooters.[21]

The passage to adult society at the age of 15 (with the Lehrerleut—at the age of 14—similar to the Jewish age of Bar Mitzvah (13)) is marked in several ways: the boys and girls stop dining with the children and join the adults in the dining hall; they stop working as babysitters and join the work cycle. Boys work with the men on specific tasks or as part of the shifting workforce, and the girls work with the women in the kitchen, garden, the dining hall, painting, etc. At this time boys receive their personal tools such as a saw and hammer, and the girls receive paint brushes, kitchen knives, a broom, a hoe and knitting needles; boys and girls receive a "private" drawer chest with a key to store their personal belongings, and also their personal Bible, a copy of the *Confession of Faith* and Hutterite song books, a present from the colony; the adult's close supervision of their religious behaviour is reduced; they do not attend German school anymore; they say their morning and evening prayers without the supervision of the German teacher and not as part of the group of small children; they are not allowed to miss the evening and Sunday prayer services; they must obey the disciplinary rules of the colony in addition to those set by their parents and the German teacher; they are no longer subject to physical punishment, and in case of a severe misdemeanor, the boy or girls may be disciplined by standing during the evening prayer service or Sunday service; the children's head covering is replaced by an adult head covering, and they all receive new clothes; they are granted the same money allowance and the same amount of cloth as the adults. However, until their baptism, the boys and girls must attend Sunday school, memorize the Bible and hymn books they receive at the age of 15 containing preparation instructions for baptism, and memorize sections from Sunday prayer services. Improper behaviour is dealt with by the German teacher and not by the minister, who handles adult misdemeanors. They must ask him for permission whenever they want to leave the colony; they are not allowed into management tasks, nor can they elect or be elected.[22]

As a rule, the Hutterites do not encourage their children to pursue their formal studies after the age of 16, but the government would like them to do so. From the Hutterites' point of view, 16-year-olds are needed in the workforce. Continuing their studies after this age not only disrupts the life of the colony, it also affects the self-confidence of boys, since at this age they are already entitled to adult work privileges, and may feel deprived of their status if they must pursue formal education beyond the age set by their culture. Some say that the reason for objecting to 12 years of formal studies might be that "the adults do not want the youngsters to be too smart."[23] However, the Hutterites get some of their professional training through correspondence courses and by reading technical literature. Another way of acquiring knowledge is through the marketers of the advanced machinery and equipment, who instruct the operators of this equipment in the colony. They, in turn, instruct the other members in the colony. Since Hutterites do not receive formal professional training, they often acquire operating skills the hard way, but those who learn from them – through training or apprenticeship – find it a lot easier.

In the last few years, boys and adults from some colonies have been sent to courses taking place in the neighbouring town, in trade subjects such as electrics, plumbing, water treatment, etc., which might be useful to the colonies. Some courses are for Hutterites only, but others are mixed. In the past, recommendations of state and district committees to integrate the Hutterites in courses relating to agriculture, crafts, industry and home economics were not followed.[24]

Today, more and more colonies regard favorably a 12-year formal education for the young members of the colony. Unlike its predecessors, the young generation understands the importance of education to the colony's economic success, especially due to the vast technological advancement in the area of machinery. A license for operating heavy vehicles, such as a semi-trailer and an advanced combine, is conditional upon a certificate of completion of 12 years of formal education, as well as participation in advanced professional courses. The growing penetration of outside world terms into the colony also creates a demand for completion of a full high school education. Therefore, "if there is no need in the colony for participation of 15- or 16-year-olds in the workforce, the colony will not pressure them not to study." However, further studies will by no means come at the expense of the youngster's duties to the colony. Since the English school in the colonies is not suitable for offering a full high school education and as the potential number of students for completing high school studies is very small, some of the teaching is done through correspondence, using feedback from the teachers (as in the "open university"), by distance learning through telephone conference and with the assistance of a visiting teacher who visits each colony. Exams are taken in the colonies and are supervised by teachers arriving especially for this. Children in grades 9-12 are assembled in each colony in a special group, separated from the children in grades 1-8. The teacher teaches through the telephone conference, and each day the lesson is given from another colony or from the local school division office. Thus the teacher gets to meet his students from time to time. Requirements and exams are identical to those in other public schools in the province, and in spite of the difficulties associated with one-classroom teaching and telephone conference teaching, the level of teaching is being preserved and it is similar to that in provincial public schools.[25]

The idea to establish a public regional school for Hutterite children, which will serve a few Hutterite colonies and will enjoy the privileges of economies of scale, as in the regional schools of the religious kibbutzim in Israel, has not been considered for many reasons. The distances between colonies and the difficulties of access could perhaps be overcome in some regions where colonies are more densely concentrated, but matters of principle are equally effective barriers. Even in cases where colonies are located less than a mile of each other, literally within walking distance for school age children, as with the case of Bloomfield and Westroc colonies, near Gladstone in Manitoba, each colony retains its own school. From an educational point of view, the Hutterites ascribe great importance to the child's staying on the colony all day long, near family, taking part in its everyday life. The family gathers twice a day for "coffee breaks" between meals, half an hour of "togetherness", and studying in a regional school would not enable this. Also, it would be impossible to employ the children in babysitting or other tasks during free time or hours during the day designated for children's work. The children would also not be able to participate in the three daily meals in the colony's dining hall. The German teacher, who accompanies and supervises the children all day, would not be able to do so efficiently if children from various colonies attended a regional school together.[26]

Two additional reasons for the decision not to establish regional schools are the Hutterite conception of each colony as a church, a whole ensemble which must contain within itself all the components necessary for life, including the school; secondly, in spite of the extensive inter-colony cooperation, Hutterites as a rule are quite obsessive about maintaining each colony's independence, a sort of communal individualism, something that is enshrined in the Hutterite Church Rules asserting that there is no mutual legal commitment between the colonies.[27] For all these reasons, the government failed in its efforts to establish high schools for Hutterite children even in Cartier municipality in Manitoba where colony density is the highest in Canada.[28]

The relationship between the Hutterite community and the public school system is complex and varies in each colony. Although the Hutterites attach importance to teaching their children the English language and math, the English teacher and the English school are considered a threat to the colony, to its lifestyle and to its chances of survival, for these bring the outside world and its values into the colony. "It is the place where the ideologies of the world and the colony compete with each other over the loyalty of the young people." The seeds of future defection of the young Hutterite, from the colony to the world that has been revealed to him during his school years, might be spread in the English school, especially among children who find it difficult to adjust to the colony's lifestyle. Furthermore, a close relationship between a teacher and a student might lead to defection, and indeed, in some cases children ran away from the colony with the English teacher, or teachers helped the young people find work outside the colony as part of their preparations for defection. For an English teacher to be a role model is very dangerous to the Hutterite community. The Hutterites must, therefore, minimize the danger, but they can do so only in informal ways, for as a rule they are not allowed to intervene in the process of appointing the teachers, and they cannot determine the curriculum. Indeed, it is customary that a new teacher who has not previously taught in a Hutterite colony to receive orientation from the minister before entering the classroom. The minister explains to the teacher what is right and what is wrong, what is acceptable in the Hutterite religion and what is not. He clarifies what material will be considered offensive and should not be taught (for example, those which contradict religious beliefs, such as texts dealing with evolution or texts which have erotic elements in them). He also explains to the new teachers that they are not allowed to use audio-visual equipment, such as a radio, tape recorder or a camera. In addition, the schedule of the English school is adapted to the daily routine of the colony. Thus the children are able to eat all their meals in the colony's dining hall and stay with their families during the colony's morning break and other breaks. It is made clear to the English teacher that if the colony needs a child to help with a task, his or her absence or late appearance in school is justified by colony needs. The school year ends as the work in the vegetable garden begins. Some days during the harvest season women and girls work there from morning to night, and the younger schoolgirls take care of babies and small children throughout the day.

The colony encourages English teachers to maintain discipline even by using corporal punishment, which is forbidden in the public school system. However, it does not allow the English school to deviate from the colony's daily routine, and thus, an order given by an English teacher to a child to stay in class during lunch break or after school, is not acceptable. Teachers who follow the colony rules are rewarded with presents, food and help. During lunch breaks they are invited to the members' homes and are a source of vital information about what goes on in the outside world. Teachers cooperating with the colony's interests, even if they are not the best of teachers, are more welcome than talented teachers who demand their pupils adopt independent thinking. As mentioned above, until lately parents did not encourage their children to excel, and they very seldom intervene in the teaching process.[29] However, not every colony maintains a good relationship with the English school; sometimes there is tension between the colony and the school. Usually it is about control over textbooks and their content, use of audio-visual methods or computers or taking the children out of school to perform various colony tasks (such as babysitting). On one occasion a teacher was expelled from a colony because of this. In some cases, the colonies decided to waive the government funding and to institute a private English school.[30]

Introducing computers into the schools in the 1980s, and the expanding use of CDs and the Internet for teaching purposes in the 1990s, placed very difficult challenges in front of the Hutterite community. The children were now able to experience the temptations of the outside world, without having to leave the colony. CDS are easily available, either through the neighbouring farmers or by purchasing them during visits to the nearby town for a doctor's appointment, marketing produce, etc. Therefore, the Hutterites refuse to introduce advanced computers into the colonies' schools. It seems that the schools in the colonies are the only ones in the world in which PCs from the 1980s are still being used. Moreover, computers are not allowed in the schools of the Lehrerleut colonies. Computers are found there only in the service of agriculture.

As a rule, the use of the Internet is totally forbidden by the leaders of the three Hutterite leut. Some colonies break this prohibition, but they are strongly criticized by the Hutterite Church. On the other hand, some colonies enable a certain member to get connected to the Internet for business purposes only, and on the condition that the connection to the Internet is made not from within the colony but form a certain store in the nearby town. Other colonies enable one person, trusted by the elders, to get connected to the Internet from within the colony, for economic purposes only. Therefore, the Internet cannot be used for constructive purposes in the schools. It turned out that the youngsters are usually successful in putting their hands on the login of that only member who received the permission to use the Internet, and thus they are able to get connected.[31] Within the more liberal Kleinsasser colonies, computers and Internet access seems to be common and Hutterite youth there have developed considerable familiarity with email and enjoy considerable facility in use of computer graphics, scanning materials and processing digital photographs.

The fact that advanced computers are used in economic branches has created a dangerous breach through which the young people find ways of listening to music and watching movies. However, lately the Hutterites made it clear to the government that they will not allow the introduction of the Internet into the schools, and they also threatened that if this is done in spite of their refusal, they will stop the operation of the English school and will establish a private schooling system, funded entirely by the colonies.[32]

College education is almost impossible, even for a teacher's certificate, except for in Group One colonies under Jacob Kleinsasser's leadership, since there is nothing like the college world to mix with the outside, sinning world. A young Hutterite who wants a college education will have to choose between leaving the colony or complying with tradition and staying faithful to his forefathers and community. A colony member stated:

> Our colony will not permit anyone to go to college although we are considered a modern colony. The experience of colonies that have sent youngsters to acquire a teacher's certificate was not successful. The graduates came back to the colony and did not want to be teachers, or they defected. If someone in the colony would like to be a doctor, we will not send him to the university for there is a danger that he will lose himself. I wanted to go to college, I was even prepared to leave, but I did not want to hurt my family. I think that higher education is something you have to sacrifice if you want to remain Hutterite... we have learned to accept things; we say that this is what God wanted, but in truth we are always in conflict with ourselves. In baptism we say that our self has to die, but we still struggle with ourselves. If we do not give up our self will, no communal life can exist.[33]

Another colony member left the colony while she was young. She wanted to go to college and see the world. After seven years she returned to the colony.[34] A similar story is that of the sisters of Tom Hofer, the minister of Deerboine. They left the colony because they wanted to study at college and nursing school, and they settled in town. Later, when they returned for the funeral of their aunt, they were seated far away from the coffin, as a sign of their defection.[35]

In the Group One colonies under Jacob Kleinsasser's leadership, a college education is possible. Group One colonies established a joint four-year Brandon University Hutterite Education Program (BUHEP) for training teachers for the English schools in the colonies.[36] But even in the more conservative colonies change proceeds. In some Group Two colonies cameras and cell phones are now openly displayed while colony leaders turn a blind eye. In late 2009, while visiting a Group Two colony, the second author noticed a teenaged girl busily text messaging her boyfriend in the presence of her parents. Some Group Two colonies have a number of common cell phones available for members to sign out when traveling outside the colony but there are signs that this practice will eventually become redundant as personal cell phones become more common.

This intrusion of advanced communications technology has several implications for colony management. Modern cell phones generally have multiple capabilities: they can receive data, access the Internet, and function as a camera or video recorder. Not only does this technology promise to speed the flow of uncontrolled information but the need to pay for subscription plans on a long-term basis ensures that the need for "side money" will continue to increase. Clearly, the problems of managing modernity in the colony will become ever more complex and will require a deft hand to manage the transition into the information age.

Notes

1. Robert Friedmann, *Hutterite Studies* (Goshen: Mennonite Historical Society, 1961), 138–140.
2. Peter Riedemann, *Confession of Faith* (Rifton, NY: Plough Publishers, 1970), 130–131.
3. Friedmann, *Hutterite Studies*, 138–140.
4. Ibid.
5. Linda Maendel, from Elm River Colony (Schmiedeleut Group One), published a children's storybook, *Linda's Glücklicher Tag*, in Hutterisch, in 2006.
6. There are, for example, many words of Ukrainian origin in the Hutterite lexicon, including *Tscheinik* (teapot), *Pasternak* (parsnip), *Tchabadan* (suitcase), *Gugarutz* (corn), and *Worsch* (beet soup); words of Romanian origin include *Gasa* (potato soup) and *Kratzavitz* (cucumber). Since their arrival in North America, they have similarly adopted many English words that have been "Hutterized." For example, *Matchstankle* (matchsticks) and *Behalf di* (behave yourself). See Michael Holzach, *The Forgotten People: A Year Among the Hutterites* (Sioux Falls, S.D.: Ex Machina Books, 1993), 37.
7. Patrick Murphy, interview by John Lehr, James Valley Colony, January 13, 2005; Donald B. Kraybill and Carl F. Bowman, *On the Backroad to Heaven: Old Order Hutterites, Mennonites, Amish and Brethren* (Baltimore and London: Johns Hopkins University Press, 2001), 24–25.
8. Linda Maendel, Elm River Colony, email communication with John Lehr, December 15, 2013.
9. John Ryan, *The Agricultural Economy of Manitoba Hutterite Colonies* (Toronto: McClelland and Stewart, 1977), 74–75.
10. Mary-Ann Kirkby, *I am Hutterite* (Saskatchewan: Polka Dot Press, 2007), 54–57, 77.
11. John A. Hostetler, *Hutterite Society* (Baltimore and London: Johns Hopkins University Press, 1974), 287–289; Donald D. Pitzer, *America's Communal Utopias* (Chapel Hill: University of North Carolina Press, 1997), 388–389.
12. For further details, see William Janzen, *Limits to Liberty: The Experience of Mennonite, Hutterite and Doukhobor Communities in Canada* (Toronto, ON: University of Toronto Press, 1990), 143–161; Ryan, *The Agricultural Economy of Manitoba Hutterite Colonies*, 13–14 and 75–78.
13. Ryan, *The Agricultural Economy of Manitoba Hutterite Colonies*, 24–25.
14. Hostetler, *Hutterite Society*, 345–346; Janzen, *Limits to Liberty*, 142–161;, Kraybill and Bowman, *On the Backroad to Heaven*; Aharon Meged, "A Christian Commune in Canada," *Mibifnim* (1947), 551.
15. See note 12.

16. Friedmann, *Hutterite Studies*, 139–140; Hostetler, *Hutterite Society*, 236; Caroline Hartse, "Social and Religious Change among Contemporary Hutterites," *Folk* 36 (1995), 112.

17. Kraybill and Bowman, *On the Backroad to Heaven*, 44.

18. John Hofer, interviews by Yossi Katz, James Valley Colony, May 2004 and August 2004; Sara Gross, Bloomfield Colony, August 17, 2004; Johnny Hofer, James Valley Colony, September 26, 2005; Peter Waldner, Castor Colony, September 14, 2005.

19. Pitzer, *America's Communal Utopias*, 338.

20. Many colony members testified to this. See also Hostetler, *Hutterite Society*, 215–220, 260–262; Kraybill and Bowman, *On the Backroad to Heaven*, 44–46.

21. Observations on visits to various colonies; Tim Croker, English teacher, interview by Yossi Katz, Castor Colony, September 13, 2005.

22. Hostetler, *Hutterite Society*, 332–335; Kraybill and Bowman, *On the Backroad to Heaven*, 44–46.

23. Mr. Lacroix, the high school English teacher in Bloomfield Colony, interview by Yossi Katz, Bloomfield Colony, September 23, 2005. Bloomfied Colony uses the telephone conference distance-learning method of instruction for senior students. At the request of the teacher who was teaching in another colony, the first author used the telephone to tell the students in classes in other colonies about the upcoming Jewish holidays.

24. Hostetler, *Hutterite Society*, 26; William Janzen, *Limits to Liberty*, 145; Ryan, *Agricultural Economy*, 76–78; Sara Gross, interview by Yossi Katz, Bloomfield, August 2004; Patrick Murphy, interview by John Lehr, note 7.

25. In 2007 two girls graduated with a Grade Twelve High School Provincial Diploma from Bloomfield Colony. In 2008, a boy and girl graduated.

26. This is based on observations and on conversations with colony members.

27. Sara and Kenny Gross, interview by Yossi Katz, Bloomfield Colony, August 2004.

28. Hostetler, *Hutterite Society*, 261.

29. Hostetler, *Hutterite Society*, 201, 218–219, 260–262; John Hofer, *The History of the Hutterites* (Elie, Manitoba: James Valley Book Centre, 2004), 74; Edward D. Boldt, "The Hutterites: Current Developments and Future Prospects," in James S. Frideres (ed.), *Multiculturalism and Intergroup Relations* (Westport Conn.: Greenwood Press, 1989), 60–63; Janzen, *Limits to Liberty*, 142 ff.; Pitzer, *America's Communal Utopias*, 336 ff.; Hartse, "Social and Religious Change," 112–116; Kraybill and Bowman, *On the Backroad to Heaven*, 22–23, 32–47; observations by Yossi Katz during a visit to Bloomfield Colony on September 21–23, 2005.

30. John Hofer, interview by Yossi Katz, James Valley Colony, September 26, 2005; Bloomfield Colony, Manitoba, for example, maintains a good relationship with the English school; the colony members express their views regarding the curriculum content, there are meetings with the teachers, and a regular contact between the parents and the school is being maintained. The nature of this cordial relationship was evident at the ceremony marking the Grade 12 graduation of two students in June 2007 attended by the second author.

31. Tim Croker, English teacher, interview by Yossi Katz, Castor Colony, September 13, 2005; Johnny Hofer, interview by Yossi Katz , James Valley Colony, May 2004. During our visit in Bloomfield Colony in May 2004, we were witnesses to a debate between the young generation and the older one, when Paul Gross, about 70 years old, claimed that introducing the computer is in itself dangerous to the colony, and all computers should be taken out from the colony, including the school computers. As opposed to him, his son, Kenny Gross, about 38, who is in charge of the colony's garage, said that "it is impossible to live as in the past, and computers are necessary, but they need to be controlled and conscientiously used, for work and school purposes only." On the prohibition to use the Internet, see the Decisions and Provisions of the Council of the Schmiedeleut stream of the Hutterian Church, Appendix 5.

32. Minister David Maendel, interview by Yossi Katz, Sturgeon Creek Colony, May 2004, who also said: "We intend to cut ourselves from the English school, and everything

will be in our hands. We do not want the bad influence of the outside world. The English school urges us to use the Internet. We do not want this. If they will press us, we will quit and set up a private schooling system without the government's aid." We have seen how a girl from a Manitoba Group Two Colony used the advanced computer her father used in his work to watch the contents of the CD which she bought in the nearby town. She did it without her father's knowledge, but her mother knew about this.

33. This informant requested anonymity.
34. This informant requested anonymity.
35. Yossi Katz, conversations with the sisters of Minister Tom Hofer during a funeral in Deerboine, May 5, 2004.
36. Barbara Gross, interview by Yossi Katz, Bloomfield Colony, August 2004.

Chapter 8

LEISURE TIME
IN AND OUTSIDE THE COLONY.

C ULTURE AND LEISURE TIME ACTIVITIES IN HUTTERITE colonies are limited and lack diversity. The outside world listens to the radio, watches television and movies, browses the Internet, attends the theatre, concerts, dances and parties, plays competitive sports, and is involved in a myriad of organizations that promote social change or community-based recreational activities. Hutterites do not engage in any of these activities. The claim that "TV brings destruction and Hollywood is the sewer pipe of the world," is one with which even many secular Canadians might have some sympathy, but few would go so far as to ban it from their homes.[1] In the colonies there are no sports fields, golf courses, swimming pools, theatres or health clubs. Fitness equipment is rare, and although not entirely absent, the equipment that is present is mostly treadmills and stationary bicycles for cardiac rather than bodybuilding objectives.

As colony work does not end until about nine o'clock in the evening, Hutterites have little free time. Most of it is spent among the family—conversations between husband and wife, reading a chapter from the Bible, telling traditional stories to the children, and visiting friends and neighbours in the colony. These visits can last for hours, consisting of discussions about faith, the colony's economy, impressions from visiting other colonies, world affairs, and so forth. Visits are informal and mostly spontaneous. The door of each house in the colony is open to visitors, and knocking on the door is not acceptable, for everyone is supposed to enter his neighbour's house as if it were his own. This, too, expresses the full community of the Hutterite lifestyle.

Listening together to liturgical music, performed by choirs composed of the young people of the colony, is a common way to spend leisure time. The number of books in the Hutterite home is usually very limited. Most of them deal with religion, and Hutterite or Anabaptist history, but professional agricultural literature, home craft magazines and more serious newsmagazines such as *Time, Maclean's, The Economist,* and *Readers Digest* may be found in some homes. Books are usually kept in closed closets. Some colonies have libraries, but their holdings are quite limited.[2]

Schmiedeleut colony members may read fine literature, except for such literature that undermines faith, or includes immoral or erotic content. The Hutterites buy books at their own expense, from their "salary" or from money made on the side. They may also read daily newspapers, except for tabloids. Some of the Schmiedeleut colonies members patronize public libraries in the nearby towns and the regional mobile library, from which they can borrow books. For example, the library of the town of Portage la Prairie, Manitoba, serves 10 colonies, and with every year that passes, the Hutterites become a more substantial element of the subscriber base. The most requested books among the Hutterites are those dealing with spiritual matters, science fiction and suspense, but they read all types of books. As a rule, it is difficult for colony leaders to supervise the books read in the library or those taken out to read at home.[3]

In spite of the injunction not to surf the Internet, recently issued by the elders of the Hutterian Church, and the lack of access to computers on the colony, Hutterites can easily have access to the Internet while visiting the public library, although the time spent in the library is short due to the fact that it should be spent for exchanging books only and is limited because of the organized ride back to the colony. There is also no supervision on the (mis) use of the computers and Internet, especially by the youth, which should be for economic/business purposes only. Conscience and self-discipline play an important role in deciding what to read or whether to buy a CD or surf the Internet:

Because we are human beings, we cannot supervise everything. Everyone must make their own decisions, and we expect them to be good ones. After years of supervising everything that they read I now trust my daughters when they go to the library, but if you want, you can reach all the bad things. Education is important, education, which tells the children that they must develop a morality and an awareness of what is right and what is wrong.[4]

As mentioned above, access to the Internet is approved only for business purposes in Group Two Schmiedeleut colonies and is restricted to one person in the colony. This arouses resentment among members who demand equal access to the Internet: "Since we are equal, members ask why one person only, and not the others, should be given access to the Internet. A decision should be made—everybody or no one. Some Bosses have an access to the Internet—what do they need it for? Some people are allowed to surf the Internet, and they don't need this."[5] In any case, access to the Internet places a tremendous challenge to self-control. In Group One Schmiedeleut colonies, colony elders are more tolerant of Internet use and some members have personal email accounts, and presumably, unrestricted access to the Internet.

Daily newspapers and weekly magazines such as *Time* and *Maclean's* are an important source of information about the outside world, and in some colonies people listen to the radio without permission. One colony minister's daughter remarked, "we know exactly what goes on in your [namely, the outside] world."[6] However, the colony does not fund the purchase of books or newspapers.

Telephone use varies considerably between colonies. Whereas almost all the Schmiedeleut and, strangely, many Lehrerleut colonies generally have a phone in every home, in Dariusleut colonies this is less common. Every colony has a phone, though it may be located in the minister's house or the Boss's office.[7] In the latter case, conversations with friends and family members in other colonies are rare.[8] In some colonies, each external phone call disconnects automatically after 10 minutes. Telephone conversations within the colony are also not common, as people live in close proximity; today some people on Schmiedeleut colonies also have cell phones.[9]

Visiting other colonies, especially by ministers, retirees and women, is a popular form of recreation. Ministers visit other colonies for consultations and sharing decision making with their colleagues on issues of education, faith, and for discussions about amending and updating the leut regulations, as well as to attend rituals such as funerals, and election of ministers. Retirees and women simply visit family members or attend celebrations and funerals. It is obvious that between adjacent colonies, there is a high frequency of visits, but visits between distant colonies are also common. The retirees' frequent visits to see their family in other colonies are a privilege of seniority. In general, the Hutterite colonies take good care of their elderly. They can change their accommodation and move to an apartment that is more suited to their needs; they receive special food, and disabled persons can expect good care and treatment by the colony's members for as long as necessary.[10]

Medical appointments also fall under the heading of recreation for they involve off-colony travel. Similarly, activities such as marketing produce, shopping for the colony, attending to necessary chores in town, and a trip to distant colonies—in fact, anything that requires spending the night in a motel—all have a recreational component. Indeed, the permission of the minister to travel outside the colony (for personal matters) or the Boss (for economic purposes) is needed.[11] While staying outside the colony, Schmiedeleut Hutterites (only) may dine in restaurants or coffee shops, and they receive an appropriate allowance for this purpose before they commence their journey. The traveling and overnight accommodation allowances given by the Schmiedeleut colonies are significantly higher than those given by the Lehrerleut colonies. Unlike the Schmiedeleut colonies, in the Lehrerleut colonies there is a fixed day each week for trips outside the colony, and on this day, called "The Black Day," all the other Lehrerleut colony members come into town for errands. Having all members in town at the same time enables community members to meet friends from other colonies, and allows the community to monitor itself when its members encounter the temptations of the city. Schmiedeleut colonies do not synchronize their visits to town in the same way. The exception is trips made by the colony girls during the summer for selling vegetables, when they often take the opportunity to make their annual visit to fabric shops or to visit friends who would not normally be seen on account of travel or visit quotas. In the restaurants, hotels and streets, Hutterites interact with the outside world, often exposed to its less savory elements such as violent television programs, immodest dress, salacious magazines, sensationalist newspapers, and so on.

Weddings and funerals provide rare opportunities for Hutterites to gather en masse. Up to 350 guests may attend a wedding, for which an invitation is necessary. Over a thousand people, many coming from far afield, may attend the funeral of a well known and highly regarded leader, for which an invitation is not required. Funerals are not only an opportunity to pay one's respects and express sympathy to bereaved family members but also to socialize with seldom-seen friends and relatives. Often such visits provide an opportunity for young people to socialize, so much so that the Hutterite Council in an 1994 Ordinance rebuked those who grasped at any opportunity to attend a funeral in order to facilitate visiting and courtship:

> There are far too many young people at wakes and funerals and weddings. It was agreed upon that unbaptized men and women should no longer be allowed to drive to such events. One would think that these events would give them reason to reflect, especially if it was an accident and God called some young people home, but the actual experience is much different. Namely, a lot of mischief occurs when so many young people get together. They don't even come in to the wakes; rather they sit in the houses or on the [colony] streets or run around and drink.[12]

When in town, if the opportunity presents itself, Hutterites will watch television, although usually they do not find it very interesting. Occasionally, they will find their way to dubious places such as bars and clubs. In preparation to the meeting of the Schmiedeleut ministers, which was scheduled to take place in June 1975, the elders of the leut issued a letter to the ministers, saying that:

> [Going into bars and clubs] is a bad, sinful pastime... Let us stay outside, as often as we are there; the female gender should not go in at all, and young women and virgins absolutely not because they are in the greatest danger of frittering away their virginity, along with Dinah, the daughter of Jacob our forefathers... Our brothers sit there in such dishonour far too often and far too long. Half-exposed women of the world are there and serve the drinks; that is not good for us

to do. The young people see it and also want to sit there, and where does the money come from? And the whole colony is maligned while some sit and drink without moderation.[13]

The letter also noted that some members would consider half an hour for prayers in the colony church to be too long but the same people would think that half an hour was not enough time to enjoy a drink in a bar. The letter pointed out that while the leadership had the power to command, it wished only to appeal to common sense and the self-respect of those who abused the privilege of having a drink in town.

Earlier, in 1960, the elders of the Schmiedeleut came out strongly against the drinking habits of the Hutterites during their trips outside the colony, and against visiting pubs and saloons. One of the decisions asserted that:

> In order to combat alcoholism it has been decided that each brother is allowed to drink one bottle of beer (the smallest one) once a day in the restaurant with a meal instead of going to the beer parlour or saloon. And each person should stay away from the beer parlours, saloons, or breweries.[14]

Smoking is forbidden, and the rules are strictly enforced.[15] Sports activities are forbidden after the age of 15 in some of the Schmiedeleut colonies, whereas in other colonies they are allowed. Swimming in the pools, dugouts or rivers is allowed for children only, on the condition that boys and girls bathe separately. Girls are also required to wear modest swimwear (a T-shirt and trunks while swimming). However, some colonies allow sports activities for all ages, and a few even have swimming pools. Lehrerleut colonies forbid sports activities for all except school children.[16]

Hutterite youth spend considerable time alone. Boys usually gather in the evenings at one of the houses to share the experiences of the day. On these occasions, they may talk about articles forbidden in the colony that they have or that they would like to acquire. A wrist watch, a camera, a CD, a walkman and photos of youth idols or friends are all hidden in a closet, locked with the key which each boy and girl receives on their 15th birthday. In the past the minister opened "suspicious" letters and packages addressed to young people. Contraband or pictures were thrown away. Today they arrive with less censorship: "Today it is different. There is no problem sending 'forbidden' stuff, the minister does not always open envelopes. In any case, they can take photos, they have cameras, and they can have the photos developed in the nearby town." [17]

Some boys visit their friends in the nearby colony after work, and some secretly make their way to neighbouring farmers to watch television. However, from our experience of the colonies it is clear that most boys and girls show self-discipline. They know the limits. Thus, they will listen to country music but not to rock and roll; they will watch television, often in the houses of neighbouring farmers, but restrict their viewing to hockey games, and educational and news programs; they might smoke an occasional illicit cigarette but mostly they do not take drugs. [18] However, in some colonies where self-discipline is somewhat loose, drugs are present, either brought into the colony by friends of colony boys who have left the colony and returned to it, or obtained from the employees of visiting contractors. [19]

There are also boys who spend the late hours of the evening reading, mainly the Bible. Some may go into the carpentry shop or another workshop to assemble a small table or some other article from scrap materials, to sell to neighbouring farmers or others who visit the colony, to generate money on the side. Nor do the girls sit idle. They make socks, slippers, pillows, and similar handcrafted items for the same purpose. [20]

In short, the recreational pursuits and regimes of most colony members parallel those of many ordinary Canadian families living in rural areas before the advent of radio and television. Without canned entertainment they look towards themselves for their amusement. Visiting and conversation still occupy a significant social role in the colonies. Hutterite youth, like their counterparts on the outside, enjoy "hanging out" together and increasingly keep in contact with their friends in other colonies via text messaging on illicit cellphones (See Appendix 4). There are, of course, wide variations between the leut and between colonies within each leut.

Notes

1. Donald B. Kraybill and Carl F. Bowman, *On the Backroad to Heaven: Old Order Hutterites, Mennonites, Amish and Brethren* (Baltimore and London: Johns Hopkins University Press, 2001), 33, citing the words of the German teacher in one of the colonies. See also Aharon Meged, "A Christian Commune in Canada," *Mibifnim* (1947): 543–53, 551.

2. This is based on observations during visits to various colonies in Canada and the United States.
3. The testimony of the librarian in the public library of Portage, August 2004; Sara Gross, interviews by Yossi Katz, Bloomfield Colony, August 2004, September 21–23, 2005; Paul Gross, interview by Yossi Katz, Bloomfield Colony, September 21–23, 2005; Minister Mike Hofer, interview by Yossi Katz and John Lehr, Sommerfeld Colony, May 2004.
4. Sara Gross, interview with Yossi Katz, August 2004.
5. Ibid.
6. It is interesting that the minister's daughter made the comment in Sturgeon Creek. Compare this to Meged, *A Christian Commune*, 551, who visited a Hutterite colony in 1947 and reported that the Hutterites did not read newspapers.
7. Hutterite phone and address books, 2004, 2005, 2006, 2007, 2008, and 2009.
8. A boy living in a Lehrerleut colony, who wants to talk with his girlfriend from another colony, must buy a dialing card from his salary ($8 a month). However, if he expended his budget, the minister and the Boss will let him use the telephone freely, within reasonable limits. Julie Waldner and Peter Waldner, interview by Yossi Katz, Castor Colony, September 13, 2005 (Castor Colony belongs to the Lehrerleut).
9. James Valley Colony, Manitoba, has six communal cellphones that are signed out when needed; a notice by the colony Boss's office states that those delivering hogs to the Brandon processing plant have priority.
10. Based on our observations and interviews with members in various colonies.
11. The minister and the Boss are the only people who do not need permission to travel outside the colony, but they must inform each other about their trip, or mention it at their morning meeting. See Caroline Hartse, "Social and Religious Change among Contemporary Hutterites," *Folk* 36 (1995) 112–13; Kraybill and Bowman, *On the Backroad to Heaven*, 32–33.
12. *Ordnungen und Konferenz Briefen*, November 24, 1994, Ordinance #12.
13. James Valley Colony Archive, Decisions and Provisions of the Council of the Schmiedeleut stream of the Hutterian Church, 1876–2004, March 12, 1975 (Appendix 5).
14. Ibid., February 9, 1960, 43–45 (Appendix 5); John A. Hostetler, *Hutterite Society*, (Balltimore and London: Johns Hopkins University Press, 1974), 267.
15. Hostetler, *Hutterite Society*, 267. On one occasion the second author visited a colony with a group of students and the minister took them into the church to explain Hutterite history. One slipped out to smoke a cigarette on the church steps. We exited to find him surrounded by a group of curious Hutterite children. The minister enquired what they were doing. The response was, "We are watching this man sin!"
16. Sara Gross in note 3.
17. This informant requested anonymity.
18. Based on the observations of Dan Katz (15 years old at the time) who visited the colonies with us in May 2004. Dan spent a lot of time with the youth, and his observations are described in Appendix 4. One farmer with whom we spoke, who wished not to be identified, said that he would often have several Hutterite youths watching television in his basement "six nights a week."
19. This informant requested anonymity. This issue is discussed in recent years' discussions and decisions of the Schmiedeleut meetings (Appendix 5). Also, Garreth Lehr, a millwright who has worked as a contractor in Hutterite colonies in Manitoba stated that, on some colonies, young Hutterite boys would attempt to obtain marijuana, offering colony wine in exchange. Garreth Lehr, interview by John Lehr, Calgary, October 7, 2007.
20. Impressions of the children's rooms in the home of the Gross family in Bloomfield Colony, May and August 2004; John Hofer, interview by Yossi Katz, James Valley Colony, May 2004.

Chapter 9
RELATIONSHIPS WITH NEIGHBOURS
AND THE HOST COMMUNITY

I NTERACTION BETWEEN HUTTERITES AND THEIR NEIGHBOURS
on adjacent farms and with the population of nearby small
towns, and between Hutterites and the Canadian establishment
has always been extremely complex. These relationships have
changed over time and there have been, and still are, considerable
variations in these relationships depending on geographical location, the leut, and the leadership of each colony.

The principles of their philosophy drive Hutterite interaction
with the host society. The tenets of their faith, their economic
orientation towards agriculture, and their quest for isolation from
the outside secular world, mandate a rural location. On the other
hand, they must react to the attitudes of the host society, which
are driven by its perception of non-conformist groups, its tolerance
of difference and its fear of a perceived economic and territorial
challenge by an alien group. Such concerns prompted protracted
efforts to restrict the colonies' territorial expansion in Canada.

During the First World War the Hutterites refused to join the
United States army and were not prepared to take any part in the
general war effort. Fueled by a wave of patriotism and xenophobia,
demands were made that they abandon German as their *lingua
franca*. They refused and anti-Hutterite sentiments exploded in
the areas where Hutterites had settled. They were harassed by

their neighbours and the United States' government, their property was seized, their stock driven off, and their young men forcibly conscripted. Two died in military prison. This led the Hutterites to leave the United States and immigrate into Canada in 1918. Twenty years later, there were only six colonies left in the United States—five in South Dakota and one in Montana (Figs. 2.1–2.5 show the diffusion of colonies from 1920 to 2014).[1]

In Canada, the Hutterites received a hospitable welcome, and in the first period of their settlement, the attitude towards them from their neighbours as well as from provincial and federal governments was positive. Indeed, the Hutterites isolated themselves and avoided any unnecessary contact with the establishment and had minimal social interaction with their neighbours. Their economic success, due to their autarkic economy in the period of the deep economic depression of the 1930s, made them welcome, for they were renowned for doing their business fairly and honestly and for discharging all their debts to neighbouring farms and the establishment.[2] However, the entry of Hutterite colonies into some rural environments disturbed the social balance. Non-Hutterite farmers feared that sale of lands to Hutterite colonies would lead to their isolation from their neighbours and foresaw the collapse of their fragile rural social and economic institutions. On the Canadian prairies, a public school generally served about half a township, some 18 to 20 square miles of territory. If a Hutterite colony occupied even a sixth of that area, because Hutterite children did not attend the local public school, there might well be insufficient children to warrant the maintenance of a school. The upshot would be that non-Hutterite children would have to travel further than the usual three-mile maximum to attend a school. The entry of a Hutterite colony also had a dramatic effect on the price of land. If a colony chose to buy in bulk from wholesale outlets in the major service centres, it threatened to undermine retailers in nearby small towns. All this fueled resentment of the Hutterites; outbursts of vandalism revealed underlying antagonisms and resentment of Hutterite economic success.[3]

When the Second World War broke out, the relationship between the Hutterites, on the one hand, and their neighbours and the Canadian government, on the other hand, soon deteriorated. Once again, the Hutterites refused to take any part in the war effort. Not only did they refuse to join the army, they also refused to buy war bonds and thereby transfer to the government and other federal institutions money designed to further the war aims of the allies. Additionally, due to the rise in agricultural prices during the war, the local farmers wanted to use the opportunity to expand their lands; but whenever they looked for lands to buy, they encountered their Hutterite rivals. Therefore, the farmers pressed their demands that the Hutterites not be permitted to expand any farther. The merchants in the small towns near the colonies supported this call. They alleged that the Hutterites were dealing mainly with the wholesalers in the big cities—where they could enjoy better deals and prices—and were avoiding small-town merchants. The principles of the Hutterite faith, which enjoin the Hutterites to engage as little as possible in trade and merchandise, fostered this tendency to concentrate their dealings with big-city merchants and avoid a myriad of lesser transactions with smaller concerns.

In 1942, their anti-Hutterite opinions inflamed by patriotic fervour, Alberta farmers living in the Raymond area (where many colonies were located) demanded that the government stop approving the sale of lands to the Hutterites. They demanded that the federal and provincial governments notify the Hutterites that unless they were "willing to accept the responsibilities of citizenship which must be accepted by other Canadians," that land title would no longer be issued to them.[4]

As a result, in 1943, the government of Alberta legislated a law forbidding the sale and lease of lands "to any enemy alien and Hutterite," claiming that the purpose of the Act was to "alley public feeling which has been aroused to the point of threatened violence in some instances."[5]

In the same year, the government of Alberta passed such a law, a draconian one from the Hutterite standpoint. The law was to be valid until one year after the war, but it was renewed and remained in force until 1947. This law had four main clauses: Hutterites were not allowed to acquire lands beyond those that they held in 1944, they were not permitted to establish new colonies within 40 miles of an existing colony; the area of any colony could not exceed 6,400 acres; in any case of sale or leasing of land to Hutterites, one should offer the right of first refusal to discharged soldiers, whom the government wished to help establish themselves as farmers. This law was strictly enforced.[6] The application of this law decreased hostility towards the Hutterites, but worsened the colonies' economic state. Their populations increased but could not supply their members with work, for they were unable to get lands either for expansion or for branching. In response, after 1948, the Hutterites began settling in the states of Montana and Washington in the United States and in the province of Saskatchewan, Canada.[7]

In Alberta opposition to the Hutterites did not subside until the 1960s, mostly because of envy of their continued economic success and colony expansion. This contrasted with the steady decline of family farms in rural Alberta. Public opinion held that it would be possible to amend the "anti-Hutterite" laws only if the Hutterites were prepared to become Canadian citizens in the full sense of the word, accepting responsibility for the national as well as local social needs. However, by the end of the 1950s, the voices of those opposed to anti-Hutterite legislation grew louder in calling for repeal of these discriminatory laws. Nevertheless, the prevailing opinion blamed Hutterites for trying to establish a state within a state, for unfairly competing with the neighbouring farmers (for, as opposed to single-family farmers, the Hutterites had many advantages, mainly the ability to exercise economies of scale), and for destroying local rural economies, which took the form of a dramatic decrease in the number of businesses in the nearby towns and a desertion of the young generation.

Although it is clear that the Hutterites did not cause the economic problems of Alberta's rural economy, the locals held them to be fully responsible for it. In most cases, the Hutterites were nothing more than scapegoats for the increasing frustration of the rural population in Canada and in the United States. Rural depopulation had little to do with the presence of Hutterites but was due to farm consolidation, highway improvements and increased accessibility to larger service centres, the migration of the young to the cities for educational and employment opportunities, farm mechanization, and the rise of agri-business. Rural depopulation resulted in closure of local businesses and consolidation of rural school districts, where pupils were bussed to large schools in larger service centres from up to 30 miles away. All these processes had invisible causes but the purchase of lands and the building of a colony in a district was a highly visible action that focused attention in a district in decline. Complex problems and their solutions are seldom seen as such by people looking for a simple explanation of their own economic failure. They grasp on to the most obvious explanations to rationalize complex events over which they had little control and which swept them in their path.[8]

During the 1960s, opposition to the discriminatory laws against the Hutterites grew. The *Lethbridge Herald*, which had always opposed anti-Hutterite legislation, wrote in September 1964 that the Communal Property Act was an assault on the "concept of freedom and tolerance upon which Canadian society is founded. The Hutterite issue has become a test case for minority rights. It's Hutterites today, Catholics and Jews tomorrow."[9] Some amendments ameliorated the impact of the law, but the Communal Property Act was not repealed until 1972. That same year, the new Conservative government of Alberta appointed a committee to re-examine the Hutterite issue. The committee concluded that the laws of the province against the Hutterites breached the federal law regarding human rights and, therefore, it decided to repeal all the laws from the 1940s that discriminated against the Hutterites. For the first time in 30 years, the Hutterites in Alberta could purchase lands without restriction. They soon took advantage of the opportunity, and within five months of the Act's repeal, they had purchased 44,475 additional acres and established seven new colonies. Between 1974 and 1988, the Hutterites built 44 more colonies.[10]

Other places in the United States and Canada shared similar concerns regarding Hutterite expansion. Restrictions on land purchase by Hutterites were imposed by other states and provinces, but Alberta's restrictions were the most severe.[11]

In Manitoba, where all the Schmiedeleut colonies had relocated after leaving South Dakota in 1918, similar arguments had advocated restrictions on Hutterite colonies' expansion since the 1940s. Manitoba did not enact any discriminatory laws, but in 1954, during the annual convention of the Union of Manitoba Municipalities, a resolution demanded that the government take steps to restrict the territory that each colony could purchase and to set a minimal distance between each two colonies. The government did not adopt these demands, but pressure to do so increased. The Union made it clear that if the government did not act, the Union would act independently to take steps to reach an agreement with the Hutterites. The Premier of Manitoba at the time supported this decision, and explained to the Hutterites that if they did not reach an agreement with the Union, the government would pass laws restricting their expansion. The Hutterites had no choice, and thus, in April 1957, the Union and the Hutterite leadership in Manitoba signed a "Gentleman's Agreement" whereby the Hutterites accepted almost all of the Union's demands, which included, among other things, limiting the territory of each new colony to 5,120 acres; establishing no more than two colonies in the area of one municipality; and keeping a distance of at least 10 miles between every colony. This agreement satisfied the Union, although its implementation met some difficulties.

In 1969, 12 years after signing this "Gentleman's Agreement," the Hutterites made it clear that they no longer considered themselves obliged to abide by it. And indeed, in 1971 they purchased land under conditions that were in clear violation of it when the provincial NDP government sold Macdonald Airport (a former Commonwealth Air Training Program air base) to New Rosedale Colony. The Premier of Manitoba at the time was sympathetic, and he declared that the Gentleman's Agreement prohibiting such a purchase constituted discrimination against the Hutterites, and was no longer valid. The Manitoba Human Rights Commission supported this decision, and claimed, as in Alberta, that the agreement was in contravention of Canadian law regarding human rights. The Union gave up its threat to prosecute the Hutterites for violation of the agreement and Airport Colony was established on the site.[12]

No further attempts were made to place special restrictions on the expansion of Hutterite colonies, although members of the Union have suggested it from time to time. The policy of the government of Manitoba has been that the Hutterites "are people the same as anyone else and they are entitled to the same rights, privileges and restrictions."[13]

In Saskatchewan, where the Hutterites arrived in 1952 following the placement of restrictions on colony expansion in Alberta and Manitoba, they encountered the opposition of local groups that called on the government to immediately take steps to restrict their settlement there. Their arguments were similar to those advanced in Alberta and Manitoba. However, the Saskatchewan government did not wish to undermine laws concerning human rights and refused to consider enactment of any measures against the Hutterites. It assumed that education and explanation eventually would lead to understanding of the real issues and tone down anti-Hutterite feelings. A government committee appointed to deal with the issue concluded that to decrease suspicion and resentment of Hutterites, the colonies must overcome their inclination to concentrate in limited areas and that they must cooperate and integrate colony economies within the economic fabric of local rural communities. This latter recommendation failed to take into account the Hutterite principles of isolation from the outside world. In August 1958, a "Gentleman's Agreement" was signed between the government of the Province of Saskatchewan and the elders of the Lehrerleut and the Dariusleut, according to which the location of new colonies would be decided in consultation with a special government committee. At the same time, the government published the summary of its policy regarding the Hutterites: new colonies would not be established less than 35 miles from an existing colony; the territory of each colony would not exceed 10,000 acres; and the social and economic needs of local rural communities would receive preference over Hutterite wishes. The policy was to be implemented as following: upon being informed by the Hutterites (according to the "Gentleman's Agreement") of their intention to establish a new colony at a certain place, a government committee would examine the request and would take into consideration the reactions of the local municipalities, the school administration and local businesses. Based on this information, the committee would then decide on the Hutterites' request.

This arrangement remained in place for only 10 years, but it caused difficulties for the Hutterites. Bureaucratic procedures were time-consuming and often forced the postponement of settlement expansion. The government sometimes deliberately delayed the process. Prior notification of intentions to purchase land caused its price to rise putting the colonies at an economic disadvantage. This led to long delays in the establishment of new colonies. In 1968, the Hutterites announced their refusal to renew the agreement, although in fact it continued to exist.

Nine years later, in 1977, one of the municipalities in Saskatchewan tried to prevent the establishment of a colony in its area by changing regional planning criteria to make communal settlement difficult, if not impossible. The municipality insisted that the changes in planning requirements were not directed against Hutterites. Unconvinced, the Hutterites began building the colony in contravention of planning regulations. The municipality prosecuted the colony, but the judge in the case accepted the Hutterites' argument that the municipality's actions to change planning regulations constituted discrimination against them and, therefore, the new regulations were invalid. After the ruling, the provincial government decided to relax the rules governing the building of new colonies. Among other things, it was prepared to cancel the demand for a distance of 35 miles between any two colonies and to keep the government committee's discussions secret so that the prices of land in the proposed area for settlement would not rise. However, this did not put an end to the struggles of the local municipalities against the expansion and concentration of Hutterite settlement. In the 1980s efforts were made in various Saskatchewan rural municipalities to change regional planning rules in such a way as to prevent the establishment of new colonies. Courts of law understood that such rule changes were targeted at the Hutterites; they ruled again that these changes constituted discrimination against the Hutterites and a breach of human rights.

Another method the municipalities in Saskatchewan employed against the Hutterites' expansion at the end of the 1980s was by pressuring the government to assert explicitly by law the restriction of the 35 miles between any two colonies, based of the argument that this is the only way "which will enable our cultures to live in harmony." [14]

Although the Hutterites still feel that their neighbours envy their economic success, at present there are no restrictions on purchasing land or regulations hampering the establishment of new colonies near existing colonies. The planning requirements that Hutterites must meet are identical to those imposed on all farmers. [15]

Examination of the daily relationship of the Hutterites with the Canadian establishment and the rural surroundings in recent decades points again to a general guideline of isolation, although the level of isolation is different in each colony. The Hutterites did not initiate integration if they did not have to do so, a result of their seclusion and their suspicious attitude towards the outside world, the world of sin. They respect the rules of the state, although they are not always comfortable with them. They pay taxes in spite of the fact that part of this is directed toward military purposes; they obey the planning rules and retain formal ties with the local, provincial and federal authorities; they celebrate Canadian holidays, except for Remembrance Day, and they pray for the well-being of the government. In some colonies, mainly the Lehrerleut and Dariusleut colonies, the Canadian flag is seen only in the English school. Hutterites do not usually take part in federal, provincial or municipal elections. They have no interest in involvement in municipal affairs and do not compete for public offices, since this is against the Hutterite conscience (for it involves taking an oath). They also refuse to participate in the Canadian pension and social security plans, claiming that this is not necessary for them as a group that takes care of all the needs of its members.

Their economic enterprises and their operation require them to retain some ties between a small group of the colony's members (usually the elders) on one side and commercial companies and the establishment on the other side. The Hutterites tend to attach an informal and friendly atmosphere to these ties, thus receiving sympathetic reactions from the other side, which somewhat diminishes the suspicious and hostile attitude towards them taken by many people in the host society.

The colonies' refusal to take part in the social activities in the local community is responsible for a good deal of anti-Hutterite sentiment in areas where colonies are located. This was the basis for many of the slanders against them, and even overt expressions of hatred, in the form of vandalism directed against colony property. The myth of Hutterite disregard for their neighbours is far from reality. In most areas the Hutterites share tools and work with their neighbours during the busy seasons, clear roads of snow together or help their neighbours fix their tools, cooperating in myriad ways. During the 1997 flood that devastated the Red River Valley in Manitoba, Hutterite colonies turned out in force, lending heavy equipment and providing hundreds of volunteers to the flood-fighting effort. Hutterite women and men worked alongside students and army personnel as volunteers, filling sandbags and contributing what they could to the common effort to protect local communities and farms from the rising waters of the Red River.[16] Misunderstandings arise all too easily, however. When the neighbours wish to repay the Hutterites for their assistance by inviting the colony's children to their homes "to enable them to listen to the radio and watch television and take them to shows, this is a break of our colony's rules. When we ask our neighbours not to do this, they are angry and it causes some friction."[17]

Today colonies are more open to their non-Hutterite neighbours; this is certainly true of the Schmiedeleut whose colonies patronize the public libraries in nearby towns (or to the mobile library serving the rural districts). Colony elders serve as members of agricultural institutions, and the colonies are involved in the charities of local communities. All this certainly contributes to a greater understanding between the Hutterites and their neighbours.[18]

Changes in the rural economy and the rise of agribusiness have also blunted some of the older complaints about the Hutterites.

There is little difference, for example, between the purchasing practices of a large corporate farm and the alleged purchasing practices of Hutterite colonies. Corporate farms buy in bulk, seek out the best price from wholesalers who are based outside the region, and do not provide many opportunities for local people to secure employment. In contrast, while they seek out the best price, colonies attempt to patronize local suppliers and, to a limited degree, participate in local affairs. Thus the complaints levied against the colonies, whether true or false, apply equally to an increasingly broad spectrum of the agricultural economy. Furthermore, in a highly competitive global agricultural market marked by low commodity prices, many individual farmers are now anxious to sell their family farms to anyone because of the low returns from farming. When Hutterites purchase them, they are thankful.[19]

Nevertheless, Hutterite colonies generally remain less integrated into the social and economic aspects of local life than their private or corporate neighbours, and they avoid political affairs as much as possible. Within the rural municipality of De Salaberry, Manitoba, for example, there are three Hutterite colonies. According to the rural municipality's Economic Development Officer, these constitute the three largest economic operations in the area, "yet we never hear from them, they just go about their business."[20]

Notes

1. Donald E. Pitzer, *America's Communal Utopias* (Chapel Hill, NC: University of North Carolina Press, 1997), 336–37.
2. William G. Laatsch, "Hutterite Colonization in Alberta," *Journal of Geography* 10 (1971): 347–59.
3. John A. Hostelter, *Hutterite Society* (Baltimore and London: Johns Hopkins University Press, 1974), 255–60; William Janzen, *Limits to Liberty: The Experience of Mennonite, Hutterite and Doukhobor Communities in Canada* (Toronto, ON: University of Toronto Press, 1990), 61 ff.; Donald B. Kraybill and Carl F. Bowman, *On the Backroad to Heaven: Old Order Hutterites, Mennonites, Amish and Brethren* (Baltimore and London: Johns Hopkins University Press), 30–31.
4. Report of the Hutterite Investigation Committee, Order in Council, Appendix C. December 8, 1958. Provincial Archives of Alberta.
5. Ibid.
6. Aharon Meged referred to these laws when reporting on his visit to Hutterite colonies in 1947. To the readers of *Mibifnim* (From the Inside), he told about the unstable relationship between the Hutterites and their neighbours. He wrote: "The relationship with the neighbors is not good. The neighbors defame them and inform on them to the government. The government is about to expropriate some of the colonies' lands in western Canada, which according to the neighbors, are held by the Hutterites illegally. Private land owners worked hand in hand and demanded that the 'brethren' not be allowed to purchase lands, with the argument that they

'conquer' all the free lands. Indeed, the government is about to publish a law-along these lines, although the average piece of land per family in a commune is 41 acres while that of a farmer's family in the same district is about 400 acres." See Aharon Meged, "A Christian Commune in Canada," *Mibifnim* (1947): 551.

7. Laatsch, "Hutterite Colonization"; Pitzer, *America's Communal Utopias*, 336–41.
8. Janzen, *Limits to Liberty,* 82–84.
9. *Lethbridge Herald,* September 23, 1964.
10. Laatsch, "Hutterite Colonization," 82–84; Janzen, *Limits to Liberty,* 66–76.
11. Janzen, *Limits to Liberty,* 60–77.
12. The conversion of a former air-training base from military to agricultural use is a source of great satisfaction for the Hutterites, who cite the Biblical prophesy: "They shall beat their swords into ploughshares and their spears into pruning-hooks; nation shall not lift up sword against nation, neither shall they learn war any more." *Holy Bible,* Isaiah 2: 4.
13. Janzen, *Limits to Liberty,* 60–65.
14. Ibid., 74–84. A geo-statistical analysis of the dispersion of the Hutterite colonies in Manitoba (see Appendix 3) shows that dispersion in the past and the present is random. Therefore, the claims that the Hutterites have a strategy of spatial "taking over," or that they intend to establish "a state within a state" are baseless.
15. John Hofer and Aaron Hofer, interview by Yossi Katz, James Valley Colony, September 26, 2005.
16. Buzz Currie, *A Red Sea Rising: The Flood of the Century* (Winnipeg, MB: Winnipeg Free Press, 1997), 53, 134.
17. Hostetler, *Hutterite Society,* 255–60; Meged, "A Christian Commune," 551–52; Kraybill and Bowman, *On the Backroad to Heaven,* 32–33; Lisa M. Stahl, *My Hutterite Life* (Great Falls: Farcountry Press, 2003), 84–85; and observations from visits to various colonies. In September 2005, during a visit to the colony of Leedale, which is close to the small town of Eckville in Alberta, townspeople were interviewed to determine their relationship with the colony. All were aware of the nearby colony, but none claimed acquaintance with any colony members.
18. Kraybill and Bowman, *On the Backroad to Heaven.* The extreme openness that the Hutterites showed toward the Katz family also proves this. Following our visits in the colonies and our long-lasting acquaintance with the small community of Chabad emissaries in Winnipeg, we brought together members of a colony and the person who is in charge of the Chabad emissaries in Winnipeg. The Hutterites began visiting the Chabad community, bringing eggs and vegetables as charitable gifts. The column published in the *Great Falls Tribune* by Maria Stahl from the Dariusleut colony of Gildford, Montana, also demonstrates increasing openness. Stahl published many notes for the "outside readers" in her column, describing everyday life in the colony. Later, these notes were collected and published. See Lisa Stahl, note 17.
19. A non-Hutterite farmer near the colony of Bloomfield, Manitoba, interview by Yossi Katz, September 22, 2005. This informant requested anonymity.
20. Leslie Gaudry, Economic Development Officer, rural municipality of De Salaberry, Manitoba, interview by John Lehr, St. Malo, Manitoba, September 20, 2008.

Chapter 10

A WOMAN'S PLACE IN THE COLONY

O N VISITS TO HUTTERITE COLONIES, MOST WOMEN from the outside world are amazed, and many are outraged, to learn that Hutterite women do not have the right to vote in colony affairs. Women do not participate in the elections held in the colony from time to time, and they cannot play any part in the election of colony officers. Election to the job of the Head Cook, a position filled by a female, is in the hands of baptized males, the only people who can vote. Members elect two women to the position of *Zeich Schneider* (material buyers), one woman to the position of Cook for Special Diets and the Sick, one to supervise the Children's Dining room and the Garden, and four to work in the kindergarten. However, a woman can never be a Colony Boss or a Farm Boss, a German Teacher or a leader of the colony. The men make decisions regarding affairs that are traditionally supposedly the women's realm, such as the planning of the kitchen and the dining hall and their equipment. They choose whether they want to let the women take part in this or not, and may solicit their opinion but the final vote is made only by men. Most visitors from the outside, however, do not find it unusual that women cannot become ministers, as this prohibition is widely subscribed to in most of the major Christian denominations and within Islam and Judaism. They are less concerned that in the ecclesiastical organization of most mainstream monotheistic religions women continue to play a subordinate role.

In the early years of Anabaptism, women were often active within the movement and sometimes expressed their faith outside traditional roles. However, in doing so they did not consciously question the subordinate role society assigned to them as women. It has been argued that the more literal the interpretation of the Bible, the greater the tendency to maintain traditional and conservative social perspectives, including the place of women in society. Although there were many radical concepts within Anabaptist theology that challenged traditional social ideals (for example, pacifism, the refusal to take oaths, separation of church and state) in regard to gender roles, among sixteenth- and early seventeenth-century Anabaptists in Europe the understanding of women's role in church and society remained traditional. Radicalism within Hutterite society was confined to the interpretation of the scriptures and the practice of their faith. Traditional gender roles within Hutterite society simply mirrored those of the outside world in sixteenth-century Europe.[1]

The status and role of women in the Hutterite community today still remains based largely on Hutterite theology as formulated by Riedemann in the sixteenth century:

We say, first, that since woman was taken from man, and not man from woman, man hath lordship but woman weakness, humility and submission (1 Peter 3: 1-6), therefore she should be under the yoke of man and obedient to him, even as the woman was commanded by God when he said to her, "The man shall be thy lord" (Genesis 3:16). Now, since this is so she should heed her husband, inquire of him, ask him and do all things with and naught without his counsel. For where she doeth this not, she forsaketh the place in the order in which she hath been set by God, encroacheth upon the lordship of the man and forsaketh the command of her Creator as well as the submission that she promised her husband in the union of marriage: to honour him as a wife her husband. The man, on the other hand, as the one in whom something of God's glory is seen, should have compassion on the woman as the weaker instrument, and in love and kindness go before her and care for her, not only in temporal but also and still more in spiritual things... Where, however, the husband doeth this

not or is careless and superficial therein, he forsaketh the
glory which was given him by God, as well as God's order.[2]

A literal reading of Riedemann's words would suggest that in the
Hutterite view the woman is inferior, "the weaker vessel," and must
be submissive and ruled by the man; he is the one who makes the
decisions. This attitude is not uncommon in Judeo-Christian theology, but this interpretation misses the nuances of Hutterite gender
relationships. Men and women, on the colony, as in everyday life
in the outside world, operate in two very different sub-cultures.
Women generally occupy a subordinate position within Hutterite
society only in the sense that they are not a part of the decision-
making hierarchy and that roles within the colony remain strongly
gendered. Their position is not materially different from that of
a woman living within a conservative religious household where
gender roles are well-defined and remain traditional. Pursuit of
different roles does not necessarily imply feelings of inferiority,
and most Hutterite women are happy with their roles in the colony:

I have never felt that the men in my life look down on me.
That includes family, friends, fellow teachers, acquaintances
and ministers. I've asked other women's opinion on this and
they feel just as I do. Over the last year I've had the opportunity to translate a set of Bible stories into our language
with a Wycliffe linguist. Over that time, I've had tremendous
support and encouragement from men as well as women. In
my work as a German teacher I never feel that the men, who
are also teachers, see me as inferior to them. I'm not saying
that men looking down on women, doesn't exist on colonies,
it probably does just like it does outside the colony, but it
certainly is not the norm.[3]

Harrison claims, however, that Hutterites understand equality
between the sexes only in the mystical dimension of faith. Practically
speaking, this means only that women as well as men can achieve
salvation. In all other spheres, the woman was to show obedience,
humility, submission, and deference, specifically to her husband and
in general to other males. The order was determined before marriage was divinely ordained.[4] Harrison's claims need qualification:

It's not so hard to understand and accept that wives should be submissive to their husbands, especially since scripture teaches us that the man is to be the head of the house, just as Christ is the head of the church (Ephesians 5: 21-33). Therefore, being submissive is not a bad thing. We do not interpret this to mean that husbands/men should lord it over or look down on their wives/women.[5]

There is no doubt that males have significant privileges and choices of more varied occupational tasks, and males also have more responsibilities than a woman. Although some conservative ministers hold the attitude that if women are entrusted with money they will waste it, namely, that women have no sense of responsibility, other Hutterite leaders think very differently.

In the summer of 2003, two of my fellow Hutterite friends and myself [from the more liberal Group One Schmiedeleut] went to Europe for a month to take part in a German language course. We had credit cards from our colonies and when I was given mine, I was not even as much as told how to spend money. I was trusted with it, just as anybody else would have been. Furthermore, I didn't even expect it to be any different. Additionally, I find it hard to believe that many Hutterite men think that women handle money irresponsibly. I would say the opposite is true.[6]

While most women generally accept their role and position, some may also harbour a sense of injustice:

We believe that original sin comes from Eve. Women are considered weaker, as Eve was, and therefore they should not be given power. Because the Old and New Testament do not believe in equal rights, we do not either. Whenever women receive power, the right to vote, they get divorced and ruin the family... [but] we are aware that our status stands in contrast to the status of the prophetess Deborah [who at one time led Israel] and this is frustrating. What's especially frustrating is that the men think that they are cleverer than we are. We are not less smart than our husbands.[7]

When Meged, while visiting the colonies, wondered about the fact that women have no voting rights, a minister responded that "we regard the woman as equal to us in everything, and maybe even superior—but we want to free her from worrying. As in the family [on the outside world] the livelihood concerns are the husband's, so is the case here: the management and organizational concerns are for the man to handle."[8] For their part most Hutterite women harbour no feelings of inferiority and commonly point out that they still influence colony governance by discussing matters with their husbands or, in the case of unmarried younger women, with their fathers or brothers. Most women will laughingly dismiss enquiries about their lack of formal voting rights with the response that "we tell our husbands how to vote," a remark usually accompanied by a broad grin. Clearly, although some would like to have formal input into colony governance, others do not see the need or are indifferent to the question.

Assigning women a lower status is common in all the monotheistic religions. Eastern Orthodox Christians, Ultra-Orthodox—even some Orthodox—Jews, and some Moslems view all women of reproductive age as inherently unclean. No Ultra-Orthodox Jewish male will touch or shake hands with a woman other than his wife; no woman of reproductive age may enter behind the iconostasis of an Eastern Orthodox Church, and even Roman Catholics carry vestiges of these attitudes in their ritual of "churching" a mother after the birth of a child. In synagogues and mosques women are secluded, not only separated from men, but screened from them. Such attitudes are not seen among the Hutterites. Women and men are seated separately in church and at meals but there is no exclusion or seclusion according to gender. Boys and girls are educated in mixed classes and until the age of 15 they eat together in the children's dining room, though they are seated at separate tables because "it cuts down on the amount of flirting between the 14-year-olds."[9] We argue that the different status of men and women on the colony is based largely on the assignment of work according to gender and is not grounded in religious notions of cleanliness and the woman's menstrual cycle. There are, however, some faint echoes of old attitudes when Eve is held to be the reason for the fall of Adam (and, therefore, the fall of humanity), and biblical passages are used to justify contemporary opinions.

Current attitudes of some Hutterite males to gender roles are revealed in their attitudes to women voting in colony affairs. Mostly they mirror those held in secular North American society some decades ago, before women obtained the franchise. One Hutterite remarked that "women should not be given any status or voting rights [in colony affairs]; not even the cook or head kindergarten teacher [should have the right to vote]. Women are responsible for sins; look what Eve did."[10] Many outsiders, and probably some Hutterites, regard these attitudes as anachronistic and sexist. Even some ministers acknowledge the difficulty of the situation. Those women who remain unconcerned with their inability to vote on colony affairs regard most of the issues discussed at colony meetings to be of little interest to them. Nevertheless, women can exert considerable influence, both direct and indirect, through their husband's vote:

> First of all, I don't ever remember a time when men got together to vote on something that I wished I could join them! It's a huge responsibility. I have never envied them. I wouldn't say it's the responsibility I shrink from, but I'm not convinced a whole lot would change if the women voted too. Most of the time when they do vote, it's something that really doesn't affect me and how I continue my life. I mean, I don't really care what kind of combines they are buying, what size shop they will be building, or what kind of grain . handling system gets put in.[11]

Given the prevailing attitudes, one doubts that even if women voted outcomes would be much different. Status on the colony is less a matter of position than regard earned by example. A colony member physically unable to maintain the work pace of her fellows was spoken of with high regard "because she works as hard as she is able and is always willing. If she could do more she would." Another remarked, "If I used my older dienne [unmarried woman] status as a way of always getting my way, which I easily could, I think it would not take long before I was asking myself, 'why doesn't anybody like me?'"[12]

Older women have a greater influence in the colony because they have proven themselves over the years:

> The young women still haven't served enough time to prove themselves even if they have good ideas. If you have proven yourself for a long time you acquire some status. The chance

it will happen to older women is high. Time is a very important factor in the colony. I am only [a short time] in this
colony. I have to prove myself. It will take time.[13]

Even in Hutterite society things are never static. A colony boss
explained that as outside influences penetrated the colony women
gained more interest in having a voice in colony affairs, something
he attributed to women's growing awareness of the change in the
status of women outside the colony. "As the world progressed
so did our women. Since they cannot vote they influence their
husbands to vote the way they want them to.... As the power of
women in the outside world grows, so does the power of women
in the Hutterite world." This inside opinion is echoed by Ingoldsby
and Smith, who report that Hutterite boy-girl sibling relationships
are typical of the Canadian norm.[14] A Dariusleut (non-Hutterite)
teacher commented to them:

> In my class everybody takes a turn sweeping the floor, etc.,
> though at first this rule was met with haughty arrogance by
> the boys. They said sweeping was women's work and their
> mothers and sisters cleaned up after them. However, over
> the years I have heard of many big strapping fathers who
> routinely make beds, wash dishes, get up in the night with
> the baby, and put little ones to bed.[15]

That colony women spend so much time together for many years
bolsters their sense of identity and self-worth. Whereas men work
mostly in pairs, or in the hog barn in total isolation, women work
mostly in groups. As the old adage has it, many hands make light
work, but group work also builds camaraderie and fosters interpersonal relationships. Women can look after their own interests
and even have some influence on the way that the colony is run
despite their lack of formal involvement in colony governance.
Pathways of influence are built through personal relationships
forged during working hours. Most women accept their gender
roles within the colony and prefer the quiet and long way for introducing changes on their behalf. It seems that this grants them
more openness to change and perhaps a greater tolerance of their
children's misdemeanors.

Despite the lack of their formal representation with the colony
administration, women can wield influence on the minister when

it comes to their children's well-being. The presence of a state-appointed school teacher on every colony ensures that, in cases affecting the children, women can pressure the minister to take action. For example, if they feel a child is subject to bullying or unfair treatment and the minister is reluctant to address the issue, a threat to notify the teacher generally impels the minister to act immediately, for if a teacher learns of any case of potential abuse, however broadly defined, he or she is legally obligated to inform the child welfare authorities.[16] No minister wants to have the world intruding into colony affairs, so this ensures that the problem is addressed expeditiously.

Married women do not usually work in the manual or trade sectors of the colony economy. In some colonies they preform light work in colony manufacturing plants, or take responsibility for bookkeeping and secretarial work, but in the Schmiedeleut colonies, at least, they seldom, if ever, tackle implement repair, carpentry, or electrical work. Nor do they work in the cow barn, pig barn, chicken barn or turkey barn. That is man's work. Women do not work in the fields during seeding or harvesting since they seldom, if ever, drive heavy agricultural equipment. They do, however, work in the colony garden under the coordination of the gardener, who may be the minister or German teacher.

At killing time married and unmarried women work alongside the men. The slaughtering and butchering of chickens, turkeys, pigs and other livestock is the men's preserve. Women pluck, eviscerate, clean and pack the birds and meat. It is hard work, disliked by many, but everyone participates and with most of the colony's labour force engaged, it is completed remarkably expeditiously. Colony members, both women and men, will relate with quiet pride the numbers of fowl prepared for market within a couple of days, evidence of their cooperative, communal spirit and strong work ethic.

High demand for labour in the Alberta oil patch and the high wages paid to oilfield workers have lured away many young men from Lehrerleut colonies, creating a labour vacuum on some colonies. Necessity has broken down gender barriers; women are now seen performing a variety of tasks formerly restricted to men.[17] This labour shortage has not yet affected the Schmieleleut colonies, and gender roles have shifted less.

In some colonies single women work in manufacturing shops on a regular basis; also, some drive tractors and work in the fields.

However, in the more conservative colonies they do not perform field labour except for the vegetable garden and the orchard. In many Schmiedeleut colonies, teenaged boys are responsible for transporting women and girls to and from the vegetable garden; in others, women do so.[18] Some colonies permit women to acquire driver's licenses so that they can help in situations where additional drivers are needed; in others, women drive trucks and vans on a regular basis, not only when male drivers are not available. This, however, contravenes the Ordinance of December 7, 1997, which states that "Driver's licenses for wives or young women should not be allowed at all, and they should not drive any vehicles."[19]

In addition to raising their children, women work in service activities, in the vegetable garden, and in the orchard. These services activities include all kitchen and dining hall chores, such as cooking, laundry,[20] sewing and weaving rugs (making clothes, linen, curtains, etc. for all the members), cleaning, and taking care of the babies and the kindergarten children. In the Group One Schmiedeleut, some 70 women are also professionally trained schoolteachers with undergraduate degrees, mostly obtained under the Brandon University Hutterite Education Program. They hold professional accreditation from the Manitoba Department of Education. Several are principals of colony schools. Attitudes towards having Hutterites as teachers in the colony schools varies, but in colonies that do not accept it the debate seems to be centered more on the policy of having Hutterite teachers than on the gender of the teacher. Nevertheless, attitudes vary and it is difficult to see this situation being embraced by the most conservative colonies.

Since the entire colony eats three times a day in the dining hall, many women will spend a significant part of their day there. A woman's work in the kitchen, dining hall and garden begins at age fifteen and usually ends when she retires at age forty-five, or when she cannot work anymore due to poor health. In addition, under the general guidance of the minister or the second minister, the women do all the work in the vegetable garden and the greenery. For the most part, when women work in the garden, there "hardly ever is a man around and if there is, he isn't there to just supervise the women."[21] Until recently in some Lehrerleut colonies, the women marketed eggs and garden produce at roadside stands located at the main crossroads near the colonies. This was stopped when it appeared that the women were absent from the colony for long periods, reducing time spent with their families and children.

Although the head cook's position is permanent, other women from the ages of seventeen to forty-five work in the kitchen as cooks or assistants about one week in ten, although this varies from colony to colony, depending on how many women are in the colony.[22] One week in three women wash dishes. Usually two women prepare and cook the meals for the colony, assisted by a crew of several younger unmarried women who are responsible for cleaning up the kitchen after cooking is finished. They also take the food to the dining hall where it is placed on each table.[23] Those at each table then serve themselves. It is increasingly common for colonies to serve their meals buffet-style.

Changes in men's lives have also affected women's lives. Women now marry four or five years later than they did a generation ago. Rozen attributes this to increased mechanization, which has eliminated many of the colony jobs previously done by young men.[24] She claims that lack of opportunity to move up into a position of responsibility delays the acquisition of status by young males, who are understandably reluctant to take on the responsibility of marriage without the requisite status. Concomitantly, young women are reluctant to give up their girlhood friends and the security of their own colony for a young man who has yet to find his position within his own colony. Many Hutterite women scoff at Rozen's ideas and claim that they are simply wrong and "almost laughable." A more likely explanation is that young people are achieving their Grade 12 so are attending school until age eighteen.

Although the later age of marriage has lowered the birth rate the average Hutterite woman today still has three to six children. During her pregnancy, she is exempt from heavy work. After giving birth, she is entitled to a maternity leave of eight weeks, during which she rests and takes care of the baby. Usually a friend or close relative (*Obwoterin*) will stay in her house for two or three weeks to take care of the house and other young children, if any.

This *Obwoterin* is automatically exempt from her duties in her own colony during the time she is helping the new mother.[25] Another relative will do the laundry for her. The new mother also receives special meals from the colony's kitchen.[26] These meals incorporate special traditional dishes that are high in protein, to build up the mother's strength. After the birth of her first child the woman will have a *sorgala* appointed to her and her family.

The *sorgala* is usually a young girl (although when there are none available it may be a young boy) from another family on the colony, who helps the mother with the baby and helps to take care of it as it grows to adolescence. The *sorgala* develops a bond with both the family and the child, becoming a kind of older sibling to the child and an adopted child to the parents. These relationships can last a lifetime.

Hostetler notes that the women play an informal but critical role in keeping the balance of power in the colony. For example, mothers have more influence than do fathers in the case of a power struggle between two brothers. Through marriage, women unite two families. This brings about an extended set of loyalties in the husband's family, which checks the exclusiveness of the relationship between the brothers. The woman is more committed to her husband's family than to her parents' family (although she maintains her loyalty to her family and keeps in touch with her parents, brothers and sisters), and she always supports her grown sons. The man tends to be more loyal to his parents' family than to the family he has built. The different loyalties of the husband and wife help to prevent the nuclear family from becoming too strong. Any negative feeling the woman may feel towards her husband for the lack of emotional support is turned against men in general.

Hostetler also suggests that the woman's loyalty to the female group offsets the emotional importance of the nuclear family in the same way that the man's identification with the colony replaces and limits his personal identification with his wife and children. When women gather power in the inner affairs of the colony, it usually is more because of the emphasis they put on their close family, and is not due to their interest in colony affairs. When a certain minister is said to be strict, it usually means that he keeps the women in their "proper place," which contributes to the smooth functioning of the colony as a unit and which protects society against self-centered familial groups which compete with each other.[27]

When she marries, the woman moves to her husband's colony. This can be quite an adjustment as the woman not only leaves behind her network of social contacts but enters a completely new social milieu because colonies differ in the way that they function and in how their women interact. As an outsider from a different colony, a newcomer bride may experience a certain degree of culture shock as she adjusts to the new environment.

The minister's wife is probably the most important woman on a colony, as she has a special role. In many colonies, she acts as the fabric buyer for the whole colony. She accompanies her husband on his trips to town and chooses the fabrics for the women's clothes. Thus, she develops unique relationships with merchants in nearby service centres. But it seems that her main role is an informal one: she acts as a channel through which women in the colony pass requests and complaints to her husband. Women expect her to use all her influence on her husband to achieve what they desire, usually things such as permissions instead of prohibitions.

Among the Schmiedeleut, although the first minister's wife often has duties such as the fabric buyer (*Zeich Schneiderin*), there are no other special duties imposed upon her when her husband is elected minister. Any duties assigned to a first or second minister's wife are most likely a result of her age or her being elected to the position, and unconnected to her role as a minister's wife.[28]

The Lehrerleut are most conservative on gender issues. The minister of Castor Colony in Alberta, for example, expressed great reluctance to relinquish control of any purchases to women.[29] In contrast, among the Schmiedeleut, and not only among the more liberal Group One colonies, women have done their own shopping for many years. One woman from a Group Two Schmiedeleut colony commented:

> When women do not have the freedom to shop for themselves they feel pressured to make money on the side, and this is frustrating for them. Some colonies listen to women, for example, regarding the design of the dining hall and the kitchen. In others, the men do not listen to the women and do not even consult them regarding these issues. Sometimes, I need convince myself that if this is for the good of the colony, then it should be accepted (for example, the minister cannot satisfy all the people all of the time). There was an exceptional case in one colony when the men were vacillating on the issue of whether to remain [a Group One Colony] or to join the Group Two of the Schmiedeleut. The women went on strike and refused to cook to force the men to reach a decision. The upshot was the minister of the colony left, and the whole colony, under the leadership of the second minister, moved to the Group Two side.[30]

Young women in the colonies are well aware of fashions in the outside world but seldom express any desire to move their traditional dress toward emulation of them. Reading a critique of their "old-fashioned clothes" in a Winnipeg newspaper, two Hutterite women offered a spirited defense of their traditional garb:

> We do not feel ashamed of our way of clothing, nor old fashioned. We feel well dressed and, of course, grown up. The clothes we wear are not to make us look attractive, nor for pride.... We wear long skirts all the time, whereas those who feel well-dressed in mini-skirts, turn around for a long old-fashioned Hutterite-styled dress and wear it on their most important day—their wedding day—to make themselves feel [adult]. So to us, every day is important.[31]

Birth control is an issue that affects women in many ways. Health is a significant concern when women bear many children. In the past some Hutterite women with large families who wanted to stop further pregnancies, but were not allowed to do so by the colony, had strokes and heart attacks that were attributed to the stress of childbirth. Today there is a greater awareness of the health risks of multiple pregnancies and use of birth control for medical reasons is now far more acceptable.

The average number of births per woman in a Hutterite colony has decreased from ten births at the beginning of the twentieth century to three to six births today. It seems that most women do not adhere to the severe prohibition against limiting birth, and that many must employ some form of birth control.[32] The birth control methods employed are usually female surgical procedures and various sterilization methods rather than use of over-the-counter non-permanent devices.[33]

Gender inequality is interwoven in Hutterite life in other ways. For example, the marriage ceremony reflects the man's superiority over the woman. During the ceremony the minister utters phrases such as "women are weaker," and "God authorized the husband to be the head for the woman." Divorce is prohibited and a woman can never leave her husband,[34] although community pressure would do much to protect a wife's rights in cases of marital turbulence. The marriage ceremony is always held in the husband's colony, to which the bride moves on the occasion of her wedding. She resides there thereafter.

Hutterite society is currently experiencing a number of macro-changes, such as the movement from agriculture to manufacturing, the later age of marriage and the smaller family size. These may have significant impact upon the role of women within colony life. Rozen argues that if the Hutterites cannot remain in agriculture and pursue real communal farming (with all its implications for community members), they may not be able to maintain the traditional role of women and the family structures that have stood them in such good stead for a hundred years.[35]

As agriculture becomes increasingly competitive and colonies operate in a globalized marketplace, familiarity with computer technology will become increasingly important. Increasingly, among the Schmiedeleut at least, more girls are completing their grade twelve education and often gaining familiarity with computer technology. Over the years with mechanization, many jobs on the colony have changed and no longer require physical strength, especially in those colonies that now rely on industrial operations to generate part of their income. As many new jobs in the "digital age" require intellectual aptitude and dexterity rather than physical endurance, an increasing proportion of jobs will be essentially gender-neutral, jobs such as programming computers, setting automated machines, dealing with accounting issues, and so forth. In Rock Lake Colony's manufacturing plant two of the 17 full-time employees are women.[36] As colonies move into more high-tech enterprises, opportunities for women to contribute to the earned income of the colony will increase. Can the colonies afford not to exploit one half of their intellectual capital? In the digital economy Hutterite women could make a significant contribution to their colony's economy while working from home, remaining physically removed from the outside world but working within it. This would certainly benefit the colonies' economies but would also shift the distribution of responsibilities within the colony. Thus, the catalyst for change in the roles of women within the colonies may come from technological innovation in the outside world and from economic necessity on the part of the colonies, rather than from any philosophical reappraisal by the church leadership.

Differences in leadership styles and strategies between the Group One and Two colonies may well govern the success of each in adapting to a rapidly changing technological world. After the governance question, regulating the rate of change within the colony is one of the principal ideological issues dividing the two groups; other elements seem, to colony outsiders at least, to be essentially insignificant. The effect on the status and roles of women in the colonies remains uncertain.

When discussing the place of women within Hutterite society a number of things seem clear. First, it is difficult to generalize because of the variation between colonies and the variation in opinions held by Hutterite women. Second, the position and role of women within each leut varies considerably, and third, as in the world beyond the colony, things are seldom static. In a 2001 study of the changing Hutterite family Bron Ingoldsby captured the essence of Hutterite familial relationships when she wrote that the Hutterite family is reminiscent of the idealized American family of the 1950s:

> Still technically patriarchal with occasional blustering on the part of the father, and the mother doing pretty much what she wants. [There is] real affection that leads to greater equality in decision making. Without the TV, families engage in easy, happy conversations. Word games and jokes are common, with extended kin dropping in and out throughout the evening. Evening walks and activities on a typical colony look like a scene from the musical State Fair.[37]

Within the Group One colonies gender roles have changed greatly over the last several decades and it is reasonable to conclude that, while these roles may have evolved less in other more conservative leute, they have evolved nonetheless and they will continue to do so.

Notes

1. Wes Harrison, "The Role of Women in Anabaptist Thought and Practice: The Hutterite Experience of the Sixteenth and Seventeenth Centuries," *Sixteenth Century Journal* 23, no.1 (1992): 49-50.
2. Peter Riedemann, *Confessions of Faith* [Originally published in 1545 as *Rechenschaft unserer Religion*] (Rifton: Plough Publishers, 1970), 97-99.
3. Linda Maendel, Elm River Colony, email message to John Lehr, February 12, 2008.
4. Harrison, "The Role of Women," 54.
5. Linda Maendel, Elm River Colony, email message to John Lehr, February 12, 2008.
6. Ibid.
7. This Hutterite woman requested anonymity. On the prophetess Deborah see *The Holy Bible*, Judges 4 and 5.
8. Aharon Meged, "A Christian Commune in Canada," *Mibifnim*, 550.
9. Telephone interview of a Schmiedeleut colony's children's dining room supervisor by John Lehr, January 17, 2014. Anonymity was requested.
10. Interview of Schmiedeleut colony member by Yossi Katz. Anonymity was requested.
11. Interview of Schmiedeleut colony member by Yossi Katz. Anonymity was requested.
12. Interview of Schmiedeleut colony member by Yossi Katz. Anonymity was requested.
13. Interview of Schmiedeleut colony member by Yossi Katz. Anonymity was requested.
14. Bron B. Ingoldsby and Suzanne R. Smith, "Public School Teachers Perspectives on the Contemporary Hutterite Family," *Journal of Comparative Family Studies* 36, no. 2 (2005): 258.
15. Ibid. Similar attitudes as to what is regarded as "women's work" by adolescent boys are frequently encountered in Canadian society, particularly among immigrants from Mediterranean and Middle Eastern countries. Kay Lehr, former teacher with Winnipeg School Division No. 1, interview with John Lehr, January 19, 2014, and numerous conversations with current and former educators in Manitoba and Ontario.
16. One such incident was related to John Lehr by an informant who requested anonymity.
17. Rod Janzen and Max Stanton, *The Hutterites in North America* (Baltimore MD: Johns Hopkins University Press, 2010), 256.
18. Linda Maendel, Elm River Colony, email message to John Lehr, February 12, 2008.
19. *Ordnungen und Konferenz Briefen*, December 7, 1997, Ordinance 7. On a visit to James Valley Colony on October 4, 2008, the second author observed a young woman driving a tractor and trailer along colony roads with great skill and confidence.
20. Every housewife is entitled to laundry hours during which all the washing machines and dryers are at her disposal. She has a choice of commercial detergent or of soap made on the colony.
21. Linda Maendel, Elm River Colony, email message to John Lehr, March 28, 2008.
22. Sara Gross, interviews with Yossi Katz, Bloomfield Colony, August 2004. Also numerous conversations by both authors with members of various colonies. Usually the wife of the Boss is elected as the head cook, under the assumption that she is in a better position to get the necessary products without difficulty. Other considerations are the character of the candidate for this job and her ability to maintain a proper relationship with the rest of the colony. Sara Gross, interview with Yossi Katz, Bloomfield Colony, September 21–23, 2005.
23. At special meals, associated with engagements and weddings, for example, it is customary for the young men to wait on the guests and serve them at their tables.
24. Frieda Schoenberg Rozen, "The Role of Women in Communal Societies: The Kibbutz and the Hutterite Colony," in Yosef Gorni, Yaacov Oved and Idit Paz (eds.), *Communal Life: An International Perspective* (Yad Tabenkin: Transaction Books, 1985), 619.
25. Jennifer Kleinsasser, "Graduation Address at the Oak River High School Graduation," *Preservings* 26 (2006): 89.

26. Caroline Hartse, "Social and Religious Change among Contemporary Hutterites," *Folk* 36 (1995):112-15.

27. John Hostetler, *Hutterite Society* (Baltimore and London: Johns Hopkins University Press, 1974), 270-73.

28. Patrick Murphy, James Valley Colony, email message to John Lehr, April 12, 2010; Linda Maendel, Elm River Colony, email message to John Lehr, April 4, 2010.

29. Peter Waldner, Castor Colony, Interview with Yossi Katz, September 13-14, 2005.

30. This woman requested anonymity.

31. Liss and Ruth Maendel, "Hutterites' Reply: 'Glad to Walk his Narrow Path,'" *Winnipeg Tribune*, January 9, 1969.

32. Bron B. Ingoldsby, "The Hutterite Family in Transition," *Journal of Comparative Family Studies* 32, no. 3 (2001): 385-389.

33. Similar forms of birth control are employed in ultra-religious Jewish society for these are methods that are permitted halachically, while men are not allowed to use birth control. See Chapter 5.

34. John Lehr has been party to conversations where Hutterite women have expressed support for the concept of divorce "under certain circumstances," but most support the ban on divorce in general terms.

35. Rozen, "The Role of Women," 620.

36. Sol Gross, Rock Lake Colony, telephone interview with John Lehr, January 15, 2014.

37. Ingoldsby, "The Hutterite Family in Transition," 391.

Chapter 11

WEGLAUFEN:

Leaving the Colony

THE HUTTERITE COMMUNITY IS NOT HERMETICALLY
sealed. Occasionally, members who have had enough of
communal life and have lost commitment to the Hutterite
faith decide to leave the colony. Defection means not only
leaving the colony itself, the Church and the Hutterite faith, but
also leaving, and perhaps losing, relatives and friends, for a true
Hutterite must be part of the colony and keep all its rules.

People defect for various reasons, but three are commonly cited.
The first is the wish to know and experience life outside the colony.
As we have already noted, the colonies are not completely secluded,
and to those considering defecting, the outside world seems one
of unlimited possibilities that they would like to enjoy. Moreover,
in the colony, young people are under the constant pressure of
work, with relatively limited opportunities to unwind after work
hours. Most of these defectors are young people who have not yet
undergone the rite of baptism, and tradition and faith are not yet
a significant part of their lives. In Lehrerleut colonies, the excess
of orthodoxy can push youngsters to leave. For free-spirited young
people, life in these colonies is very hard. Constant frugality, and
the fact that upon marriage young couples receive almost nothing

except for a house, encourages many young people to make money on the side, and this exposes them to the outside world, its luxuries and its temptations.[1]

Some of the youth in every leut make acquisition of money their central concern, lose all interest in the colony and look for ways to enjoy their savings—something that is possible only in the outside secular world. In such cases, they sometimes leave with several thousand dollars that they have put aside.[2] Most return to the colony after they have experienced life outside. After they confess and are disciplined, the colony welcomes them back into the fold.[3]

The desire for self-fulfillment is another reason for defection. Achieving personal goals is not an objective in Hutterite life and they may be impossible to attain within the colony. For example, some girls want to train as nurses in hospitals, some boys would like to acquire a teacher's certificate, but such decisions belong to the colony, not the individual. Fulfillment of community needs rather than those of the individual are the rule, and those who wish for personal fulfillment are always under pressure to adjust to the needs and ideals of the colony. If they decide to remain in the community, it is after they have convinced themselves that they have made the right choice. Colony life does have its attractions: lifelong care, a place in society, financial security, fellowship and, for many, a sense of spiritual purpose; however, it also demands sacrifices, particularly abandonment of self-will, ambition and, for some, personal goals.

The problem of self-fulfillment also arises over employment in the colony. Young people may aspire to jobs that they have no hope of attaining because the position is already occupied by someone a few years older. Since there are many young people in the colony as a result of high birth rates, these jobs may not open up within their working life unless the colony branches.

A third reason for leaving is a spiritual quest. Some become dissatisfied with the Hutterite faith, and wish to follow another Christian sect that is more evangelically inclined. In such cases, if the follower chooses to stay in the colony and worship openly according to his new faith, the colony will expel him. Today, religious motives are behind most of the defections, and there is little chance that these people will return to the colony.[4]

Samuel Hofer, born in 1962, who in 1983 left the Lehrerleut colony of Baildon, near Moose Jaw, Saskatchewan, for religious reasons, gives a fascinating description of defectors in general and explains why religious belief can trigger defection. Some consider the use of the word "defection" or "desertion" to be inappropriate and prefer to use the Hutterite terms *weggelufene, wecchglufne* or *weccklufna* (runaways) for those who leave the colony. These terms have a broader meaning than their literal translation. They are generally applied to all Hutterites who leave the colony either temporarily or permanently and also include anyone who "leaves home, departs from the shelter of the parents' house and community, or is assimilated by mainstream society."[5] According to Hofer, the terms likely came into use years ago when young men, anxious to experience life on the outside before accepting baptism, literally ran across fields to their non-Hutterite neighbours or to rendezvous with a friend who would drive them to their destination. Mostly, these runaways return to the colony after a few months.[6]

For a colony member to leave is a traumatic act, for leaving implies much more than the physical act of removing oneself from the colony. It involves rejecting one's culture and cutting ties with friends within the colony. For a modern Hutterite, one is either in the colony as a part of the fabric of its society, or outside it with little real connection to it. Although those who leave the colony may continue to regard themselves as Hutterites because of their cultural background, in a strict sense they are not, because leaving the colony means leaving the Hutterian Church. Since the absorption of the Prairieleut into the United States' Mennonite community in their early years in North America, there have not been any non-communal Hutterites, so moving to independent life within the Church is impossible.

Hofer compares the act of leaving the colony to the act of emigration overseas for a non-Hutterite. Thus, the decision to leave is intensely personal. Plans to leave are generally not revealed, although some discuss their intentions with friends. Regardless, fellow colony members may have their suspicions that someone is troubled and is contemplating abandoning the colony.

Many Hutterite runaways, especially young men not yet baptized, intend to return after sampling life in the outside world, but Hofer chose to leave his colony because an evangelical sect had proselytized him two years earlier. He realized that once he left there was no going back to the colony, as the two years prior to his defection had been difficult for him from a theological standpoint. His new beliefs and interpretations put him in conflict with Hutterite teachings and he went through a crisis of conscience, feeling that he was alone and unable to share his ideas with anyone in the colony:

> The truth was that my Hutterite faith consisted mostly of boundaries, colony rules, and fears of condemnation by God on Judgement Day. The doctrine of *Gelassenheit* (surrender and service to the community) for the love of God wasn't something I understood from the heart. God and Love seemed to exist on vastly different planes. The words were certainly there in songs, prayers, and sermons, but they seemed empty against the fearsome vision I had of God, who would condemn me for having an interest in art and psychology. When I became disenchanted with the Christian religion, I believed it to be a little more than a system of mind control. I have since become aware of the wider implications of this great religion and have made peace with it, although my belief in God is not based on the Bible's tenets of Original Sin and Eternal Damnation. As for the Hutterite version of Christianity, I didn't remain in the colony long enough to become fully indoctrinated into the communal faith.[7]

Hofer left the colony with a job waiting for him. Before he left he spent two months arranging for employment on the outside. This is quite usual as most runaways have a job arranged before they take the final step. At the very least they will have a "safe haven" arranged, often by the members of an evangelical sect who encourage runaways to leave the colony and join their church.

After overcoming all doubts and fears about the social and spiritual implications of leaving the colony, *weggelufene* must deal with the harsh realities of economic survival in the outside world. To go from the cocoon of the colony to exposure in the outside world is a daunting prospect; having a job, preferably one with living quarters supplied, or a sympathetic evangelical "sponsor" waiting to help with the transition to the outside world, takes much of the financial and emotional uncertainty out of the equation. When they leave, runaways sever all financial ties with the colony. According to Hofer, most people leave with less than $100 in their pocket, although others who planned well ahead have reportedly had several thousand dollars stashed away in "illicit" bank accounts.[8] Nevertheless, many younger runaways take with them only the bare necessities such as clothes, shirts, and socks—whatever will fit into a small bag or suitcase.

When the time comes to leave, young adults tend to make a break for it and seem to be most afraid of the shame of apprehension by an adult colony member before they are clear of colony property. Samuel Hofer described waiting until the adults were eating breakfast in the dining hall. "With my stash of clothes under my arm, I dashed to the garages where one of the boys was warming up the 706 International tractor. Minutes later we were bumping along the gravel road leading to the highway." [9]

Farmers with property bordering on to colony lands frequently relate stories of young runaways appearing at their house asking for shelter or a ride to an acquaintance's place. One told that over a period of several years, up to a dozen young Hutterite runaways from a nearby colony had appeared at her door asking permission to use the phone to contact a friend in order to get a ride. On one occasion, two young runaway Hutterite girls were in the farmhouse kitchen using the phone when they saw the colony Boss driving down the nearby section road. Fearing discovery they ran out and hid in a culvert until the Boss had left and their ride arrived. [10] Another Manitoba farmer told of a Hutterite youth of about 18 knocking on his door asking for a ride to a nearby farm where he had arranged for live-in employment as a hired hand. He told the youth that he would give him the ride but did not want to get involved in internal colony affairs or to wreck his relationship with the colony, so he would later notify the colony Boss of the incident. While en route to the bus station the runaway took off his suspenders and threw them out of the truck window. When asked what he was doing, he replied, "I won't need these anymore, I'm never going back." To the Hutterite youth, this was both a practical and symbolic gesture. Ironically, within a month he returned to the colony. [11]

Before leaving, *Weggelufene* go through emotional swings of doubt, fear, guilt, excitement, anticipation, and hope. If they confide their intent, they risk having family and friends try to dissuade them, complicating things even more. Someone leaving the colony to pursue a dream has a difficult time communicating this desire. Ideas of obtaining a university degree, becoming an airline pilot, or a nurse, are discouraged—even ridiculed. "What good will it do, when you lose your salvation?" is a typical response. [12] To those remaining on the colony, a *Weggelufener's* departure is both shocking and worrying. Samuel Hofer described it as leaving a hole akin to someone dying. Mary-Ann Kirkby wrote, "To a Hutterite nothing is more shameful than the word *weglaufen*, 'running away'."[13] In her case, her entire family left the colony over a dispute between her father and a colony elder; their leaving was equally traumatic for these who left and those who remained. In her biography, she paints a vivid picture of the emotional stress placed upon the family's children, wrenched out of their secure and peaceful world into an alien and uncertain future.

Colony members are shocked when someone leaves, especially if it is a youth entrusted recently with a new responsibility such as the operation of a tractor or other piece of farm equipment, for this is something that young Hutterites prize greatly. This pales in comparison to the dismay felt when an entire family leaves, as it throws the colony's future into doubt. Who will be next to leave? Is this the end of commitment to the communal ideal? Samuel Hofer noted that when two of his female cousins left Baildon Colony in the 1980s, people were very concerned because it was rare for women to leave Lehrerleut colonies. "The colony's future looked grim. Where would it end? Was this the beginning of women leaving the colony as was common among the Schmiedeleit [*sic*]?"[14]

Hutterites believe that someone born a Hutterite cannot expect salvation outside the colony. For those baptized into the Church, the implications of leaving are far greater socially, physically and spiritually. By leaving they break their baptismal vows (confession of faith) by which they promised to die a martyr's death rather than "sin willfully" (which in the eyes of Hutterites encompasses defection). It is quite understandable, therefore, that almost all baptized adults who leave the colony do so for theological reasons and usually after they have committed to another faith—most often to a brand of evangelical Christianity—rejecting the basic Hutterite belief that communal living is essential for salvation and replacing it with one that emphasizes an intensely personal relationship with Christ. Hutterites committed to communal life consider baptism and confession of faith as evidence of such an "intense personal relationship" and argue "we live in a community because we believe that God calls us to do so in Acts 2. It is an expression of faith; just simply living communally will not buy salvation."[15]

In the 1960s the main reason for leaving the colony was to experience life on the outside, to see if the grass really was greener on the other side of the fence. Young Hutterites wanted to have fun, watch television and movies, and have some money and private property. Others left to pursue their ambitions and fulfill their dreams, or to exercise their freedom of choice. Some simply balked at what they saw as unfair decision-making by colony elders, especially when they perceived a bias in favour of a particular family.[16] These issues are common in most societies but they can be addressed, if not largely overcome, in Hutterite colonies by strong organization and wise leadership. The real threat comes from a seemingly unlikely source: charismatic evangelical Christianity. A number of charismatic Christian Evangelical Churches see the Hutterite colonies as fertile ground for their proselytizing efforts. They offer personal salvation through a direct relationship with Christ, salvation that comes without communal living or removal from the world. One Dariusleut minister described one such evangelist as "worse than the Devil himself," adding that he was not allowed onto colony property. Nevertheless, he acknowledged that members of his colony would sometimes sneak off the colony to attend revival meetings.[17] To some proselytes the old Hutterite prayers, songs, and sermons lack spontaneity and the excitement of the evangelical preaching. They also consider Hutterite garb immaterial to their belief, seeing it merely as a tradition, having nothing to do with true Christianity.[18]

Today, Hutterites have access to religious teachings, other than those they receive from their ministers in the colonies, through books, magazines and even radio. There is, perhaps, less reluctance than previously to challenge the precepts of their faith. When a colony minister cannot provide satisfactory answers, the temptation is to seek them from outside, thus increasing their vulnerability to evangelists.

Evangelical sects not only promise salvation but also encourage Hutterites to leave their colonies by offering assistance if they leave and enabling the runaway to make a smooth transition from the shelter of the colony to the shelter of the evangelical community.

Others have noted that Hutterites who leave the colony often gravitate to a similar kind of environment, one that offers security, order and discipline. Perhaps the most extreme example is that of two young men who recently left a North Dakota colony and enlisted in the United States Army, where they served a tour of duty on active service in Iraq.

When Hutterites leave they generally do well in the outside world. Their moral values and strong work ethnic make them valued employees. Young men often have a variety of practical skills that enable them to fit as easily into industrial situations as into farm-related or agricultural operations. Samuel Hofer claims that one Calgary oil company's employees are all former Hutterites and cites a host of occupations held by former Hutterites, including welders, carpenters, computer programmers, nurses, truck drivers, ranchers, bakers, agricultural sales representatives, veterinarians, and police officers. Hofer feels that experience of the outside world is not entirely a bad thing. He argues that experience outside the colony enables people to grow and develop self-confidence: "[those] who return to the colony are often very anxious to take on responsibilities because life outside may have stretched them and made them more aware and appreciative of the care provided by the colony..." [19]

Hofer also questions whether the Hutterites' quest for a new spirituality is related to technological advances. Technology has enabled one person to do the work of many but the specialized knowledge required in certain trades often means that a person works alone. When group work is reduced, camaraderie is lost. Elders admit they have a problem: "All we can do is keep the secular and spiritual in balance." [20]

Until about 50 years ago, the number of those who left the colonies permanently was very low. A study published in 1955 found that between the years 1880–1950, only 106 men and 8 women out of those who were born in the North American colonies during those years left the colonies permanently. The researchers used to ascribe the defection to leadership problems, internal conflicts, economic or social problems, age, and so forth. The study also found that between the years 1950–1955, 141 men and 3 women left the colonies, but most of them returned after some time. These returning defectors were usually young people who had wanted to experience the luxuries of the outside world.

As implied by Samuel Hofer, the number of permanent defectors in the last 30 years has increased dramatically, mostly triggered by a search for religious fulfillment. A study published in 1982 claims that in one year, 300 colony members out of a total population of 21,800 left due to religious causes. Also, between the years 1983–1993, 600 Hutterites left their colonies for the same reasons. These were not only young, unmarried men, but people from all ages, including women and even whole families.[21] In recent years, the rate of defection has increased tremendously, and now the defection rate exceeds the birth rate, though many defections are not permanent. The introduction of new industries into colonies makes defection easier, for the acquisition of industrial skills gives young people a chance to acquire trades and skills that enable them to find work in urban areas without difficulty.

Regardless of the skills held by any defector the act of leaving the colony is a traumatic event, for the defector is required to restructure his or her life in virtually every aspect. Contact with their friends and family remaining on the colony is difficult if not impossible. Not only a new job and new co-workers, but also a new circle of friends must be assembled who share the same fundamental values, interests and attitudes as the defecting Hutterite. The defectors must learn to manage their own financial affairs, purchase their own clothes and, in the case of males, to cook their own food. Not surprisingly, many defectors gravitate to other defectors with whom they share much in common.[22] The pull of other Christian groups promising a different path to salvation is understandably also great.

Indeed, as noted earlier, the main cause for defection in the last decades is the search for spiritual realization, a road paved by Evangelical Christianity and the appeal of charismatic evangelists and their missionary allure. This happened, for example, in the Dariusleut colony of Red Rock in the United States, which suffered from severe economic problems and received no assistance from its neighbouring colonies. Evangelists influenced most of its members, who apostatized, and later testified that they experienced rebirth and heard the voice of God. Formally, they remained members of the Hutterite colony in order to try to convert Hutterites from their own and other colonies, but they denied the belief that communal life promises salvation. To them, the internal and personal experience was the road to salvation. Slowly, the whole character and religious customs of the colony changed. Neighbours were invited to prayer services; Bible lessons took place in the church, colony members attended services in a church in town, etc. In spite of the significant changes from the Hutterian tradition, the members claimed that they are the true Hutterites. The Hutterian Church no longer recognizes Red Rock Colony as a member colony.[23]

The issue of defection came to national attention in 2013 with the publication of *Hutterites: Our Story to Freedom*, a book authored by nine former Hutterites who left Forest River Colony in North Dakota and Hillside Colony in Manitoba to follow a charismatic evangelical preacher.[24] Intended to be a celebration of their newfound freedom and an explanation of their decision to leave their colonies, the book is a rationalization of their rejection of communal life, a catalogue of grievances, and a list of the alleged spiritual shortcomings of the Hutterite way. Nevertheless, it offers some valuable insights into the mindset of those who leave for spiritual reasons; clearly they did not choose to leave because of a crisis of faith. Their decisions, it seems, were triggered by myriad factors: perceived lack of opportunity within the colony system, lack of spiritual stimulation, a need to express their individuality, a wish to experience recreational activities available only outside the colony, and for some, a conviction they were treated unfairly by the colony leadership. The book ignited a firestorm of controversy.[25] Some former Hutterites saw it as a truthful account that identified the issues that drove them to leave their colonies, but many within the colonies were outraged at what they considered to be a vindictive and inaccurate portrayal of colony life.[26]

Caroline Hartse who, together with other scholars, studied the phenomenon of defection due to religious causes during the 1980s and 1990s, analyzed the events in Red Rock Colony and concluded that the Hutterites there came to believe that personal worship of God rather than the worship of God within the framework of a religious institution is the key to salvation. In other words, they became convinced that their choice should be for "internalized religion" and not "institutionalized religion" that demands submission of individualism to community. However, the present religious Hutterite way of life does not facilitate this. Some Hutterite preachers, usually new ministers, seldom offer their own interpretation of religious or biblical precepts. Generally, Dariusleut and Schmiedeleut ministers will clarify meanings and comment on theological ideas in the church service but the Lehrerleut ministers are more reserved and do not comment or clarify to the same degree. Sermons are read verbatim as written in the 16th century, usually without change of any kind. In church services at least, prayers are memorized and recited "with little evidence of conscious reflection, and hymns are chanted in the same centuries-old fashion. The net effect is a church service devoid of any meaningful personal involvement, a ritualistic affirmation of, and acquiescence to, the submission of the individual" to the collective will.[27]

Today, operation of modern machinery is based on individual work as opposed to the agricultural group work of the past, so there is more space today for personal expression in Hutterite life. This reinforces the inclination to regard the religious purpose of life as a part of the personal rather than the communal realm. As a result, people look for alternative ways in Christianity to make this possible. Second, the Hutterites are increasingly asking more questions about their faith. If the ministers are unable to answer these questions the believers turn outside, often to charismatic evangelical preachers, in their search for answers. Hutterite doctrine cannot provide an answer that permits the spiritual searcher to go his or her own way outside of the communal system. Third, the expansion of various religious movements in North America since the 1970s, mainly Evangelistic Christianity that rooted itself near the colonies, took advantage of dissatisfaction within the colonies generated by organizational and economic problems. In the "market of faiths" outside the colonies, Evangelistic Christianity seemed the most appropriate to the Hutterites. The disappointment of Red Rock with its neighbouring colonies that offered it no assistance at its time of need, namely, the feeling that the leut conformism had collapsed, was exchanged for a an emphasis of internal spirituality—the acceptance of Jesus the saviour—rather than emphasizing external behaviour. The defectors concluded that adherence to traditional Hutterite clothing and communal life cannot alone promise salvation. Only the personal, internal acceptance of Jesus Christ will promise that.[28]

The Hutterite leadership in the colonies is very sensitive to any possibility of defection, whatever the reason is, and it acts to prevent it. Thus, a Hutterite who gets engaged in theological discussions and deep philosophical issues, always arouses the suspicion that he might be on his way to adopt another faith and leave the colony. As already mentioned, the Hutterites, like most other Anabaptist faiths, are tolerant toward young people who have not been baptized yet, who purchase forbidden articles such as cameras or radios. Thus, Schmiedeleut members going to town receive a greater per diem than they really need. The Hutterites do this because too much restriction might lead to defection, even if it is for a limited period of time. Those who left the colony and returned to it might also have a negative influence on their friends, for their impressions of the outside world inspire others to experience it. The Group One Schmiedeleut colonies under Jacob Kleinsasser's leadership permit young people to attend classes in nearby towns, perhaps as an attempt to reduce defections by those who feel spiritually unfulfilled.[29]

Hutterites who leave the colony permanently are regarded as people who left the Church and repudiated the Hutterite faith, and therefore there are some restrictions placed on their interaction with their former colony and its members. Some colonies do not permit the defector to visit relatives in the colony, and his relatives cannot meet with him outside the colony. When a defector attends the funeral of a relative in the colony, he is not allowed to sit in the inner circle together with the family members of the deceased. The distancing of the defectors is clear, their placing at the funeral a symbolic replication of the geographic, religious, and social gulf created by the act of leaving the colony.[30]

Oil sands development in Alberta and a boom in the oil and gas industry in recent years has created a high demand for skilled labour. Hutterite males who leave Alberta and Saskatchewan colonies find it easy to secure a high-paying job, as often as not working with other ex-Hutterites in the oil and gas industry. Not surprisingly, the number of runaways has increased, especially among the Lehrerleut, who have many colonies set among the gas wells and oil rigs of southern Alberta. Most who leave are non-baptized males between 18–25 years of age, but it is also increasingly easy for women to secure work in a cafeteria or personal care home, and increasing rates of defection among Lehrerleut women reflect this. As yet, the Schmiedeleut have not been affected to any great degree by the recent boom in North Dakota's oil and gas industry, perhaps because Canadian Hutterites find it difficult to obtain permits to work in the United States.

High defection rates affect the colonies in many ways. So many young men left one Alberta Lehrerleut colony that "the last marriage was conducted in 1987; the last two children were born in 1993."[31] Some colonies lack sufficient males to undertake the heavy labour of jobs that were formerly performed exclusively by males. Women step in to the fill the gap: "They paint, gather eggs, milk cows, feed animals, and assist in the birthing of livestock. Women clean garages, assist in the carpentry shop and barns, and wash vehicles. They also drive into town for vehicle and equipment parts. Some help with cattle branding and garden plowing."[32]

Defection remains a concern among Hutterite leaders. They realize that it is the nature of all societies to have divergent views.

The negotiation of the fine line between the concept of community of goods as the road to a truly Christian way of life and the inherent human tendency towards individualism and self-expression is a test of the collective wisdom of the Hutterian Church leadership.

Notes

1. This informant requested anonymity.
2. Mike Hofer, interview by Yossi Katz and John Lehr, Sommerfeld Colony, Manitoba, May 12, 2004.
3. John Hofer, interviews by Yossi Katz, James Valley Colony, May and August 2004.
4. Samuel Hofer, *The Hutterites: Lives and Images of Communal People* (Saskatoon, SK: Hofer Publishers 1998), 159–67; John Ryan, *The Agricultural Economy of Manitoba Hutterite Colonies* (Toronto, ON: McClelland and Stewart, 1977), 14–15, 81–82. See also *Winnipeg Free Press,* June 14, 2008, A3.
5. Samuel Hofer, *The Hutterites,* 159.
6. Mike McGarry, "Sam Made It—On the Tough Outside," *Winnipeg Tribune,* December 28, 1968.
7. Samuel Hofer, *The Hutterites,* 159–60.
8. See Samuel Hofer, *The Hutterites,* 159; Mike Hofer, note 2.
9. Samuel Hofer, *The Hutterites,* 159.
10. Manitoba farmer, interview by John Lehr. This informant requested anonymity.
11. A Manitoba farmer, interview by John Lehr. This informant requested anonymity.
12. Ibid.
13. Mary-Ann Kirkby, *I am Hutterite* (Saskatchewan, SK: Polka Dot Press, 2007), 109.
14. Samuel Hofer, *The Hutterites,* 160–61.
15. Linda Maendel, Elm River Colony, email message to John Lehr, March 29, 2008.
16. Samuel Hofer, *The Hutterites,* 164–65.
17. Paul Stahl, Smoky Lake Colony, Alberta, Telephone interview by John Lehr, September 5, 2000.
18. *Winnipeg Free Press,* June 14, 2008, A3.
19. Samuel Hofer, *The Hutterites,* 166.
20. Ibid., 159–67.
21. For an account of a family's defection from Fairholme Colony in Manitoba, see Kirkby, *I am Hutterite,* 109–20.
22. For an account by one of the apostates involved in this incident, see Rebecca Hofer, *Removing the Hutterite Kerchief* (Kelowna, Collegium, 2009).
23. Karl Peter, Edward D. Boldt, Ian Whitaker and Lance W. Roberts, "The Dynamics of Religious Defection among Hutterites," *Journal for the Scientific Study of Religion* 21, no. 4 (1982): 327–30.
24. The Nine, *Hutterites: Our Story to Freedom,* Kearney, Nebraska: Risen Son Publishing, 2013.
25. The story of the nine runaways was carried by dozens of television and radio stations and appeared in newspapers across the Northern Plains and Prairies. Much of the coverage resulted from an aggressive book promotion tour that included virtually every major centre in areas where colonies are located. See, for example, *Brandon Sun,* September 7, 2013; *Bismarck Tribune,* August 26, 2013; *Calgary Herald,* November 22, 2013; *Grand Forks Herald,* October 12, 2013; *Medicine Hat News,* November 22, 2013; *Red Deer Advocate,* October 23, 2013; and *Yorkton News Review,* October 30, 2013.
26. Carol Maendel, Forest River Colony, letter to the *Grand Forks Herald* posted online at *http://www.hutterites.org/beliefs/nine-misrepresentation/*; Johnny Hofer, James Valley Colony, letter to Jason Waldner, a former member of Forest River Colony, October 14, 2013.

27. Christof Brumann, *Die Kunst des Teilens: Eine vergleichende Untersuchung zu den Überlebensbedingungen kommunitärer* (Gruppen, Hamburg: LIT, 1998), 113. This criticism of Hutterite sermons was a common theme in the reasons for defection given by the authors of *Hutterites: Our Story to Freedom*.

28. Caroline Hartse, "Social and Religious Change among Contemporary Hutterites," *Folk* 36 (1995): 109–28; Ryan, *The Agricultural Economy of Manitoba Hutterite Colonies*, 14, 15, 81–83; Edward D. Boldt, "The Hutterites: Current Developments and Future Prospects," in James S. Frideres (ed.), *Multiculturalism and Intergroup Relations* (New York and London: n.p., 1989), 61–71; Donald E. Pitzer, *America's Communal Utopias* (Chapel Hill, NC: University of North Carolina Press, 1997), 325–35; John Hofer, interview by Yossi Katz, James Valley Colony, September 26, 2005.

29. Aaron Hofer, John Hofer and Johnny Hofer, interviews by Yossi Katz, James Valley Colony, May and August 2004; Boldt, "The Hutterites: Current Developments and Future Prospects," 68–70.

30. John Hofer, interviews by Yossi Katz, James Valley Colony, May and August 2004; our observations at a funeral which took place in Deerboine Colony in May 2004, and our conversations with the relatives of the deceased, some of whom had left the colony and returned only briefly to participate in the ceremony.

31. Rod Janzen and Max Stanton, *The Hutterites in North America*, Baltimore MD: Johns Hopkins University Press, 2010, 256.

32. Ibid.

Chapter 12

GLOBALIZATION, DIVERSITY
AND CHANGE

I N THE 130 YEARS SINCE THE HUTTERITES ARRIVED IN NORTH
America, both North American society and the Hutterite community have undergone many changes. The practice of the
Hutterite faith demands separation from the outside world
but the complete detachment they desire is impossible to achieve.
Although one can live in a Hutterite world when inside a Hutterite
colony, the colony itself is always set in a non-Hutterite milieu. The
colony is analogous to a heavenly ark on an often-stormy secular
ocean. Hutterites *cannot* totally disengage from the world surrounding them, so changes that occur outside the Hutterite Ark
affect, one way or another, everything that occurs within the Ark.

The development of transportation, for example, in the three
provinces of Manitoba, Saskatchewan and Alberta in the first half
of the 20th century, the dramatic increase in the quality of roads,
and the mechanization of agriculture after the 1940s, reduced the
physical isolation of the colonies. It placed them nearer to the outside world and brought them closer to the cities. Hutterites' visits
to towns or to their neighbours' farms became more frequent. This
was not without effect. Rural electrification on the prairies in the
late 1940s and early 1950s, and the concomitant development of
telecommunication networks also thrust the secular world to the
very threshold of the colonies. Regardless of their wishes, Hut-

terite colonies were beset by a wave of secular values that leaked into their closed society in a thousand ways. The Hutterites of the late 20th century found it far more difficult to avoid exposure to the secular world than did their brethren who lived in the same colonies some 60 years previously.

This chapter will limit its survey mainly to the changes that occurred in the Schmiedeleut colonies, although it will also make some generalizations regarding the Hutterite Church as a whole. Even within the same leut the Hutterites today are not the same monolithic body they used to be in the past. There are numerous differences in the changes that have occurred among colonies within each leut. This alone constitutes a significant break with the past.

The last three decades have witnessed tremendous changes in five aspects of life: economic, religious-traditional, social, educational, and the degree of openness to the outside world. Perhaps the greatest change seen in the Hutterite world was the schism that fractured the Schmiedeleut into Group One and Group Two colonies. This sad tale appears to revolve around personalities, although it perhaps is better seen as lying in philosophical disagreements over the approach to be taken to managing the onrush of modernity.[1]

The Schmiedeleut Schism

DURING THE 1980s and the 1990s, internal issues of the Hutterites reached once again the courts of the "outside world," this time as a result of a deep crisis among the Schmiedeleut. Thus, today there are arguably four Hutterite leute instead of three. This is a difficult subject both for Hutterites and outsiders because the two sides in the dispute do not agree on some of the basic facts of the issue. It is clear, however, that passions run high on both sides of the issue. As early as 1992 it became apparent, even to outsiders, that rifts were developing within the community over concerns about the leadership style of Jacob Kleinsasser, his "high degree of interest in the affairs of individual colonies, and most importantly with a group of nouveau Hutterites based at the Woodcrest Colony in New York."[2] According to Preston, Kleinsasser believed strongly that if the Hutterites were to survive they had to change. This meant embracing higher education, moving into manufacturing, and adopting a new, more aggressive business model. A part of this strategy involved integration of the Schmiedeleut with the Bruder-hof from New York,[3] a communal group founded in Germany in 1920 by Eberhard Arnold with traditions and behavioural norms very different from those of the Hutterites.[4]

Arnold wanted to establish a utopian society during the chaotic times following the First World War. He gathered people sharing the same opinions, many of them graduates of the German youth movement who believed in the internationalism of pacifists, so-cialists and Christians. They knew nothing about the existence of the Hutterites in North America although they studied the old writings of the Hutterites. In 1930, when Arnold found the Hut-terites in North America, he made a journey to South Dakota and the Hutterite colonies in Western Canada, where he spent about a year and was ordained as a minister in Standoff Colony, Alberta. The Hutterites authorized him to "announce the word of God" and "gather the zealots" in Germany.

At the beginning of the 1940s, Arnold's Bruderhof emigrated to Paraguay; 20 years later, all the Bruderhof colonies left there in favour of the United States. Even before that, in the middle of the 1950s, one of their colonies became united with Forest River (Schmiedeleut) Colony in North Dakota, a union that was devas-tating for the Hutterites. The relationship between the Hutterites and the Bruderhof remained tense for about 20 years.

In 1973, the Bruderhof initiated some contact with the Hut-terites and hoped to reach formal reconciliation. A year later the Hutterites were persuaded to re-accept for a trial period the Bru-derhof and the rebellious Hutterites who had remained with the Bruderhof after the quarrel of the 1950s. It was a very difficult decision for the Hutterites, but they hoped that the union would flourish. The Dariusleut and Lehrerleut, suspicious about this process from the beginning, remained cautious.

With one foot inside the Hutterite world, the Bruderhof looked for people among the Hutterites to defend its principles. It found the person it was looking for in Jacob Kleinsasser, a charismatic and persuasive minister who was (and still is) the leader of Crystal Spring Colony in Manitoba. Kleinsasser had the power to move things among the Hutterites in the West, especially after he was appointed in 1978 to lead the Schmiedeleut council, and later the whole Hutterian Church, receiving the title of Bishop. Although many Bruderhof members had no wish to join the Hutterites, dress in their traditional manner and adjust themselves to their ideology, the Bruderhof leadership convinced the majority to adjust to and accept Hutterite culture.

At first it seemed as if the Schmiedeleut had done the right thing. Some Hutterite ministers "fell head over heels in love" with the Bruderhof's system of community life. They especially liked "the childlike submission and unreserved obedience by the common people to a hierarchy-type government." Another aspect of the Bruderhof communities was power, which the Hutterites respected, although with some reservations. The leaders of the Bruderhof communities were prepared to test their beliefs and their children's beliefs against the world. They were not afraid to send people with doubts outside, to the world, to put their faith to the test. Some Hutterites saw that as a symbol of praiseworthy vitality and as a sign of confidence in their faith.

Younger Hutterites were especially enthusiastic. In the Bruderhof communities, women were allowed to take part in the community's discussions, children were allowed to study at local schools outside the community after they finished Grade 9, and men were given more opportunities to make use of the education and skills they acquired besides implementing them in agriculture. In addition, the warm and enthusiastic faith of the Bruderhof members encouraged a cheerful prayer, community singing and playing. People showed more openness and expressed their feelings. In comparison, the old-fashioned spirituality of the Hutterites seemed cold, formal and homogenous.

Since the Schmiedeleut had lived in Canada for many years in an atmosphere reminiscent of their golden period, during which they experienced no persecutions except for some restrictions on land purchase, many of them became complacent and less strict in their religious observance. Other members, feeling a much greater desire for spiritual growth, left the Hutterian faith in favour of experiences of spiritual "rebirth" within the bosom of a vigorous evangelical church, which did not necessarily require formally joining a church, submission to its authority, or living in a community. Some Hutterite elders thought that maybe the energy and infusion of new ideas on the part of the Bruderhof might be the answer to their prayers. But many Hutterites in the Schmiedeleut colonies feared at a very early stage that the union with the Bruderhof would lead to chaos. "Nothing good will turn out of this," they said.

When Jacob Kleinsasser was elected Bishop, he assumed responsibility for guiding the Church. Although Hutterites believe that God appoints a bishop to hold the church's reins of government, he is not considered infallible. Since he is obliged to report directly to God he must be obeyed but an occasional mistake in a bishop's judgment is considered inevitable. A Hutterite bishop faces huge challenges: he must exercise skill, tact and decisiveness.

Kleinsasser was something of a visionary, progressive and liberal in his opinions. Aware of the challenges facing the Church, he saw a need for it to move beyond some of the traditional attitudes that had served it well in the past. He thought that the Church should adapt to changing circumstances and so pushed for Hutterites to enter higher education, which he believed was necessary for the economic and social progress that Hutterites needed. This conflicted with traditional Hutterite attitudes. In Bruderhof communities, children were expected to graduate from high school; often they continued their education in college or university. Kleinsasser wanted the traditional Hutterites to follow suit. He wanted to have Hutterite teachers, who were all college graduates, teaching the government curriculum at the colonies' schools. Indeed, much of his vision has materialized. Hutterite colonies in Manitoba that accepted his leadership reached a new stage in the educational system. Nowadays, parents and elders encourage the young to resume their studies in high school and to graduate with a Grade 12 certificate. In 1994, 21 Hutterites began their studies at a special new education program (BUHEP) for Hutterites in Brandon University, in western Manitoba.[5]

Supporters of Kleinsasser, now the leader of the Group One colonies, regard him as a charismatic, God-fearing leader who genuinely cares for his people and "who is hurting more than anybody else" about the schism in the Church.[6] They are distressed that Kleinsasser, who is known fondly by his supporters as "Jake Vetter" [Uncle Jake], is portrayed in a less than flattering light. While conceding that everyone makes mistakes, they strongly refute any implication that Kleinsasser was motivated by anything other than a concern for the well-being of the Hutterian Church. The account of events leading to the schism presented below relies heavily on court documents and legal opinions, which ultimately favoured the Group Two position, and the published accounts given by Alvin Esau and Samuel Hofer. Both of the latter are sympathetic to the

Group Two position. Interviews with some of the principals on the Group Two side supplemented this account.

The tensions within the Schmiedeleut surfaced in the early 1990s when a dispute broke out over a feeding device that Daniel Hofer, from Lakeside Colony in Manitoba, had invented some years before. Crystal Spring Colony, led by Kleinsasser, appropriated the design and registered a patent for it with the government patent office. The Hutterites, used to sharing their knowledge freely with other colonies, never saw any need to register a patent for any innovation developed in the colonies, for according to the principles of their faith they are not allowed to file a suit at court. Copying an innovative idea of a colony was nothing new. Indeed, Daniel Hofer claimed that his original intention had been to share the feeding device design with the other Hutterian colonies, with the royalties going to Lakeside.

Crystal Spring found itself as the owner of a worthless patent, for the colonies surrounding it copied the design and manufactured their own feeding devices. Crystal Spring decided to deal with the problem by selling the patent for one dollar to an outside non-Hutterite company. This company refused to let Lakeside and the other colonies continue manufacturing and selling the feeding devices. This triggered a spate of legal suits. Some colonies that were anxious to avoid confrontation settled out of court and paid $10,000 each. All the lawyers' bills were divided between the outside company (the holder of the patent) and Crystal Spring, and they also shared the payments received from the settlements. Crystal Spring Colony thus profited from the arrangement.[7]

Daniel Hofer accused Kleinsasser and other Schmiedeleut elders of making dubious financial deals that were designed to be a cover for other, less successful business ventures. In retaliation, Kleinsasser excommunicated Daniel Hofer, who refused to acknowledge Kleinsasser's authority and obey his demand that he leave Lakeside. Kleinsasser filed a legal suit, demanding the Hofer family and its supporters be expelled from the colony. For Hutterites this was a major step, as they avoid litigation and any recourse to the courts of the outside society on ethical and religious grounds. Hofer filed a counter suit, and lost. But by doing so he opened some complicated issues for discussion when he presented accusations against Kleinsasser and his supporters in court. Kleinsasser, not too wisely, stepped into a trap when he was forced to reveal more about his business deals, probably far more than he wished to reveal. Daniel Hofer appealed to the Supreme Court, which ruled in his favour in 1992. Meanwhile, it was revealed that under Kleinsasser's leadership several unsuccessful business deals had led to losses that ran into the millions of dollars. According to his accusers, Kleinsasser and others had allegedly invested unwisely and adopted financial management practices that, although seemingly above-board, were actually intended to exploit other colonies. Kleinsasser vigorously repudiated these accusations, insisting that his intention has always been to redistribute colony assets and assist the poorer colonies.

Kleinsasser's opponents also alleged that he interfered with the internal matters of individual colonies in an inappropriate way. During a dispute in one of the colonies, Kleinsasser allegedly refused to let the colony elect its minister according to the customary manner. He dispatched his observer to the colony but the colony's members rejected him. In response he seized the colony's bank account of $250,000 and ordered its people to evacuate the colony. They refused to do so. His actions exacerbated the rift and polarized opinions. Colonies, and even families, were divided, as people were required either to affirm their support for him or risk excommunication. Ministers were allowed to preach in their colonies only if they agreed with his position. Opponents were removed from their positions. People who protested risked expulsion from the Church. Some marriages were broken, when women left their husbands and returned to their parent colonies.

The leaders of the Dariusleut and Lehrerleut were dismayed by the turn of events and decided to act to resolve matters during their biennial meeting in 1990. However, Kleinsasser did not appear at the meeting despite his obligation to do so as the president of the three leute. He instead sent a written power of attorney. As a result, the Dariusleut and Lehrerleut removed Kleinsasser from his high position as the head of the Schmiedeleut and the Hutterian Church. Later, in a letter addressed to "Whom It May Concern," the Lehrerleut elders described Kleinsasser's demeanour as "one of arrogance; aloofness and overbearing superiority to say the least; belittling the Lehrerleut and Dariusleut."

Customs entering the Schmiedeleut colonies from contact with the Bruderhof generated criticism from the Dariusleut and Lehrerleut. They were alarmed when they heard that in some Schmiedeleut colonies, people took babies to church (children under the age of six do not attend church in traditional Hutterian colonies); they were also alarmed to find out that during rituals and weddings, live music was played, and that torches and candles were lit for the worship of God. In 1990, when they revealed the origin of all these customs, the leaders of the Dariusleut and Lehrerleut presented before the Bruderhof a list of 10 concerns regarding non-Hutterite customs and a list of other grievances. By doing so they formally cancelled the union of the Hutterites and the Bruderhof of 1974, "out of fear that such forbidden sins may slowly infiltrate into our colonies," and they asked the Bruderhof "to stop using and tarnishing the Hutterite image with your anti-Hutterian deeds."[8]

By 1992, Kleinsasser's actions aroused a growing concern among the Schmiedeleut colonies. For some time it seemed as if Kleinsasser had succeeded in changing the old style of leadership conduct. After all, he was the bishop appointed by general vote. However, his wish to introduce customs of the Bruderhof meant dismantling and discarding some of the traditions and culture of the Hutterites. Eventually, the more traditional Schmiedeleut colonies began to side with Joseph Wipf of South Dakota, Kleinsasser's opponent. Wipf was formally elected as the bishop's assistant. He called the elders of the Lehrerleut and Dariusleut colonies for help, and after a few meetings, they assured him of their support in a letter signed by 78 ministers, including the elders of the two leute.

In December 1992, more than 160 Schmiedeleut ministers met and placed 12 grievances against the leadership. Kleinsesser demanded a vote of confidence. His supporters, knowing what the outcome of such a vote would be, tried to dissuade him, but he insisted on calling the vote. In a vote, 90 of the 168 delegates present supported his removal from his post, and agreed that he should no longer have the status of an elder in the Hutterite Church, while 78 supported him. Kleinsasser disputed the vote results, arguing that the 90 delegates present did not constitute a majority of those eligible to vote when those not present were counted. He excommunicated those who rejected his leadership. The Schmiedeleut became divided into two factions; each insisting it was the genuine one. The ministers who accepted Kleinsasser's leadership met in Crystal Spring in March 1993, and were told that they would not be allowed to serve as ministers in colonies that rejected his authority. At the same time, Kleinsasser refused to renew the letters of reference for ministers who did not accept him as leader, letters that they needed in order to perform marriage ceremonies.

Canadian Vital Statistics permits to perform marriage ceremonies expire every two years, and Kleinsasser, as the elder Schmiedeleut, was the only one authorized to renew them. Therefore, most of the Hutterian colonies agreed to amend the 1950 Constitution of the Hutterian Brethren Church in a way that enabled them, among other things, to appoint two ministers to management positions in the Hutterian Church, and these ministers were authorized to appoint ministers to perform marriage ceremonies.

The two factions of the Schmiedleut have not yet resolved their differences, and there is doubt whether they will be able to do so in the future. The group of colonies under Kleinsasser's leadership [Group One colonies] tends strongly towards Evangelist ideas. They claim that they represent real Christianity, while the colonies outside their group do not. At the same time, their members adopted a more liberal way of life as Hutterites. They are less rigid in their adherence to traditional Hutterite clothing, their children are allowed to take university courses, they also allow the use of radio, television, cameras, computers, the Internet, and so on. The traditional faction of the Schmiedeleut [Group Two], as well as the Dariusleut and Lehrerleut forbid these. In 2014 there were 125 (64.1%) traditional Group Two Schmiedeleut colonies and 64 (32.8%) Group One colonies under Jacob Kleinsasser's leadership. A further six colonies (3.1%) remain unaffiliated with either group.[9]

The Split and Its Effect: Changes in the Constitution of the Hutterian Brethren Church

IN FACE OF the severe split among the Schmiedeleut, the leaders of the Lehrerleut, the Dariusleut, and the traditional faction of the Schmiedeleut, decided to amend the 1950 Constitution of the Hutterian Brethren Church. The Hutterian leadership wanted to use this opportunity to include in the new constitution amendments needed after 40 years of experience. These changes were needed especially in relation to the union with the Bruderhof, and were also required to address issues that came out of the legal suits launched in the 1960s by expelled members demanding their share of communal property.

The principal changes from the Constitution of 1950 were: first, the colonies of the three leute were obliged to sign the constitution if they were willing to be part of the Hutterian Church and its leut. By doing so, all the colonies that followed Kleinsasser were technically expelled from the Hutterian Church; the Schmiedeleut had split, and a kind of new Hutterite leut was created that legally lay outside the Church.[10] Second, to prevent the concentration of too much power at the hands of one leader, as happened with Kleinsasser, it was determined that the president (bishop) of the Hutterian Church—the head of the board of managers—cannot at the same time be the head of one of the three leute. As mentioned above, Jacob Kleinsasser had held the two positions simultaneously. It was also decided that in the case of tied votes at the board of mangers of the Church (where all three leute are represented), the vote of the president will not decide the issue (as written in the Constitution of 1950), but the decision will be made by drawing lots. As for the resolutions of the council of the leut, which is its supreme institution, the Constitution of 1993, clarified that "To the extent that the decisions of the Conference might affect the Church generally then such decisions shall be subject to review by the Board of Managers who have the right... [in accordance with its being the supreme body in charge of all principles and discipline in the Hutterian Church] to overrule any such decision pertaining only to matters which are of concern to the whole of the Church or which may affect the working, administration or operation of the Church generally."[11]

Elder John Wipf now leads the traditional faction of the Schmiedeleut. Jacob Kleinsasser still leads the liberal faction. John Wipf, the minister of Willow Creek (Lehrerleut) Colony, Alberta, now heads the Hutterite Church.

The Constitution of 1950, which was copied in part from standard regulations of business corporations, included among other things a clause enabling each colony to purchase patents, licenses and concessions. This clause opened the door to Kleinsasser's dubious deals and to the scandal of the theft of a patent from Daniel Hofer. In the Constitution of 1993, the permit to purchase patents, licenses and concessions was completely erased. Also, the clauses relating to the prohibition to hold private property were emphasized again and again and even expanded, the full ownership of the colony of all the assets was also emphasized, and similarly the fact that a member who was expelled or left the colony out of his own will, is not entitled to any share in the colony's assets. The constitution makes this very clear:

All property, real and personal, of a Colony, from whomsoever, whensoever, and howsoever it may have been obtained, shall forever be owned, used, occupied, controlled and possessed by the Colony for the common use, interest, and benefit of each and all of the members thereof, for the purposes of such Colony... All the property, both real and personal that each and every member of a Colony has, or may have, own, possess or may be entitled to at the time that he or she joins such Colony, or becomes a member thereof, and all the property, both real and personal, that each and every member of a Colony may have, obtain, inherit, possess or be entitled to, after he or she becomes a member of a Colony, shall be and become the property of the Colony to be owned, used, occupied and possessed by the Colony for the common use, interest and benefit of each and all of the members thereof... None of the property, either real or personal, of a Colony shall ever be taken, held, owned, removed or withdrawn from that Colony, or be granted, sold, transferred or conveyed otherwise than by such Colony in accordance with its by-laws, rules and regulations and the provisions of these Articles and if any member of a Colony shall be expelled therefrom, or cease to be a member thereof, he or she shall not have, take, withdraw from, grant, sell, transfer or convey, or be entitled to any of the property of the Colony or any interest therein; and if any member of the Colony shall die, be expelled therefrom or cease to be a member thereof, his or her personal representatives, heirs at law, legatees or devisees or creditors or any other person shall not be entitled to, or have any of the property of the Colony, or interest therein, whether or not he or she owned, possessed or had any interest in or to any of the property of the Colony at the time he or she became a member thereof, or at any time before or thereafter, or had given, granted, conveyed or transferred any property or property interest to the Colony at any time.[12]

The trauma of the union with the Bruderhof and the improper conduct of some Hutterian colonies, including colonies under Kleinsasser's leadership, also found its expression in one of the clauses of the Constitution of 1993. While the Constitution of 1950 declares that the board of managers of the Church may accept to the Church each suitable community "which complies with and conforms to the religious doctrine and faith of the Hutterian Brethren Church," the parallel clause in the Constitution of 1993 has been expanded to include some conditions. The same clause also dealt with the need to reaffirm from time to time existing colonies, something that did not exist in 1950. The Constitution of 1993 says:

> The Board of Managers, may admit to membership or continue in membership in the Church any Colony which affirms or reaffirms that it complies with and conforms to the authority of the Board of Managers and the religious doctrine and faith of the Church as expounded by Peter Riedemann, and the Board of Managers may join any such Colony to one of the Conferences as it deems appropriate. The Board of Managers may from time to time request that each Colony reaffirm that it complies with and conforms to the authority of the Board of Managers and the religious doctrine and faith of the Church as expounded by Peter Riedemann, provided always that any Colony which does not, upon request of the Board of Managers, affirm or re-affirm that it complies with and conforms to the authority of the Board of Managers and the religious doctrine and faith of the Church shall cease to be a Colony of the Church and shall cease to be in the Conference to which it was joined. Any affirmation or reaffirmation provided to the Board of Managers may be accepted or rejected by the Board of Managers and a Colony which has submitted a reaffirmation that was rejected by the Board of Managers shall not be a Colony of the Church.[13]

This last clause authorized the expulsion of the colonies that remained loyal to Kleinsasser from the Hutterite Church on the grounds that they failed to comply with the above regulations.[14]

Economics and Globalization

HUTTERITE DETERMINATION TO succeed economically, always one of their characteristics, has been tested recently by strong competition from extra-regional markets in the new globalized agricultural economy. The general increase in the standard of living throughout North America forced them to achieve comparable growth and grant similar increases in material comforts to their members, lest dissatisfaction increase defection rates or, at the very least, engender strong feelings of frustration. The Hutterites, therefore, became more materialistic and economically ambitious. Today, economic conditions in most the colonies are more than reasonable, and the standard of living is high. As there are now no legal restrictions affecting land purchase, they can expand their holdings and strive for greater efficiency through economies of scale, replace and improve their agricultural machinery, and compete with advanced industries. Newly built daughter colonies have well-appointed colony buildings (the school and the dining hall) and family houses are spacious, with the wife's sewing room and husband's office located in separate rooms in the house.

The old parent colonies have also undergone a process of building and renovation. Old houses are either dismantled and replaced or renovated. In some cases colony plans are also in the process of change, as when older buildings are replaced they are repositioned to place all residential buildings in a semi-circle, all fronting onto the communal dining hall and kitchen. It is telling that the rationale for this reorientation is to place all colony residences at an equal distance from the dining hall and the circular plan permits each house to be accessible by motor vehicle.[15] It should be noted that only a few decades ago, they used to draw water from wells in the yards, bathrooms were outside the house, there were no kitchens in the houses, sewing was done in the living room and men also worked from the living room, and houses in general were much smaller.[16] A house in James Valley Colony that today is occupied by a family of four might have been home to 17 people only 40 years ago. Most colonies also provide special houses for the elderly, renovate their communal buildings and modernize agricultural operations.

Materialism is one of the factors most affecting the decrease in religious adherence. Increasingly, members find excuses for not attending evening services or other religious gatherings, due to their need to be on business outside the colony. Some, who are present in the colony at the time of the service but do not wish to attend it, say that they listened to it through the public address system which is connected to each house and is intended to transmit the service to the sick and elderly who are physically unable to attend. Some colony ministers will cancel prayers due to prior engagements involving colony matters, as is clear from a reading of the Conference Ordinances. When the whole colony is focused on economic success, its members find it difficult to concentrate on spiritual and religious matters, and to make time for them. On the contrary, in an atmosphere and reality where individuals bearing the burden are not rewarded for their work by receiving money or other benefits, they find it hard to resist the allure of individualism, and the consequent desire to make money on the side, which is a sin in Hutterite eyes.

Exposure to the outside world is inevitable and it comes at a moral cost. Sara Gross captured the sad conundrum faced by the Hutterite leadership:

> Since we are human—forbidden values do penetrate. We have to be more secluded from the world. In the last ten years, we do more business with the outside world, we travel more, and this affects us. We need to isolate ourselves more if we wish to survive as Hutterites in the future. But how is this possible? A better balance needs to be kept between advancing technology and our Hutterite values. Change can be positive but the cultural impact needs to be better thought through. The economic success, technology and technological needs forced us to expose ourselves. If we had not advanced technologically, we would have been forced to leave the market and adopt a lifestyle very similar to that of the Amish. The colonies have changed so much in the last ten years, and if they continue to change at the same rate in the next decade, we will be in a lot of trouble. In other words, we might disappear religiously if we put ourselves in the economic front, and we might disappear economically if we isolate ourselves and perfectly stick to our faith.[17]

The Hutterite birth rate has also undergone a tremendous change. In the past Hutterites adhered almost without exception to the religious prohibition to limit births, but today there has been a dramatic decline in observance of this prohibition. The average number of births dropped precipitously over the last few decades. Similar findings have been observed in other religious-traditional societies that experienced economic success and material abundance. A possible explanation for this phenomenon might be that people are less likely to sacrifice their personal comfort as their economic situation improves. In any case, the explanation that Hutterite ministers are more aware today of the medical risks involved with many births and that they are now prepared to accept medical advice to limit the number of births cannot fully account for such a precipitous decline in the birth rate. It seems, therefore, that colony members are exercising their own judgment about birth control that would seem to reflect a lessening of the influence of church doctrine and ministerial authority, if not religious adherence.[18]

There has also been a loosening of traditional ways and observance of Hutterite traditions, for example, in clothing styles, especially in women's clothing. Many changes have been introduced into the traditional homogenous clothing patterns, and thus, despite instruction to the contrary, women stopped wearing traditional aprons, and the use of modern and floral fabrics has increased. The effect of exposure to the outside world can be seen clearly, and the annual pronouncements of the Schmiedeleut councils, demanding that women return to the old traditions have not been heeded. For example, in March 1975, all the ministers of the Schmiedeleut colonies were urged not to allow the fabric buyers to be influenced by the entreaties of other women on the colonies:

Those sisters who have been ordered to buy the fabric, and who chose the proud patterns that have already become far too prevalent are not the only guilty ones who have willfully disobeyed and pushed too hard. No, the sisters and the mothers are just as guilty, and perhaps even more so than the cutters. They should not be excused, rather they should get rid of everything that is not good for the colony so that the colony may once again resume the old ordinances. They should erect the old cornerstone again that our dear ancestors loved and protected before our time, and which was pleasing and loved by our dear God also before our time, otherwise they would not have pleased him. If we think that we are still humble now, think where we would be today if already during their time they had torn down the foundation and had become proud with their prideful clothing? Why do we love to buy and have such big flower prints on our clothes? This will only harm us along with our children, and our children's children, and the young women, but maybe it is already too late. One must put out the fire when it starts.

If it is already in the attic it is too late. Where is the covenant that we made with God to help to build his church? We have all promised him, on bended knee, that we would help to build up his house, not to tear it down. Now, many of the dear brothers and sisters who held watch and built it up before us are already in eternity, and not only can we not maintain what they built, but we try to break it apart and tear it down? What sort of reward would our God give us for such a thing? With bound hands and feet the useless servant will be thrown into the farthest darkness—may God protect us all from such a fate.

Let us stop for a moment and consider the purchase of floral-printed fabric. Where the flowers are too big or too many, or too obvious, then arrogance is shown. Let us only go back 30 years, when our mothers purchased fabric for the colony, then the dear Lord will see more humility among us, if we will do as they did. Let us first begin by buying dark fabric and garb. First only black fabric, or dark blue, dark green, dark brown, and white fabric may be purchased, according to the ordinance.

And if there are little flowers on the fabric, they may not be bigger than a human's eyeball, and may not be too close together. And the fabric may not be shiny, or glittery. Striped fabric has also been taken to an extreme, particularly with light coloured stripes and shiny fabric. That is not allowed to be purchased and will not be tolerated. Also, no multi-coloured accessories are allowed.[19]

Materialism fosters inequality between colony members. Making money on the side has become common, and has been facilitated by certain tasks that require longer stays away from the colony. Access to money in some colonies, namely, money received for personal discretionary needs, also contributes to inequality by heightening tensions and decreasing communal intimacy:

In the past, when we traveled for various needs, we tried to travel together with as many people as possible. This builds better community spirit. Today, too many people travel by themselves or with their own family. Two years ago, a decision was made by the Schmiedeleut council to forbid the use of Internet in the colonies, but no specific rules were formulated. Some colonies must have access to the Internet for operating the machinery and marketing. But as soon as the Internet entered some colonies, the other colonies want it too. And since we are equal, people in the colony complain why only some members have access to the Internet and the others do not. In other words, a decision should be made—everybody or no one. Some members have access to the Internet. What do they need it for? They don't need it.[20]

Introduction of new technologies forces colony members to specialize in new professions and to become proficient very quickly. Other professions become redundant or their skills required only on an occasional basis. For example, 25 years ago the colony's shoemaker made all the shoes for everyone. It was a full-time job. Today it is much cheaper to buy ready-made shoes, many of which have bonded rubber soles that are difficult to repair. While a colony shoemaker may still make some shoes in the winter, most of the time he merely repairs them. At the very best, shoemaking is now a part-time job, and the shoemaker today also functions as a plumber, an electrician, a goose herder or a tractor operator. The market economy transferred the members' skills to where they are most needed for the colony's economy, and we might suppose that the need for professional mobility caused some social tension, replicating the situation in the outside world.

Adoption of advanced technologies also brought about changes in women's work patterns. Twenty years ago, women gathered together once or twice a week for potato peeling to prepare enough to last for a few days. Today, one woman can perform the same task in less time using an automatic peeling machine. Similarly, women used to sit for long hours in the evenings separating feathers for filling pillows, blankets and mattresses. This activity helped the women to maintain social contacts during the long winter nights. Other home group activities consisted of weaving and making rugs. Today, women make rugs with the help of their computerized sewing machines, which are able to make diverse and complicated patterns. The result is more time spent at home with the family and less time spent with the other women. Family ties become stronger, and parents are closer to their children, but group solidarity is weakened.[21]

The introduction of advanced machinery and technology also brought about dramatic changes in education. Changes in the outside world affect the young generation and their parents and cause them to push towards completing a high school education. Also, some of the ministers understand that extending German school education is vital to keep the young generation attached to Hutterite faith. The elders are aware of the necessity to be open to the needs of the young people who experience a continuous tension between adherence to the centuries-old laws and traditions on the one hand, and the modern world, which cannot be avoided, on the other. They understand that they cannot disengage from the world and hermetically seal off the colony if they want to keep the young generation's loyalty. And thus, while in the past the Hutterites did not permit formal schooling to exceed eight years (and under the pressure of the Canadian and American laws, 10 years), there is today a far greater willingness to allow young people to finish high school, and even take professional courses. Federal, provincial, and state regulations demand certification for certain trades and this certification may require attendance at a specialized technical institution. Thus the colony is faced with the choice of sending away one of its members for training and certification or to rely on outside contractors who would oversee and "sign-off" the work performed by colony members. The latter course is expensive, inefficient and still introduces the outside world into the colony.

Instead of electing a member who does not have any other job in the colony to the position of German teacher, today colonies elect the most appropriate man for the job; parents take a greater interest in their children's achievements in school and in the quality of teaching, both in the German school and the English school; German teachers introduce advanced teaching techniques and participate in professional education programs carried out by the Schmiedeleut; and some ministers, driven by a sense of mission, copy and distribute religious-educational materials and have established book stores in both Group One and Group Two colonies, where one can find historical, theological and educational materials.[22]

Exposure to the outside world is perhaps the most dramatic and continuing change that the Hutterite community is experiencing today. In the past, the Hutterites avoided any contact with the outside world, as Aharon Meged wrote after visiting a Hutterite colony in 1947: "Usually the brethren refrain from mingling with people who are not members of their leut, and they seldom leave the colonies. Only those who hold central positions go to town for their business, and this, too, not on a daily basis."[23] Today, things are different. It seems that never before have the Hutterites been so exposed to the outside world from which they sought to isolate themselves. This has profound significance for their chances of long-term survival.[24]

Trips outside the colony are now routine, although they still require the approval of the elders. However, whereas until the mid-1970s an exact record was kept of every vehicle that left the colony, including the names of the travelers, their destination and purpose of travel, in later years this practice stopped altogether.[25] As noted earlier, rural depopulation and the decline of small service centres were triggered by improvements in the rural road system. As the small centres patronized by isolated colonies were bypassed by farmers able to haul their grain to other centres offering a wider array of services, businesses failed and the drawing power of the small centre was eroded further. As small centres collapsed, colonies were forced to take their business to the large cities where they were exposed to the North American secular world of the 21st century and to its lax moral values so diametrically opposed to Hutterite faith and principles.

Hutterites visiting the city are now exposed to the outside world far more than their parents were a few decades ago. Along the highways, billboards advertise a variety of products and promote the values of the secular materialistic world; in the cities and towns they are confronted by display windows, various shops, pubs, newspapers and books, which they may read freely and even purchase; they may watch television and movies; they can look at fashionable articles of clothing, fabrics, CDs, radios, cameras, cellular phones, etc.; products that are no longer unfamiliar to them. The Hutterites' familiarity with advanced technology makes every member highly aware of the existence of such products. Not everybody resists the temptation to acquire them. If they wish, they may—regardless of the prohibition—purchase at least some of these items with money made on the side or by using the per diem given for their stay outside the colony. Since many electronic items are small and relatively inexpensive, it is easy to make a clandestine purchase.

In recent years, the onrush of technology has accelerated. Attempts to manage change in communications technology are seen in the regulations and minutes of the Schmiedeliet, which increasingly focus on such things as use of camera phones, cellphones, and the Internet. The problem is compounded by the practical applications of such items for business and agriculture and their ability to bring the "sinful" world into the colony, as is made clear by the reiteration of the ban of Internet use in the *Ordnungen und Konferenz Briefen* of 2006, 2007, 2008 and 2009. The ban and its rationale is made clear in the regulations of 2009:

> *It was recognized that Internet cannot be in homes, including the homes of ministers and colony managers, and where it is found that the Internet is being used for manufacturing without means to block it so that only email is accessible and someone commits a sin through it, he shall be punished with shunning, regardless of whether it is a minister or colony manager.* Because the order clearly states that it shall not be put into houses, which has been punished before, and that who sins with such an unclean spirit must be punished with shunning. It is and remains a great ruse of Satan to catch us into his net; *it shall also not be used without consent from the council of elders.* [Emphasis in original.][26]

Some of the colonies pay for agricultural newspapers for their members, and encourage both young and adults to use the public library. The Hutterites may borrow any book they wish to read, or sit in the library and read books and newspapers. They can also use the Internet there. The English school, which has always served as a bridge between the children and the outside world, tries to bring in foreign news as part of the curriculum. Sometimes the school finds itself in a struggle against the leadership of the colony, which opposes the improvement of learning methods through the use of computers and access to the Internet. In spite of the prohibition against television in colony houses, some colonies permit them in their schools to show educational programs and videos, but this is not their only use. It is not uncommon for someone in the colony to keep a radio at home, and some members find it hard not to listen to the radio in rented vehicles.[27] On some colonies, clandestine satellite television has made an appearance.

Advanced technology leaves Hutterites more time for reading (whereas in the past they spent much time performing farm and domestic chores). Some of the tasks, like operating a combine-harvester guided by GPS, enable the operator to listen to audio-cassettes during work hours. With a little effort, one can use the computers in the colony, which are designated for farm business purposes, to watch or listen to CDs purchased in town or received from neighbouring farmers. There are initial signs of connections to the Internet; indeed, among the Group One Schmiedeleut, Internet use and email communication is fairly common. Furthermore, the new generation of cellular phones, with direct connection to the Internet, is already there. Even the more conservative Schmiedeleut colonies will not be able to refrain from using email and limit themselves to fax machines for business communications for much longer.

Ironically, it is not the vulgar and lewd secular world that poses the greatest threat to the Hutterite way of life, but the deeply religious yet non-communal evangelical Christian sects that proselytize among the Hutterites. Mose Stoltzfus, an ex-Amish evangelist, has targeted Hutterites in his search for proselytes, and has had some success by promising salvation without commitment to communal life. One Dariusleut Colony minister described him as "worse than the Devil himself," and refused to let him set foot on colony property. Colony members were forbidden to attend his church services or associate in any way with him, his church, or its members.[28] Thus, both the secular and the religious outside worlds threaten the future of Hutterite communal life, but the greater danger comes from the evangelical religious world.[29]

The increasing level of contact with the outside world and the reduction in anti-Hutterite sentiment within the host community has created a silent threat to the Hutterite way of life. Paradoxically, outside hostility restricted interaction with members of the host community, but strengthened group cohesion, thus reducing the temptation for defection and doing much to ensure the longevity of the Hutterite system in North America. To use a biblical analogy, when the flood subsides, the Ark is no longer necessary as a refuge, and the need to remain within it fades.

Today, in a culture increasingly tolerant of diversity and difference, long-lasting business relationships with suppliers in town develop into strong social ties, the colonies' doors are not closed to visitors from the outside, the bookstores in the colonies welcome visitors, too, and current news about the daily life in one of the Dariusleut colonies in Montana was published in one of the local newspapers by one of the colony's girls. Later, these articles were published as a book. There is no doubt that this was done with the approval of the elders of the colony and the leut, and perhaps even with their encouragement.

The writer, Lisa Marie Stahl, tells, among other things, that many colonies in the region participate in blood-donor drives in the nearby town, the colony's garage serves as a repair centre for the neighbours, and in general, business ties with the outside world have generated long-lasting friendships:

> Visits to the colony are frequent. There are few days when meals are eaten at the communal kitchen that an English friend isn't there to join us. On a lazy summer evening, you'll likely find a couple of the guys going fishing with a friend. Or on a Sunday afternoon, a family from town will come out to the colony to spend the day with friends. When a colony has a celebration—a wedding, shivaree [hulba], harvest party, Christmas or graduation program—it's the perfect chance for neighbours and friends to gather and share the evening... In the last decade, more Hutterites started volunteering for their local fire departments. Others, women as well as men, have joined the ambulance team and trained to become first responders. Colony tours are frequent and can range from one person to a group of one hundred. People touring the colony come from all over the United States, as well as other parts of the world. On tours, people who have never visited a colony get to see how such a large organization works, and also ask questions. A lot of times, it's a chance to clear up some of the misunderstandings they may have about Hutterites and colony life.[30]

It should be noted that Lisa's colony belongs to the Dariusleut, a leut that is regarded as more conservative than the Schmiedeleut. For the latter, the problems are equally serious.

Although the intensity of the pressures from the outside world has increased yearly since the Hutterites first arrived in North America, their leadership has managed to negotiate a fine line between maintenance of Hutterite traditional values and the changing expectations of their community members. Eaton termed this a process of "controlled acculturation."[31] He noted that Hutterites hardly ever rescind one of the directives written in the *Ordnungen und Konferenz Briefen*. Most commonly, a series of regulations passed over a number of years will call attention to a practice that the leadership feels to be inappropriate or contrary to the community's interests. When it becomes clear that repeated exhortations have failed to squash the practice and that it has now become commonly accepted, a new regulation will attempt to re-define the issue so that the leadership can continue to exercise a measure of control. The rules bend but they do not break. Control is maintained and the threat managed. Change is thus managed so as to be incremental, not sudden, thus it never threatens the system's stability.

Notes

1. This issue is one that few Hutterites wish to discuss. Many feel that this is an internal dispute, "family business," and are reluctant to have outsiders advance their own interpretations of events.
2. B. Preston, "Jacob's Ladder," *Saturday Night* 107, no. 3 (April 1, 1992): 30–31.
3. On the Bruderhof, see Yaacov Oved, *Witness of the Brethren: A History of the Bruderhof* (New Brunswick, NJ: Transaction Books, 1996), 6.
4. The description of the Schmiedeleut schism is based mainly on Samuel Hofer, *The Hutterites: Lives and Images of a Communal People* (Saskatoon, SK: Hofer Publishers, 1998), 131–40 (all citations are from there), and Alvin J. Esau, *The Courts and the Colonies: The Litigation of Hutterite Church Disputes* (Vancouver: UBC Press, 2004), as well as on interviews held with John Hofer, the minister of James Valley Colony, and Aaron Hofer, the Boss of James Valley, in May 2004.

   It should be noted that the schism strained relations between the Schmiedeleut and the Hutterian Church in general; it also tore families apart, when one brother found himself in a Group One colony while the second brother's colony affiliated with Group Two. Moreover, some Group One colonies do not allow their members to visit and keep in touch with the Group Two colonies. This harms, among other things, family relationships. Despite their differing alignments, James Valley Colony (Group Two) and its neighbouring colony, Starlite (Group One), retain an exceptional cordial relationship. The reason lies in the geographic proximity of the two colonies and Starlite's origin as a daughter colony of James Valley. Interviews by Yossi Katz and John Lehr with members of both Starlite and James Valley colonies, 1998–2009.
5. Brandon University Hutterian Education Program.
6. Linda Maendel, Elm River Colony, email message to John Lehr, March 29, 2008.
7. For an excellent impartial and detailed account of the legal background to the schism within the Schmiedeleut see Esau, *The Courts and the Colonies*.
8. Samuel Hofer, *The Hutterites*, 131–40.
9. See Appendix 1 and *Hutterite Directories, 2005–2013*.
10. Group Two Hutterites legally carry the Hutterite name but members of Group One colonies have little regard for the legal distinctions of what constitutes the true Hutterite Church. Regardless of legal niceties they simply describe themselves as Hutterites, which of course, they are. The distinction is *de jure* rather than *de facto*. Linda Maendel, Elm River Colony, email message to John Lehr, March 1, 2007.
11. James Valley Colony Archive, Constitution of the Hutterian Brethren Church and Rules as to Community of Property, 1993.
12. Ibid.
13. Ibid.
14. John Hofer, interview by John Lehr, James Valley Colony, September 4, 2008.

15. Patrick Murphy, interview by John Lehr, James Valley Colony, September 27, 2007.
16. Based on our observations on visits to colonies; Sara Gross, interview with Yossi Katz, Bloomfield Colony, August 2004.
17. Many members in the colonies told us the same thing. For example, Johnny Hofer, the German teacher in James Valley, said in May 2004: "The more our economic situation improves, the more our worship of God is disturbed." Interview by Yossi Katz, May 2004. See also, Edward D. Boldt, "The Hutterites: Current Developments and Future Prospects," in James S. Frideres (ed.), *Multiculturalism and Intergroup Relations* (New York and London, 1989), 62, 63.
18. Donald B. Kraybill, and Carl F. Bowman, *On the Backroad to Heaven: Old Order Hutterites, Mennonites, Amish and Brethren* (Baltimore and London: Johns Hopkins University Press, 2001), 48–53.
19. *Ordnungen und Konferenz Briefen*, March 12, 1975 (see Appendix 5). At a funeral in Deerboine Colony, there were a variety of over-decorated dresses. Women wore dresses of various colours. Photographs of school graduates were displayed on the walls of the entrance hall. People were quite willing to be photographed. Some women did not observe the rule against a one-piece outfit. See the regulations in Appendix 5, re-emphasizing the often-disregarded orders regarding clothing.
20. Sara Gross, interview by Yossi Katz, Bloomfield Colony, August 2004; Johnny Hofer, interview by Yossi Katz, James Valley Colony, May 2004.
21. Samuel Hofer, *The Hutterites*, 125–30.
22. James Valley Colony has a small bookstore housed in its own building. It carries biblical literature, books on Hutterite history and life, and an array of office supplies.
23. Aharon Meged, "A Christian Commune in Canada," *Mibifnim*,552.
24. Kraybill and Bowman, *On the Backroad to Heaven*, xii–xiii, 8–9.
25. Minister Michael Hofer, interview by Yossi Katz and John Lehr, Sommerfeld Colony, May 2004.
26. *Ordnungen und Konferenz Briefen*, Item 7, May 8, 2009.
27. Lisa M. Stahl, *My Hutterite Life* (Great Falls: Farcountry Press, 2003), 81; Kraybill and Bowman, *On the Backroad to Heaven*, 32–39. During visits to the colonies, we accompanied members to the public library in the town of Portage La Prairie (in the centre of Manitoba, between Winnipeg and Brandon), and we realized that a large number of Hutterites use the library. Regarding the fear about the English school's access to the Internet, see Minister David Maendel's words, Chapter 7.
28. Paul Stahl, Smoky Lake Colony, Alberta, telephone interview by John Lehr, February 12, 2001.
29. Lisa Stahl, *My Hutterite Life*, 82; James Valley Colony Archives in Note 5; our observations during visits to colonies and from conversations with colony members. Compare to Meged, "A Christian Commune," 551, who reported that the Hutterites do not read newspapers.
30. Stahl, *My Hutterite Life*, 92.
31. J.W. Eaton, "Controlled Acculturation: A Survival Technique of the Hutterites," *American Sociological Review* 17 (1952): 331–40.

Epilogue and Prognosis

THE HUTTERITE COMMUNITY TODAY REMAINS THE LARG-
est communal society in the world. Its population numbers
about 48,500 people, living in over 500 colonies in Canada
and the United States.[1] Although the number of kibbutz
members in Israel exceeds this, many kibbutzim no longer lead a
full communal life, so the Hutterites remain the largest communal
society in the world. Their communal way of life, as well as the
institutional organization of the Hutterite Church with its three
(or four) leute, is firmly based on principles tested in the courts
and is protected by the Canadian and United States legal systems.
Similarly, both Hutterite internal rules and the legal system of the
outside world regulate and protect the organizational structure of
individual colonies.

Three Hutterite leute arrived in North America in the second half of the 19th century. For more than a decade now, the
Schmiedeleut have been split into two factions, and there are now
four *de facto*, if not *de jure*, leute. A common misunderstanding is
that Hutterite colonies are all the same but they are by no means
homogenous and have never been so in the past. Even within a
leut, there are significant social and economic differences between
colonies, as well as differences in the level of their religious adherence. Among the leute, the Lehrerleut are considered the most
orthodox, followed by the Dariusleut, the conservative Group Two

Schmiedeleut and the liberal Group One under Jacob Kleinsasser's leadership. Economic advancement and the level of social conservatism are essentially juxtaposed, so the more liberal Dariusleut and Schmiedeleut are considered the most economically advanced leute, while the conservative Lehrerleut are generally recognized as less technologically advanced.

To understand the character of the Hutterite community (or Church) one must first understand the principles of its unique Christian faith. This is also the basic difference between Israel's kibbutzim, the world's other major communal movement, and the Hutterite community. The kibbutz movement grew out of a secular socialist ideology entirely separate from Jewish religious belief. The religious kibbutz movement, a relatively small element of the kibbutz movement, also embodied socialist ideology; it merely wished to enable Orthodox Jews who were attracted to it to practice full communal life while maintaining full Jewish religious observance. Communal life is not a component of the Jewish religion. In contrast, Hutterite religious faith, formulated in the first half of the 16th century, is the *only* basis for the full communal lifestyle practiced by Hutterites. Socialist ideology is not a consideration.

Hutterite Christian faith is not only the basis for their communal way of life; it also determines the daily routine of every member of the community, the division of tasks and gender roles in the colony, the principle of seclusion from the outside world and hence the basic geography of Hutterite settlement in North America. That most colonies are located far from towns and cities and rely principally on agriculture, the principle of branching, the attitude towards education and the structure of the education system, all reflect Hutterite values that are determined by the fundamental tenets of their faith. Their religious outlook and belief system determine women's status, the prohibition of birth control, their moral precepts and concepts of sin, the issue of punishment and repentance, rituals and daily religious routines, and their attitudes towards the state. Indeed, their religious beliefs govern their entire world and rule every moment of their waking lives.

From the foregoing discussion of the structure of Hutterite society it would be easy to conclude that life in a colony is strictly regimented and that apart from the fulfillment of religious beliefs it offers little in the way of personal satisfaction or fulfillment. Nothing could be further from the truth. Hutterites live in community

Agricultural machinery, James Valley Colony.

Bloomfield Colony houses from the front.

Bloomfield cemetery.

Born in Ukraine, childhood in South Dakota, died in Manitoba.

Baking bread.

Bloomfield choir.

Bloomfield Colony showing the backs of houses.

Carpenter's shop, Rock Lake Colony.

James Valley Colony kitchen.

James Valley Colony, boiling tomatoes.

Colony school, Rock Lake Colony.

James Valley original house.

Colony gas station, Rock Lake Colony.

Dining room, Rock Lake Colony.

Grain bins, Rock Lake Colony.

Colony fire engine, Rock Lake Colony.

High school graduation, Bloomfield Colony.

Herding geese, James Valley Colony.

Children's play structure made by colony carpenter, Rock Lake.

Kindergarten, James Valley.

Girls in colony playground.

Minister's wife sharing a book with young child, James Valley.

Lunch room, manufacturing plant, Rock Lake Colony.

Making noodles, James Valley Colony.

Leaving Sunday School, Bloomfield Colony.

Minister's wife wearing a "wanick."

Retirement years.

Bloomfield Colony school.

*Straining dumplings,
James Valley.*

The next generation.

James Valley kindergarten.

Two Hutterite girls, James Valley Colony.

and maintain strong family ties and derive a quiet satisfaction from their work, family and friends and the knowledge that they are serving their community every day. Because they believe that they are fulfilling God's will by living and working communally most Hutterites feel spiritually fulfilled. Like other people, Hutterites enjoy good food, good times and good friends. They are by no means puritanical in their views and they share a good and often earthy sense of humour. Although their commitment to their faith is always evident on colonies through their everyday actions, they seldom proselytize, preferring to lead by example. To them, life on the colony is Christianity lived.

The personal freedom of the individual Hutterite in particular and of a colony in general, is nevertheless relatively limited. All colony officials, parents, the German teacher, the minister, the Boss, the elders and the leaders of the Church, have all zealously acted for hundreds of years to preserve a strict socio-religious framework that strives to maintain values, commandments, order, and traditions that date back over four hundred years. The religious components, the historic basis, and the traditional Hutterite world are the Hutterite community's conscience and its moral authority. Together they will determine the future of the community.

Despite the overwhelming presence of religion in Hutterite daily life, spiritual concerns are tempered by the community's commitment to economic achievement and its desire to maximize the returns of its investments in labour and capital. A spiritual orientation does not preclude concern with worldly comforts or economic security. The worship of Mammon is allowed, albeit reluctantly, but only for the benefit of the colony as a whole. The problem is that principles that are advantageous when applied to the community are deleterious when adopted by individuals, because they then run counter to community interests. Individualism, with all its implications, has leaked into the Ark, and if the flow is not checked, it may well sink it. Hutterites are no different from other people, religious or not. They are not perfect. Lust, greed, envy, gossip, deception, and desire for revenge walk among them, as in all societies.[2] They differ fundamentally from secular communities in their open recognition of their vulnerability and their desire to overcome it through devotion to Christian principles and the practice of communal living. Secular communities, on the other hand, rely on the authority of the law backed by the violence of the state to maintain order and justice. In this regard even the Israeli religious kibbutz has more in common with the secular world than with the "communal-religious" world of the Hutterites.

The Hutterites clearly understood that a precondition for maximizing economic achievement and building the colony's profit margin is the use of advanced technology and modern marketing systems. Unfortunately, integration of advanced technology into colony operations leads inevitably to increased exposure to the outside world. Implement dealers, parts specialists, fuel, fertilizer, and herbicide agents, all work closely with their clients. Marketing produce is no longer a simple transaction between the buyer and seller but involves various levels of government that determine production quotas, check the quality and safety of produce, and operate marketing boards through which specific commodities must be traded.[3] No matter what level of interaction with the outside world that the colony leadership may wish for, their ability to determine it is limited by circumstances far beyond their control.

Improvements in roads, the quality and reliability of motor vehicles and the relative decrease in the cost of operating motor transport has effectively shrunk the distance between the most isolated colony and the nearest town or city. Whether this is a real factor in increasing the inflow of alien ideas into the colony is a moot point, but there can be no doubt that colony members are now exposed to the secular world on a more frequent basis than before. The North American secular world to which they are exposed promotes liberalism, egalitarian values, multiculturalism and mobility, all values that threaten the Hutterite system that depends on conservatism, respect for religious authority and ethnic integrity, difference and isolation.

This is the world from which the Hutterites wish to escape by retreating into their Ark. There is no doubt that today, the Ark is leaking. The problems faced by a leadership that is attempting to manage the relationship between the Hutterite world and the secular world are now exacerbated by the revolution in information technology. Computers and the Internet are about to inject the outside world into the heart of the colonies. The challenges posed by the new means of communication will cause earlier dilemmas faced by the Hutterite leadership attempting to keep the world at bay to pale into insignificance. Modern technological communication—the cellular phone connected to the Internet—does not even require access to a computer within the colony. Advanced technology, used for the economic benefit of the colony, becomes a huge window to the secular outside world that the Hutterites try so hard to avoid.

Inevitably, Hutterites today, more than ever, are caught between their loyalty to a religious, conservative lifestyle that was determined in the 16th century and the values of an ever-intrusive outside world. In other words, they are torn between resignation to the inevitable and commitment towards the principles of the colony.[4] This tension is not unique to the Hutterites. It probably exists in every traditional-religious society exposed to modernity, as is, for example, the Jewish ultra-Orthodox society.[5]

Under these circumstances, and in spite of the communal-religious strict framework and indoctrination through their own German-school educational system, not everybody in the colonies (to put it mildly) remains loyal to the religious-conservative lifestyle established hundreds of years ago. The annual discussions of the Schmiedeleut council regarding deviations from the laws, and the regulations published following these discussions, are probably the best proof of this. The sincere testimonies of people we interviewed in the colonies during the preparation of this volume, and our more casual personal experiences of life on the colonies over a decade or more also support this contention.

Defection is the extreme expression of the inability to stay loyal to the Hutterite way of life. Defections, especially of the baptized, signify this more than anything does, for defection actually means giving up life as a Hutterite. Many defections reflect a desire to practice alternative evangelical Christian beliefs where communal life is not seen as a prerequisite for Salvation. Those attracted to what they regard as a more relevant path to the worship of God but choose to remain in the colony must reach their own compromise with Hutterite religious demands and the traditional lifestyle.

There is no doubt that there has been a reduction in religious adherence and a weakening of the church authority in the last few decades. This is indicated by the dramatic decline in the average number of children per family. In other words, there appears to be increasing use of birth control in spite of a strict prohibition against it. The annual decisions of the Schmiedeleut council and the regulations it issues provide numerous examples for compromises by individuals: wearing non-traditional clothing, skipping prayer services, possession of forbidden articles (such as radios and jewelry), excessive consumption of alcohol, and even non-marital sex and use of so-called recreational drugs. The ever-present dilemmas posed by making money on the side and the rise of individualism compound these issues.[6] Even some colony leaders are themselves making compromises, for they are aware of the great tension between the individual and the community and between the community and the surrounding world. Thus, for example, it is very rare for sinners to be expelled from the colony, even if they were guilty of grave sins; sins of the youngsters and those who have not yet been baptized are accepted by turning a blind eye; people going to town, especially young ones, are given more per diem than they need for the bare necessities so as to reduce the temptation to acquire things in an underhanded fashion; absence from the evening prayer service is tolerated and leaders do not perhaps pursue the issue as diligently as they might.[7]

Samuel Hofer commented in 1998:

Elders, alarmed that so many young people were leaving the colonies, had to relax a few rules. Fifteen years ago, young people caught with skates and hockey sticks were punished. Today, they walk across the yard with their hockey sticks and skates in broad daylight. Our crew once rented a car to travel to other colonies to play hockey. At one Hutterite community in southern Alberta, the preacher ordered that the ice on the dugout be destroyed. I don't think that would happen today. The elders look the other way, hoping that by giving in a little, the young people will stay in the colony.[8]

Defections, decline in religious adherence and the incessant compromises made to accommodate new attitudes constitute a threat to the Hutterite way of life, and are a real danger to the Hutterites' survival as a community and a religious commune. We have already noted that their annual growth rate is declining. During the years 2003-2005, defections exceeded births. It is unlikely that colony leaders will try to reduce contact with the outside world and restore the colony's role as an isolated ark; indeed, one wonders if it would be possible to do so at this stage. In fact, the opposite seems likely, as in all probability, interaction with the outside world will continue to increase. Even if defection rates stabilize, there is a risk that further openness will weaken religious discipline and erode the traditional way of life.

Whether the annual regulations issued by the Schmiedeleut will improve the situation is debatable, as an analysis of the discussions and regulations issued in the last 130 years reveals that the same reproof was made time and again concerning some misdemeanours, and these statements become increasingly severe over time. In other words, it seems that even without the demographic problem, the Hutterites, and most certainly the Schmiedeleut, are about to face a faith and identity crisis at a time when their economic situation is at its best and there are no restrictions on land purchase. The recent schism in the Schmiedeleut during the last decade seems to be a clear expression of this.[9]

Increasingly liberal attitudes to religious observance combined with the radical changes in the demographic structure of Hutterite colonies may be the precursor of more significant changes. It is not impossible that the core of Hutterite life could erode to the extent that communal living disintegrates with colony members relocating on to individual family farm units. When so many principles of the Hutterite faith appear to be changing or at least weakening, it may be asked why should the communal component be the only one to remain sacrosanct? There are other associated issues surrounding the perpetuation of communal life within an economic and cultural environment where communal living is extremely rare and where individualism is seen as a prized virtue. Mechanization has also affected the social balance of the colony system since manpower demands have decreased and the issue of providing meaningful employment to all colony members becomes a concern for the leadership.

In the past, the Hutterite community's leaders have proven remarkably adept at managing change and preserving the integrity of their way of life. The question is whether they will be able to cope with what must be an unprecedented rate of change in the outside world that is echoed within their own system.[10] In order to avoid uncontrolled change and the deterioration of the present system, the Hutterite leadership might consider the wisdom of introducing some steps to manage and even counter the pressures bearing upon the colonies.

First, all the leute must acknowledge the new reality of modern communications and accept that there is no way to avoid the outside world, for it is already inside the colonies. Second, it must reconsider the contents of education and the religious messages that are being passed on to the young generation in face of the reality of the 21st century. The leaders must devise a strategy to enable the individual to filter the messages received from the secular world. Third, the leadership must equip the members with appropriate tools that will make it easier for them to cope with the many tensions they experience. This is far more easily said than done, but it seems that a solution might lie in the strengthening of religious commitment and communal ideology among colony members. Thus, the question must be asked whether the daily two hours of German school is sufficient to inculcate the sense of purpose and religious values that are central to the continuation of communal life. Perhaps the time has come to deal with priorities regarding investment in the colony's economy versus investment in education. The question of the role of parents in their children's education might also be reviewed.

The majority of Canadians support the concept of human rights and religious freedom and the courts generally uphold these rights, but there are, in fact, legal limitations on both group and individual rights. Fringe groups that claim the right to openly practice polygamy, for example, run afoul of the law, as do cultural groups whose traditional practices and traditions conflict with liberal "Canadian values." Groups such as observant Hassidic Jews, who in maintaining their values are seen as imposing their religious standards on secular mainstream society, often trigger hostile reactions from the majority. On the whole, though, Canadian society, it seems, is content to "live and let live" and, as a rather reclusive society generally out of the public eye, living in isolated rural areas, the Hutterites have benefitted from the liberal social values and tolerance espoused by secular community leaders. This is a fragile situation and any suspicion that Hutterites enjoy an unfair advantage in any of their economic endeavours or that they are acting in a manner seen as contrary to the greater good of the wider secular society could quickly reverse prevailing attitudes towards them. Indicative of the latent suspicion of "the other" is a recent opinion voiced in the *Globe and Mail*:

> Today, there is a small minority of parents who refuse vaccination for "religious reasons," dubious interpretations of scripture. The handful of measles cases that usually occur in Canada tend to spring up in Hutterite communities or, as occurred recently, in some fringe Hasidic sects near the Quebec–New York State border. In Canada, we are too polite and politically correct to say so, but that's the reality.[11]

Similarly, there are rumblings in some areas about the Hut-terites having an unfair advantage in their industrial operations because they do not pay into worker's compensation insurance (though neither do they draw from it) and their labour is "free."[12] Their labour is not free, of course. Colony operations have to feed, clothe, and house all their members and provide for the children, the sick, and aged. Perception is all-important and public opinion is notoriously fickle.

A further issue that is problematic for the Hutterites is the ques-tion of individual versus group rights. As yet the courts have ruled in favour of the group when defectors have sued for a share of the colony assets, but there is no guarantee that this will always be so. Like all religious institutions the survival of the Hutterite Church depends on inculcating its values and belief systems into the young and impressionable. When other more mainstream religious groups living in the secular world impose their values it excites little com-ment, but the Hutterian community is more easily identifiable and spatially concentrated. It is thus more vulnerable to criticism as an institution that imposes its philosophy and insists on conformity. If the Hutterian church becomes regarded as an illiberal religious institution suppressing the right of the individual to free expression, support for the integrity of the colony could wane. For example, a legal decision that awarded a share of colony assets to any who wished to leave would be a financial disaster for the colony, and the precedent would threaten the survival of the church.

The recent highly publicized departure of nine Hutterites from their colonies in Manitoba and North Dakota has brought issues of individual rights and social justice within Hutterite colonies to the attention of outside society. For those unfamiliar with the nuances of colony organization it would be easy to conclude that Hutterite colonies are deeply flawed social entities. Developed over centuries and founded on principles of equality, fairness, and co-operation, colony organization has its weaknesses, but the shortcomings identified by its most vocal critics are generally those of individuals rather than any inherent defects of the system of colony governance. The continued health of the colonies thus depends on leaders and colony members practising what they preach and adhering to the basic tenets of the Hutterian church.

It is also vital that the Hutterite leadership learns from the recent experiences of other communal communities (such as the kibbutz) and Jewish ultra-Orthodox communities as they face challenges posed by the modern world. One approach that would address some of the issues raised here would be to separate the religious and economic roles of colony leaders. Today, the minister fulfills both.[13] There is no doubt that a society whose way of life is rooted in religious faith must invest in its religious philosophy and develop a theological literature that addresses the spiritual issues involved in coping with modern life and the changes it engenders. Colony ministers, as well as the heads of the leute and the Hutterian Church, have not yet invested in this in a meaningful way. Releasing ministers from their economic duties and making them focus on their religious tasks, permitting them to be spiritual leaders only, might change the situation. There is no doubt that their religious authority will increase, their religious-spiritual knowledge will broaden, and they will be able to supply clearer answers to religious distress and address the questions of faith which, if ignored, may cause colony members to turn to other religions. At the same time, the heads of each leut and the church will be able to allocate time for frequent meetings of all the ministers in order to formulate a revised Hutterite religious philosophy, whose basis lies in the original Hutterite theology, but which takes into account the new reality of a world of unprecedented information flows.[14]

There is no doubt that only a high level of faith will maintain the Hutterite colony system. What should concern the leadership is the proportion of defectors who leave the colony for spiritual reasons rather than from a desire to experience life on the outside. Those who leave to "sow their wild oats," and to experience a different way of life, often return to the fold. Those who leave to join an evangelical church seldom return; in fact, they tend to be the defectors who are most critical of the Hutterite way of life.[15] It seems, therefore, that a real challenge for all Hutterite leaders is to prevent their religion from becoming one of rote rather than conviction. This is difficult to do when living in community is seen as a basic fulfillment of one's religious duty. The minister's role thus becomes doubly important, requiring wisdom, flexibility and a certain amount of charismatic leadership from all the colony leadership. It is no easy challenge to re-invigorate a theological philosophy first articulated in the 16th century. That colony members are inculcated with the ideology of communal life may be an insufficient foundation on which to build a new enthusiasm and religious zeal. Better knowledge of the drawbacks of unrestrained individualism and materialism would be advantageous in the quest to generate a more enthusiastic embrace of the spiritual benefits of communalism that can counter the spiritual blandishments of evangelical churches. There are risks to this approach, since it means greater exposure to the secular world and not just the world of their rural neighbours who are not really typical of broader North American society. In some instances, progressive leaders from both the Group One and Group Two Schmiedeleut are engaging with this world through charitable activities, donations of food, and so on. Social outreach may be a road worth exploring in the quest for spiritual reinvigoration. Secular issues also come to bear upon spiritual well-being. Colony leaders are not exempt from reconsidering their future farm structure, for high rates of unemployment endanger the colony and might lead to the erosion of the communal feeling of "togetherness." Thus a crucial issue for the Hutterite community is the role that industrial activities should play within the colony economy. What should be the ratio of industry to agriculture in the colonies' economy? What role should other economic activities play? To what extent will a re-orientation of economic endeavours accelerate or reduce the rate of integration with the outside world? These are fundamental questions with religious and social implications that may well determine colony branching and the general health of Hutterite society.

The changing nature of agriculture and the need to adopt the most advanced technology means that colonies must not only maximize use of their land, infrastructure and capital, but also in order to compete in a global economy they must exploit all of their intellectual capital. This more than anything will push for the re-examination of some responsibilities on the colony and a concomitant shift in gender relations.

The Hutterites are acutely aware of their limited gene pool. There are now less than 20 surnames found among the Hutterites, a reflection of the relatively few families that constituted the initial colonies in North America and from whom virtually all Hutterites are descended. Proselytes are rare, and rarer still are those who stay and marry into the group. The Hutterite leadership has concerns about the genetic consequences of intermarriage. In consequence, marriage between cousins is forbidden and marriage between second cousins is discouraged. Since 1996, when two young people have shown an interest in marriage every Schmiedeleut colony minister has been able to consult a copy of the *Schmiedeleut*

Family Record (known jokingly as "the spy book") detailing the genealogy of all colony members.[16]

The effects of intermarriage are exacerbated by the division of the community into the three leute. Marriages between the leute are not common, further reducing the genetic diversity within each community. Immigration regulations, of both Canada and the United States, and the attendant bureaucracy, make even intra-leut cross-border marriages difficult. While they do not prevent such marriages, bureaucratic issues generally delay them by up to two years. Since the schism in the Schmiedeleut their opportunity for genetic diversity has shrunk even further. A recent Group Two regulation forbade marriage between members of Group One and Group Two colony members.[17] This has proven difficult to enforce and an estimated ten intergroup marriages take place each year.[18] One Hutterite from a United States Group Two colony philosophically remarked, "people fall in love, so what can you do?"[19] In practice, the Group Two regulation seems to apply only to Group Two members leaving to marry in the Group One colonies; there is less of an issue when Group One members leave to marry into a Group Two colony.[20] Nevertheless, the likelihood of intermarriage between members of a Group One and Group Two colony is still less than before the schism. In practical terms, this means that members of Group One colonies in the United States must in all likelihood find their marriage partner on one of only ten colonies. Of a total population of about 1500 people, no more than 400, probably far fewer, would be eligible marriage partners. The problem is less serious for the more numerous Group Two colonies in the United States, but the long-term implications of the international boundary and, for the Schmiedeleut, their internal schism, must remain a concern for the Hutterite leadership.

The Hutterian church clearly faces some significant issues. The loose structure of the Church as a whole, where the various leute operate as virtually independent institutions, means that strong central leadership is not possible. The recent schism within the Schmiedeleut further exacerbates this situation. On the positive side, the structure of colony operations, with a division of responsibilities between the minister(s), *Haushalter* (Secretary-Treasurer) and *Weinzedel* (Farm Boss) offers each colony the opportunity for the integration of secular and spiritual concerns and the maintenance of religious zeal. This model of governance has enabled

Hutterite communities to survive for hundreds of years with their religious principles still intact.

Hutterite resilience in the face of adversity has been remarkable. Although the problems now facing the colonies are of a less violent nature than even 50 years ago, in their way they are more intense and more difficult to counter by appeals to in-group solidarity. Nevertheless, despite the rather forbidding inventory of problems facing them at the beginning of the 21st century, their history of adaptation and survival gives good reason to think that the Hutterite colonies will remain a feature of the diverse North American social landscape well into the next century.

Notes

1. There are a few "Hutterite" colonies that are not technically members of the Hutterite Church, although members consider themselves Hutterites, practice community of goods and maintain the dress and beliefs of Hutterites. An example is Rainbow Colony in Manitoba, which has about 30 members.

2. Donald B. Kraybill, and Carl F. Bowman, *On the Backroad to Heaven: Old Order Hutterites, Mennonites, Amish and Brethren* (Baltimore and London: Johns Hopkins University Press, 2001), 12.

3. In the past, Hutterite colonies milled wheat for their own use. Today, in Canada, all wheat must pass through the Wheat Marketing Board; therefore, the flour used on a colony does not necessarily originate from there. All milk must be marketed under strict quota limits through the Milk Marketing Board. Colonies were formerly permitted to use milk from their dairy herd to produce their own cheese for on-colony consumption. This privilege was rescinded when the Milk Marketing Board learned that colony-produced cheese was traded to other colonies and some actually entered the marketplace, in contravention of Marketing Board policy. Johnny Hofer, interview by John Lehr, James Valley Colony, September 27, 2007.

4. Kraybill and Bowman, *On the Backroad to Heaven*, 8–9, 24–25.

5. See, for example, Nurit Reichal, "The Development of the Education System in Kfar Kame," *Galei Iyun Umchechkar* 14 (June 2005), 15–45.

6. Samuel Hofer, *The Hutterites: Lives and Images of a Communal People* (Saskatoon, SK: Hofer Publishers, 1998). See the annual decisions of the Schmiedeleut council, Appendix 5; Sara and Kenny Gross, interview with Yossi Katz, Bloomfield Colony, August 2004; John Hofer, Johnny Hofer, Aaron Hofer, and Sara Hofer, interviews by Yossi Katz, James Valley Colony, May 2004.

7. Based on our observations and conversations with colony members.

8. Samuel Hofer, *The Hutterites*, 130. Similarly, on colony visits, children were seen playing war games and using toy guns.

9. Amitai Niv, "The Residue of a Social Novelty," *Hakibutz* 6/7 (1979), 115–30.

10. James S. Frideres, "The Death of Hutterite Culture," *Phylon* 33, no. 3 (1972): 260–65.

11. André Picard, "The return of measles: Where did we go wrong," *Globe and Mail*, June 8, 2011, http://www.theglobeandmail.com/life/health-and-fitness/the-return-of-measles-where-did-we-go-wrong/article598566/.

12. Over their religious objections, Big Sky Colony in Montana was recently ordered to purchase workers' compensation insurance. See John Garvey, "Reining in Religious Freedom: A Hostile Government Chips Away at the Faith-based Life," *Washington Times*, July 1, 2013.

13. During visits to colonies (2004–2006), we raised the idea of releasing the minister from dealing with economic issues. Mike Waldner, the German teacher in the Lehrerleut Colony of Castor, opposed this idea, claiming that if the economic situation in the colony is not good, it will have a religious-spiritual effect on the colony and, therefore, it is extremely important that the economic issues, too, be part of the minister's responsibility. He also added that if the economic situation deteriorates, the other ministers and the head of the leut will know about it soon enough ("information travels fast among the colonies"), and they will ask for explanations. If necessary, congregations will remove the minister and will elect a replacement. In contrast, Johnny Hofer, the German teacher in James Valley, observed that the time has come for the ministers to deal with spiritual matters only. Tom Hofer, the minister of Deerboine, noted that this idea has been implemented in his colony. He added that, as a minister, he deals with all the spiritual issues, and the Boss is responsible for all the farm-economic issues. In general, during conversations with members of various colonies during visits in the colonies in September 2005, there was some sympathy for these ideas. During the visit of the Hutterite delegation to the Eighth Conference of the Study of the Kibbutz at Yad Yaari, Israel, in May 2006, it was clear that colony leaders were well aware of the need to address these issues. However, the structural organization of the Hutterian Church does not provide for a strong central leadership to lead this process. The difficulties the Schmiedeleut experienced with their schism—a crisis from which they are far from recovering— makes it difficult for them to start this process of reappraising leadership roles within the colonies for fear of triggering additional turbulence.

14. Edward D. Boldt, "The Hutterites: Current Developments and Future Prospects," in James S. Frideres (ed.), *Multiculturalism and Intergroup Relations* (New York and London, 1989), 66–70; Caroline Hartse, "Social and Religious Change among Contemporary Hutterites," *Folk* 36 (1995), 116–28.

15. See, for example, Ian Hitchen, "Ex-members Slam Hutterite Colonies' Rule, *Winnipeg Free Press*, June 14, 2008.

16. David Gross, *Schmiedeleut Family Record* (High Bluff, Manitoba: Sommerfeld Digital Printing Centre, 2012).

17. *Ordnungen und Konferenz Briefen*, 2012. Ordinance 1 states in part: "If it can go according to the advice given and the approval of the parents and the congregation, and they are wedded according to Christian standards and our community manual, we will allow them to be wedded until January 1, 2013. And then there should never be marriages between the two groups." (Underlining in original.)

18. Anonymous informant, telephone interview with John Lehr, June 10, 2014.

19. Ibid.

20. Canadian Group Two colony members, conversations with John Lehr, June 17-20, 2014.

Appendix 1

HUTTERITE COLONIES IN NORTH AMERICA IN 2014
List by province/state, parent colony, year of establishment and group[1]

ALBERTA

COLONY (Alberta)	PARENT	YEAR	LEUT
ACADIA (Oyen)	Crystal Springs, AB	1952	L
ALBION RIDGE (Picture Butte)	Keho Lake, AB	2010	D
ALIX (Alix)	Erskine, AB	1993	D
ARMADA (Lomond)	Spring View, AB	2003	L
ARROWWOOD (Blackie)	Springvale, AB	2007	D
ATHABASCA (Athabasca)	Rosebud, AB	1962	D
BEISEKER (Beiseker)	Rosebud, AB	1926	D
BENTLEY (Blackfalds)	Leedale, AB	1999	D
BERRY CREEK (Hanna)	Wildwood, AB	1981	D
BIG BEND (Cardston)	New Elmspring, AB	1920	L
BIRCH HILLS (Wanham)	Ridge Valley, AB	1996	D
BIRCH MEADOWS (Eaglesham)	Sandhills, AB	2009	D
BLUE GRASS (Warner)	Elmspring, AB	1999	L
BLUE RIDGE (Mountain View)	Waterton, AB	2000	D
BLUE SKY (Drumheller)	Starland, AB	1996	D
BOW CITY (Brooks)	Sunnyside, AB	1964	L
BRANT (Brant)	Rock Lake, AB	1968	L
BRITESTONE (Carbon)	Roseglen, AB	1994	L
BYEMOOR (Byemoor)	Pleasant Valley, AB	1986	D
CAMERON (Turin)	Ewelme, AB	1969	D
CAMROSE (Camrose)	Springvale, AB	1948	D
CARMANGAY (Carmangay)	Waterton, AB	1975	D
CASTOR (Castor)	Hutterville, AB	1965	L
CAYLEY (Cayley)	West Raley, AB	1936	D
CLEARDALE (Cleardale)	Holden, AB	2001	D
CLEAR LAKE (Claresholm)	Rockport, AB	1982	L
CLEARVIEW (Bassano)	Newell, AB	1975	L
CLOVERLEAF (Delia)	MacMillan, AB	2008	L
CLUNY (Cluny)	Tschetter, AB	1961	D
CODESA (Eaglesham)	Warburg, AB	2002	D

COLONY (Alberta)	PARENT	YEAR	LEUT
COPPERFIELD (Turin)	Cameron, AB	2014	D
CRAIGMYLE (Craigmyle)	Tschetter, AB	1984	D
CRYSTAL SPRING (Magrath)	New Elmspring, AB	1937	L
DEERFIELD (Magrath)	Hutterville, AB	1992	L
DELCO (New Dayton)	Sunny Site, AB	2004	L
DONALDA (Donalda)	Red Willow, AB	1978	D
EAST CARDSTON (Cardston)	Warren Range, MT	1918	D
EAST RAYMOND (Raymond)	Wolf Creek, AB	1996	D
ELK WATER (Irvine)	Spring Creek, AB	1979	D
ELM SPRING (Warner)	Elm Spring, SD	1929	L
ENCHANT (Enchant)	Ewelme, AB	1989	D
ERSKINE (Erskine)	Stahlville, AB	1976	D
EVERGREEN (Taber)	Midland, AB	2008	L
EWELME (Fort Macleod)	East Cardston, AB	1927	D
FAIRLANE (Skiff)	Rosedale, AB	1986	L
FAIRVIEW (Crossfield)	Beiseker, AB	1944	D
FAIRVILLE (Bassano)	Springside, AB	1986	L
FERRYBANK (Ponoka)	Sandhill, AB	1949	D
GADSBY (Stettler)	Veteran, AB	1987	D
GRANDVIEW (Grande Prairie)	Fairview, AB	1977	D
GRANUM (Granum)	Standoff, AB	1930	D
GREEN ACRES (Bassano)	Newell, AB	2003	L
GREENWOOD (Ft. MacLeod)	Big Bend, AB	1999	L
HAIRY HILL (Hairy Hill)	Plain Lake, AB	1996	D
HAND HILLS (Hanna)	MacMillan, AB	1957	L
HARTLAND (Bashaw)	Pleasant Valley, AB	2010	D
HIGH RIVER (High River)	East Cardston, AB	1982	D
HILLRIDGE (Barnwell)	Lakeside, AB	1994	D
HILLVIEW (Rosebud)	Rosebud, AB	1990	D
HINES CREEK (Hines Creek)	Pincher Creek, AB	branching	D
HOLDEN (Holden)	Cayley, AB	1970	D
HOLT (Irma)	Granum, AB	1949	D
HUGHENDEN (Hughenden)	Athabasca, AB	1973	D
HUTTERVILLE (Magrath)	Rockport, AB	1932	L
HUXLEY (Huxley)	Stahlville, AB	1959	D
IRON CREEK (Bruce)	Camrose, AB	1979	D
JENNER (Jenner)	Winifred, AB	1983	L

COLONY (Alberta)	PARENT	YEAR	LEUT
KEHO LAKE (Barons)	Wilson, AB	1981	D
KINGS LAKE (Foremost)	Elmspring, AB	1976	L
KINGSLAND (New Dayton)	Miami, AB	2010	L
LAKESIDE (Cranford)	Wolf Creek, AB	1935	D
LATHOM (Bassano)	Bow City, AB	2003	L
LEEDALE (Rimbey)	Pinehill, AB	1977	D
LITTLE BOW (Champion)	New York, AB	1983	D
LIVINGSTONE (Lundbreck)	Spring Point, AB	2000	D
LOMOND (Lomond)	Turin, AB	1984	D
LONE PINE (Stettler)	Handhills, AB	branching	L
LOUGHEED (Lougheed)	Veteran, AB	2010	D
MACMILLAN (Cayley)	Big Bend, AB	1937	L
MANNVILLE (Mannville)	Vegreville, AB	1988	D
MAYFIELD (Etzikom)	Wildwood, AB	1981	D
MIALTA (Vulcan)	Brant, AB	1998	L
MIAMI (New Dayton)	Milford, AB	1927	L
MIDLAND (Taber)	Miami, AB	1981	L
MILFORD (Raymond)	Beadle, SD	1918	L
MILTOW (Warner)	Milford, AB	1992	L
MIXBURN (Minburn)	Holt, AB	1960	D
MORINVILLE (Morinville)	Sandhills, AB	1971	D
MOUNTAIN VIEW (Strathmore)	Cluny, AB	1994	D
NEU MUEHL (Drumheller)	Verdant Valley, AB	branching	L
NEUDORF (Crossfield)	New Rockport, AB	1992	L
NEW ELM SPRING (Magrath)	New Elmspring, SD	1918	L
NEW ROCKPORT (New Dayton)	Rockport, AB	1932	L
NEW YORK (Lethbridge)	West Raley, AB	1924	D
NEWDALE (Milo)	Rock Lake, AB	1950	L
NEWELL (Bassano)	O.K., AB	1962	L
O.B. (Marwayne)	Thompson, AB	1957	D
O.K. (Raymond)	Rockport, SD	1934	L
OAKLANE (Taber)	O.K., AB	1994	L
OLD ELM SPRING (Magrath)	Elmspring, SD	1918	L
PARKLAND (Nanton)	MacMillan, AB	1972	L
PIBROCH (Westlock)	Wilson, AB	1953	D
PINCHER CREEK (P. C.)	Felger, AB	1927	D
PINE HAVEN (Wetaskiwin)	Scotford, AB	1997	D

COLONY (Alberta)	PARENT	YEAR	LEUT
PINE HILL (Red Deer)	Lakeside, AB	1948	D
PINE MEADOWS (Glendon)	Manville, AB	branching	D
PLAIN LAKE (Two Hills)	Scotford, AB	1970	D
PLAINVIEW (Warner)	O.K., AB	1975	L
PLEASANT VALLEY (Clive)	Veteran, AB	1970	D
PONDEROSA (Grassy Lake)	New Elmspring, AB	1974	L
PRAIRIE HOME (Wrentham)	Plainview, AB	1997	L
PRAIRIE VIEW (Sibbald)	Ferrybank, AB	1984	D
RAINBOW (Innisfail)	Pine Hill, AB	1999	D
RED WILLOW (Stettler)	Stahlville, AB	1949	D
RIBSTONE (Edgerton)	Camrose, AB	1960	D
RIDGE VALLEY (Crooked Creek)	Spring Point, AB	1977	D
RIDGELAND (Hussar)	Clearview, AB	1991	L
RIVER ROAD (Milk River)	Rock Lake, AB	1985	L
RIVERBEND (Mossleigh)	Newdale, AB	1976	L
RIVERSIDE (Fort Macleod)	Standoff, AB	1933	D
ROCFORT	Morinville, AB	2013	D
ROCK LAKE (Coaldale)	Old Elmspring, AB	1935	L
ROCKPORT (Magrath)	Rockport, SD	1918	L
ROSALIND	Byemoor, AB	2011	D
ROSEGLEN (Hilda)	Crystal Spring, AB	1970	L
ROSEBUD (Rockyford)	Tschetter, SD	1918	D
ROSEDALE (Etzikom)	Hutterville, AB	1953	L
SANDHILLS (Beiseker)	Springvale, AB	1936	D
SCOTFORD (Fort Sask.)	New York, AB	1953	D
SHADOW RANCH	Little Bow, AB	2009	D
SHADY LANE (Wanham)	Fairview, AB	2003	D
SHAMROCK (Bow Island)	Kings Lake, AB	1997	L
SILVER CREEK (Ferintosh)	Red Willow, AB	2008	D
SILVER SAGE (Foremost)	Sunrise, AB	branching	L
SKY LIGHT (Vulcan)	New Dale, AB	2012	L
SMOKY LAKE (Smoky Lake)	Beiseker, AB	1969	D
SOUTH BEND (Alliance)	Winnifred, AB	1965	L
SPRING POINT (Pincher Creek)	Granum, AB	1960	D
SPRING RIDGE (Wainwright)	O.B., AB	branching	D
SPRING VALLEY (Spring Coul.)	West Raley, AB	1997	D
SPRING VIEW (Gem)	Bow City, AB	1979	L

COLONY (Alberta)	PARENT	YEAR	LEUT
SPRINGSIDE (Duchess)	New Rockport, AB	1955	L
SPRINGVALE (Rockyford)	Jamesville, SD	1918	D
STAHLVILLE (Rockyford)	Spring Creek, MT	1919	D
STANDARD (Standard)	Acadia, AB	1987	L
STANDOFF (Fort Macleod)	Spinks, SD	1918	D
STARBRITE (Foremost)	Crystal Spring, AB	1989	L
STARLAND (Drumheller)	Lakeside, AB	1972	D
SUNCREST (Castor)	Castor, AB	1983	L
SUNNY BEND (Westlock)	Cayley, AB	1991	D
SUNNY SITE (Warner)	Elm Spring, AB	1935	L
SUNRISE (Etzikom)	Sunnyside, AB	1978	L
SUNSHINE (Hussar)	Cayley, AB	1956	D
THOMPSON (Fort Macleod)	East Cardston, AB	1939	D
THREE HILLS (Three Hills)	Wilson Siding, AB	2006	D
TOFIELD (Tofield)	Carmangay, AB	1998	D
TSCHETTER (Irricana)	Rosebud, AB	1948	D
TURIN (Turin)	West Raley, AB	1971	D
TWILIGHT (Falher)	MacMillan, AB	1986	L
TWIN CREEK (Standard)	Riverbend, AB	1998	L
TWIN RIVERS	Huxley, AB	2013	D
VALLEY VIEW (Torrington)	Huxley, AB	1971	D
VALLEY VIEW RANCH (Valley View)	Thompson, AB	1973	D
VEGREVILLE (Vegreville)	Pibrock, AB	1970	D
VERDANT VALLEY (Drumheller)	Handhills, AB	1974	L
VETERAN (Veteran)	West Raley, AB	1956	D
VIKING (Viking)	Warburg, AB	1985	D
WARBURG (Warburg)	Ferrybank, AB	1964	D
WATERTON (Hillspring)	Wilson, AB	1961	D
WEST RALEY (Cardston)	Beadle, SD	1918	D
WHEATLAND (Rockyford)	Stahlville, AB	1998	D
WHITE LAKE (Barons)	Granum, AB	1973	D
WHITESAND	Gadsby, AB	2013	D
WILD ROSE (Vulcan)	Old Elm Spring	1990	L
WILLOW CREEK (Claresholm)	Parkland, AB	1995	L
WILSON SIDING (Coaldale)	Richards, SD	1918	D
WINIFRED (Medicine Hat)	Milford, AB	1953	L
WINTERING HILLS (Hussar)	Sunshine, AB	2002	D

COLONY (Alberta)	PARENT	YEAR	LEUT
WOLF CREEK (Stirling)	Wolf Creek, SD	1930	D

BRITISH COLUMBIA

COLONY (British Columbia)	PARENT	YEAR	LEUT
PEACE VIEW (Farmington)	South Peace, BC	2002	D
SOUTH PEACE (Farmington)	Mixburn, AB	1977	D

MANITOBA

COLONY (Manitoba)	PARENT	YEAR	LEUT
ACADIA (Carberry)	Riverbend, MB	2002	S (1)
AIRPORT (Portage la Prairie)	New Rosedale, MB	1972	S (2)
ASPENHEIM (Bagot)	Huron, MB	1988	S (U)
AVONLEA (Greenridge)	Glenway, MB	2013	S (1)
BAKER (MacGregor)	Rainbow, MB	1973	S (1)
BARRICKMAN (Cartier)	Maxwell, MB	1920	S (1)
BLOOMFIELD (Westbourne)	Riverside, MB	1957	S (2)
BLOOMING PRAIRIE (Graysville)	Rose Valley, MB	2010	S (2)
BLUE CLAY (Arnaud)	Blumengard, MB	1998	S (2)
BLUMENGART (Plum Coulee)	Milltown, MB	1922	S (2)
BON HOMME (Elie)	Bon Homme, SD	1918	S (2)
BOUNDARY LANE (Elkhorn)	Plainview, MB	1997	S (1)
BRANTWOOD (Oakville)	Grand, MB	1995	S (2)
BRIGHTSTONE (Lac du Bonnet)	Maxwell, MB	1959	S (1)
BROAD VALLEY (Arborg)	Lakeside, MB	1974	S (2)
CANAM (Margaret)	Wellwood, MB	2005	S (2)
CASCADE (MacGregor)	Bon Homme, MB	1994	S (1)
CLEARVIEW (Elm Creek)	Whiteshell, MB	1983	S (1)
CLEARWATER (Balmoral)	Poplar Point, MB	1959	S (1)
CONCORD (Winnipeg)	Crystal Spring, MB	1987	S (2)
COOL SPRING (Minnedosa)	Newdale, MB	1988	S (2)
CRYSTAL SPRING (Ste Agathe)	Sturgeon Creek, MB	1954	S (1)
CYPRESS (Cypress River)	Homewood, MB	1975	S (2)
DECKER (Decker)	Brightstone, MB	1981	S (1)
DEERBOINE (Alexander)	Riverdale, MB	1959	S (2)
DELTA (Austin)	Sturgeon Creek, MB	1987	S (2)
ELM RIVER (Newton Siding)	Rosedale, MB	1934	S (1)

COLONY (Manitoba)	PARENT	YEAR	LEUT
EMERALD	Sunnyside, MB	2012	S (1)
EVERGREEN (Somerset)	Rose Valley, MB	1975	S (2)
FAIRHOLME (P la P)	New Rosedale, MB	1959	S (1)
FAIRWAY (Douglas)	Spruce Woods, MB	1995	S (1)
GLENWAY (Dominion City)	Milltown, MB	1966	S (1)
GOOD HOPE (P la P)	Poplar Point, MB	1988	S (1)
GRAND (Oakville)	Bon Homme, MB	1959	S (2)
GRASS RIVER (Glenella)	Grand, MB	1972	S (2)
GREEN ACRES (Wawanesa)	Spring Valley, MB	1991	S (1)
GREENWALD (Beausejour)	Barrickman, MB	1957	S (1)
HARMONY	Shady Lane, MB	2013	S (U)
HEARTLAND (Hazelridge)	Lakeside, MB	1995	S (2)
HIDDEN VALLEY (Austin)	Sturgeon Creek, MB	1968	S (2)
HILLSIDE (Justice)	Rosedale, MB	1958	S (2)
HOLMFIELD (Killarney)	Riverdale, MB	1975	S (2)
HOMEWOOD (Starbuck)	Lakeside, MB	1962	S (1)
HORIZON (Lowe Farm)	Starlite, MB	branching	S (1)
HURON (Elie)	Ranch, SD	1926	S (2)
IBERVILLE (Cartier)	Rosedale, MB	1919	S (2)
INTERLAKE (Teulon)	Rock Lake, MB	1961	S (2)
JAMES VALLEY (Elie)	James Valley, SD	1918	S (2)
KAMSLEY (Somerset)	Oakridge, MB	1998	S (2)
KEYSTONE (Meadows)	Rock Lake, MB	1995	S (1)
LAKESIDE (Cartier)	Maxwell, MB	1946	S (1)
LITTLE CREEK (Marquette)	Waldheim, MB	2002	S (1)
MAPLE GROVE (Lauder)	Ridgeland, MB	1981	S (1)
MARBLE RIDGE (Hodgson)	Bloomfield, MB	1972	S (2)
MAXWELL (Cartier)	Maxwell, SD	1916	S (2)
MAYFAIR (Killarney)	Riverside, MB	1970	S (2)
MIAMI (Miami)	James Valley, MB	1966	S (2)
MILLSHOF (Glenboro)	Cypress, MB	1994	S (1)
MILLTOWN (Elie)	Milltown, SD	1918	S (2)
NETLEY (Petersfield)	Interlake, MB	1996	S (1)
NEW HAVEN (Argyle)	Clearwater, MB	1977	S (1)
NEW ROSEDALE (P la P)	Rosedale, MB	1944	S (2)
NEWDALE (Brandon)	Bon Homme, MB	1974	S (1)
NORQUAY (Oakville)	Milltown, MB	1993	S (2)

COLONY (Manitoba)	PARENT	YEAR	LEUT
NORTHERN BREEZE (P la P)	Woodland, MB	1998	S (2)
OAK BLUFF (Morris)	Elm River, MB	1952	S (1)
OAK RIVER (Oak River)	Deerboine, MB	1998	S (1)
OAKLAND (Carroll)	Marble Ridge, MB	branching	S (2)
OAKRIDGE (Holland)	Barrickman, MB	1969	S (2)
ODANAH (Minnedosa)	Grass River, MB	1995	S (1)
PARKVIEW (Riding Mtn.)	Huron, MB	1964	S (2)
PEMBINA (Darlingford)	Blumengard, MB	1962	S (2)
PINE CREEK (Austin)	New Rosedale, MB	1972	S (2)
PINELAND (Piney)	Iberville, MB	1996	S (1)
PLAINVIEW (Elkhorn)	Waldheim, MB	1973	S (2)
POPLAR POINT (P la P)	Huron, MB	1938	S (1)
PRAIRIE BLOSSOM (Stonewall)	Oak Bluff, MB	1994	S (2)
RAINBOW (Ile de Chenes)	Elm River, MB	1964	S (U)
RIDGELAND (Dugald)	Springfield, MB	1967	S (1)
RIDGEVILLE (Emerson)	Maxwell, MB	1994	S (1)
RIVERBEND (Carberry)	Oak Bluff, MB	1969	S (1)
RIVERDALE (Gladstone)	James Valley, MB	1946	S (1)
RIVERSIDE (Arden)	Iberville, MB	1934	S (2)
ROCK LAKE (Grosse Isle)	Iberville, MB	1947	S (2)
ROLLING ACRES (Eden)	Riverside, MB	2005	S (2)
ROSE VALLEY (Graysville)	Waldheim, MB	1958	S (2)
ROSEBANK (Miami)	Hidden Valley, MB	1998	S (2)
ROSEDALE (Elie)	Rosedale, SD	1918	S (1)
SHADY LANE (Treherne)	Barrickman, MB	1993	S (1)
SILVER WINDS (Sperling)	Ridgeland, MB	1998	S (1)
SKYVIEW (Miami)	Miami, MB	1993	S (1)
SOMMERFELD (High Bluff)	Rock Lake, MB	1977	S (2)
SOURIS RIVER (Elgin)	Maxwell, MB	1977	S (2)
SPRING HILL (Neepawa)	Sunnyside, MB	1963	S (1)
SPRING VALLEY (Brandon)	James Valley, MB	1956	S (2)
SPRINGFIELD (Anola)	Poplar Point, MB	1950	S (1)
SPRUCEWOOD (Brookdale)	Springhill, MB	1976	S (2)
STARLITE (Starbuck)	James Valley, MB	1991	S (1)
STURGEON CREEK (Heading.)	Blumengard, MB	1938	S (2)
SUNCREST (Touround)	Crystal Spring, MB	1969	S (2)
SUNNYSIDE (Newton Siding)	Milltown, MB	1942	S (1)

15

COLONY (Manitoba)	PARENT	YEAR	LEUT
TREESBANK (Wawanesa)	Hillside, MB	1984	S (2)
TRILEAF (Baldur)	Parkview, MB	1987	S (1)
TWILIGHT (Neepawa)	Maple Grove, MB	1997	S (2)
VALLEY VIEW (Swan Lake)	Elm River, MB	1986	S (1)
VERMILLION (Sanford)	Homewood, MB	1990	S (1)
WALDHEIM (Elie)	Bon Homme, MB	1935	S (1)
WELLWOOD (Ninette)	Spring Valley, MB	1967	S (2)
WESTROC (Westbourne)	Bloomfield, MB	1992	S (2)
WHITESHELL (Riverhills)	Iberville, MB	1960	S (1)
WILLOW CREEK (Cartwright)	Greenwald, MB	1982	S (2)
WINDY BAY (Pilot Mound)	Fairholm, MB	1978	S (1)
WINGHAM (Elm Creek)	Sunnyside, MB	1991	S (1)
WOODLAND (Poplar Point)	Rosedale, MB	1971	S (2)

SASKATCHEWAN

COLONY (Saskatchewan)	PARENT	YEAR	LEUT
ABBEY (Abbey)	Tompkins, SK	1971	L
ARM RIVER (Lumsden)	Spring Creek, AB	1964	D
BAILDON (Moose Jaw)	Springside, AB	1968	L
BEECHY (Beechy)	Main Centre, SK	1981	L
BELLE PLAINE (Belle Plaine)	Holt, AB	1990	D
BENCH (Shaunavon)	Old Elmspring, AB	1952	L
BIG ROSE (Biggar)	West Bench, SK	1984	D
BONE CREEK (Gull Lake)	Tompkins, SK	1991	L
BOX ELDER (Maple Creek)	Pine Hill, AB	1960	D
BUTTE (Bracken)	Sand Lake, SK	1991	L
CARMICHAEL (Gull Lake)	Cypress, SK	1985	L
CLEAR SPRING (Kenaston)	Bench, SK	1971	L
CYPRESS (Maple Creek)	Big Bend, AB	1953	L
DINSMORE (Dinsmore)	Glidden, SK	1978	L
DOWNIE LAKE (Maple Creek)	Wolf Creek, AB	1958	D
EAGLE CREEK (Asquith)	Sandhills, AB	1987	D
EAR VIEW (Gull Lake)	Downie Lake, SK	1997	D
EATONIA (Eatonia)	Haven, SK	1987	L
ESTUARY (Leader)	Riverside, AB	1958	D
FORT PITT (Lloydminster)	Ribstone, AB	1969	D

COLONY (Saskatchewan)	PARENT	YEAR	LEUT
GARDEN PLANE (Frontier)	Jenner, AB	2002	L
GLIDDEN (Glidden)	Miami, AB	1963	L
GOLDEN VIEW (Biggar)	Southbend, AB	1981	L
GRASSY HILL (Gull Lake)	Carmichael, SK	2007	L
GREEN ACRES	Newell, AB	2003	L
GREEN LEAF (Marcelin)	Fort Pitt, SK	1999	D
HAVEN (Fox Valley)	Acadia, AB	1967	L
HILLCREST (Dundurn)	Leask, SK	1969	D
HILLSVALE (Cutknife)	Springvale, AB	1961	D
HODGEVILLE (Hodgeville)	Box Elder, SK	1971	D
HURON (Brownlee)	Big Bend, AB	1969	L
KYLE (Kyle)	Rosedale, AB	1970	L
LA JORD (White City)	Arm River, SK	1979	D
LAKEVIEW (Unity)	Hillsvale, SK	1973	D
LEASK (Leask)	Sandhills, AB	1958	.D
LOST RIVER	Hillcrest, SK	2012	D
MCGEE	Glidden, SK	2013	L
MACMAHON (MacMahon)	Waldeck, SK	2004	L
MAIN CENTRE (Rush Lake)	Rockport, AB	1963	L
MILDEN (Milden)	Dinsmore, SK	2006	L
PENNANT (Pennant)	Abbey, SK	2002	L
PONTEIX (Ponteix)	Downie Lake, SK	1973	D
QUILL LAKE (Quill Lake)	Riverview, SK	1977	D
RAYMORE (Raymore)	Ewelme, AB	2003	D
RIVERBEND (Waldheim)	Leask, SK	1996	D
RIVERVIEW (Saskatoon)	Fairview, AB	1956	D
ROSE VALLEY (Assiniboia)	Baildon, SK	1986	L
ROSETOWN (Rosetown)	Milford, AB	1970	L
SAND LAKE (Val Marie)	Old Elmspring, AB	1966	L
SCOTT (Scott)	Lakeview, SK	1997	D
SIMMIE (Admiral)	New York, AB	1964	D
SMILEY (Smiley)	New Rockport, AB	1968	L
SOVEREIGN (Rosetown)	Rosetown, SK	1995	L
SOUTHLAND (Herbert)	Beechy, SK	2010	L
SPRING CREEK (Walsh)	Lakeside, AB	1956	D
SPRING LAKE (Swift Current)	Hodgeville, SK	1991	D
SPRING WATER (Ruthilda)	Valleyview, AB	1982	D

COLONY (Saskatchewan)	PARENT	YEAR	LEUT
SPRINGFIELD (Kindersley)	Smiley, SK	1991	L
STAR CITY (Star City)	Estuary, SK	1978	D
SUNNY DALE (Perdue)	Hillsvale, SK	1990	D
SWIFT CURRENT (S.C.)	Simmie, SK	1978	D
TOMPKINS (Tompkins)	New Elmspring, AB	1954	L
VALLEY CENTRE (Biggar)	Golden View, SK	2004	L
VANGUARD (Vanguard)	Waldeck, SK	1980	L
WALDECK (Swift Current)	Elmspring, AB	1963	L
WEBB (Webb)	Box Elder, SK	1993	D
WEST BENCH (East End)	East Cardston, AB	1959	D
WHEATLAND (Cabri)	Kyle, SK	1987	L
WILLOW PARK (Tessier)	Springvale, AB	1979	D
WYMARK (Vanguard)	Vanguard, SK	2010	L

MINNESOTA

COLONY (Minnesota)	PARENT	YEAR	LEUT
ALTONA (Henderson)	Fordham, SD	2001	S (U)
BIG STONE (Graceville)	New Elm Spring, SD	1956	S (2)
ELMENDORF (Mountain Lake)	Upland, SD	1998	S (U)
HAVEN (Dexter)	Rolland, SD	1989	S (1)
HEARTLAND (Lake Benton)	Plainview, SD	1996	S (2)
LISMORE (Clinton)	Big Stone, MN	2004	S (2)
NEUHOF (Mountain Lake)	various colonies	1994	S (1)
SPRING PRAIRIE (Hawley)	White Rock, SD	1980	S (2)
STARLAND (Gibbon)	Pembrook, SD	1993	S (1)

MISSOURI

COLONY (Missouri)	PARENT	YEAR	LEUT
GRAND RIVER (Gallatin)	Elmendorf, MN	2014	S (U)

MONTANA

COLONY (Montana)	PARENT	YEAR	LEUT
AYERS RANCH (Grass Range)	Kings Ranch, MT	1945	D
BIG SKY (Cut Bank)	Milford, MT	1978	L
BIG STONE (Sand Coulee)	Cascade, MT	1986	L

COLONY (Montana)	PARENT	YEAR	LEUT
BIRCH CREEK (Valier)	New Elm, AB	1948	L
CAMROSE (Ledger)	East End, MT	2002	L
CASCADE (Sun River)	Glacier, MT	1969	L
DEERFIELD (Lewistown)	Wolf Creek, AB	1947	D
DUNCAN RANCH (Harlowtown)	Birch Creek, MT	1963	L
EAGLE CREEK (Galata)	Rimrock, MT	1982	L
EAST END (Havre)	Hilldale, MT	1977	L
EAST MALTA (Malta)	Turner, MT	1981	D
ELK CREEK (Augusta)	Milford, MT	2010	L
FAIR HAVEN (Ulm)	Duncan Ranch, MT	1980	L
FLAT WILLOW RANCH (Roundup)	Kings Ranch, MT	1980	D
FORDS CREEK (Grass Range)	Ayers, MT	1980	D
FORTY MILE (Lodge)	Spring Creek, MT	1980	D
GILDFORD (Gilford)	Deerfield, MT	1974	D
GŁACIER (Cut Bank)	Elm Spring, AB	1951	L
GLENDALE (Cut Bank)	New Rockport, MT	1969	L
GOLDEN VALLEY (Ryegate)	Springdale, MT	1978	L
HARTLAND (Havre)	Hilldale, MT	1999	L
HIDDEN LAKE (Cut Bank)	Big Sky, MT	1996	L
HILLCREST (Power)	Springdale, MT	2013	L
HILLDALE (Havre)	Rockport, MT	1963	L
HILLSIDE (Sweetgrass)	Sunnyside, AB	1951	L
HORIZON Hillside	MT	2012	L
KILBY BUTTE (Roundup)	Fords Creek, MT	1992	D
KINGS RANCH (Lewistown)	Beadle, SD	1935	D
KINGSBURY (Vanier)	Miller, MT	1981	L
LORING (Loring)	North Harlem, MT	1982	D
MARTINSDALE (Martinsdale)	New Miami, MT	1959	L
MIDWAY (Conrad)	Miller, MT	2008	L
MILFORD (Wolf Creek)	Milford, AB	1947	L
MILLER (Choteau)	O.K., AB	1949	L
MOUNTAIN VIEW (Broadview)	Golden Valley, MT	2002	L
NEW MIAMI (Conrad)	Miami, AB	1948	L
NEW ROCKPORT (Choteau)	New Rockport, AB	1948	L
NORTH HARLEM (Harlem)	Deerfield, MT	1960	D
PLEASANT VALLEY (Belt)	New Rockport, MT	1989	L
PONDERA (Vanier)	Birch Creek, MT	1994	L

COLONY (Montana)	PARENT	YEAR	LEUT
PRAIRIE ELK (Wolf Point)	Surprise Creek, MT	2006	D
RIM ROCK (Sunburst)	Hillside, MT	1963	L
RIVERVIEW (Chester)	Sage Creek, MT	1980	L
ROCKPORT (Pendroy)	Rockport, AB	1948	L
SAGE CREEK (Chester)	Miller, MT	1960	L
SEVILLE (Cut Bank)	Rockport, MT	1983	L
SPRING CREEK (Lewistown)	Wolf Creek, SD	1912	D
SPRINGDALE (White Sulphur)	Milford, MT	1959	L
SPRINGWATER (Harlowtown)	Martinsdale, MT	1982	L
SUNNY BROOK (Chester)	Riverview, MT	2010	L
SURPRISE CREEK (Stanford)	Kings Ranch, MT	1963	D
TURNER (Turner)	Ayers, MT	1959	D
TWIN HILLS (Carter)	Glendale, MT	2002	L
ZENITH	Glacier, MT	2011	L

NORTH DAKOTA

COLONY (North Dakota)	PARENT	YEAR	LEUT
FAIRVIEW (La Moue)	Rockport, SD	1984	S (2)
FOREST RIVER (Fordville)	New Rosedale, MB	1950	S (2)
GRANT (Enderlin)	Deerfield, SD	branching	S (2)
MAPLE RIVER (Fullerton)	Blumengarth, SD	1969	S (2)
SPRUCE LANE (Blanchard)	Millbrook, SD	branching	S (1)
SUNDALE (Milnor)	Spring Creek, ND	1985	S (2)
WHEATLAND	Fairview, SD	2013	S (2)
WILLOW BANK (Edgely)	Fairview, ND	1985	S (2)
WOLLMAN RANCH (Elgin)	Ayers Ranch, MT	2000	D

SOUTH DAKOTA

COLONY (South Dakota)	PARENT	YEAR	LEUT
BLUMENGARD (Faulkton)	Blumengart, MB	1952	S (2)
BON HOMME (Tabor)	Russia-Ukraine	1874	S (2)
BRENTWOOD (Faulkton)	Thunderbird, SD	1987	S (1)
CAMERON (Viborg)	Rosedale, SD	2010	S (2)
CAMROSE (Frankfort)	Glendale, SD	2010	S (2)
CEDAR GROVE (Platte)	Bon Homme, SD	1972	S (2)
CLAREMONT (Castlewood)	Poinsett, SD	1995	S (2)

COLONY (South Dakota)	PARENT	YEAR	LEUT
CLARK (Raymond)	Jamesville, SD	1955	S (2)
CLEARFIELD (Delmont)	Greenwood, SD	1996	S (2)
COLLINS (Iroquois)	Spink, SD	2010	S (2)
DEERFIELD (Ipswich)	Plainview, SD	1971	S (2)
EVERGREEN (Faulkton)	Blumengard, SD	1992	S (2)
FORDHAM (Carpenter)	Huron, SD	1974	S (1)
GLENDALE (Frankfort)	Bon Homme, SD	1949	S (2)
GOLDENVIEW (Salem)	Cedar Grove, SD	2013	S (2)
GRACEVALE (Winnfred)	Tschetter, SD	1948	S (2)
GRASSLAND (Westport)	Long Lake, SD	1990	S (2)
GRASS RANCH (Kimball)	Platte, SD	1990	S (2)
GREENWOOD (Delmont)	Jamesville, SD	1970	S (2)
HILLCREST (Garden City)	Riverside, SD	1979	S (2)
HILLSIDE (Doland)	Huron, SD	1961	S (2)
HURON (Huron)	Jamesville, SD	1936	S (2)
HUTTERVILLE (Stratford)	Spink, SD	1982	S (1)
JAMESVILLE (Utica)	Roseisle, MB	1936	S (2)
LAKE VIEW (Lake Andes)	Maxwell, SD	1988	S (2)
LONG LAKE (Westport)	Pearle Creek, SD	1967	S (2)
MAXWELL (Scotland)	New Elm Spring, SD	1949	S (2)
MAYFIELD (Willow Lake)	Clark, SD	1987	S (2)
MILLBROOK (Mitchell)	Rosedale, SD	1982	S (1)
MILLERDALE (Miller)	Milltown, SD	1949	S (2)
NEW ELM SPRING (Ethan)	Maxwell, MB	1936	S (2)
NEWDALE (Elkton)	Hillside, SD	1979	S (1)
NEWPORT (Claremont)	Deerfield, SD	1988	S (2)
NORFELD (White)	Spring Valley, SD	2010	S (2)
OAK LANE (Alexandria)	Rockport, SD	1986	S (2)
OLD ELM SPRING (Parkston)	New Elm Spring, SD	1998	S (2)
ORLAND (Montrose)	Jamesville, SD	1995	S (2)
PEARL CREEK (Iroquois)	Huron, SD	1949	S (2)
PEMBROOK (Ipswich)	Tschetter, SD	1974	S (2)
PLAINVIEW (Leola)	Spink, SD	1957	S (2)
PLATTE (Platte)	Bon Homme, SD	1949	S (2)
PLEASANT VALLEY (Flandreau)	Big Stone, MN	1977	S (2)
POINSETT (Estelline)	New Elm Spring, SD	1968	S (2)
RED WILLOW (Toronto)	Riverside, SD	branching	S (2)

COLONY (South Dakota)	PARENT	YEAR	LEUT
RIVERSIDE (Huron)	Rockport, SD	1948	S (2)
ROCKPORT (Alexandria)	Bon Homme, SD	1934	S (2)
ROLLAND (White)	Gracevale, SD	1978	S (2)
ROSEDALE (Mitchell)	Rockport, SD	1945	S (1)
RUSTIC ACRES (Madison)	Wolf Creek, SD	2003	S (2)
SHAMROCK (Carpenter)	Huron, SD	2002	S (2)
SHANNON (Winfred)	Rockport, SD	2010	S (2)
SILVER LAKE	Hillcrest, SD	2011	S (2)
SPINK (Frankfort)	Bon Homme, SD	1945	S (2)
SPRING CREEK (Forbes, ND)	Maxwell, SD	1964	S (2)
SPRING LAKE (Arlington)	Wolf Creek, SD	1978	S (2)
SPRING VALLEY (Wessington)	Platte, SD	1964	S (2)
SUNSET (Britton)	Glendale, SD	1977	S (2)
TSCHETTER (Olivet)	Barrickman, MB	1941	S (2)
THUNDERBIRD (Wecota)	Glendale, SD	1964	S (1)
UPLAND (Artesian)	Spring Valley, SD	1988	S (2)
WESTWOOD (Britton)	Newport, SD	2010	S (2)
WHITE ROCK (Rosholt)	Rosedale, SD	1968	S (2)
WOLF CREEK (Olivet)	Tschetter, SD	1964	S (2)

WASHINGTON/OREGON

COLONY (Washington/Oregon)	PARENT	YEAR	LEUT
MARLIN (Marlin, WA)	Pincher Creek, AB	1974	D
SCHOONOVER (Odessa, WA)	Spring Creek, MT	1979	D
SPOKANE (Reardan, WA)	Pincher Creek, AB	1960	D
STAHL H.B. (Ritzville, WA)	Huxley, AB	1980	D
STANFIELD (Stanfield, OR)	Stahl H.B., WA	2008	D
WARDEN (Warden, WA)	Spokane, WA	1972	D

Note

1. Leut/Group designations:

    D...........Dariusleut
    L...........Lehrerleut
    S (1) ......Schmiedeleut (Group One)
    S (2)......Schmiedeleut (Group Two)
    S (U).....Schmiedeleut (Unaffiliated)

Appendix 2

HUTTERITE COLONY BRANCHING

The Branching Process from James Valley

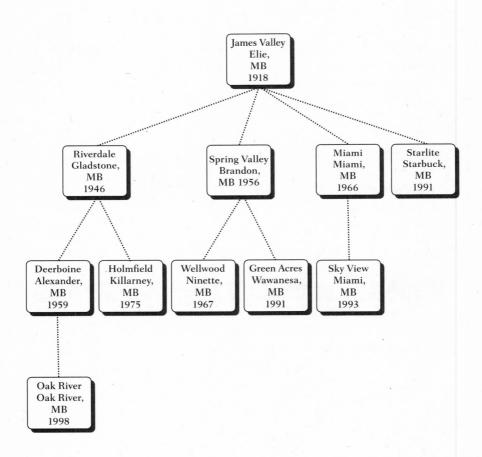

Appendix 3

DEMOGRAPHIC ANALYSIS
of SCHMIEDELEUT COLONIES

The Schmiedeleut Family Record, 2003, is a very detailed genealogy record that is updated annually. It is a rich source of demographic information about the Hutterite population. At our request, Amichai Feigenboim analyzed the data for the 180 Schmiedeleut colonies in North America as of 2003.[1] These Schmiedeleut colonies constituted about 38% of the then 474 Hutterite colonies in North America. The Schmiedeleut then numbered about 18,000 people.

Age at Marriage, 1890–2003

1. Average age at marriage: 24.
2. Average age at marriage—men: 25.
3. Average age at marriage—women: 24.
4. 90% of the population gets married between the ages of 19 to 29.
5. The average age of marriage has increased between 1890 and 2003, as shown below:

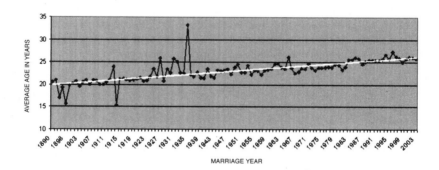

GRAPH 1. Average age at marriage, 1890–2003

X = year of marriage; Y = average age

CONCLUSIONS: The age of marriage is relatively high in the Hutterite community compared to other traditional societies.

The increase in the age of marriage throughout the years has been affected by the outside world.

Family Size, 1884–2003

1. The average number of children per family: 6.
2. The number of children in the largest family: 22.
3. The number of children in the smallest family: 1.
4. In 70% of the families there are 3–9 children, in 39% of the families there are 4–6 children.
5. A decrease in the time between births in the family can be identified throughout the years, as shown in the following diagram:

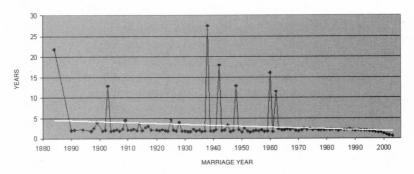

GRAPH 2. Average Interval between Births, 1880–2003

X = year of marriage; Y = average time in years between children

Throughout the years, there is a decline in the number of children per family, as shown in the following diagram:

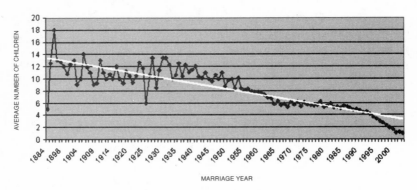

GRAPH 3. Number of children per family, 1884–2003

X = year of marriage; Y = average number of children

Premature Births/Premarital Conceptions, 1891–2003

1. Average number of weeks between marriage and the birth of the first child: 78.

2. 12% of the firstborns were born before the 35th week after marriage.

3. The number of the firstborns born before the 35th week after marriage increases with time, as shown in the following diagram:

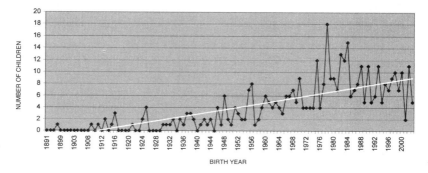

GRAPH 4. The number of firstborns born before
the 35th week after marriage, 1891–2003

X = year of birth; Y = number of children

4. In 74% of the years since the Schmiedeleut settled in North America, there were firstborns who were born before the 35th week after marriage. Since 1945, no year has passed without such births occurring.

5. The relative percentage of early firstborns out of all firstborns at a certain year indicates an almost fixed inclination—a very small rate of growth, as shown in the following diagram:

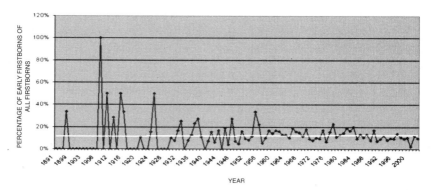

GRAPH 5. Percentage of births before
the 35th week after marriage, 1891–2003

X = year of birth; Y = percentage

CONCLUSION: In spite of the religious prohibition against sex before marriage, premarital pregnancy occurs. This phenomenon increases quantitatively and not relatively as we are nearing the present (see regulations of 1985 in Appendix 5; regulation 5 of 1988; regulations 1, 2 of 1990; regulations 1, 3 of 2002; regulations 1, 2 of 2003; regulation 15 of 2004).

Percentage of Children Under 15 in Colonies[2]

1. A total of 23% of the Hutterite population is under the age of 15

2. In 86% of the colonies, children are more than 17% of the population.

3. In one colony (Rainbow, Manitoba), there are no children today (according to the Hutterite definition).

4. A correlation was found between the year of the colony's establishment and the average percentage of children in the colony. The younger the colony, the more children in the colony, as shown in the following diagram:

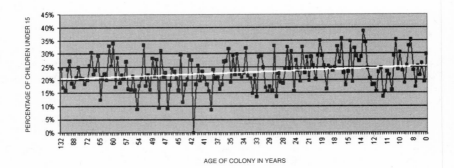

GRAPH 6. Percentage of children in the colony
in relation to the colony's age

X = colony's age; Y = percentage

Branching of Colonies[3]

1. Each colony branches on average once in 31 years.

2. 46% of the colonies have branched at least once. One colony has branched eight times.

3. The shortest period before branching occurred was one year after the colony's establishment.

4. The longest period before branching occurred was 98 years after the colony's establishment.

5. 76% of the colonies branch within 13 to 49 years.

6. The average time between colony branching is 17 years.[4]

7. The younger the colony, the longer it takes before first branching.

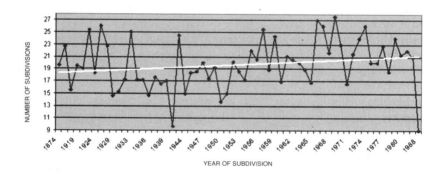

GRAPH 7. Branching of colonies, 1874–1988
$X = year;$ $Y = number \ of \ subdivisions$

CONCLUSIONS:

a. The economic burden of a colony's branching becomes heavier each year.

b. The actual execution of branching is a task that carries with it an advantage of seniority.

Colony Defections, 1842–1976[5]

1. The average percentage of defectors from a colony is 18.

2. Since 1919, there have been defections every year.

3. Since 1919, defection rates increased.

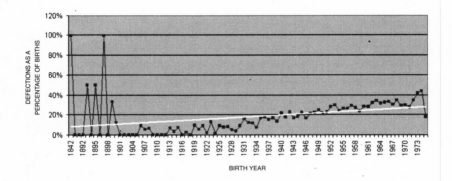

GRAPH 8. Colony defections as a percentage
of natural increases by year

X = year of birth; Y = defectors as a percentage of births

Distances Between Parent and Daughter Colonies[6]

1. The average distance between a parent colony and its daughter colony is 167 km.

2. The shortest distance measured between a parent colony and its daughter colony is 3 km.

3. The longest distance between a parent colony and its daughter colony is 1,454 km (from South Dakota to Alberta, Canada).

4. 90% of parent colonies are less than 392 km from their daughter colonies.

5. Over time, the average distance between the parent colony and the daughter colony has decreased, as shown in the following diagram:

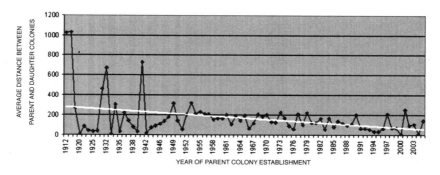

GRAPH 9. Average distance between parent and daughter colonies by year of parent colony establishment

X = year of parent colony establishment; Y = average distance

Notes

1. Mrs. Nikola Goldschmit entered the data.
2. According to the Hutterites, any colony member under 15 is a child.
3. Mr. Ian Gorsky helped with entering data.
4. When a colony branches for the first time, it is the time elapsed between its establishment and its first branching, but from the second branching, it is the time elapsed between the first and second branching.
5. The percentage of defectors is the ratio of newborns to defectors in any year.
6. Analysis based on colonies' distribution maps.

Appendix 4

A VISITOR'S PERSPECTIVE

DAN KATZ WAS a religiously observant Israeli teenaged guest in the Schmiedeleut colonies in May 2004. He accompanied his parents, Ruthie and Yossi Katz, on one of their visits to the Hutterite colonies. Dan was 15 years old at the time. At his father's request, he wrote down his impressions immediately after the visit, printed here in an essay entitled "Behind the Scenes: The Impressions of Dan Katz." Seven years later, Dan returned to the James Valley Hutterite Colony. The second essay in Appendix 4, entitled "Coming Full Circle: James Valley Hutterite Colony, Spring 2011," is Dan's account of that second visit, this time from the perspective of a married man in his twenties.

BEHIND THE SCENES:
THE IMPRESSIONS OF DAN KATZ

THE DAILY ROUTINE of the members of James Valley starts at 6:30 a.m., after they wake up, organize themselves and go to breakfast at 7:00 a.m. After breakfast, at 8:00 a.m., the adults (15 years old and up) begin their daily work, while the children younger than 15 years go to school until 3:30 p.m., and then they help with the simpler tasks (working in the garden, chicken coop, etc.). The adults have a tea break of 20–30 minutes at 9:30 a.m., and afterwards they resume their work until 11:30 a.m., when it's lunch time. After eating lunch, they take a break until 1:00 p.m. Then they continue to work until 2:30 p.m., when they have another coffee break, and again work resumes until 5:45 p.m., the time of the evening prayer service in church, which lasts for half an hour. The service is followed by dinner, and after dinner they finish everything that needs to be finished at work. at 9:00 p.m. the workday is completed. In the evening they usually visit friends in the colony or in other colonies. Bedtime depends on how tired they feel or upon their mood.

As an active worker, I also shared the social life of the workers (both young and adult), the jokes, hardships, grievances and all the usual things that arise during a normal workday. My job was to work in the dairy barn: feed the cows and the calves, make sure that they all had enough straw, help with the milking of the cows three times a day, and other such tasks. Working in a Hutterite colony means working without pay, for the benefit of society. The workers work for free, in exchange for food and residence given to them by the colony. Although one may think that because they are not paid, they will neglect their work and will not do it properly, it is not so. I have never seen such devoted workers, arriving on time, answering every call and trying to do their work the best they could. Also, some of the significance of such work is that you don't really have a regular job. Everyone knows where he is supposed to be at 8:00 each morning, but his job is not regular, and whenever he is called through the intercom to do something else or help someone, he immediately goes to answer the call. For example, the guy I worked with in the barn, for whom this work was his regular job, was also responsible for a tractor, and every time he finished some task in the barn, he took his tractor and went to do something else: move straw, sand, etc.

During the breaks, I spent time with one of the workers, about 18 years old, and every time I sat with his family, I heard another Bible story, or was asked questions about Judaism—why we do things this or that way. It was nice to listen to stories about characters you know, or be at the centre of things and be surprised that there are people who are interested in Judaism, even more than some Jews are. But after some time it started to be crazy; it seemed as if they try to convince me how good it is to be a Christian and why it is worthwhile, and what will happen to me if I try following another religion and stuff like that, but I already decided that I am quite happy with what I am and they cannot change anything. Personally, I admire them for working so hard, and for how they manage to keep their children away from the bad things outside: television, internet, radio, etc., and at the same time advance so much technologically in order to increase their profits from agriculture. I also admire greatly their hospitality; at least to judge from our reception in James Valley. People told us that it has never happened that outsiders stayed in the colony for more that two or three days, therefore I was very impressed with the attention we received. I was almost never left alone.

Slowly, I grasped the work I had to perform, and advanced from being a timid boy regarding a cow with apprehension, to letting the calves suck at my fingers. I fell in love with the work, the farm and everything in it, from driving the various tractors to helping in the carpentry shop, from sowing to daring to enter the pig barn and look at the pigs.

After the long, tiring, but enjoyable workday, you go into the shower and get ready for the last part of the day—gathering with the guys with a bottle of Coke in one hand and some chips (kosher) in the other, and full of answers for the questions I might be asked. In theory, after 9:00 p.m. everyone can spend their time as they wish. Some go to visit friends, some study or read the Bible, and some go straight to bed. I was with the first group. At the beginning, every night I went somewhere else, always with the guy I worked with in the barn. Later, I stayed in one place, and it seemed to me that the guys easily find out where all the action takes place, and they all arrive there together. At the beginning, there were all the regular questions: "Is it kosher?" "Why are you wearing a skullcap?" or, "Can I, too, be a rabbi and make that bacon kosher?" I answer all the questions patiently, and after an evening or two, they already become half Jewish and I become the first Hutterite Jew in history. Then, when people start to arrive, the questions take another direction: about home, friends and Israel, why we are at war all the time, etc. Sometimes I feel as if I am banging my head against an imaginary wall when I don't know what to say to them. They don't understand why we are like that, and I don't fully understand them. Little by little, we all come to understand that we have a different belief and outlook and there is no point in arguing, and we can also speak of more enjoyable things. That's why I loved these gatherings. On the one hand, they are less curious than the adults are about the way we are, for I am a boy like them, and therefore there was no problem, no troubling questions. On the other hand, it was fun to spend time with them and see what interests them, and really there are not many differences. For example, they are also interested in sports. Indeed, they don't know much about world sports, but they are still interested in baseball and hockey games, like regular Canadian boys, and they are also curious about places in the world they would like to visit, but they can't because they are Hutterites and this is not something a Hutterite is allowed to do.

In my visits in houses and rooms of Hutterite boys, I wasn't surprised to find out that there are some deviations from what they are allowed to keep in their rooms. Each boy receives at the age of 15 a closet with a key where he can keep everything he wants. The laws in the colony forbid to them keep all sorts of "spoiling" stuff, such as cameras, radios, iPods, CDs, pictures, etc. When I saw all these things in their rooms, I wasn't surprised at all. I wonder what the elders of the colony really · think about such laws that forbid the keeping of stuff like that, when facing an influence from the outside world that penetrates under the wall put up by the colony. The world is going forward, they must understand this, and with it all sorts of bad things enter the colony, so why be surprised when you find such things in the closets of the boys and girls? And if they are not allowed to keep forbidden things, why are they given a closet with a key, to keep all this stuff so that nobody finds it? What's the reason behind this? The elders of the colony must consider this earnestly. I believe they are right to be blocking the Internet and television, but what's wrong with a Discman with quiet country music, or a camera to remind you of good moments?

The issue of the wristwatch also makes me crazy. What's wrong about a simple wristwatch, showing the time? In any case, they wear the wristwatch whenever the elders are not around, so why does it matter?

In each closet I was shown there were photos of friends, cassettes and cameras. Also, in the last evening I spent with them, one of the boys came to me with a sophisticated camera and said that he bought it in the nearby town and he must take my picture as a souvenir, so what's wrong with that? Why is it so hard to understand that the prohibition in the Bible "Thou shalt make no graven images" speaks about idolatry and not about a photo taken with a new Nikon camera in 2004? There were no cameras 4,000 years ago, and even if they say that God knew what would be 4,000 years later, there is no connection between the prohibition and taking pictures as souvenirs.

Personally, I enjoyed very much being in the farm, experiencing a different lifestyle, getting to know a different and interesting society, and seeing how much we are alike in spite of the differences. I represent their side of the story. I have seen things from a different angle, from behind the scenes of the adults, those who know everything and hold everything in their hands. Behind them, there are those who want to enjoy life. Indeed, they do enjoy themselves very much even under the present circumstances, but they hide too much and it's a pity, because it destroys the "togetherness" of the Hutterite colony.

I promised them that I would be back in about 10 years, maybe earlier. I hope very much that it will really happen, because I enjoyed my visit tremendously and I would like to repeat it again in James Valley.

—Dan Katz, Efrat, Israel 2004

Coming Full Circle

James Valley Hutterite Colony, Spring 2011

I FIRST VISITED JAMES VALLEY COLONY when I was only 14, and received the nickname "the first Jewish Hutterite." Seven years later, now married, and immediately after I finished my army service, my parents invited my wife Hadar and me to join them for another visit to James Valley Colony. Of course, we were delighted to do so. Even though we did maintain some telephone contact from time to time I was very keen to see how my friends there were doing after all those years. Hadar was also anxious to finally see all those people she has heard so much about from me and my parents. She was also curious to see how people can live such a secluded life in the modern world, and how they succeed in raising children in the face of all the challenges that threaten their customs and values. And, of course, she was curious as to how they manage their economy: making their own clothes and linens, preparing their wholesome foods and being remarkably self-sufficient.

Unlike Hadar, who heard much about the Hutterites but had not met them, my parents and I were already well-acquainted with Hutterite life. We were all looking forward to this visit, wishing to discover a deeper level of their culture and to learn more about their everyday life, and therefore we looked out for small details that show the inevitable clash between the Hutterite way of life and the modern world.

Our visit was scheduled for the spring, when the Canadian prairies and especially the Hutterite colonies start to emerge from a long winter, and the prairies are wet with the snow-melt.

When we arrived at the airport, we were warmly received by the family of the colony's minister, John Hofer. Naturally, there is no such thing as a trip from the colony that has only one purpose, even if it is for meeting visitors—no matter how important they are. Driving out of the colony involves cost of fuel, and therefore the trip should be used for performing other tasks as well. Such was the case with us. We joined our hosts in running additional errands in Winnipeg—buying kosher food for us, purchasing fabrics for the women of the colony, closing deals with a regional tractor company, and also taking advantage of a local factory's liquidation sale to buy items at bargain prices.

When we finally arrived at the colony everybody was glad to see us. People were coming and going in and out of the minister's house, and every few minutes some member of the colony, of various levels of acquaintance, came to see an unusual sight in a Manitoba prairie colony—visitors from Israel.

My close friend William, with whom I spent much of my time during my last visit seven years ago, was very happy to see me again. He introduced us to his wife and one-year-old daughter. Together with him, and his sister Rhoda, we spent our time in the colony. They took us on a tour of the colony to show Hadar what a Hutterite colony is like. I enjoyed seeing the colony again and was glad to notice the progress it had made since my last visit.

Hadar was greatly impressed by the exemplary order and cleanliness, the smooth operation of the colony, the large dining halls, the efficient production methods and all the foods preserved and stored in the kitchen's basement. She was also impressed by the colony's organization and discipline—everybody knows exactly what he or she should do every minute, and there is no open or hidden unemployment. Everybody works.

We saw the new technologies adopted by the colony. Hutterites insist on uncompromising progress in everything that is connected to production and marketing. The colony employs a computer specialist, whose task is to handle all computer systems and to deal with the technological connections of the colony, and provides him with a technologically advanced office. This person was not born a Hutterite but is a rare example of someone who has joined their ranks and married into Hutterite society. The Hutterites are very satisfied with his expertise. Now every workshop in the colony has advanced and powerful computers operated by well-trained workers who monitor and control production.

During my last visit to the colony I was shown the locked chests that all youths receive when they reach fifteen years of age. In this chest they keep all the objects they are not allowed to possess according to Hutterite rules: cameras, a *Discman*, photographs, and so forth. I was wondering then to my father and myself how the colony leaders expect the youth to keep the rules if they give them access to such a chest. It is clear that a youngster in the colony, as every other youngster in the world, will want to push the boundaries.

Today, with rapid technological progress and the options for sharing on-line information, everyone owning a computer can connect to everything that happens outside the Hutterite colony with the push of a button. When we were invited to watch the powerful computer that controls the whole production of feed mix in the colony, we met its operator, whom I recognized from my former visit—William's brother. His job then was to weld iron, but today he sits in his own office, working on the computer on plans for iron welding. He manages client contacts through a Google mailbox. He showed us proudly his private mailbox, and how it can be used for sending him photographs from the Holy Land.

I noticed that another friend of mine, Derek, was no longer on the colony. When we met in 2004, he was 12 years old. In 2011 as a young man of 19, he decided community life no longer suited him, and left the colony to live in a large city. I was surprised to hear that the slim boy I remembered from my visit had spread his wings, but I was told that it is a well-known phenomenon, and usually the young people that leave the colony return to it after they realize how complex the world outside is. Later, we were told, he did return to the colony.

Derek's younger brother, a high school student, showed us his "school"—a small room containing a table and a chair, equipped with an advanced internet camera and a screen, which are connected to a shared educational system operated by the regional education authority. Sitting in this room every day, he participates in a virtual class, and receives a full education from teachers of the whole region through the Internet.

The day after we arrived we received great honor when our friends, William and Rhoda, took a day off and received a vehicle from the colony to take us for a visit to colonies in the area. As we know, this is not usual.

Hadar noticed that William was given some cash from the colony for the day's expenses, and he made a great effort to spend it all on us. We realized having cash is not something that a Hutterite experiences very often. William wanted very much to buy Kosher wine, so that we could all have a glass of wine together in the evening.

Another innovation I noticed during this visit was the arrival of the cell phone. Until a few years ago only the minister had a telephone line. Today, every vehicle that leaves the colony, as well as key people in the colony, are all given cell phones.

We visited many colonies in the area; each shares the common characteristics of the Hutterite community. Yet, at the same time, each is unique. Differences are created by each colony's financial state and their economic enterprises. For example, Sommerfeld colony specializes in the design and manufacture of amazing wood furniture, another colony has an aluminum plant, and a third colony operates a new plant for manufacturing using lasers. Our trip was long but interesting, and we felt that our hosts wished to show us as much as possible, in order to share more of their life with us, but also because they wished to stretch the day as much as they could before they returned to everyday life in the colony.

In the evening—as I remembered from my last visit—real life begins. Each age group assembles at some place and enjoys a pleasant social evening. Our visit certainly contributed to the fun.

We arrived at the house of George, the brother of William and Rhoda. He is also married with a few kids. We shared with them our experiences and taught them how to play *Taki* (a card game), and at the end of the evening left it with them as a present. Each Hutterite is allowed to take pictures only once in his life, and keep them. They do it on their wedding day. It was very important for them to show us their photo album from their wedding, and they even gave us one photograph of the couple as a souvenir.

During the evening some discussions arose about the common and different characteristics of our life as observant Jews, in comparison to their life as Christian Hutterites. The main issues that were discussed involved relations between couples and intimacy. It seems that these issues reveal that we have a lot in common, for instance, abstention from sexual relationships before the wedding, matchmaking customs, raising children, etc.

Our hosts were very anxious to hear about my service in the Israeli army. We brought with us a laptop full of short films and pictures from the army and some of our wedding, and these generated a lot of interest. The Hutterites are pacifists, but they enjoyed seeing the military pictures that are part of Israeli cultural life, and we tried to convince them of our need to defend ourselves in the Promised Land.

Meal time in the colony is a very social time. In addition to serving plenty of superb dishes, it is used for meaningful community discussions, mainly among the women. The minister's wife sits in her house, her dining room window open to the colony's center, and from there she manages the whole colony. Women have apparent power in the colony—not because of their work, but by virtue of their influence on their husbands and the respect shown to them by all the men.

After three days full of experiences we gathered on Friday at the minister's house to say goodbye. Women from the colony arranged for us a spontaneous farewell ceremony, consisting of Hutterite religious songs. We even "sang" in sign language, which the Hutterites in James Valley know well because they have children suffering from deafness at birth, the result of inter-marriage over generations. In response we sang the Jewish grace to them after meals.

Based on our experience from our former visit, this time we brought with us two giant bags, for we knew that one does not leave James Valley empty-handed. We are used to living in a world were everything is synthetic and artificial, so we were glad to receive some original wedding presents. During our stay at the colony the women sewed for us a full double bedding set from the fabrics we bought in Winnipeg on the day we arrived, and they even showed us the goose feathers that filled the down comforter and the pillows that they insisted that we should take home with us. They tried to teach Hadar how to sew, in order to turn her into a real Jewish Hutterite woman, but failed!

Every friend and acquaintance we met during our visit came to say goodbye and gave us a farewell present. We promised to meet again in the future. We returned home to Israel full of experiences. One question remains unanswered, however: Is it really possible and/or desirable to totally shield our children from the influence of the outside world?

Dan Katz
Israel, 2013

Appendix 5

ORDINANCES AND CONFERENCE LETTERS
OF THE SCHMIEDELEUT,

1762–2012

Translated from the German by Robyn Sneath,
Adrian Vannahme, and David Fuss.

THE NUMBERS IN square brackets refer to the page number in the original German-language manuscript. English words in the original are italicized. All underlining is as in the original manuscript.

To exclude financial details of colony affairs and to protect the privacy of individuals the authors of this book have lightly edited this document. Some commentary dealing with sensitive personal material is summarized.

[1] **This is a Collection of the Ordinances that still apply and are still in effect.**

IN THE YEAR 1762 the servants of the Word, Mathias Kleinsasser and Joseph Kleinsasser, brought this proclaimed ordinance of the congregation, given by Maertel Roth, teacher of Alwinz in Siebenburg, to us on an old paper, which was most diligently recorded in the year 1781.

1) **Quiet and Modest among one another.** Each one ought to consider why it is to be this way and why the Lord ordered it that way.

So that his own would know what is ordered of them, and whom they are serving, namely, the Lord in heaven and his own in the congregation. And because God, through counsel and knowledge of his own, arranged each one in its place, that each might be compatible and friendly, not gossipy or fractious in the kitchen, neither at the table, nor anywhere, rather that each would lead a quiet and modest life, as is befitting the brothers and sisters, that they might serve as a good example or role model.

2) **Servants of the Word [Ministers].** The servants are not appointed to rule, to berate, or to drive over the Lord's heirs with force, rather to be humble, friendly, and kind to each. For what has been given into their hands is not theirs, but belongs to the Lord and the godly, so that they should handle and deal with things in the way that they will have to answer before the Lord.

The servant should also take diligent care to handle his position as one who goes ahead of the congregation, which was commanded to him by God and the congregation.

Because we are your servants of the Word, you are our helpers in the service of the congregation's temporal needs, who hold the congregation's possessions in your hands, the first of which is...

3) The position of Manager [*Haushalter*]

A. He must see to it that the needs all throughout the congregation are brought to the attention of the congregation and cared for in a timely matter. And also that everything in the kitchen is laid out in the most faithful manner and given out for the corporate benefit and that the people are cared for. Therefore he should see all positions as equal and watch so that each one fulfills his command, service, and post with a well-disposed attitude.

B. He should go into the kitchen himself to look at the lights and the hearths in order to see how they are being cared for and to ensure that they are all being kept in good condition.

He should also go into the kitchen to look in on the cook to see that she uses the lard, eggs, cabbage, meat, and other food sparingly and that she doesn't give out wood according to her own will rather that she approaches it with the fear of God.

And also warn the one who cares for the cattle not to spill the milk and the seamstress not to be negligent with the cloth or the garments and the baker not to give out soft bread according to her favour, to whomever she chooses, for it is not her duty to divide, but to bake.

C. [2] The manager should record all debts and debtors so that whether the account is with the rulers or other people, he will be able to deal on good ground and with a good conscience, so that no injustice occurs and so that one does not work toward loans and allow such big debts to accrue.

For a lot is placed on the manager, both to the benefit and the detriment of the congregation. If, however, a manager has trouble, and cannot get rid of it on account of having too much work, and goes from morning to night with no help, then he should let the *Farm Boss* or another brother know how the good of the congregation might be achieved through all of the work.

D. A manager should look in the barns daily and should care for them even at night, and should check with the watchmen to see how they are doing. He should also see how the cattle are being fed, especially regarding hay and straw, and he should also see to it that big expenses are not being employed for the cattle.

E. A manager should not accustom himself to sitting in solitary places. The manager should consult every evening with the *Farm Boss,* so that the work would be carried out at the right time and so that the people would be properly directed. And if it is difficult work then to share a drink, and to share the burden, so that the young people wouldn't be led to speak profanity.

F. The manager's assistants, such as the *Farm Boss,* should do all things with good counsel, nicely asking and nicely advisable, lest one go one place and one to another, for the people will see and out of it much good will occur if it is done in this way.

4) The Farm Boss's Position.

A. The Farm Boss should not go to bed until he has heard from the manager how he is to arrange all the subordinate people early the next morning. In summary, when he comes from the field or from his work, he is to pay diligent attention to the yard and to see to it that all that applies to industry such as the feeding pig and all the wagons are brought under the roof, so that nothing is ruined and nothing goes missing. He should also pay careful attention to rakes, ropes, ploughs, shovels and other little things so that nothing is ruined and nothing is stolen. The same is required of the shop because it takes a lot of money to buy things again.

B. The Farm Boss is required to coordinate the people for all of the work, and also to see to it that the work is carried out with faithfulness and diligence, and so that people do not take too many freedoms in the vineyard or the orchard.

C. The Farm Boss should also diligently consider that should the colony find itself in a position without enough food and drink because of poverty, he should not become impatient and speak about food, as people are wont to do, and be inclined to place blame and open one's mouth to gossip. Rather, out of compassion he should exhort people to have patience, and try to mitigate [3] the situation as he is able, and thereafter bring the matter forward in quietness with humility! For wherever the Bishop among a people begins to place blame and shows or demonstrates a poor example, then what are those to do who rely on him? He should also diligently help out around the house and be a good example to the people, and does everything that has been assigned to him in his God ordained position, and handle things according to the fear of God so that evil will no where arise.

5) **A Manager should seek counsel.** A manager should seek counsel from his elders and should not trust himself too much because an elder is not working for his own interests and because he diligently safeguards his position. In the same way the manager does not have freedom to pursue his own likes, a fact that the elders are expected to know.

6) **If the Manager should leave.** If the manager goes somewhere on account of the affairs of the colony, he should report to the minister and tell the purpose of the trip and also what needs to be purchased and should give his key to the minister, so that if something arises he can notify others about the need.[1]

7) **The Manager's account.** Every manager, if he goes somewhere on account of the affairs of the colony, must give a clear and precise account to the minister when he returns, regardless of whether it is small or large he should write down what he spent and what he took in.

8) **Ordering goods.** If something needs to be ordered, whether through an agent or by letter, the manager should not order anything without consulting the minister. Neither should a brother order anything without requesting permission from the manager.

9) **Lending Money.** If a credit note is to be signed, no manager should do so alone, rather the minister and the manager both. No large amounts of money are to be lent without the counsel of the colony. If, however, a note is to be renewed, it must be done with the knowledge of the witnesses. If, however, for a short period of time a small amount of money like $300.00 or $500.00 needs to be lent for an emergency, then the minister and the manger should do this together.

10) **Coats for Baptized Brethren.** All married and baptized brethren should receive from the congregation a coat worth about $5.00 or $6.00, and if after a time another needs to be purchased, then this should be a matter of general counsel.

11) **Spirits.** Every year, around harvest time, all souls over 15 years are to be given a quart of spirits.

12) **Linoleum.** The linoleum is to be simple, no longer speckled blue or other colours.

13) **Cradles.** [4] One should keep to the old practice, namely simple cradles with homemade rocking parts.

14) **Cloths and Shirts.** Regarding markings on cloths [headscarves] and shirts not so much pride is to be shown. A large woollen cloth should not have any markings larger than one inch long and for a head scarf the marking should not be more than half that size and for a common headscarf or shirt or other garment the markings should be smaller than half an inch and there should be no ornamentation other than the name and year. Current larger markings should not be unstitched but should be made dark.

15) **Aprons.** Aprons with borders should not be sanctioned, and the existing ones should be worn inside out. We are going to stay with the pressed aprons and no gingham or light coloured ones will be tolerated.

16) **Mailing Letters.** Letters that are to be mailed should be brought to the minister before the post, according to the old ordinance. Youth not yet baptized should not be allowed to send letters or packages in the mail, and the minister and the manager should examine whatever is sent to them in order to intercept unseemly things.

17) **Driving to go visiting** with one's own money, whether money earned from selling feathers or otherwise should not be allowed. If one wants to go driving and needs money, the matter ought to be discussed and permission sought with the deacons, and should happen with common money. But if one wishes to drive to Manitoba or Alberta, for visiting, then it ought to be decided by the whole colony.

18) **Wearing a Beard.** The Brothers should let their beards grow and not cut them too short, rather should remain as a Brother according to the old practice. That is the evidence of the obedient.

19) **Widows and orphans** should not be forgotten but should be kept equal through allowance.

20) **Taking Brethren into Counsel.** All married men should be accepted into the general counsel, as should all baptized single men when they are 25.

21) **When Runaways return.** If someone comes from the world and brings clothes with them, they ought to be used as work clothes and the clothes from the colony should serve as Sunday clothes.

22) **Mealtime at the Common Table.** Everyone who is able and not ill should come for meals and should not take out the food without cause.

23) **Shunning those who have fallen away.** Those who have been baptized and accepted into the congregation and then leave the congregation

again, they should be shunned and one should not shake their hand, neither should one embrace them, nor kiss them, nor eat with them.

24) [5] **Drinking at weddings.** It is recognized that if someone is not at home during a wedding or a pig slaughter, where wine or other drink is normally drunk, he is not allowed to take any home, unless he has gone out on the fields on account of the colony.

25) **Pocket watches.** It is recognized by the congregation that if someone has a pocket watch, he should bring it to the manager and he should sell it. They are not allowed. Only the Farm Boss is allowed to have a watch.

26) **Cook.** No one should take or carry anything out of the kitchen, unless it is a bucket, a spoon, or dishes. It should be seen to that things are run punctually and cleanly, and that not too much lard is used and that the food is prepared cleanly and expediently. The cook should also be faithful and diligent as is encouraged and she should not deal with people according to appearance but according to need and to distribute according to what the need demands. And she should pay special care and attention to the sick. And if the food carriers want something for sick children or the elderly then the cook should do what she can. And she should faithfully exhort her helpers that they should not gossip and laugh so much when they are together but should be peaceable toward one another and wherever a quarrel wishes to arise, they should speak nicely so that one cannot hear the yelling from far away.

27) **For the Food Servers or the Bread Cutters.**[2] He should pay careful attention to his position and diligently serve the people in the dining room and carry the food to the table with good will and should not try to use his subordinates for his own ends, rather during mealtimes he should remain in the dining room or the room so that one need not look long for him when it is mealtime.

The food carrier should also take the bread to the places. And after the meal the bread should not be left lying in the dining room on the tables and the benches but he should also see to it that not all the full slices or loaves are taken from the tables. Special attention should be given to this.

A carrier should pay careful attention to the people regarding gossiping, and should warn them and diligently speak to them if it is too loud, and should be careful to be humble around the Brothers and Sisters.

And he should pay careful attention to whatever he has in his hands, whether it is bread, meat, or salt. And if people from outside the congregation should come into the kitchen, then he should respectfully receive them.

The bread cutter should not slice the bread in too big of pieces and should carefully cover up the sliced bread lest spider webs should fall on it.

He should also not sneak anyone—neither from the outside nor from among us—into the bread house to drink.

[6] One must also pay careful attention to the baker that she does not bake too much bread, especially in summer, so that the bread doesn't get mouldy, but also not to wait too long so that one cannot eat the bread when it is warm and fresh, because great harm will come to the colony in both instances. The bread should be exchanged twice a week during the serious heat. And to wipe off the mouldy bread with a clean cloth through which diligence the bread might be protected. And when the bread cutter has finished his task then he should look around in the colony house to see if everything is being properly done and should honour his position.

THESE ORDINANCES WERE passed in the year 1927 on the Benard Colony in Canada by the elder, Joseph Kleinsasser, and several others of the then elders and ministers, and were then given over to the congregations in order to be verified and were thus accepted. Of the ordinances from that time some have been altered or lifted entirely. Those are not to be found here.

1876

1) **Taking Dishes out of the kitchen.** On March 24, 1876 it was recognized that no one should take anything out of the kitchen, except buckets, spoons, or other dishes.

2) **Mealtime at the Common Table.** It was also recognized that everyone should come to eat who is able and should not take out the food without cause.

1877

1) **Cousins marrying each other.** In August of 1877 it was recognized, through a majority of votes, that if two cousins find themselves together and wish to marry, then they should do that because there is no injunction against it in the Holy Scripture (see notice below).

Note: Our former godly Elders Joseph Kleinsasser and Joseph Waldner and the ministers before them determined that although there was no existing recorded ordinance regarding this matter, it is certain that the above ordinance was lifted in the year 1878 and was done so because of two important matters: 1. Because experience has taught us that it can be very detrimental to the offspring. 2. Because the law in South

Dakota (which was called Dakota Territory until 1889) strictly forbade it and still does and punishes it harshly.

And this decision made by the above-mentioned elders, was remembered by all of the elderly as long as they lived and remained in effect, and should serve for us all as [7] evidence that the marriage of cousins is still forbidden and should remain forbidden so that our race does not degenerate, and we be charged and punished by rulers as lawbreakers (This ordinance was again changed. See below: Marrying Relatives).

2) **Going to your brother before going to the Minister.** It was also decided that if someone wishes to go to the minister, before he does so he should go to obey the command of Christ and should rebuke his brother once or twice according to Matthew 18:15: "Moreover if thy brother shall trespass against thee, go and tell him his fault between thee and him alone: if he shall hear thee, thou hast gained thy brother."

1879

1) **Shunning those who have fallen away from the faith.** On May 26, 1879 it was decided that regarding those who were baptized and had been integrated into the congregation,[3] and then left the colony, one should not shake their hand, neither should one embrace them, nor kiss them, nor eat with them.

Note: This previously mentioned ordinance is often disobeyed. For those who disobey it read Ps. 50:21-22.

1883

1) **Horse Harnesses.** It was recognized that neither ivory rings nor red ribbons or bands should be allowed for horse harnesses.

1884

1) **Sending letters, postcards and keeping stamps.** It was decided that no one should send letters that have not been read by the manager or ministers.

Also, no one should keep a stock of stamps, envelopes or postcards, rather should get them from the minister or the manager.

2) **Opening Letters.** It was also decided that no one is allowed to open letters that have not been sent to them.

3) **Moustaches.** IT was decided that no brother is allowed to grow a moustache, much less grow one that curls.

4) **English clothing.** If someone comes from the world and brings clothes with them, they ought to be used as work clothes and are not to be spared. The clothes from the colony should serve as Sunday clothes.

[8] 1886

1) **Baby Carriages.**[4] On August 9 it was decided by the congregation that no baby carriages with four wheels are to be permitted.

1891

1) **Money received as Gifts.** On December 26 it was decided that whoever has received or receives money as a gift should give it over to the manager. 25 cents of that may be kept and used as allowance.

2) It was decided that **smoking or taking snuff or chewing tobacco etc.** must be stopped shortly.

1909

1) **Shirts without Creases.** It has been recognized by all of the colonies that shirts may be worn without creases. But no pockets should be put on the front to hold pencils etc., rather only plain shirts, just without creases.
  But if someone wishes to follow the old ordinance, he is free to do so.

2) **Children's caps.** Regarding children's caps the following has been decided: they may be made without a little peak in the front instead of the tuft. But also no roll caps are to be made. Also there are to be no brims or bands in different colours.

3) **Punishment for Youth.** It has been decided by the whole congregation that if unbaptized young people leave the colony and the congregation, the fathers may go after them once in order to bring them back.
  Then the father or another appointee from the brotherhood should bring the young man before the brotherhood in order to be punished. And that should also be his punishment for sex outside of marriage[5] and serious theft.

1911

1) **The ordinances that are still in effect for the manager.**

A. **Should the Manager leave.** If the manager goes somewhere on account of the affairs of the colony, he should report to the minister and tell the purpose of the trip.

B. **Purchases.** He should also report what needs to be purchased, and should leave his key at home with the minister.

C. **The Manager's account.** [9] Every manager, if he goes somewhere on account of the affairs of the colony, must give a clear and precise account to the minister when he returns. Regardless of whether it is small or large he should write down what he spent and what he took in.

D. **Ordering goods.** If something needs to be ordered, whether through an agent or by letter, the manager should not order anything without consulting the minister.

E. **Signing credit notes—lending money.** If a credit note is to be signed, no manager should do so alone, rather the minister and the manager both. No large amounts of money are to be lent without the counsel of the colony. If, however, a note is to be renewed, it must be done with the knowledge of the witnesses.

   If, however, for a short period of time a small amount of money such as $200 or $300 needs to be lent, then the minister and the manger should do this together.

F. **If the manager is sending someone somewhere.** The managers should notify the minister if they are sending someone somewhere on account of the business of the colony.

1917

1) **Purchased pelts.** On October 16 it was decided that small fur coats may be purchased for Brothers and boys, but not all kinds, only those which are compatible with the ordinances.

2) **Going to Funerals.** It has been decided that when traveling because of a funeral, one should travel by train with the ticket paid for by colony money. Funerals for one's father and mother, sister and brother, daughter-

in-law and son-in-law,[6] brother-in-law and sister-in-law and children are allowed, but not more.

Children traveling. In 1921 it was also decided that children should also be allowed to go along but only if it is the funeral of grandparents or siblings.

1921

1) **Hairstyles.** Each one should wear his hair as the Brothers are supposed to, and should wear it with a part. From the front the sides should be even with the eyes and half the ear should be exposed.

No tuft is allowed, and neither are layers.[7] If a Brother or son will not obey then he will be disciplined, and if necessary even as far as being sent to a different congregation.

2) **Christmas tree.** No Christmas tree should be set up. If, however, the teacher wishes to give the children some candy or whatever, then he may.

3) **Making spirits or wine.** Making spirits or schnapps or wine for one's personal use should be stopped entirely.

4) **Aprons** [10] with trim are not to be allowed, and those that are still in existence should be worn inside out until they are worn out.

5) *Fleckenschuhe.*[8] The decision was newly revived to stop purchasing these shoes.

6) **Shoes.** It was also decided that boots may be purchased, but that they ought to be made of rubber and may be purchased every 3 years.

1925

1) **Picnics.** It was decided that the picnic for ministers' children in Rosedale shall be discontinued as unnecessary, and that having picnics for school children is not to be allowed.

If, however, the teacher wishes to give the children ice cream, candy, peanuts, and so forth, then he is free to do so. But no one is to leave the schoolyard to seek amusement with the children.

2) **Canning for personal use** is to be stopped entirely, for it does not belong to true community. And herewith everyone is faithfully requested to cease this abuse.

3) **Collecting drinks at Weddings.** If there is a wedding no one should take the freedom to try to save drinks to then take home, or to do the same after the wedding is over, for the nature of the two is different.

Each one should only drink as much as he is able in order to maintain a pure conscience. For all excess and misuse is sin.

Exception: If someone is away because of work when it is poured, then he can go later and claim it from the giver, but he may not carry it home.

If people are ill so that they are not able to come to the wedding then the manager should give them their due according to what is fair.

1926

1) **Colours of household appliances.** Different colours are not allowed for household appliances, including the chest,[9] not even the lacquer or oil.

The chair seats and the cover of the sofa beds should remain according to the old custom, namely, black or the same colour as the rest of the piece. Do not try to rub off the chair seats, rather first use up the colour or the oil. In the future, however, paint things according to the ordinance.

Linoleum. [11] The carpet or floor covering should not be mottled or multicoloured.

2) **Cradles.** With the cradles one should stick with the old style, namely, simple cradles made with rocking runners.

3) **Cloths and Aprons.** One should not show pride through the markings on clothes or aprons. No big woollen cloth should have a marking on it that is bigger than one inch. They should be no bigger than half of half that size.

Markings on a headscarf, apron, or other garment should be somewhat smaller than half an inch. And there should be no ornamentation, just the name and year.

4) **Aprons of the Servers.** The aprons worn by the waiters and the servers[10] are not to be tolerated.

5) **Cakes for the Bride and Groom.** No special decorated cakes are to be baked to honour the bride and groom.

6) **Gas Mantle Lamps (Incandescent Gas Lights).** These are to be disposed of.

7) **Driving to go visiting.** Driving for visits should be kept fair. If someone who has the opportunity wants to drive to the other congregations, then he should ask the minister for permission. If, however, an extra drive

is taken to have a vehicle fixed in a nearby community, then it should happen with the manager's knowledge.

If, however, a longer drive to the colonies up here (in Canada) is undertaken, either to all of them, or to Blumengart, Riverside or whichever, then the brotherhood should decide.

And if colonies from there come up here, it should also be decided by the brotherhood.

8) Gifts. Clothing or footwear that was given as a gift must be shown to the minister and will be credited to you if the colony hands out the same item later. Other gifted items must be shown to the minister and the manager who will decide what to do with them.

9) Aprons. Aprons with trim are forbidden and will no longer be tolerated. Existing ones should be worn inside out.
It has also been decided to stay with the pressed aprons and that any light colours or gingham prints will not be tolerated.
Note: This number 9 was lifted in 1941 but applies again.

10) Skirts. With respect to our dresses we will stay with our traditional garb and will not start new fashions with pleats and the like.
[12] The dress should fall 5-6 inches from the ground.

11)Pants. The men's pants should fall 3-4 inches from the ground.

1927

1) Annunciation. The holiday, Annunciation, should be observed from now on.

2) Matters of the Post. All incoming mail should be brought to the manager. The minister, according to the decree from 1884, should still read outgoing letters. Unbaptized young people are not allowed to send letters or packages in the mail; if something should be sent to them, then the minister must read it in order to prevent unrighteous things.

Note of Explanation or Encouragement: The above ordinance, number 3 from 1884 (regarding moustaches) was presented to all colonies in 1927 to vote on, and the majority, which was not expected, accepted it and validated it. And thus it is still in effect. We ministers would have preferred for it to be lifted because this is the most commonly violated ordinance. It is, however, still in effect.

3) **Ordinance regarding chairs.** A family with six souls or more may have seven chairs; one with 4-5 souls may have four; one with three or less may have three.

1928

1) **Driving to go visiting.** Driving to go visit friends or relatives in other colonies with money has been discussed and it has been decided that driving to go visiting with one's own money, whether earned or gifted, should not be allowed.

Should someone want to go driving and needs money, it should be the colony's money and should occur with the approval of the brotherhood.

Should someone want to drive to Alberta or South Dakota, the decision should be made by the whole colony.

1929

1) **Wedding.** If there is a wedding in a colony, neither a relative nor a sibling nor anyone else is allowed to come other than people from the Mother or Daughter Colony or colony of the Bride.

Otherwise, however, it is not to be allowed. One should not even come if someone else is on his or her way, or even try to find a way to come ahead of time.

[13] 1930

1) **Weddings.** At weddings no songs should be sung that the minister has not agreed to or allowed. And no songs should be allowed that are not fitting for us.

2) **Fur pelts.** Fur overcoats are to be given every ten years. If they last longer than that then they are to be replaced after they wear out.

3) **Rubber boots** should be given every three years.

4) **If a young girl**[11] **marries.** On February 2, 1930 is was decided that if a *Dirne* from one colony marries someone from a different colony then in the next year the colony from which she comes must provide her new clothes for the coming year, regardless of which month it is in which the wedding was held.

5) **Driving Trucks.** No unmarried men under 25 should drive a truck.

1931

1) **Dishes.** No dishes are to be placed on the counter as a sign of finery. Only dishes that are being used may be placed there, such as one or two bowls. Everything else should be placed in cupboards or cabinets out of sight.

2) *Hulba.*[12] It has been recognized by all of the colonies that no more *Hulbas* will be allowed during the engagement. No young people may sing or get together with the bride and groom or anywhere else. Also, no alcohol is to be given as a gift, other than what the bride and groom give to their parents or siblings who are attending the actual engagement.

1932

On January 15 1931 various abuses were recognized and discussed, as follows:

1) **Sweaters.** Sweaters will soon be done away with as they are not a part of our garb, and because they help to a considerable extent to promote unjust dealings. Those that are still in existence should be unstitched or disposed of in a different manner. Whoever does not obey will have their sweaters taken from them and burned and the disobedient will be punished.

2) **Taking Credit (for personal goods to sell for personal profit).** Taking out wool in order to knit stockings or to make blankets and then selling them at a profit does not belong to community, and should not be allowed.

3) **Ordinances.** The ordinances of the colony should be read aloud yearly.

[14] 4) **Colours of Household Appliances.** Different colours of the chests and all other household appliances are not allowed. And the linoleum should not be mottled or multi-coloured.

1935

1) **Linoleum.** It has been recognized that buying linoleum should not be allowed, and the existing linoleum should be dyed with paint or wood stain, so that they are plain.

2) **Sofas and Sleeping Benches.** Resting benches and the folding beds should be disposed of. One should keep to the simple beds that have been the custom until now.

Sleeping bench. The handmade sleeping bench was given to the seniors who have none, and the childless families of old were given one too. And it should remain that way.

3) **Punishment for Youth.** Regarding punishment for youth it has been recognized that unbaptized youth who are over 21 years old may stand for at Sunday service or evening service instead of being disciplined with the rod. It must, however, be decided by the colony.

1936

1) Regarding **cabinets, dressers, and corner shelves,** the following has been decided: A big shelf or commode, that is used to store clothes instead of a chest, may be kept. But the ornamentation and cut-outs must be done away with and they must be made plain.

But one family may not keep both, rather only one of the two, either a shelf or commode.

The smaller piece, whether the cabinet or the dresser, should be disposed of according to this ordinance.

The small corner shelves without doors may be kept.

2) **Winter blankets.** In order to achieve greater equality regarding the winter blankets, it was decided at the annual meeting in January 1936 that matter should be handled in the following way:

A. Every eight years these blankets will be given out.

B. The situation with the newlyweds is to be handled in the following manner: Those who marry in the year in which the blankets are to be given out will receive those blankets and no other, just as the other families.

C. Those however, who marry in year 1, 2, 3, or 4 after the blankets have been handed out receive the blankets along with the other families.

D. Those however, who marry in year 5, 6, or 7 after the blankets were handed out, they only receive half of the blankets.

1938

1) **Caps.** No caps other than black ones are to be purchased in the future. [See the 1948 ordinance regarding caps.]

2) **Zippers.** Zippers, in place of hooks and eyes, are not to be allowed.

3) **Ornamentation on Jackets.** Exposed chests or unbuttoned shirts for church or prayer or for school are not to be allowed. The vest should be buttoned closed and the jacket should be closed at least at the top.

4) **Collars.** Coming to teaching, prayer or to Sunday school with a woollen or any other sort of collar is not allowed.

5) **School.** The ban on going to engineering or Beekeeping School is to be lifted.

6) **Eating at home.** Eating at home in the night or the evening is forbidden. Eating at home in the evening or the night when a young couple gets engaged or marries should not happen. It is not allowed on other nights either.

7) **Belts.** The wearing of belts is forbidden. Because there is no ordinance permitting the wearing of belts and because they were not worn or used according to Christian custom, they are to be disposed of. Nothing other than suspenders will be tolerated.

8) **Hats.** Nothing other than black hats will be tolerated, with the exception of straw hats which may be black or white. The white or grey hats that are still in existence in this year, 1938, may be worn until the end of this year.

9) **Shop Aprons.** Women are allowed to wear shop aprons. Each woman is permitted one plain work apron, but it must be without pockets or ornamentation. The band should be the same as it is for other aprons and should not be anything other than black or dark blue.

10)

A. **Distribution of the feathers.** The annual distribution of the feathers should be done away with.

B. **Feather allowance.** No one should receive more feathers than what the old ordinance permits, which, since 1941, is 48 pounds.

C. [16] **The sale of feathers.** Also the ordinance permitting the sale of feathers, except on behalf of the colony has been lifted. The individual cannot sell.

D. **Personal use.** The sale of anything for personal use is also forbidden, other than wool, soap, mittens, stockings, or other similar things. Also, no edible things should be sold other than carrots, melons, popped corn, or whatever it is called. These things are not allowed to be sold except to the colony.

Note: The 1925 ordinance number 1 that permitted this is hereby lifted, because it only encouraged and strengthened self-interest.

11) **Profiting.** Earning a profit through buying and selling is forbidden.

The selling of eggs, honey, or other things for profit is not to be permitted. Peter Riedeman forbids it in our account book under the title: *From the Dealer.*

12) **Sewing Machines and Wall Clocks.**

A. Each family is allowed one of each.

B. If, however, 2 sewing machines or 2 clocks are to be given, it must be done with the permission of the brotherhood.

1940

On January 31, 1940, at the annual ministers' meeting, the following was decided:

1) **Clothing.** In order to defend us against, and to stop, pride, from now on only single-coloured and matte fabric should be purchased for our garb.

The colours that the things should be include: black, dark blue, coffee brown, or grey for the outer garment. Light and gingham may be used for children under five, also for sleeping clothes.

All fabric that is multi-coloured or floral should be dyed. The minister and the manager from each colony should decide what needs to be dyed. Where there is only one minister, the Farm Boss should also help so that there are three who are checking.

Whoever hides their clothes and does not allow them to be examined will have them taken away and the person will be punished.

Note: See ordinance number 1 from 1949 regarding garments about the reduction of one-coloured garments.

[17] **2) Hats.** Straw hats that look like soldiers' hats, or helmets, should not be purchased or worn. The existing ones should be put away and not worn.

3) **Shoes.** The leather shoes for women should have a heel no higher than one inch, which is to be measured from the front.

4) **Coffee and Tea** may now be purchased with one's allowance as may some other foods or drinks.

1941

The following should be added to the Clothing Ordinance #1 from 1940 in order to complete it:

1) **Aprons.** The aprons for women should be no other colour than black, dark blue, dark green, or coffee brown, but may be only one colour.

Clothing. The garments for women should only be the colours that are mentioned above in the 1940 decision, and that applies to girls at the age of 10. Under the age of 10 children's colours will be tolerated. Young boys'[13] garments should be the same colour as the others.' The shirts should be one colour, but not red or yellow.

2) **The distribution of feathers.** Regarding the distribution of feathers it has been decided that upon marriage each spouse should receive the feathers from the colony from which they come.

Each spouse should receive 24 pounds of feathers. Together each couple should have 48 pounds of feathers.

If a young man or young woman is still unmarried at the age of 25, then they should receive the same portion as a married person, namely, 24 pounds per person. And if they then later marry, then they should not receive any feathers, because they already received their portion.

A baby should receive 8 pounds. And when a child is 10 years old, then it should receive two more pounds so that it has 10 pounds in total.

And if the child is 15 years old, it should receive two more pounds so that in total it has 12 pounds.

3) **Pocket watches.** It has been decided that a colony may have several pocket watches if it is considered necessary. They should then be given to those who work during the night and also to some who work on the fields. And after the work is finished the watches should be taken off.

4) **Allowance.**[14] All people older than 15 years are entitled to 20 cents a month in allowance. This should be given out once a month to the head of the household. But this allowance should only be used for edible things. Children under the age of 15 [18] receive 15 cents a month. For all unbaptized children the money is to be given to the parents.

1943

1) **The distribution of clothing after someone dies.**

A. Everything that a person received in the last round of distribution, whether clothing or footwear, is to be collected.

B. If a family dies out then the bedding is to be distributed throughout the colony.

C. If a child dies, then things are to remain the way they were with the clothing distribution.

D. If, however, it is the last child in the family, then the clothes are to be distributed according to the same manner as it is done for adults.

1944

1) It has been discerned that no other **Washing Tables** in the homes are to be allowed other than those with the basins as has been the custom, either along the wall or on a stool that has been made for it.

Those who have been saving money to buy a different kind should be examined and all other kinds will be taken away.

2) **All Plaques on the Walls with Sayings** are to be done away with and are not to be tolerated.

3) **Shoes.** Buying shoes is allowed, but only shoes that are approved by the minister, the manager, and the cobbler may be purchased. There is to be no ornamentation on them in accordance with the long held ordinance.

4) **Household Appliances.** Regarding household appliances and floor colours, things are to be kept according to the long held ordinance, namely, simple with no strands.

1946

1) **Punishment for those who buy Linoleum.** Whoever buys or acquires in any way linoleum that is contrary to the ordinance after January 1, 1946 will be examined and the flooring will be taken away.

[19] 1947

1) **Those who have fallen away or run away.** When those who have fallen away or run away, whether they are baptized or unbaptized, wish to convert, and wish to return to the colony and be accepted, then they should declare themselves to the minister that they desire acceptance. And then, according to the ordinance they should be accepted by the brotherhood and the colony.

1948

On January 27 the annual ministers' meeting was held on the Elm River Colony in Manitoba, where the following was decided:

1) **Linoleum.**[15] Floor coverings were discussed and it was decided by the majority to allow in the first room, whether it is big or small, linoleum to cover the whole floor, as long as it is of a single colour.

Otherwise the previous ordinance is still in effect: one colour, not multicoloured, and no ornamentation.

With this, the vast majority was in agreement.

2) **Caps.** The plain black caps without straps may either be bought or made—but only the black ones.

3) **Concerts.** It has been decided that Christmas concerts should be done away with and should not be allowed anymore in the schools, for such things do not belong to Christianity (see 1950 #4 regarding this matter).

1949

1) **Ordinance regarding fabric.** Alleviation of the ordinance insisting on a single colour. The minister, the manager, and the pattern-cutter should exhort the congregation to be assiduous when purchasing fabric, and to remain in true humility and lowliness.

Clothing. That means that clothing no longer needs to be one colour, there can be small markings, but they should be small, no bigger than a dime, as is fitting for God's people. Also small flowers are allowed in about the same size but not bigger.

Note: The one purchasing the fabric as well as the distributor can sin terribly and blemish and burden their own consciences and lead the colony into the abyss if they willfully and boldly seek to plant seeds of devilish arrogance in the hearts of the younger and the older members of the colony, and thereby lay waste to the Lord's vineyard and plant themselves on the side of the devil. If this matter is not curbed it just shows that they care too little for the ordinance and all the preaching against arrogance and [20] the spirit of the world is in vain. It is already a matter of weeping and lamenting how blind some of the ministers and the managers are on the inside and how they seek to please the people and thereby deny the Saviour and crucify humility. They should therefore consider and improve themselves, for otherwise something thorough will have to be done. This work of Satan is already being carried on and cannot be denied. The innocent are exempted but all others should consider themselves for the great holy God will not be mocked and will not allow anyone to spit in his face. The Jewish peddlers who come to the yard are a bigger threat and plague than the Jesuit Delphini was in the History book. That one was an overt enemy of the colony, but these ones appear in the likeness of a businessman. These fleas can work themselves into the fur very easily but getting them out is a much more serious matter. Therefore we must be careful and must apply this well-meant admonition so that things will improve. Explanation of the expression 'work of Satan': it means every time pride and a worldly mind are promoted and every conscious, frivolous violation of the word of God and the ordinances of the colony. Conscious disobedience is a sin of magic and antagonism, it is idolatrousness and idolatry. And these sins bring us into disgrace before God.

2) **Small Buttons.** It has also been decided that small buttons may be used on shirts, but must be the same colour as the shirt or fabric or garment.

3) **Sewing machines.** It has been decided not to set a price for sewing machines, but to try to purchase them as cheaply as possible, but only second-hand. The timing should also be changed from the old ordinance: when a family marries, then a machine may be purchased from the manager.

4) **Mirrors.** Also regarding mirrors a step ought to be taken: and they may be 12 inches by 12 inches.

5) **Skirts.** If skirts are purchased or made they should not have more than two pouches and no belt; and they should be dark blue or black, and not mottled.

6) **Buying more land.** In Canada and the United States it is done accordingly: if a colony in South Dakota wishes to add about 100 acres, then it need inform only the South Dakota colonies. And the same goes for Manitoba, only the Manitoba colonies need be informed.

1950

THE FOLLOWING ORDINANCES were decided on during the annual meeting that was held January 31, 1950, at the Sturgeon Creek Colony near Headingly, Manitoba, Canada.

1) **Bonnets.** REGARDING bonnets it has been decided that sisters and young women may not go around the colony bare-headed or with bonnets, let alone wearing bonnets to the table for meal-time. That is shocking!

Dress Collars. No virtuous, honourable, or god-fearing Sister or young woman should allow himself or herself to be seen with an open collar. For that is not appropriate for them.

[21] As far as we know, it was never allowed. For there will be a time when nothing is left over, when we will one day have to stand before the great and strict judge and will have to give an account.

2) *Fleckenschuhe* were also discussed because of the long-standing prohibition. In many colonies they were bought anyway without a second thought even though they are forbidden. Each one should guard himself against should things!

3) **Linoleum.** And the same goes for the ornamented, splashy linoleum.

That some colour or decorate their linoleum with various ornaments without a second thought, and seek to get around the ordinance by every possible means, is directly contrary to the ordinance. Closer attention should be paid to this and should not become an annoyance to others. And not even a thought is given to the words of Christ: "Woe unto the world because of offences! For it must needs be that offences come; but woe to that man by whom the offence cometh!" (Matthew 18:7)

Note: An offence is a wrongdoing or any kind of bad deed or bad example that tempts one to sin, or with which others become trapped, misled or infected.

For that reason this must be taken more seriously.

4) **Weddings.** And as for going to weddings, there should be the same order in Manitoba as in South Dakota. Why should the colonies in the United States have different customs and ordinances than here in Canada? And the ordinance states thus: In January of 1929 it was discerned that if there is a wedding in a colony then no relative, or sibling, or anyone, is to be given permission to attend, other than the two usual colonies, or if a bride is from a different colony. Otherwise it should not happen.

Neither is it permitted to drive to the wedding, even if someone is already on the way there, nor is it allowed to diligently seek a way ahead of time to get there. That is particularly evil.

And that is the ordinance to which we will hold and conform.

5) Concerts. The minister from the colony should keep to this ordinance and should not permit concerts to be approved or held.

We must stand our posts and keep better guard and watch. Yes, we must all keep to the ordinance, which was discerned lest such evil creep in. For these are the sorts of evils that are the foxes which destroy the vineyard (Song of Songs 2:15).

1951

1) **Ordinance regarding mattresses.**

    A. In the future the colony should buy the mattress for the married couple; it should be worth about $20 to $25.

    B. The newly married couple should give eight of their 48 pounds of feathers for the mattress.

    C. The ordinance regarding the distribution of feathers should remain the same. Only the wing feathers should never be distributed but should be stripped and sold along with the other colony feathers.

    D. When a bed is purchased for the children, a mattress may also be purchased with it, about $5 to $7 but not more, and only one until they get married.

    E. Only the manager, or whomever he appoints, may purchase the mattresses.

2) **Electing a Servant of the Word.**

    A. An election is held one Sunday after the sermon from Deuteronomy 17, which addresses the issue. And from those Brothers, who each have 5 or more votes, one will be chosen through a draw.

    B. Regarding the witness brothers from a colony, an earlier vote should be held, according to the wishes of the servant, and two or more brothers should be nominated who are considered capable of the position.

    C. Then every other colony should send four brothers—from the ministers, managers, witness brothers, etc. to the voting colony. And together with the delegates from the other colonies a vote may then be held in the voting colony and one or more new brothers may be voted in, but only from those who were nominated.

And of those brothers who have five or more votes, then one, or however many are to be selected, will be chosen through a draw.

D. In the nominations only those receive more than one vote should be considered for election. If more than one person considers someone who took part in the earlier vote capable, then two people may nominate him, but not more than two.

Note: The ordinance regarding nominations was made in the year 1904.

1952

The following was discerned during the annual ministers' meeting on February 25, 1952, at Lakeside Colony in Manitoba.

1) **Mailing Letters.** The ordinance from 1884, which stated that no one is allowed to send letters without the leadership reading them first, is to be lifted, because dishonourable letter writers circumvented the ordinance and thus it has not served its purpose.

[23] 2) **Sewing Machines.** The sewing machine ordinance is to be changed so that from now on, brand new sewing machines may be purchased, in so far as a colony thinks it is good and accepts it.

3) **Ordinance regarding Mattresses.** Elaboration of the ordinance regarding mattresses for married couples: in the future the feather mattress that is purchased for the married couples should cost $20-$25 without the sales tax or other taxes.
  Distribution of Feathers. The newlyweds should give up eight of their 48 pounds of feathers.
  Otherwise the ordinance regarding the distribution of feathers should stay the same. Only the wing feathers should never be distributed but should be stripped and sold along with the other feathers.
  Mattresses for Children. When beds are purchased or are to be purchased for children, an adequate cotton mattress may be purchased but only one without spring coils and only one until they marry.
  Beds for Children. The first bed is only to be purchased for the 5th child. The assumption is that until then cradles and the sleeping benches that were previously used should suffice.

1953

The following was debated and discerned at the annual conference, which was held on February 16, 1953, at the Huron Colony in Canada.

1) **Linoleum.** From now on (1953) linoleum may be purchased, but it must be plain, not mottled or floral. And it should be sought out and purchased by the minister and the manager.

If a colony purchases mottled, floral print, or decorative linoleum, contrary to this ordinance, it should be disposed of, and those who purchased the illicit linoleum will be investigated and punished.

The already existing linoleum, which is not plain, rather has a floral print, or is mottled, flecked, painted, or otherwise ornamented, should be painted over, in accordance with the 1935 and 1950 ordinance; otherwise it belongs to the illicit linoleum and should be disposed of.

2) **Wristwatches.** Wrist watches are not permitted rather they should be taken off and done away with, because they are mostly worn out of pride and are acquired by dishonest means.

[24] 3) **Resting benches.** The padded resting benches seem to be taking over in the colonies. These were prohibited in the 1935 ordinance #2, because they do not belong among us and should from now on be done away with.

4) **Driving to funerals.** It has been discerned that this should be restricted as much as possible and the main vehicle should no longer be driven, other than in exceptional circumstances, such as where there are a lot of relatives of the deceased.

5) **Driving trucks.** It has been discerned that the old ordinance of 1930 should be upheld, namely that no unmarried men under 25 should drive a truck. Now, however, it has been decided that in inevitable situations or emergencies, others who are considered reliable, may also drive trucks.

6) **Allowance.** Everyone over 15 years old is entitled to 20 cents of allowance per month. This should be given out once a month by the head of the household.

But this allowance is only to be spent on edible things. Children less than 15 years old and over half a year receive only 10 cents a month. The parents are to be given the allowance of all unbaptized children.

7) **Work aprons.** The work aprons that were allowed in 1938 should not be worn without the proper ties, and the proper ties are not to be replaced or removed, as is already happening in some colonies, where the proper apron is not even worn anymore, rather only the short work aprons. This work apron should be plain, without pockets or ornamentation, should not be store-bought or plastic, and must be black or dark blue, or must be the same colour that is allowed for the proper aprons. If this does not happen with the wives' work aprons then they must be done away with.

8) **Clothing.** Because in nearly all colonies, but in particular the colonies in South Dakota, too much arrogance and high spirits are being displayed in the clothes, all of the ministers should earnestly concern themselves and try to curb arrogance and to resist pride in clothing by holding the fabric buyer and the pattern cutter firmly to the ordinance and not allowing anyone to wear clothing that has been prohibited, such as multi-coloured and floral printed fabrics, or light-coloured and shiny fabrics or whatever else does not belong among us, a people of God that preaches and ought to practice humility. Otherwise such behaviour cries out to the world that we are becoming worldly, and the outsiders will take comfort in the fact that soon we will be the same as them and as the world.

It will require constant fighting and vigilance, because the trash has grown over our heads and has taken root inside. It must be done, however, otherwise both cow and calf will be corrupted and we will cease to be a people of God, and will be rejected by God as lukewarm Christians and as flavourless salt. The arrogance with the clothing is already too great—already so blatant. Those who are the most to blame are the fabric buyers and the pattern cutters who plant this evil and stick this hellish fire into hearts. They will have much to answer for, and we along with them, because we did not stop them and hold them to account. Through this the Lord's vineyard will be destroyed and the enemy sows his accursed weeds of arrogance through us, his instruments. Woe to him who does such things, according to [25] the Holy Scripture (Galatians 6, 7). Let us blow the trumpets in all seriousness and warn ourselves, for God will not be mocked and what a person sows is what he will reap.

1954

It was discerned during the annual conference on February 16, 1954 at the Milltown Colony at Benard in Manitoba, Canada that ordinances regarding the following matters are necessary:

1) **Young people going away.** Young unbaptized women and men, as well as baptized women and men (under 25 years) in all of the colonies in Canada are not allowed to drive across the border to South Dakota to the colonies there in order to pick grapes or because of the *Besenkraut* or Broomcorn, etc., because nothing good come of it for the young people. And the same goes for the young women and men from the colonies in South Dakota—they are not allowed to come across the border to the colonies in Canada.

2) **Young people going visiting.** Young unbaptized people (women and men) from our colonies in Canada are not allowed to drive across the border to go to South Dakota, and the reverse holds true as well that

the young people from our colonies in South Dakota are not allowed to drive to Canada in order to work. Neither are they allowed to ride along with baptized young people, because this practice has been very overdone, and through it the ordinance regarding driving to go visiting has been grossly mishandled and the relevant colonies in Canada and South Dakota are in general very troublesome and annoying because of their frivolous ways, and their doings and strivings. At home they can never be restrained and when away they act like they are allowed to do anything, so that some colonies are shocked by what comes on to their yards. Besides, each colony has enough to do trying to suppress its own young people—and is often at a loss as to where to start with them.

We ministers need to be diligent to hold ourselves more closely and firmly to the ordinances of the colony as the necessary guide so that later we will not have to regret that we were too careless and indulgent when the vineyard of the Lord is laid waste and the affliction and atrocity of the desolation is upon us. Even with the best attention things go downhill enough.

1955

The following was decided during the 1955 minister and managers' conference at the Sunnyside Colony in Canada.

1) **Making Schnapps and Spirits** should now be completely stopped and is prohibited, even if for the colony's use because it is forbidden by law and therefore it is not seemly for us as children of God to make it secretly.

2) **Christmas programs.** Those teachers from the world who have been hired should not be allowed to arrange and rehearse a Christmas program because in so doing they waste so much valuable school time and do not sow anything Christian into the children through it.

[26] The colony teacher should diligently use the pre-Christmas period to impress and to practice something godly with the children and explain the purpose of Christmas time to the children and make it meaningful to them, and also explain why Christ became a human or why he was born as a child.

In the worldly programs there is not even a kernel of Christianity and they are only performed for amusement and frivolity. Through such programs Christ is generally dishonoured. Therefore we should not allow them to do this because they already plant enough worldly things into the minds of our children—more than we believe.

3) **Driving to funerals.** The ordinance from 1953 regarding driving to funerals should be more carefully observed, lest more people come to the funerals than can be accommodated.

4) Photographs. Taking photographs has been prohibited among us up until now—and rightly so—because it was forbidden by the all-wise God in the holy 10 commandments, because it only leads to vanity, just as it led Israel to idolatry. Therefore, those who allow their picture to be taken in the future will be punished. We should not make ourselves equal to the world in this matter, and in so doing violate God's godly laws, for how do we know where to draw the line?

5) Electing a minister. It has also been recognized as a high priority that the Beadle Colony in South Dakota choose a second minister, and that this should happen this year. The establishment of a new colony has been handled too lightly—they have no minister who is ready to serve, who has studied somewhat and prepared himself and who has had some experience with the laws. How is someone to assume leadership of the colony who is so inexperienced in this regard? This has been handled unwisely, and shows just how little we have planned for the work of the kingdom of God.

1956

1) Establishing a new minister. At the annual ministers' conference, which was held on February 12, 1956, at the Bon Homme Colony in Manitoba, the issue of selecting ministers was discussed. The question is whether it is proper that a brother who through the draw in the previous election found himself in the minister's position but who thereafter was found to be incapable should be allowed to be reinstated again. After lengthy consideration it was unanimously decided: He should not be reinstated in the next election period. And those who are selecting the ministers should take note of this.

2) Help for the Ministers. It has also been discerned that if a colony wishes to buy land for a new yard it should select two ministers at least one year before, so that the two have some time to adjust to their positions and to prepare themselves, and to learn and to gain experience. It is not right to put off selecting a second minister as long as possible, as is too often the case.

3) Hunting. It has been discerned that shooting moose, deer, and so forth is to be totally stopped because it is against the law, and also because it is not fitting for us as Christians to hunt like a hunter with a shotgun. It is fitting for us, who are supposed to be Christians, [27] to be subject to the rulers in all things which are fair, and not to live as poachers and frivolous lawbreakers and as a poor light to the world, which watches us closely and does not expect that sort of behaviour from us, that we would be caught and found to be rogues, wildly skulking about. Then our benefactors would no longer come to our defence and say: "The Hutterites are loyal and law-abiding citizens."[16] Rather, we are to chase after with eagerness that which Paul teaches us: "Do all things without murmurings and disputing: That ye may be blameless and harmless, the sons of God, without rebuke, in the midst of a crooked and perverse nation, among whom ye shine as lights in the world; Holding forth the word of life" (Phil. 2:14-15).[17] Read also 1 Peter 2:12-13 and Titus 3:1. For these reasons we ought to be diligent, and not with hunting lust, so that we become like Nimrod, who lusted after hunting, just as the people of the world and the people of the flesh do.

Shotguns. Shotguns do not belong among us, except for the purpose of defending against dangerous predatory animals; each colony is allowed to own one for this purpose, but it must be properly acquired and must be under supervision and must not be used for hunting, as is described above. The hunters ruin the colony;[18] just like the frivolous Esau, they go down crooked paths, and neglect their position at home and pursue a disorderly business, which is detrimental to both themselves and the colony. Experience has proven this.

Hulba. It has been decided that it is necessary to impress upon each colony again that the ordinance regarding the prohibition the *Hulba* is to be renewed and enforced. Read this aloud each time a couple is married. This ordinance is found in the year 1931, #2.

Great sins occur at the *Hulba*, as everyone should know, and that is why we had to stop them. The enemy finds his way in among the frivolous young people. God is disgraced and driven from among us, for instance, during a dance. In this we do not let people see that we are children of God.

The *Hulba* is not allowed during any part of the engagement, neither before nor after. Neither is it allowed on any day before or after the wedding, nor during the week. Let us do our best to eliminate the evil which has taken such strong root among us and which has already grown above our ears.

1957

The following is a report regarding what was decided during the ministers' and managers' conference that was held in January, 1957, at the Sturgeon Creek Colony in Manitoba, Canada.

Headscarves. The following is to be an ordinance regarding headscarves. The headscarves are no longer to be stitched with fancy monograms. Those that are already marked should be done away with in one year.

1) **Tables and Chairs.** For now the iron tables and chairs should be done away with. If it is necessary to do so, we will reconsider this later.

[28] 2) **Collections.** In nearly all colonies there are figurines of birds, dogs, cows, horses, and other creatures and figures, and even beer bottle advertisements that were purchased by individuals and are displayed in the houses. This is nothing but idolatry. These should be disposed of by the minister and totally wiped out.

3) **Electronic Appliances.** Electric irons, sewing machine motors, and clocks are the only things that are allowed, nothing else.

4) **Washing.** Washing on Sunday afternoon or holidays is not to be permitted or sanctioned.

5) **Driving to Funerals.** Going to funerals has been highly excessive, and therefore obedience to the 1955 Ordinance should be encouraged.

6) **Going to Evening Service and to meals.** If people go driving at any time, then they no longer go to meals and neither to prayer. The minister should tell people when they ask for permission to go somewhere that they must go to prayer and meals and that they may not sit at home alone and take out their food.

7) **Parkas.** Parkas may be worn for one more year and then things should remain as they had been until now.

8) **Wristwatches.** It must also be noted that wristwatches are not to be tolerated but must be removed. These have been appearing in some colonies. And thus one evil after another comes into the colony, and ravages it, so that nothing is considered sin and we have made ourselves equal with the world.

The above-mentioned article 7 is not an ordinance. Rather it is a serious admonition, and ought to be announced in all of the colonies. And so all of the parkas are to be done away with by the ministers and the managers.

Yes, let us work with diligent earnestness in order to accomplish all of our obligations. We will have our hands full, but let us work toward the praise from Deuteronomy 4:8: "And what nation is there so great, that hath statutes and judgments so righteous as all this law, which I set before you this day?"

And along with that goes what God says in Deuteronomy 5:29: "O that there were such an heart in them, that they would fear me, and keep all my commandments always, that it might be well with them, and with their children for ever!" That should be our seal and our aspiration, and not that we would desire to make ourselves equal to the world through our character, customs, and practices, and thereby become enemies of God and summon God's wrath and disfavour upon us.

1958

Conference Report to all of the colonies in Manitoba and South Dakota
The following was discussed and approved during the 1958 conference that was held on February 4 at the Maxwell Colony in Manitoba.

1) **Electric Appliances.** The #3 resolution from 1957 regarding the regulation of electric appliances or instruments remains in place with one addition, that is, that electric ovens for household use are not prohibited, neither are electric pads or heaters for the sick, as long as they are introduced by the colony in an orderly way.

Water Heaters. After much discussion back and forth it has been discerned that it is up to each colony to decide whether or not it wishes to adopt water heaters. Everything else that has not been approved through an ordinance is still prohibited.

2) **Parkas.** Parkas may no longer be purchased or acquired, rather only those jackets which were allowed in #5 ordinance from 1949, without a belt or a zipper, and which are neither light-coloured nor multi-coloured. Those parkas that are still in existence may be worn until they are worn out, but without a hood or a cap, and without a zipper or elastic around the waist, and without offensive pockets on the chest like the jackets that the soldiers wear. But under no circumstances are new ones to be purchased or acquired.

3) **Resting benches and Folding Beds.** It has also been decided that the ordinance #2 from 1935 regarding padded and other types of resting benches and folding beds is to be renewed. These beds are being made locally are directly contrary to the ordinance and should be disposed of for they do not belong to the household furnishings that have been approved by the colony and they are being acquired by dishonourable and clandestine means.

4) **Dishes.** In ordinance #1 from 1931 it was determined that no dishes may be displayed for it is a sign of pride and this is happening in too many houses.

5) **Driving to Funerals.** Neither baptized nor unbaptized young men and women are allowed to go to funerals or wakes in other colonies—other than the exceptions listed in Ordinance #2 from 1917 and 1921—because nothing good comes of it, because they do not behave properly and it only leads to frivolity.

6) **Hairstyles.** It was discerned as highly necessary that ordinance #1 from 1921 be renewed. See #1, from 1921 and read it aloud.

7) **Shirts—hats—headscarves.** Not only is no one allowed to work either at home or on the field without a shirt but it is to be seriously punished, for that is something that the wild primitive people do, and is a sign of boldness and shamelessness, as is the fact that in Winnipeg and other cities and places, and also at home, men run around without hats and women without headscarves like half-wild and unconverted people of the world, [30] among whom we are to shine like a light in the world "that [W]e should shew forth the praises of him who hath called [us] out of darkness into his marvellous light" (1 Peter 2:9).

8) **Suspenders—Hats.** Boys and man are not to be allowed to go without suspenders as some are starting to do, because in so doing they violate ordinance #7 from 1938. Also the men folk are not to wear any hats of any other colour than those which are permitted—black felt hats and white, black, or straw-coloured straw hats.

9) **Ministers' coats.** The ministers are not to go to Sunday sermon at home without their coats.

10) **Newsletter.** The newsletter written by the respective Bishop regarding the proceedings or regulations of the annual conference, as well as any other newsletters that are directed to the colony, are to be read aloud by the minister in a public meeting.

Yes, let us, particularly we ministers, follow the example set by Zacharias and his Elizabeth who "And they were both righteous before God, walking in all the commandments and ordinances of the Lord blameless" (Luke 1:6), and under which our laws are also included, and according to 1 Peter 1:13 so that we will be able to remain a people of God with right customs and laws according to Deuteronomy 4:8 and will be able to keep ourselves unspoiled by the horrors and excesses of the world.

1959

To all the *Schmieden* colonies in South Dakota and Manitoba

The following, beginning with #1 is the report of the proceedings from the 1959 conference of the *Schmiedeleute* which was held on February 10 at the Glendale Colony in South Dakota, where the colonies were encouraged anew to eliminate and abolish abuses and the evil that is brazenly sneaking in and to come against them with all seriousness and total resoluteness so that we may be a blameless and set apart people, unspoiled by the horrors and excesses of the world, so that it may be rightly said of us as it is written in 1 Peter 2: 9-10 [sic]: "And, lo, the angel of the Lord came upon them, and the glory of the Lord shone round about them: and they were sore afraid. And the angel said unto them, Fear not: for, behold, I bring you good tidings of great joy, which shall be to all people."[19] In order to make this a reality, our greatest concern and mission should be to shine with true piety and living Christianity, and to fight with godly earnestness and eagerness against all ungodly beings and worldly, fleshly lusts and works of darkness, and to seek after the kingdom of God and his justice.

1) **Striking the Bell.** It has been discerned that the ordinance from 1921 regarding bells should be renewed and that the bells should only be used accordingly—to call to eat and to work, and no longer to the teaching, to prayer, or to Sunday school. Blowing the whistle should not be used either.

2) **Shunning.** If someone is being punished and is in discord or exclusion, shunning is to occur or to be used according to the discretion of the colony.

[31] 3) **Sleeves.** A reminder should be given to all of the womenfolk who wear short sleeves that they are not to be shorter than to the elbow and it goes without saying that the sleeves are not to be rolled up[20] past the elbow.

Clothing. Also sheer garments are not allowed, neither are they to be tolerated, rather should be done away with and the guilty should be punished.

Hairstyles. The same goes for wearing one's hair according to worldly fashions, such as the beehive,[21] which is a Moabite[22] custom and temptation, as is depicted in the Easter lesson.[23]

My point to the above is the sincerest admonition to all, especially to the ministers, to hold firmly to God's Word, and to everything that is preached before us from time to time and to our ordinances, and to do so without wavering, for this will keep us on track and will protect us from excess, that we might do everything according to Philippians 2:14-15, "without murmurings and disputing: That ye may be blameless and harmless, the sons of God, without rebuke, in the midst of a crooked and perverse nation, among whom ye shine as lights in the world." We do not learn this in beer parlours or saloons, or sneaking after televisions or movies, or if we seek to amuse ourselves with such things like the young people desire to do and secretly do, or if we turn away from the teaching and prayer, which is one of the greatest atrocities before God, or if we turn our backs to the Word of God or if we only read his word grudgingly. Such a people God wants to spit out of his mouth, just as he did to the lukewarm church in Laodicea, and take away and abolish his entire blessing.[24] And the colonies are have been infected almost all the way through with this Laodicean plague, and it is no wonder that there are so many ministers among us who have no guilt about omitting so many prayers a year because of traveling or seasonal work. How much more we need to follow and to take to heart the words that Paul teaches us in Philippians 4:8: "Finally, brethren, whatsoever things are true, whatsoever things are honest, whatsoever things are just, whatsoever things are pure, whatsoever things are lovely, whatsoever things are of good report; if there be any virtue, and if there be any praise, think on these things." Do not think about how we can please the world by being modern and up-to-date, and how we could make the way ever-wider,[25] and thereby deny our beliefs and the living Christianity and extinguish the goodness and love and go down wrong paths. Paul tells us that "those things, which ye have both learned, and received, and heard, and seen in me, do: and the God of peace shall be with you."[26] And that, my dear brothers and sisters, is the right key to our spiritual and temporal well-being and happiness, according to Psalm 1:1-2 and Jeremiah 17:7-8, and other writers also.

Alas, in the hope that this will be duly considered, I remain your humble servant and fellow worker, with sincere greetings and wishes for everything good from above, and especially that the God of peace and comfort will be with us and remain with us to the end, Peter Hofer.

[32] The following is the due for the nursing mothers[27] according to the 1929 record from Bishop Joseph Kleinsasser, which has not been changed and therefore is still applicable. It states:

Due for Nursing Mothers:
2 quarts of spirits
¼ pound of tea
3 pounds of fine sugar
1 bowl of *Kim*   (Herb)
9 baked eggs
2 times baked zwieback
1½ pounds of coffee
4 pounds of crumbled sugar
4 ounces of cinnamon[28]
20 pounds of chicken
1 quart of wine

And for a weaned child,[29] one pound of sugar and one schnapps' glass of tea.

Note: For one quart of spirits, three and one half pounds of coffee will now be substituted because spirits can no longer be purchased.

It has been discerned that wives who have miscarried should be dealt with in the following way: the first three months do not give anything. But in the 4th month give them half of what the nursing mother receives.

Nursing Mothers. According to the 1959 conference report the nursing mothers should only stay at home 6 weeks from the day of the birth. Take note of this from now on.

This was all changed again in 1960.

1960

The following is the conference report from the *Schmiedeleute* that was held on February 9, 1960, at the Waldheim Colony in Manitoba.

1) **Parkas.** Those who have purchased new parkas or still not done away with their parkas or made them over to be similar to the jackets that were allowed by the 1958 ordinance are to be examined and disciplined.

2) **Caps.** Those who wear a cap with a label or anything else other than what is allowed are to be examined and punished. These should be made over to look like the caps that are allowed, and then they may be worn.

[33] Whoever is guilty of the above violations but was not at the conference so that he could be disciplined must appear at a ministers' conference in order to receive discipline.

3) **Drunkenness.** In order to combat alcoholism it has been discerned that each brother is allowed to drink one bottle of beer (the smallest one) once a day in the restaurant with a meal instead of going to the beer parlour or saloon. And each person should stay altogether away from the beer parlours, saloons, or breweries. In small towns like Elie, Oakville, or such places, where there is no need to go to a restaurant, because one is only there for a short while and should do his work there as quickly as possible and then go home, it is not in any way permissible to drink intoxicating drinks because that happens in forbidden places and hideouts, and has the same effect on alcoholics as parlours and saloons.

The reason for this long overdue ordinance is that a godless disorderly life of drunkenness is being pursued by too many, and is done so with the scant colony money or was thievishly stolen from the colony or the dishonestly acquired money from the followers of *Gehasi* who are already spiritually leprous and morally depraved and degenerate, and are governed, ruled, and possessed by the spirit of gluttony, and have fallen into various vices because of it.

Let us rescue those who are not yet bound with Satan's cords by the fetters of gluttony and debauchery, and let us do our job in accordance with sobriety, temperance, respectability, and self-control, and be a light of the world and salt of the earth. Let us strive with godly, continuous fervour against the gluttony of extravagance and excess, which are pursued in the drinking establishments, where the smokers, the blasphemers and the card players, the gamblers and the godforsaken carousers, yes, the scum of humanity attend and amuse themselves, like an eagle with scavengers. We should be repulsed by what goes on in there, and that the frivolous among us run in there and that they enter the way to Hell with drinking and take part with the mockers and the drunkards and make themselves equal to them.

Also, a warning to all against buying intoxicating drinks anywhere in order to take them in their trucks or wherever and to drink them on the way, for this is strongly forbidden by the law and only the foolish drinkers that cannot help themselves do this, and thereby blindly hasten towards their ruin.

Let us all, especially ministers, managers, and elders,[30] unanimously work with God's assistance and with patience to enforce this long overdue ordinance, because drinking and drunkenness has become a cancer and has wrought woeful consequences, which will be difficult—if it is even possible—to eradicate. Let us no longer take part in foreign sins which we have excused or justified until now—by allowing the debauched to go into taverns in order to carouse or to drink for pleasure, and thereby allowing a piggish people to be raised up. We and our offspring will have to pay for it with impoverishment and immorality and we will have to give an answer for why we allowed our people to run wild and to decline spiritually and to offer themselves up to gluttony and to the devil of drink. Our fame is never good. Let us blow the trumpets against [34] this blatant sin and abominable gluttony and frivolity and debauchery that so many pursue in the taverns.

4) Projectors, Movies, Radios.[31] Agents or others with film projectors, movies, radios, or musical instruments are not allowed to come on the yard or to show their products, wares, machines, or whatever, for because of that the young people will go that much more boldly into the cities and other places to movies, the theatre, and to watch television. In the schools we must not allow such things for they will only be to our detriment and harm. And we want to show them in our schools and our churches that preach and teach against such things. What a contradiction!

4) Driving around with Agents.[32] Our people are not allowed to ride around the colonies or anywhere else with agents or the equivalent, because that only breeds mischief and corrupts our people with worldly ways and customs and tempts them to participate in them. We must forcefully guard against such harmful influences, temptations, and impurity and must do what we can to evade them. The spirit of worldliness is forcefully pressing upon us to our detriment and harm, and we ought to be frightened that the power of darkness is all around us and is coming ever closer in order to blind us.

The above statement does not prohibit us from riding somewhere with decent people from the world, as long as one has permission, in order to survey some land or something else that the colony has deemed useful.

5) Engagements. After getting engaged, couples are not to eat in their own homes, which is now contrary to ordinance #6 from 1938. Rather, instead of this disorder, a common meal is to be served in the dining room for all who wish to take part. And this is not to happen later than 10 in the evening, and after eating everyone is to go home. The engaged couple is also to eat at this common meal and is not to eat at home.

The engaged couple is to be given one gallon of wine and one bottle of schnapps that is approximately 26 ounces in order to give this out at the parents' house according to the custom and ordinance #2 from 1931.

Hulba. The *Hulba* ordinance remains in effect and should be adhered to. After the engagement it should be read aloud.

6) Wool blankets. Regarding the wool blankets it has been decided that each family only receives one, and that is upon marriage. Only the stuffing[33] is to be given every 15 years, if it is deemed necessary.

Nursing Mothers. The ordinance that all of the colonies received in 1959 regarding the dues for nursing mothers remains in effect with the following changes: the two quarts of spirits are crossed out and stopped. In its place 20 pounds of sugar or four pounds of coffee are to be given. Also no more schnapps is to be given, just as some colonies have already implemented. All colonies and managers are now to take note of this.

[35] This year the following may be cut: for men: one pair of pants and one jacket. Girls under 15: one tunic and two aprons.

7) Confirmation of Ministers. The following ministers are to be confirmed in their roles as ministers, if no one has anything against it and if the colonies approve.

Elias Maendel, Sturgeon Creek Colony
Jacob Waldner, Grand Colony
Jacob Waldner, Spring Valley Colony
Johann Hofer, Hillside Colony

All of the above are in Manitoba

In conclusion, it is my earnest wish and desire that all ministers would read the conference report aloud to the colonies and that they would work diligently as loyal watchmen and keepers of souls, and would conduct themselves and go ahead as examples for the flock, and exhort their subordinates to follow after them just as Peter exhorted us to do (1 Peter 2:13): "Submit yourselves to every ordinance of man for the Lord's sake: whether it be to the king, as supreme" and that applies especially to the ordinances of the colony about which the frivolous speak mockingly and disparagingly, as if they had been made by children. Paul speaks about this in 1 Thessalonians 4:8: "He therefore that despiseth, despiseth not man, but God, who hath also given unto us his Holy Spirit."

To you all, dear brothers, I wish you unending grace, help, power, and assistance from God, the all-powerful one and I remain now and at all times with sincere greetings, your humble fellow worker and pilgrim, Peter Hofer.

1961

The following was decided during the 1961 ministers' and managers' conference that was held on February 8 at the Rosedale Colony, in Canada.

1) **Bedding.** A change has been made regarding the 4th, 6th, 8th, and 10th child. No cradle or knit blanket is to be given, rather only 6 yards for a cover.

The 5th, 7th, 9th, and 11th do not receive a cradle or a knit blanket because they receive bedding.

2) **The distribution of feathers.** In order to make a change and to clarify: each child should receive eight pounds of feathers, and 12 pounds for the bride and 12 pounds for the groom so that the newlyweds should have 40 pounds of feathers. The young men and women who are not married should also receive 12 pounds when they turn 25. They are to receive the mattress from the colony where they marry and do not receive any feathers for a pillow.

3) **Lining.** It has also been discerned that no lining is to be given for the women's jacket and coat [*Wanick*, *Mieder*, and *Jupp*.]

4) **Children's Prayers.** Each minister is to ask his schoolteacher if he is praying the long children's prayer in the evening and the morning. There is already so much [36] change and modernization that many no longer know what they were taught. Look on page 122 in the big history book, where we are taught about how Jeronimus Kaels made the Children's Prayer. Let us follow his example with great diligence.

5) **The Manager's Account.** When the manager gives his account to the minister, he should also bring the account from the Brothers to the minister in order to avoid spending too much on eating and drinking, or other unnecessary things. The minister and the manager can inspect the account and can notify the member who has gone into excess that he is causing the widows and the orphans to lose the sweat of their brows.

6) **Movies.** Also, after the teaching the minister should keep the Brothers and should ask them if they have gone to the movies. Then every colony will see if it has obedient members or Brothers.

7) **Sunday Suits.** When the boys come out of school [at 15 years of age], they each receive six yards of fabric and three yards of lining for a Sunday suit. The men and the boys are no longer to receive vests.

8) **Blanket.** Unmarried men and women and widowers are to each receive one blanket, but not doubled, which is the size that the married couples receive.

9) **Sleeves-Stockings.** Women should be reminded that for short sleeves the cuffs should come to the elbow and that white stockings should be done away with.

10) **Hairstyles.** Something should be done regarding haircuts. See the relevant ordinance from 1921 and how strictly it was imposed.

1962

Conference report of the *Schmiedeleute*.

1) **Curtains.** Long curtains are to be put away. Curtains may only be as long as the windowsill.

2) **Work Aprons.** The work aprons may remain, but only with the condition that womenfolk should also wear the aprons. If not then the work aprons should be done away with. The colours of the same, according to the ordinance, are black or dark blue.

3) **Stockings.** White stockings are now allowed; other than that the colours of stockings remain the same as the 1938 ordinance stipulates: black, dark blue, or grey. Take note of this.

4) **Fairs.** The large majority has decided against going to fairs.

5) **Pockets.** Pockets on shirts are not to be tolerated or worn.

[37] 6) **Reading the Conference Report Aloud.** The ministers should diligently concern themselves with reading aloud everything that was discussed at the conference.

7) **Resting Benches.** In accordance with the ordinance from 1935 the resting benches are to be done away with.

8) **Rocking chairs.** Neither will rocking chairs be tolerated.

9) **Parkas.** Those who have still not complied with that which was requested a long time ago regarding the parkas are to do away with them, and if they still do not obey, they are to be disciplined even more.

Caps with visors. Caps with logos and visors are not to be tolerated, rather only those hats and caps which are allowed may be worn.

Skirts. Short skirts have been forbidden for a long time and are not to be tolerated. The ordinance states that the skirt is supposed to be 5-6 inches from the ground. It is a shameful, brazen thing that our clothes are never good enough and that we always want to please the world and to make ourselves equal with it. Compared to the world we are looking ever poorer and we are becoming spiritually and physically debauched, so that the reason for this is already a cause for alarm.

10) **Drunkenness.** Also regarding drinking, and going to beer parlours and saloons, more earnestness needs to be taken. It is an evil that other even worse things are coming to fruition, and must be combated with all earnestness and diligence. It is running rampant like an incurable cancer. In Isaiah 62:6-7 that Lord says: "O Jerusalem, I have set watchmen upon thy walls, which shall never hold their peace day nor night: ye that make mention of the LORD, keep not silence, and give him no rest, till he establish, and till he make Jerusalem a praise in the earth." That is our job as watchmen and as brothers and sisters. Let us prove ourselves as loyal watchmen so that not too much garbage and evil be carried through Jerusalem's gates, and do not let us be mute dogs who cannot bark, which the Lord so fiercely laments in Isaiah 56:10, who cannot be disciplined, are lazy, and lie around and love to sleep. When that occurs, then the vineyard of the Lord will be destroyed and we will cease to be a people of God.

1963

The following is a report about what was discerned during the annual conference that was held on January 27, 1963 on the **Sturgeon Creek Colony**, in Manitoba.

1) **Clothing.** It has been noticed that too many floral[34] clothes are being worn by and the same goes for aprons, and this is directly contrary to the ordinance which stipulates that no colours other than black, dark blue, or coffee brown may be worn, and that aprons must be one colour. As far as dresses are concerned, women may wear a print with roses that are no larger than a dime. This is often violated. Therefore we are adding to this ordinance and putting a stop to this garbage. [38] The fabric buyer should not dare to buy the forbidden fabric and thereby to spread arrogance and pride through one's clothing and to enable such things.

2) **Shoes.** The ordinance regarding the purchase of shoes was also discussed and it was decided that the ordinance from 1944 would remain in effect. But in order to clarify the ordinance and to make it more understandable, it has been discerned that the minister, the manager, and the cobbler should all go to buy the shoes and what they deem good should be accepted.

3) **Skirts.** It was also mentioned in 1962 that the skirts seem to be getting shorter from year to year, in spite of the fact that the ordinance clearly states that the hem is supposed to be 5-6 inches from the ground.

Caps. Caps are worn without bands and are made smaller so that they sit on the back of the head. This is also an evil that needs to be eliminated. The headscarf and the apron are no longer good enough and people try to force them out and to make themselves equal to the world. And it has gotten so bad, one weed after the other creeps up in the Lord's vineyard to destroy it, and we are not watchful enough to exterminate the evils when they show themselves.

4) **Borrowed Money.** It has also been discerned that where one colony has borrowed money from another or owes another, it should drive to the colony where the money is owed and should discuss it with that colony until both colonies are satisfied. Read about it in Sirach 29 and Psalm 37:21.[35]

5) **Usury.** Regarding usury or interest on money it has been discerned that a child of God is not allowed to take part in it because too many of the Holy Scriptures are against it. See Psalm 15:5 and Matthew 5:42 which states: "Give to the one who asks you and do not turn away from the one who wants to borrow from you." Also read Jeremiah 5:10, Ezekiel 18:8.

Alas, dear brothers and sisters, we remain your fellow workers, and we wish you all God's love, grace, and favour, and the best health, as we all do our duty and prove our faithfulness and faithfully and diligently keep the ordinances according to Isaiah 58:1 as we strive against sin and transgressions and fight to go ahead in goodness, Peter Hofer and George Wipf.

1964

The following was decided at the annual conference of the Hutterian Brethren that was on February 16, 1964 at Waldheim Colony in Manitoba.

1) **Trucks and Vans.** The vans should only be one colour, but not red. Those who have vans that are two colours should paint over them so that they are one colour. Also the trucks that are purchased in 1964 are not to be red.

2) In 1964 no fabric is to be cut, not even in emergencies.

[39] 3) **Shunning.** The Woodcrest and Julius or Ontario people are to be shunned because in so many ways they have made themselves equal to the world and wreaked so much havoc among us and still might do so.

4) **Garb for Girls.** More due diligence needs to be taken by us and by the parents regarding the girls, the way that they wear their hair, their apron and headscarves, so that they do not run around so unbridled and shameless to their own destruction, and to the frustration of those who still seek to build up and preserve the colony.
    Hairstyles. The same goes for boys and men who are to wear their hair according to ordinance #1 from 1921. Read that ordinance.

5) **Witness Brothers.** It has been raised that there are too few brothers sitting in the Counsel of the Witness Brothers. There are some colonies that have only one, or some even no one on the counsel other than the minister, the manager, and the farm boss. This will only serve to make us deviate, not to build us up and make us better. Those who are guilty should consider themselves and do something about it.

6) **Keeping the ordinances.** As ministers let us be more diligent and strive even more to keep the ordinances. Let us not say as the foolish do, we do not need a conference or ordinances. Read Jeremiah 2:20. For Peter says in Acts 15:28: "FOR IT SEEMED GOOD TO THE HOLY GHOST, AND TO US, TO LAY UPON YOU NO GREATER BURDEN THAN THESE NECESSARY THINGS."[36] No people on earth can be governed or survive without order; how much less so, a people of God, or a colony, which is supposed to stand in obedience and true serenity. Therefore it is written in Psalm 32:9: "Do not be like the horse or the mule, which have no understanding but must be controlled by bit and bridle or they will not come to you." Yes, let us keep to what we have. And let us walk, so that we may

honestly be able to say: We have walked according to the example set before us (Philippians 3, 17).

1965

The following is a report about what was decided at the ministers' and managers' conference that was held February 14, 1965 on the Huron Colony in Manitoba.

1) **Electric Appliances.** In almost all of the colonies people have purchased for themselves electric pans, kettles, *Kruegel*, and toasters. These should all be taken away by the minister and should be completely eliminated.

2) **Aprons for the food carriers.** The wearing of aprons at weddings by food carriers and pourers should not occur and should not be tolerated.

3) **Bicycles and Baby Carriages.**[37] Bicycles and baby carriages should be taken away by the ministers and should be completely eliminated.

4) **Weddings.** In 1964 it was discerned and established as an ordinance that from now on weddings should stop at 6 o'clock.

[40] 5) **Caps.** Also, the new style caps that the boys have are to be done away with. One should stay with the old style caps that have been in use until now.

6) **Jackets.** The jackets of the wives and also the young women and girls should be done away with. We must do our best to eliminate the evil that has already rooted itself so deeply. It has already grown above our heads.

7) **Driving to the *Juliusleut* and Woodcrest.** It should also be reported if someone wants to drive to Ontario to the Julius people or Woodcrest to visit those who have fallen away, and it is to be discussed with the old ministers.

8) **Zippers.** Zippers, instead of hooks, to fasten clothing, are not to be allowed.

Note: The eight above articles are a serious admonishment regarding what is allowed and what is not allowed and what ordinances are being introduced. And they are to be presented and reported to all of the colonies and are to be enforced by the ministers and the managers.

In conclusion, we are obligated to keep everything that the above ordinances entail, just as Paul teaches in Philippians 4:8: "Finally, dear
brothers, whatever is true, whatever is noble, whatever is right, whatever is
pure, whatever is lovely, whatever is admirable—if anything is praiseworthy—think about such things." And let us not be like the modern people,
gawking after the world and making the way ever wider and stepping
farther and farther off of the narrow way. But as it is said: What God has
commanded I must obey. 1 Timothy 1:8 says: "We know that the law is
good if one uses it properly. We also know that the law is made not for
the righteous but for the lawbreakers and rebels," for those who violate
and transgress our ordinances, and who pursue their own self-interest
through electric kettles, toasters, and electric pans. And there are those
among us who try to justify them and like the wasteful servant they
come to the conference and try to make disorder out of an ordinance.

They do this by first bringing such things home and then at the conference they try to get permission. We preach a lot about Ananias and
his wife Saphira. But many do not think about how closely related their
situation was to ours, and about how they were struck by the Spirit of
God and gave up their spirits.

We must become very sober, lest the candle of Israel go out and we be
forced to walk without any light. Let us allow ourselves to be instructed
by the Word of God as we are taught in Acts 15:28: "It seemed good to
the Holy Spirit" to make the ordinances for the colony, which we, the
brotherhood, are obligated to obey. Those, however, who go against
them, go against God's ordinances and invite judgment upon themselves.

Let us as ministers work that much more diligently to keep the ordinances of the colony, and to hold to them as an essential guide so that
later when the vineyard of the Lord has been destroyed and the misery
and horror of the destruction stands before us we do not have to regret
that we were too careless or yielding and that we saw too much with
our hands covering our eyes. Things decline enough even with the most
careful watching.

[41] Alas, dear brothers, we wish you God's unending love and mercy
as a greeting. Amen. Peter Hofer and George Wipf.

1966

The following is a report about what was discerned during the ministers' and managers' conference that was held on March 8, 1966 on the
Rosedale Colony in Manitoba.

1) **Toboggans (also called Snow Planes).** It has been decided and
established as an ordinance that no toboggans (snow planes) may be
purchased or used on the colonies.

2) Ordinance regarding Cooking for the Sick. The following is to be an ordinance regarding cooking for the sick, which is happening in some colonies. The waffle batter and waffle irons are being sent home in order to make waffles at home for the sick or for the nursing mother. This is not to happen or to be allowed. Such things only serve to separate us not to build us up or make us better, and should be stopped by the minister or the manager.

3) Aprons. It has also been reported that in some colonies the women-folk are wearing or going around with multi-coloured or floral-printed aprons, just as the dresses are. This is not allowed and is to be stopped by the minister. Let us keep to the old ordinance that was discerned in 1941. The aprons for womenfolk are to be no other colours than black, dark blue, dark green, or coffee brown, but only one colour.

4) Work Aprons. Those work aprons that were allowed in the 1938 ordinance must be worn along with the proper apron and are not meant to replace the proper apron, as is happening in some colonies, where the proper apron is no longer being worn, rather only the short work aprons. If this matter is not corrected then work aprons will no longer be allowed.

It will require constant fighting and watchfulness, for the garbage has grown over our roots and has rooted itself deeply. It must be done, however, lest the cow and the calf go to ruin and we cease to be a people of God, and we be rejected by God as lukewarm Christians and flavourless salt, for God will not be mocked and what the person sows is what he will reap.

Alas, we wish you God's unending grace, love, and mercy, and the most precious peace and the best welfare. We remain your humble fellow workers,

Peter Hofer and George Wipf.

1967

The following is a report about what was discerned during the ministers' and managers' conference that was held on February 23, 1967, on the New Elmspring Colony in South Dakota.

1) Work Aprons. The white work aprons for womenfolk are to be allowed.

[42] **2) Tea Pots.** The electric tea pots [kettles] are to be allowed.

3) Skirts. The short skirt has been forbidden for a long time and is not to be tolerated. The ordinance from 1962 states: The skirt is to be 5-6 inches from the ground. It is a shameless, brazen thing that our garb is never good enough, and that we try to please the world and to make ourselves the same as it. Because of this we are becoming ever poorer and more debauched, both spiritually and physically, so that one must start to wonder where we are headed.

Admonishment regarding the *Hulba*. It has been deemed necessary that it must be impressed upon every colony that the ordinance regarding the Hulba should be renewed and held to. The ordinance ought to be read every time a couple gets engaged. This ordinance is found in the year 1931.

At the Hulba a lot of sinning happens, as everyone should know, which is why we had to stop the Hulba. Let us do our best to eliminate the evil that has so deeply rooted itself. It has already grown above our heads. Yes, let us be diligent, especially we ministers. It is our duty as ministers, just as it is the duty of every Brother and Sister. Let us prove ourselves to be loyal watchmen so that not so much garbage be carried in through the gates of Jerusalem, and let us not be the mute dogs who cannot bark, about which the Lord so fiercely laments, and which no longer touch his heart (Isaiah 56:10) and who cannot be disciplined, are lazy, and love to lie around and sleep. When that happens, the vineyard of the Lord will be destroyed and we will cease to be a people of God.

In conclusion, I bid you all sincere greetings and the love, grace, and mercy of our great God and I anticipate your child-like obedience. I remain your humble fellow worker and pilgrim, George Wipf.

1968

With this newsletter we are notifying everyone that the 1968 conference of the Hutterian Brethren will take place on June 20 at the Huron Colony in Manitoba. That is, if it is God's will and if nothing stops us in the meantime.

May God grant that our conference would serve to improve us and build us up that we might better eliminate and put a stop to abuses and disorderly beings that try, with all their power, to creep in and to implant themselves and to make themselves at home. The words of Paul apply to us: "Your boasting is not good. Don't you know that a little yeast works through the whole batch of dough?" And he advises us: "Get rid of the old yeast that you may be a new batch without yeast."[38] As for the best way for us to do this—that is what we will discuss at the conference, with God's help, as long as we are united in this matter.

[43] Therefore it is the purpose of the ordinances to make the things well-known that are not fitting for us and that do not exclaim or enable us to boast that we are a people of God which does not see itself as the same as the world.

But these ordinances, as inevitably necessary and indispensable as they are, do not help us if we do not uphold them, and if the ministers do not stand more firmly and loyally behind them and uphold them themselves. Soon it may be said: Already new ordinances. But who is more to blame than those who walk in a disorderly way according to the flesh and always want to make the way wider for the colony and because of their own self-interest and always seek after fleshly freedom. Those are the ones we must oppose and they don't like that.

It is no wonder that even among us there are always more ordinances. And those ordinances are mostly in the way of those who walk in a disorderly way in the house of God, and who are always trying to introduce something new. They say in their hearts: I will not submit. But it is a joy for the righteous to do what is right, but it is dreadful for evildoers. We need only read what Paul has written about the law (1 Timothy 1:8-10). The righteous, the child of God, is always under the education and discipline of the Holy Spirit and follows without compulsion what the spirit teaches through Peter: "Submit yourselves for the Lord's sake to every authority instituted among men" (1 Peter 2:13).

And that pertains especially to ordinances regarding the church, which we have made at the conference to honour our great God and for the welfare of the colony, so that the latter may continue on and be upheld.

Yes, look closely at the criticizers of the ordinances. Who are they? What sort of condemnable life are they living? Their lives are the ones that are to be criticized the most. It is because of them that we are always making new ordinances. Therefore Scripture says: "Do not be like the horse and the mule, which have no understanding but must be controlled by bit and bridle or they will not come to you" (Psalm 32:9).

May the loving, gracious, and faithful God have mercy on all of the colonies and awake us to the battle that has been decreed to us, that we might look to Jesus, the author and finisher of our faith, and seek to walk in his footsteps of humility and child-like obedience and trust in God.

Alas, dear brothers, I wish you all God's unending grace, love, and mercy, and especially the most precious peace, that in all things it would go well in the house of God, his congregation. Your humble fellow servant, Joseph Kleinsasser.

1968

The following is a report regarding what was discerned during the ministers' and managers' conference that was held June 25, 1968 at the Huron Colony in Manitoba.

1) **Tables and Chairs.** It has been discerned and decided that from now on steel tables and chairs with chrome feet may be acquired.

[44] 2) **Trucks and Vans.** The trucks no longer need to be repainted, rather may remain the way they were purchased but single-coloured trucks ought to be purchased as often as possible.

3) **Family Allowance and Old-Age Pension.** From now on Family Allowance and Old-Age Pension may be accepted.

4) **Schnapps for the bride.** It was discerned on February 23, 1967 at the New Elmspring Colony in South Dakota that the bride should also be given a 26 ounce bottle of schnapps, just as the groom is, to give out at during the engagement at the parents' house.

5) *Hulba.* It was also discerned that on Saturday evening before a wedding, as well as the evening of an engagement, a lunch is to be prepared, but it is to be enjoyed in the common kitchen or dining room.

6) **Jackets.** It has also been discerned that a stop should be put to the long and wide jackets, which are gathering momentum in some colonies. It is a shameless, brazen thing that our garb is never good enough, and that we try to please the world and to make ourselves the same as it. Because of this we are becoming ever poorer and more debauched, both spiritually and physically, so that one must start to wonder where we are headed. And thus the weeds sneak into the vineyard of the Lord in order to destroy it. And we are not watching closely enough to eliminate this evil where it shows itself. The women should observe the old custom.

7) **Runaways.** Also, those who have fallen away or run away are not allowed to play their radios or guitars or musical instruments on the yard or on the colony, because through it the young people will be led astray. We do not allow such things in the schools because it will be to our detriment and harm, and yet we want to allow them in our homes. What a contradiction! Let us protect ourselves with force from such destructive influences, temptations, and stains, and avoid such things. The spirit of the world is pressing upon us with force, to our own destruction and harm; it ought to scare us that the power of darkness is all around us and is coming ever closer in order to blind us.

In conclusion, let us diligently pursue true unity in the innocence of Christ, and to practice Christian love and reconciliation one with another, so that our heavenly father would take more pleasure in us. That is what we wish for you all in Jesus Christ. Amen. Your humble fellow helper and pilgrim, Joseph Kleinsasser.

1969

The following is a report regarding what was discerned during the ministers' and managers' conference on July 2, 1969 at the Maxwell Colony in South Dakota.

1) **Splitting.** It has been discussed and decided that if a colony splits, two ministers may not stay with one group.

[45] 2) **Purchasing Land.** Regarding the purchase of land the old custom should be upheld, other than in emergencies, where it must be done quickly, in which case the minister should be notified and permission should be sought and thereafter all of the colonies should be notified.

3) **Punishment and Acceptance.** It has also been decided that no minister who has not yet been confirmed in the service of the Word has the power to reinstate or to vindicate one who is being punished, whether through prayer time or teaching. Neither does he have the power to exclude someone and much less to accept them from the state of exclusion because such peace must be extended in the name of the colony.

4) **Jackets.** Wives and womenfolk may wear jackets but they may have no improper decorations or colours, rather they must be simple as is fitting for an honourable sister. Just as Paul says: "I also want women to dress modestly, with decency and propriety,"[39] not with red or green as some are wearing already, which is a sign of brazen high-spiritedness. For the outward appearance bears witness as to what is on the inside, and what is on the inside governs what is on the outside. Therefore, my sister, consider your clothes as well as your heart and what is on the inside, that it is in keeping with your words and your deeds.

5) **Allowance.** Everyone, including children, as soon as they are born, is to receive 25 cents per month in allowance.

6) **Twins.** It has been decided that if twins are born that the second twin is to receive as many clothes as the first child in the family.

7) **Lining.** Lining is also to be given where it is needed.

Admonition regarding wristwatches. It must be mentioned that wristwatches will no longer be tolerated but are to be removed. These have appeared in some colonies and are worn freely, as if they were allowed. And so one evil after the other appears in our colonies, and destroys them so that nothing is considered sin anymore and we make ourselves the same as the world. Also wristwatches are normally worn out of pride and acquired by dishonest means.

Suspenders. Also, boys and men are not allowed to go without suspenders for it is contrary to the ordinance and seems to be appearing in the colonies again.

Yes, let us, particularly we ministers, diligently pursue the example of those who came before us. Let us be faithfully ordered by the colony, and diligently keep watch over it, while we carefully see to that the way is not entirely lost and the old marking stones are not displaced in spite of the fact that ruin is moving in to the colonies in full force. Rather, let us see to it that the good old ordinances are always upheld, so that the colony may be kept upright and in good peace, for it is insured and sealed with the blood of martyrs with a good foundation which is not to be doubted. And if we follow in the path of the pious and our ancestors, then we will not come to harm.

[46] **The confirmation of ministers.** It must also be mentioned that the following colonies have discussed it and have agreed to confirm the followers ministers in service:

Minister David Decker, from the Tschetter Colony in South Dakota
Minister George Waldner from the Spink Colony in South Dakota
Minister Mike Waldner from the Rosedale Colony in South Dakota

Alas, in conclusion, it is my wish and my desire that we ministers become more diligent, and strive even harder to uphold the ordinances. Let us not say as the foolish do: We do not need a conference or ordinances. For Peter says: "It seemed good to the Holy Spirit and to us not to burden you with anything beyond the following requirements."[40] For no people on earth can be governed or survive without order, and how much less so a people of God or a colony that is supposed to stand in obedience and serenity. Therefore it is written (Psalm 32:9): "Do not be like the horse or the mule, which have no understanding but must be controlled by bit and bridle or they will not come to you." Yes, let us uphold what we have. And let us walk so that we may be able to honestly say (according to Philippians): we have walked according to the example set before us.

And that is the ordinance that we are to uphold and according to which we are to orient ourselves.

1969

The following is a report regarding what was decided and accepted during the ministers' and managers' conference at the Home Wood Colony on November 30, 1969.

Consolidating Money. Every colony in Manitoba should give $200.00. The exceptions are Riverside Colony which should give $1000.00, Blumengart Colony, $1000.00, and Greenwald Colony, $2500.00. This money should be devoted to covering the expenses for the Interlake Colony. They are feeling so burdened because they have already paid the lawyers $50,000.00 and they still have to pay them another $25,000.00.

And because it has been unanimously decided, let us raise the money and put it aside, and give it to the minister, Jacob Hofer from the Rosedale Colony. Collecting money is an uncomfortable thing, especially when the request falls on deaf ears and when those who are being asked always put it off and make things difficult for the collector.

Therefore every minister to whom this is directed should see to it that either he or his manager sends the full sum of money either by cash or cheque so it may be passed on to the appropriate people.

It should also be mentioned that there are a number of South Dakota colonies that have still not paid what was requested of them during the conference at the Maxwell Colony.

Therefore I would like to advise all of those who still owe money that it is expected without exception. Paul says: give to each what is owed him.

Hoping for the best and trusting in God, I remain your most humble servant, Joseph Kleinsasser.

[47] 1970

The following is a report regarding what was decided during the ministers' and managers' conference that was held on April 29, 1970 at the Sturgeon Creek Colony in Manitoba.

1) **Parkas.** It has been decided that those who still have not put away their parkas, even though they were asked to do so both now and a long time ago, are to be punished even more.

2) **Kindergarten.** It has also been decided and has been established as an ordinance that kindergarten should and must be held. It is a shame that some colonies have not had a kindergarten for years now. Yes, we must all work diligently, especially we ministers, to follow in the example of our ancestors. Let us be faithfully ordered by the colony as we diligently care for and watch over it.

Aprons. It must also be mentioned that in some colonies that womenfolk are wearing and going around with multi-coloured and floral-printed aprons, just like their dresses. This is not to be permitted, rather should be abolished by the ministers. And let us uphold the old ordinances that were already decided in 1941. The aprons for womenfolk may only be black, dark blue, dark green or coffee brown, but only a single colour.

Headscarves. Sisters and young women going around the yard bare-headed or with caps on are appearing in the colonies with force. That is wrong. No virtuous, honourable, or God-fearing Sister would allow herself to be seen that way for it is not fitting. Paul says to Titus: "You must teach what is in accord with sound doctrine. Teach the older men to be temperate, worthy of respect, self-controlled, and sound in faith, in love and in endurance. Likewise, teach the older women to be rever-ent in the way they live, not to be slanderers or addicted to too much wine, but to teach what is good. They can train the younger women to love their husbands and children, to be self-controlled and pure, to be busy at home, to be kind, and to be subject to their husbands, so that no one will malign the word of God" (Titus 2:1-5). Paul says: "And every woman who prays or prophesies with her head uncovered dishonours her head—it is just as though her head were shaved. If a woman does not cover her head, she should have her hair cut off; and if it is a disgrace for a woman to have her hair cut or shaved off, she should cover her head.... For this reason, and because of the angels, the woman ought to have a sign of authority on her head.... Judge for yourselves: Is it proper for a woman to pray to God with her head uncovered?"[41]

Runaways. Also, those who have fallen away or run away are not allowed to play their radios or guitars or musical instruments on the yard or on the colony, because through it the young people will be led astray. And even the fathers and mothers can listen and watch. We do not allow such things in the schools because it will be to our detriment and harm, and yet we want to allow them in our homes. O, what a contradiction. Let us protect ourselves with force from such destructive influences, temptations, and stains, and avoid such things. The spirit of the world is pressing upon us with force, to our own destruction and harm; it ought to scare us that the power of darkness is all around us and is coming ever closer in order to blind us.

[48] Thus says the Lord of hosts, the God of Israel: Improve your lives and your ways and then I will live with you in this place. "Since my people are crushed, I am crushed; I mourn, and horror grips me. Is there no balm in Gilead? Is there no physician there? Why then is there no healing for the wound of my people?"[42]

Confirmation of Ministers. It must also be mentioned that the Bloom-field Colony has decided to confirm their Minister Joseph Gross in service.

Consolidation of Money. It has also been decided that each colony in Manitoba should put in $50.00 and deliver it to Minister Jacob Hofer of the Rosedale Colony, so that the existing as well as upcoming debts may be paid. And because it has been unanimously decided, let us come up with the money and deposit it.

Collecting money is an uncomfortable thing, especially when the request falls on deaf ears and when those who are being asked always put it off and make things difficult for the collector. For trucks and vans and rubber tires you have a lot of money. But when it comes to something church-related then you have no money and then you complain so much about how hard the times are. The innocent are exempt. Therefore every minister to whom this is directed should see to it that either he or his manager sends the full sum of money either by cash or cheque so it may be passed on to the appropriate people. Therefore I would like to advise all of those who still owe money that it is still expected without exception. Paul says in Romans 13:7: "Give everyone what you owe him: If you owe taxes, pay taxes; if revenue, then revenue; if respect, then respect; if honour, then honour. Let no debt remain outstanding, except the continuing debt to love one another, for he who loves his fellow man has fulfilled the law" (Romans 13:7-8). Therefore it is good to be subject to law not only for discipline's sake, but for the sake of your consciences.

Hoping for the best and trusting in God, I remain your most humble servant, Joseph Kleinsasser.

1971

The following is a report regarding what was decided during the ministers' and managers' conference, which was held on April 20, 1971 on the James Valley Colony in Manitoba.

1) **Parkas.** Parkas may be worn.

2) **Zippers.** Zippers may be used in jackets.

3) **Kindergarten.** Each colony should diligently work to have a kindergarten.

4) **Annunciation.** The celebration of Annunciation is abolished, and the sermon which pertains to it is to be preached the following Sunday.

[49] 5) **Aprons.** The aprons may be the same colour as the dresses, as long as they are one of the permitted colours. The aprons for womenfolk may only be black, dark blue, dark green, or coffee brown, but must be a single colour and not multi-coloured or floral printed like the dresses. This is not be tolerated, but should be stopped by the minister. And let us keep

to the old ordinance. The work apron is not supposed to replace the proper apron, as is already happening in some colonies, where the proper apron is not even worn anymore, rather only the short work apron. If this does not happen with the wives' work aprons then they must be done away with.

6) Jackets. It has also been discerned that a stop should be put to the long and wide jackets, which are gathering momentum in some colonies. It is a shameless, brazen thing that our garb is never good enough, and that we try to please the world and to make ourselves the same as it.
Drunkenness. An admonishment regarding drunkenness: each person should stay altogether away from the beer parlours. The reason for this long overdue ordinance is that a godless disorderly life of drunkenness is being pursued by too many, and is done so with the scant colony money or was thievishly stolen from the colony or the dishonestly acquired money from the followers of Gehasi who are already spiritually leprous and morally depraved and degenerate, and are governed, ruled, and possessed by the spirit of gluttony, and have fallen into various vices because of it.

Let us rescue those who are not yet bound with Satan's cords by the fetters of gluttony and debauchery, and let us do our job in accordance with sobriety, temperance, respectability, and self-control, and be a light of the world and salt of the earth. Let us strive with godly, continuous fervour against the gluttony of extravagance and excess, which are pursued in the drinking establishments.

Let us all, especially ministers, managers, and elders,[43] unanimously work with God's assistance and with patience to enforce this long overdue ordinance, because drinking and drunkenness have become a cancer and have wrought woeful consequences, which will be difficult—if even possible—to eradicate. Let us blow the trumpets against this blatant sin and abominable gluttony and frivolity and debauchery that so many pursue in the taverns. Yes, let us diligently work to comply with this and if we do we will have our hands full. Let us do our best to eliminate this evil which has taken such deep root and which has already grown above our heads.

Hoping for the best and trusting in God, I remain your most humble fellow helper, Joseph Kleinsasser.

1972

The following is a report regarding what was decided during the ministers' and managers' conference which was held on February 22, 1972, at the Sturgeon Creek Colony in Manitoba.

1) **Committtee.** It has been decided that a committee is to be named. Those who have been named are:

1. Bishop Joseph Vetter from Sunnyside

2. [50] Joerg Vetter from Lakeside

3. Joseph Vetter from Huron

4. Fritz Vetter from Poplar Point

5. Jakob Vetter from Woodland

6. Samuel Vetter from Sturgeon Creek

7. Jakob Vetter from Crystal Spring[44]

2) **Refrigerators** are not allowed other than in certain instances where they are necessary and have been permitted by the committee for the elderly and the sick and also senior ministers who have to take out a lot of food.

3) **Purchasing land.** If a colony in Manitoba or South Dakota wishes to purchase new land in order to start a new yard then the financial situation and the land must be examined by the respective committee, the Manitoba committee in Manitoba and the South Dakota committee for South Dakota and the committee's report should be circulated to all of the colonies.

4) **Manager.** It was also decided that if a manager is removed from his position for any reason, the committee must examine him to see if he has had a good witness to decide whether he may be re-elected to the position.

5) **Naming a Manager.** It has also been decided that if a colony does not have a manager, it should have a vote to name one. It should also be done in those instances where the manager has become the minister.

6) **Skirts.** The skirts for women may be black, grey, brown, and dark blue.

7) **Discord.** If a brother or sister is in discord, and is supposed to apologize during the teaching or prayer, then he or she may not come to the teaching or word of God until he is once again at peace with the colony.

8) **Pardoning.** If someone is to be pardoned during the teaching or prayer, then he may be inside during the teaching or prayer. And the pardoning should not be pushed back for too long.

10)[45] **Hairstyles.** Also, we should not allow or tolerate our boys and men to run around with long hair like hippies in the godless world. It is as it says in the Communion teaching: Some of the men desire[46] long hair, just as the people of war, and like the locusts that ascend from the abyss. It is pure nonsense and unclean to conform so much to the world and to the hippies. Let us grow our hair and wear it in a way that is fitting for a Brother or Sister and pleasing to God.

We ministers need to be diligent to hold ourselves more closely and firmly to the ordinances of the colony as the necessary guide so that later, when the vineyard of the Lord is laid waste and the affliction and atrocity of the desolation is upon us, we will not have to regret that we were too careless and indulgent. Even with the best attention things go downhill enough. Let us consider the encouragement given by the dear Brother Klaus Breidl in his last sermon, which he preached before his end along with some other brothers of the Word (during [51] the time when he was sick): Dear brothers, I ask you earnestly, see to it that you hold firmly to the good old ordinances of the colony, and that the old cornerstone does not move. Hold as firmly as you are able to the Christian community and protect against pride and self-interest. For pride is a root of all kinds of evil and a disruption of all good things. Joseph Kleinsasser.

1973

At first I wish you all from my heart the peace of the Lord, the community of his Spirit, his unending love, faithfulness, grace, and mercy, as well as the priceless health in body and soul.

Herewith we are informing all of the colonies that the annual ministers' and managers' conference is to take place March 16, 1973 at the Spink Colony in South Dakota, so that nothing will interfere.

All of the colonies are sincerely invited to attend, and to take part in making the conference a blessing and useful. Yes, may the gracious God and Lord be among us with his spirit of counsel, understanding, wisdom, and order so that it would go smoothly and praise, honour, and glory would be to his holy name, and that each one would have God's honour and pleasure and the welfare of the colonies, spiritually and physically in mind and that an actual improvement would follow among us and that we would be and remain a people of God and not fall away like the erstwhile Raditschewa.[47] Things are sadly headed that way among us.

1) **Drunkenness.** Like the horrid drinking that goes on in parlours and hideouts.

2) **Smoking.** Horrid smoking is also becoming prevalent among us.

3) **Radios.** There are also too many radios in houses, vans, and trucks.

4) **Games.** Playing hockey is also becoming prevalent.

5) **Hairstyles.** Some of the young people are growing long hair, like the people of war and the locusts that ascend from the abyss.

6) **Wristwatches.** The wristwatches are also becoming prevalent.

Let us often consider the last sermon of the dear brother Klaus Braidle: Dear brothers, I ask you earnestly, see to it that you hold firmly to the good old ordinances of the colony, and that the old cornerstone does not move. Hold as firmly as you are able to the Christian community and protect against pride and self-interest. Beware that you don't implement any innovations or adopt anything new.

[52] **Confirmation of Ministers.** It has also been mentioned that the Rose Valley Colony has decided to confirm their minister, Joseph Waldner, in service.

May God the all-powerful one, the giver of all good and perfect gifts, grant all of us heavenly wisdom and peaceful and united hearts, so that everything might happen according to his honour and for our welfare. Your most humble fellow helper,

Joseph Kleinsasser.

1973

I greet you with God's love, grace, mercy and precious peace, and priceless health in body and soul.

We are all happy because of the comfortable weather. Thanks be to God for that. Those of us leaders who were from South Dakota left Manitoba and said goodbye to as many people as possible.

But that was after we had cared for our loved ones and discussed the situation of the poor among us and our community living. Read about it in 2 Mak. 4 (Sic).

Dear brothers, we have decided to tell you about our meeting here in South Dakota on May 27, 1973, regarding the Forest River Colony in North Dakota.

A good part of our meeting in Manitoba was occupied with the aforementioned abuses, and people trying to make themselves the same as the world through wristwatches, radios, shunning, and allowing young people out into the world for a long time to work. One also hears that the Hutterite custom of going to prayer will be changed and now only "prayer meetings" will be held.

According to our decision the above-mentioned abuses will not pass without being investigated. The Minister . . . is disobedient because he was unable to come for the examination, which is disagreeable to us, though we have heard that he has been confronted and punished and we must accept that.

Dear brothers, it is our responsibility to wake each other up, to warn, and to punish one another, so that we might protect the colony from corruption. We will do this with the help and assistance from God, according to Exodus 32. Sincere greetings, Jospeh Hofer and Joseph Wipf.

1973

The following is a report about what was decided during the ministers' and managers' conference, which was held March 16, at the Spink Colony in South Dakota.

1) **Seeking Counsel.** It has been decided that from now on in each colony the manager and the Farm Boss are to hold counsel every morning with the minister. See the small History Book on page 537.

[53] 2) **Common Account.** Also, the manager is to bring the bank statement and the cheques to the minister every month.

3) **Naming a Manager.** If a manager falls away and is found incompetent for his position, so that he must be removed from the position, then he may not be re-elected during the first election.

4) **School.** The German School and Sunday School are so poorly run that sometimes people cannot read, write, or sing. Also during mealtime in the school the children's prayers are no longer prayed according to the old ordinance. Every minister should employ more diligence to improve the Sunday and German Schools in his colony.

5) **Clothing.** Clothing that is too brazen is being purchased and the ministers and managers are standing quietly by and allowing it to happen.

6) **English Clothing.** The purchased and English clothing, such as pants, Shirts, wind-breakers, and jackets with zippers are still not allowed and should be done away with.

7) **Cameras-Photos.** The same goes for cameras and taking pictures, such as the bridal couple driving to the city and having their picture taken in a studio, as well as the pictures on the walls in houses. The

same goes for **wristwatches, finger rings**, and **chains** around the neck. These are all Moabite customs and practices, and are a horror to the Lord. Also the ordinance prohibiting **big mirrors** and **floor lamps** is to be renewed, because these things lead to idolatry, as do **projectors**; these are all abuses and are not fitting for a child of God.

8) **Caps.** Regarding caps it has been decided that they may be worn until a boy marries, but not to teaching and to prayer. The old ordinance regarding hats should remain standing.

9) **Hairstyles—Beards.** This is an admonishment regarding men's and women's hair—both men and women should uphold the old ordinance of the colony. It is also dishonourable that young brothers, so to say, are no longer wearing beards. Married men are also going too long after the wedding without growing a beard. A brother without a beard should be taken into counsel.

10) **Shunning.** The ordinance regarding those who have fallen away is too often neglected, particularly through shaking hands, eating with them, and driving around with them.

11) **Runaways.** If a runaway dies or is injured while in the world: if it is a young unbaptized man or woman then they may be brought home and a funeral may be held but no wake and they may be buried in the colony cemetery, but if it is a baptized member who has run away then neither a wake nor a funeral may be held and they may not be buried in the colony cemetery.

12) **Shoes.** Also regarding the purchase of shoes one must try harder to uphold the ordinance. The high **leather boots** that are worn by the young women and wives should not be tolerated; it is only brazen high-spiritedness and a way of being the same as the world.

13) **Shirts.** The shirts for the wives and young women should only be white, and not blue or green as is gathering momentum in some colonies. It is a shameless, [54] brazen thing, that our garb is never good enough, and that we always want to please the world and to make ourselves equal with it. Compared to the world we are looking ever poorer and we are becoming spiritually and physically debauched, so that the reason for this is already a cause for alarm.

14) **Bodices-jackets.** Wives and young women's bodices should be tucked in. The jackets can stay out, but may not be as long as the white ones that the disobedient and those without virtue wear.

15) **Radios—TV—Tape Recorders.** The radios in the houses, in the schools, in the vans, trucks, tractors, pickups, and combines, as well as TVs and tape recorders, should be abolished in all seriousness.

16) **Games,** such as hockey rinks, hockey suits, and ballgames played by young men and women in the city have been shamefully exposed and are as shameless as the world.

17) **Ministers and Managers.** A shortage of leaders occurs when children are baptized so that some colonies do not have a complete leadership, and so a colony should seek to replace the leadership [the witness brothers] during the children's baptism.

18) **Eliminating Evil.** It has also been decided that because so many violations are occurring among us, and are passing unnoticed, against all warning and the ordinances of the colony, then such colonies should be given a two month period in which to improve and to eliminate these evils and the disorder. And if the colony is not obedient then it should be examined and seriously punished by the senior minister. And if the minister does not receive any help from the leadership to improve the problem, then he should go to the Bishop or to the senior minister for assistance.

Yes, let us all work diligently, especially we ministers, according to the example of Zacharias and his Elizabeth who "were both upright in the sight of God, observing all the Lord's commandments and regulations blamelessly" (Luke 1:6), and under which our laws are also included in order that we will be able to remain a people of God with right customs and laws and will be able to keep ourselves unspoiled by the horrors and excesses of the world.

Thus says the Lord of hosts, the God of Israel: Improve your lives and your ways and then I will live with you in this place. "Since my people are crushed, I am crushed; I mourn, and horror grips me. Is there no balm in Gilead? Is there no physician there? Why then is there no healing for the wound of my people?"[48] O Lord, do not let us be put to shame.

In conclusion, I bid you all sincere greetings and the love, grace, and mercy of our great God and I anticipate your child-like obedience. I remain your humble fellow worker and pilgrim, Joseph Kleinsasser.

[55] 1974

The following is a report about what was decided during the ministers' and managers' conference on June 12, 1974, at the Bon Homme Colony in South Dakota.

1) **Bodices.** The wives and the young women do not need to tuck in their bodices.

2) **Weddings.** It has been decided that from now on if a young woman from one colony marries into a different colony, then the siblings from the young woman's colony may come to the wedding, regardless of whether they are baptized or not.

3) **Fairs—Rodeos—Exhibitions.** Going to fairs, rodeos, and exhibitions has been long forbidden. And oh how this ordinance has been violated, with entire vans full driving to these things. Let us ministers and managers keep better guard and watch and not allow it. It is, after all, nothing more than lust of the flesh and the eyes and is as the Lord says through the prophet Jeremiah: It is nothing but a vain and beguiling thing. And as the Lord says through the prophet Isaiah: "If only you had paid attention to my commands, your peace would have been like a river, your righteousness like the waves of the sea."[49]

4) **Aprons.** The aprons worn by the womenfolk have also been discussed and it has been decided that the old ordinance from 1941 will be upheld. The aprons for womenfolk should only be black, dark blue, dark green or coffee brown, but may only be one colour.

5) **Two Way Radio—Walkie Talkie.** It has also been decided that from now on the two way radios sets or walkie-talkie sets, which some colonies have acquired for their pickups, trucks, combines, or wherever else, are not to be allowed, rather they are to be done away with. It is only a worldly thing and horror that will lead us astray from the right way. And thus one injustice after the other sneaks into the vineyard of the Lord. Let us see to it that it does not go the way it did for Eve, who said to God: the serpent made me do it, so that Paul had to say (2 Corinthians 11:3): "But I am afraid that just as Eve was deceived by the serpent's cunning, your minds may somehow be led astray from your sincere and pure devotion to Christ."

Election of Ministers. For the future we want you all to know that you can let your colonies know that Minister Andrew Wollman from the Ridgeland Colony in Manitoba desires that there be another minister in order to help him. So according to custom we will fulfill this request, and set the date of the election of a new minister to November 24, 1974.

May the all-powerful God grant that our conference would serve to improve and build us up, and help to eliminate abuses and disorderly beings which try with all their might to sneak in and take root.

But these ordinances are of no help to us if we do not live according to them and if the ministers do not stand more closely and faithfully behind them and uphold them themselves.

[56] Let us think often consider the words of the dear brother, Klaus Braidl's final sermon: Dear brothers, I earnestly ask you to guard yourselves against disunity, for you can well imagine what terrible sorrow would develop because of it. Hold firmly to the good old ordinances of the colony, and see to it that the old cornerstone is not moved.

Hold as firmly as you are able to the Christian community and protect against pride and self-interest. For pride is a root of all kinds of evil and a disruption of all good things. Guard yourselves lest you implement any innovations or adopt any new things.

Let us all turn therefore to God with prayer and supplication that he would awake among us faithful, steadfast, earnest men and that he would equip them with the power of his spirit for this lofty work and duty. Let us all sing together and think with proper devotion about that song of the father so that we might be reminded of the importance of faithful shepherds who allow themselves to be properly used, even if there comes a time when the people or the colony falls into disfavour with God.

We ministers need to be diligent to hold ourselves more closely and firmly to the ordinances of the colony as the necessary guide so that later we will not have to regret that we were too careless and indulgent when the vineyard of the Lord is laid waste and the affliction and atrocity of the desolation is upon us. Even with the best attention things go downhill enough. In conclusion, I greet you all sincerely and bid you the mercy of God. Your humble fellow worker,

Joseph Kleinsasser.

1974

Consolidating Money. With this newsletter all of the Manitoba colonies are being informed that at the meeting for ministers and managers, which was held on December 10, 1974 at the Milltown Colony, it was decided that presently each colony in Manitoba is to contribute [a specified sum of money] to the Lakeside Colony. Exceptions include Whiteshell, Plainview, Greenwald, and Riverdale; these four only need to give [a lesser amount], namely for alms.

And it was also decided by those at the meeting that 25 of the colonies, namely: Barrickman, Bloomfield, Blumengart, Bon Homme, Crystal Spring, Clearwater, Grant, Glenway, Grass River, Hillside, Hidden Valley, Interlake, James Valley, Milltown, Oakbluff, Oakridge, Riverbend, Rosedale, Riverside, Rose Valley, Sturgeon Creek, Suncrest, Woodland, Wellwood, and Mayfair are each to loan the Lakeside Colony [a specified sum of money] in order to help them out of their difficult situation in order to appease the school officials who are threatening them.

It was also decided by those at the meeting that the other colonies should approve if the Lakeside Colony cannot pay back the borrowed money, the other colonies should pay it back. Namely, the [money] that was lent to the Lakeside Colony.

Let us not criticize them too harshly, for it is our Christian duty to stand by them and to help them in their difficult situation, regardless of whether or not they deserve it.

[57] Sirach provides us with good teaching on this matter: "The merciful lend to their neighbours; by holding out a helping hand they keep the commandments. Lend to your neighbour in his time of need; repay your neighbour when a loan falls due. Keep your promise and be honest with him, and on every occasion you will find what you need. Many regard a loan as a windfall, and cause trouble to those who help them. One kisses another's hands until he gets a loan, and is deferential in speaking of his neighbour's money; but at the time of repayment he delays, and pays back with empty promises, and finds fault with the time. If he can pay, his creditor will hardly get back half, and will regard that as a windfall. If he cannot pay, the borrower has robbed the other of his money, and he has needlessly made him an enemy; he will repay him with curses and reproaches, and instead of glory will repay him with dishonour. Many refuse to lend, not because of meanness, but from fear of being defrauded needlessly. Nevertheless, be patient with someone in humble circumstances, and do not keep him waiting for your alms.

Let us accept this teaching as a great treasure of silver, and keep it like a mound of gold. Rejoice in the mercy of God, and do not be ashamed to praise him. Do what has been asked of you because now you still have the time and then at the time he will reward you. May God be gracious and bless us; may his countenance be light for us by and by. That is our wish for the all-powerful God. Amen.

Alas, I wish you the best in spirit and body. Your humble servant,

Joseph Kleinsasser.

March 12, 1975

To be observed at our ministers' conference by all of the ministers in our *Lehrer* colonies.

A message to all of the brothers, sisters, young men and young women in our *Lehrer* colonies, may we all take note of it: We, the ministers, all together are asking for obedient hearts and inclined minds, and that everyone would be subject to the word of God, our only father, in the high heaven, who sees us with his holy eyes and knows everything that is done, even before it is done (may he help us all to be inclined to obedience and humility).

Drunkenness. We all, the above-mentioned must hold ourselves responsible that we have not stood in the gap enough in spiritual watchfulness. Yes, in part we have been outright sleepy. But we can all still do something and help. We do not know what sort of great danger awaits us, and can and will hurry upon us if we do not stop going into the taverns and sitting in there and wasting time. It is a bad, sinful pastime, to which the holy name of God is unnecessarily bound. Let us stay outside, as often as we are there; the female gender should not go in there at all, and the young women and virgins absolutely not, because they are in the greatest danger of frittering away their virginity, along with Dinah, the daughter of Jacob our forefather. In these suspicious many have hurt their honour and were shamed before God and all the pious, and who knows what else will come out of such places?

[58] Our brothers sit there in such dishonour far too often and far too long. Half-exposed women of the world are there and serve the drinks; that is not good for us to do. The young people see it and also want to sit there, and where does the money come from? And the whole colony is maligned while some sit there and drink without moderation. Great harm may come as a result of it, and eternal consequences may follow for those who are overcome by their desire for it. Half an hour is considered a long time to come to prayer, to come and to clear one's conscience without falling asleep. In the saloons, and taverns, however, that is not long enough to be there among the perverse crowd. That is not allowed and is not to be tolerated dear brothers and young people. We ask you and encourage you, let yourselves be helped out of this indecent evil (the young women should not allow themselves to be enticed inside and should not go inside at all, rather they should protect their honour). Along with Paul we have the power to command you, but instead we ask you, do not let it come so far that we have to begin to judge and punish people because of this violation. Each one should guard himself and take care and follow this well-intended advice. The best penance is to never do it; chase after that and you will be blessed.

Purchasing Fabric. Also regarding purchasing fabric one can never be quiet. Like mute dogs, says the prophet, which cannot bark, and cannot be disciplined, as it is written in Isaiah 56:10. The fabric cutters are the most guilty and should take a good portion of the guilt on themselves, because they have been ordered by the colonies to be careful when purchasing fabric. But because of carelessness, and sleepiness, and out of selfish arrogance, and also because they wish to please the other women, they always buy proud fabrics. The respectable old fabric and clothing worn by our mothers is no longer good enough: those with their daughters now think that they are better than the old sisters were. Those sisters who have been ordered to buy the fabric, and who chose the proud patterns that have already become far too prevalent are not the only guilty ones who have wilfully disobeyed and pushed too hard. No, the sisters and the mothers are just as guilty, and perhaps even more so than the cutters. They should not be excused; rather they should to get rid of everything that is not good for the colony so that the colony may once again resume the old ordinances. They should erect the old cornerstone again that our dear ancestors loved and protected before our time, and which was pleasing and loved by our dear God also before our time, otherwise they would not have pleased him. If we think that we are still humble now, think where we would be today if already during their time they had torn down the foundation and had become proud with their prideful clothing? Why do we love to buy and have such big flower prints on our clothes? This will only harm us along with our children, and our children's children, and the young women, but maybe it is already too late. One must put out the fire when it starts. If it is already in the attic it is too late. Where is the covenant that we made with God to help to build his church? We have all promised him, on bended knee, that we would help to build up his house, not to tear it down. Now, many of the dear brothers and sisters who held watch and built it up before us are already in eternity, and not only can we not maintain what they built, but we try to break it apart and tear it down? What sort of reward would our God give us for such a thing? With bound hands and feet the useless servant will be thrown into the farthest darkness—may God protect us all from such a fate.

Let us stop for a moment and consider the purchase of floral-printed fabric. Where the flowers are too big or too many, or too obvious, then arrogance is shown. Let us only go back 30 years, when our mothers purchased fabric for the colony, then the dear Lord will see more humility among us, if we will do as they did. Let us first begin by [59] buying dark fabric and garb. First only black fabric, or dark blue, dark green, dark brown, and white fabric may be purchased, according to the ordinance.

And if there are little flowers on the fabric, they may not be bigger than a human's eyeball, and may not be too close together. And the fabric may not be shiny, or glittery. Striped fabric has also been taken to an extreme, particularly with light coloured stripes and shiny fabric. That is not allowed to be purchased and will not be tolerated. Also, no multi-coloured accessories are allowed.

Aprons. Regarding the aprons the ordinance is also to be upheld. To the teaching and the funeral service, and for weddings, one may wear all black with a black apron. But they may not be worn just any time out of pride or arrogance, as we sometimes hear of today as some act with such arrogance. As soon as the dresses with big flowers are forbidden women will begin to defy the prohibition. That is not being obedient according to the word of God. They will want to wear the same colour apron and skirt.

The clothing that has already been sewn with this fabric with flowers that are too big and which is too proud, and is already in use, should never be seen again after a period of 3 years. It should never be worn again. Whatever is left over in 3 years must be burned or dyed black. And nothing new is to be made, and the existing clothes may only be worn for work, and never if one leaves the colony and never to teaching or prayer.

In one of his evangelical parables (Luke 13:6-9) of the unfruitful fig tree, Christ talked about having patience. He says: "Why should it use up the soil?" And in the same way we say, according to this example, in three years, this should all be eliminated, and now only worn for working. All fabric or clothing that was purchased alone must be given to the minister to be burned. Where this is not brought to the minister or worn out, then it will be detrimental to one's faith and baptism. And even on the deathbed. We eat our daily bread and drink water in the same way that the man of God did every day. But because he ate what he was not supposed to eat until he returned home, and therefore violated God's law, he had to be killed by a lion. This lion is chasing after us, trying to kill us in our disobedience. Even those little kerchiefs that were purchased alone, and the shirts that were purchased alone should all be brought to the minister to be burned.

Jackets [as in pea jacket]. From now on the hanging jackets or the open jackets are not to be seen again. They make people appear as if they no longer have hands with which to sensibly clothe themselves. That has never happened among us. Our old ministers taught us: Pride and arrogance always starts in the cradle or the crib. We firmly believe in their wise admonition. And so we must be careful not to plant arrogance into our little children, so that when they grow up we will be without blame because they are not arrogant. Because then they would be able to say to us: You showed us and taught us.

Furthermore: With this we are commanding the ministers that it be in three years time, as is mentioned above. Clothe the small children in the fear of God, which is right, and just in little flowers, as the ordinance of old, from our forefathers' time allows, but without arrogance.

[60] **Shirts.** The bought yellow shirts and all too see-through shirts are forbidden, and must remain that way. Our God and Creator was not so fool-hardy that he covered our bodies with spots and with several colours.

He brought us forth with uniform skin. But, then, we must ask ourselves: **What have we made out of GOD'S image?**

It should be sufficient for us that God created, his creation, with white skin, that is our clothing from God, which he prepared through his omnipotence and wisdom. He gave it to us without spots; he didn't need our foolishness or our arrogance. We would have been found to be incompetent counsellors in such a situation. Therefore we ask all of those who are guilty: Put away all of the fabric and shirts that you bought for yourselves. Use and wear only the shirts that the beloved colony buys and gives to you, and those in charge of selecting those should also be humble if they wish to please God, and should not be too bright or too light which could wreak havoc and make things difficult for the minister and all of the insightful brothers and sisters. And such a thing would have to be punished appropriately according to the violator's status.

Vests. Disorder has also begun to appear regarding the vests, which we cannot allow to creep any further in. Those jackets which have been stitched on or insulated, or lined vests with zippers instead of hooks like those that are being worn in the world are excessive and have no place among us. This cannot be tolerated; a stop must be put to it. If someone wants to wear a jacket, then he should wear one like our fathers also wore (under the jacket). It would be a very rare sheep whose covering was half wool and half fox or wolf fur. The same goes for us if we want to be half brother and half in the world. A dove only has dove's feathers, not those of an eagle or vulture. No one can serve two masters as the words of Christ say in Matt. 6:24. Neither can one walk two streets at once. We cannot serve both God and Mammon. The Judge will declare the pure, but not the transgressors.

Hats. Great disorder has also crept in through the matter of the big hats, which are brazenly purchased and are worn contrary to the colony's ordinance. These types—the tall kind with the long feather—have never been allowed. The Indians and the Mexicans wear this kind of hat.

Riding Boots. Riding boots (cowboy boots) with the pointed toes and high narrow heels also belong to the Indians and the Mexicans. But among us they have never been allowed. Whoever introduced this disorder into our colony should consider his conscience to see where he stands with God. He has invited much judgment onto himself as well as the guilt of those whom he has led astray through boots and hats. Our dear Brother, Jakob Hutter, was a hat-maker and we know that he never made such hats without virtue for his beloved congregation.

Beards. As for cheek beards (side whiskers), and moustaches, no humility is to be found in such things, especially when they are long. Rather, they ought to be kept short, as is right and which is in keeping with our ordinance. The side whiskers must be even with the top of the ears, not the bottom. He who wishes to follow must do so for himself. The minister cannot follow for the disobedient.

If we, as men and women, brothers and sisters, young men and young women, big and little, wish to meet our great God wearing pointed boots and big hats like the world (and the Indians and the Mexicans) wear, and also wearing worldly clothing which has been mentioned in this announcement, [61] then we must look for a new god, as the Holy Scripture has shown us.

He will not be dressed in the way he was when Moses saw him on Mount Sinai, three times for forty days and nights. Neither will he look as he did when Isaiah saw him sitting on his high and exalted throne. Nor will he look the way Daniel saw him sitting on his Judgment Seat with all of the godly before him. Neither will he look the way Ezra saw him, handing out crowns to all the godly who walked justly before him. Nor will he look the way he looked to Stephen: God with the Son sitting on his right side. And neither like the son who was transfigured on Mount Tabor (Matt. 17), nor like the way he looked to the Apostle and theologian John, who saw him various times in Revelation (Rev. 1:10-18; 6:16-17; 20:11-12; 21:1-7, 22-23; 22:3-4).

A pure, holy, all-powerful God of heaven and earth, with his beloved Son, Jesus Christ, in the power of the angels and archangel, will meet the godly and will lead them into their eternal dwelling place.

But to those of us who are not following his word (Micah 6:8): "He has showed you, O man, what is good. And what does the Lord require of you? To act justly and to love mercy and to walk humbly with your God."

Jeremiah 13:15-17:[50] "Hear and pay attention, do not be arrogant, for the Lord has spoken."

And for those of us who will not follow and be obedient, we will also meet the one whom we have served, with disobedience, pride, and all arrogance. May God protect us and our children, and our children's children, all the way to our thousandth member. May he only do good and blessed things to us and all of our descendents, through Jesus Christ. Each one has been faithfully warned against all disobedience.

Wristwatches. Watches for the hand have never been allowed among us; it is only pride and arrogance. It is comfortable enough to wear the watch at the waist, for no one needs to know the time more than that.

Leather boots. The leather boots, with the rounded toe and low, wide heel, which have been worn for 60, 70, and 80 years, are not included in the above announcement, and are not forbidden.

As for the big hats: cut the feathers off and cut off the big tops to make them better, and then don't buy any more.

What might we expect if the Apostles Peter and Paul were to preach to us today? Both preached about women's costumes.

James and John, who were called the children of thunder by Christ, did as well. In his epistle John preached: Do not love the world, or the lust of the eyes or arrogance.

1. **Clothing.** In the children's school, clothing which is forbidden may not be used.

[62] 2. **Jackets (pea jackets).** The jackets, which have been taken like the hussies wear, are not godly, rather are arrogant. The mothers should forbid their daughters to wear such a thing. Taking in clothes to form to one's figure must be stopped, because where clothes are taken in the fear of the Lord is cut off and lost.

3. **Suspenders.** The menfolk should always wear suspenders. The young men should only wear black pants, not multi-coloured or the worldly overall style.

1975

The following is a report about what was decided during the ministers' and managers' conference, which was held on June 12, 1975, at the Sturgeon Creek Colony in Manitoba.

1) **Two-Way Radio.** Regarding the two-way radios it has also been decided that the old ordinance should remain in effect—they should remain banned. The car and truck radios should be done away with as well.

2) **Little School.** Each colony should work diligently to hold a Little School. It is a shame that in some colonies no Little School has been held in years. But in some colonies no one hears. Just like the doves that do not want to listen. Yes, let us all work, especially we ministers, to follow the example of our ancestors. Let us be faithfully commanded by the colony, and diligently care and watch over it.

3) **German and Sunday School.** More diligence needs to be expended regarding the German and Sunday Schools, and if there are 30 or more children, then a second teacher should be selected in order to help.

4) **Raising Children and putting them to sleep.** Also according to the old custom the children should be kept together in the summer months and should be put to sleep together.

5) **Discord.** If a fight or conflict arises between the minister and the manager, the daily prayer or teaching should be discontinued until they reconcile themselves, which is in accordance with the Holy Scripture.

6) **Ordinances.** By the way, all of the ordinances and customs that were made at previous meetings are still fully in effect.

Confirmation of Ministers. It must also be mentioned that the Millerdale Colony in South Dakota discussed it and has decided to confirm their minister Jacob Hofer in service.

In conclusion, I bid you all sincere greetings and the love, grace, and mercy of our great God and I anticipate your child-like obedience. I remain your humble fellow worker and pilgrim,

Joseph Kleinsasser.

[63] 1976

The following is a report regarding what was decided during the Ministers' and Managers' conference that was held on March 17, 1976 at the Sturgeon Creek Colony in Manitoba.

1) **Aprons.** It was discussed and decided that womenfolk are not allowed to wear multi-coloured or flowered aprons in the same print as their dresses; rather, it should remain according to the old ordinance which was decided in the years 1941, 1966, 1970, and 1971.

2) **Aprons.** The matter of some women no longer wearing any aprons has also been discussed and it has been decided that it is not to be allowed; rather, things should remain according to our custom and ordinance.

3) **Skirts.** Short skirts have been forbidden for a long time and are not to be tolerated. The ordinance states that the skirt is to be 5-6 inches from the ground. It is a shameless, brazen thing that our garb is never good enough, and that we try to please the world and to make ourselves the same as it. Paul says to the Romans: "And be not conformed to this world: but be ye transformed by the renewing of your mind, that ye may prove what is that good, and acceptable, and perfect, will of God."[51]

4) Nursing Mothers. It has also been discussed and decided that regarding that which is due the nursing mothers everything should remain according to the old ordinance.

5) Wristwatches—Radios—Tape Recorders—Pictures. Wristwatches, radios, tape recorders, and taking photos were also discussed and it was decided that none of those things are allowed; rather, the old ordinance is to remain in effect.

6) Games such as hockey and skating should be handled according to the ordinance and such evil should be stopped entirely.

7) Allowance. The allowance ordinance from 1954 has been changed slightly so that now each soul receives $1.00 per month.

8) Cap for young boys. The cap ordinance from 1973 has been changed so that now the married men may wear the cap but it must be black, and not red, or green, or blue. But as for going to prayer and to service, the old hat ordinance remains in effect.

9) Purchasing Land. It has also been recognized that if a colony wishes to purchase land for a new colony, then the colony in question should elect a second minister at least one year before, so that the new minister has time to adjust to his position and to prepare himself, to study somewhat and to gain experience. Each colony should pay close attention to this. Just as the Lord said to Baruch: 'Hear, O Israel, the laws of life. Pay attention to them, and keep them.'

Yes, let us all uphold the ordinances, lest too much evil creep in. For this evil is like little foxes, which ruin the vineyard, for our vineyards, are being watched.

[64] In conclusion, I bid you all sincere greetings and the love, grace, and mercy of our great God and I anticipate your child-like obedience. I remain your humble fellow worker and pilgrim,

Joseph Kleinsasser.

1978

The following is a report regarding what was decided during the Ministers' and Manager's Conference which was held on July 26 at the Woodland Colony in Manitoba.

1) Sending Out. Firstly, the matter of sending out was discussed and it was recognized that we are failing the whole command of Christ in the area of the commission to go into all the world to preach the gospel to all nations and to baptize them in the name of the Father, the Son, and the Holy Spirit, and to teach them to obey all that Christ commanded us.[52] We need to wake up and try to do more, for the command of Christ remains the same as long as the world is still standing.

2) **Committees.** It was also decided that the committees are not necessary and that things should remain as they were before. But regarding the question in South Dakota things should remain as they were before. First Minister Joseph Wipf should be the first one asked, namely, regarding the election and confirmation of new ministers, and also regarding the purchase of land for a new colony.

3) **Coolers.** As for the considerable amount of discussion both for against coolers, it has been decided that each colony may decided for itself which coolers it wants to allow, for such outward matters do not belong among spiritual matters. Several other outward matters will also be left up to each colony to decide for itself.

4) **Two-Way Radio—Walkie-talkies.** As for two ways, or walkie-talkies, it was decided that a one year's grace period would be implemented.

5) **Raising Children.** Not enough seriousness is being shown in the matter of the raising of children, and the colony's future depends on this. The colony teacher should use this important time to impress and to inculcate something godly into the children so that God's church would be sustained and built up. The dear Brother Jeroninus Kaels gives a good teaching about this: "O, Holy Father, we small and underage children, ask with our whole hearts that you would give to our parents, whom you gave to us out of mercy and appointed to raise us, mercy and strength, understanding and wisdom, so that they might raise us up according to your godly will, and that they would protect us from evil and teach us what is good." And dear parents, what can the schoolteachers do if the parents will not help? From where else have these bad times of lukewarm and corrupted Christianity come if not from a lack of good child rearing?

Unity. Dear brothers, let us strive for peace, love, and unity and precious reconciliation. Let no one carry bitterness or anger in their hearts against another, particularly not us who are servants of the Word. Amen. [65] Herewith I bid and wish you all, dear Brothers, the all-powerful God's unending mercy, help, strength, and assistance, and I remain now and at all times, your humble fellow worker and pilgrim,

Joseph Kleinsasser.

1979

The following is a report regarding what was decided during the Ministers' and Managers' Conference which was held on July 10, 1979, at the Woodland Colony in Manitoba.

1) **Ordinance regarding the Cutting of Fabric.** The cutting of fabric was discussed briefly and the following was decided according to which the fabric cutters may judge themselves: the opinion was restated and expressed that fabric is still not being purchased in accordance with the fabric ordinance. This is not in keeping with the innocence of Christ, rather smacks of gawking after the world, which is not fitting for the children of God.

2) **Church account.** It was discussed at length whether a church account should be set up, in order to handle the many interests for which the colonies give out money. It was decided, however, to push it back for one year in order to become better acquainted with the matter, and to discuss it again later.

3) **Electing Ministers.** A change is to be made regarding the appointment of ministers. Namely, one week before the election two ministers are to be called to the colony where the election is to take place. The teaching from Deuteronomy 17 should be read the day of the nominations in order to give those who have been nominated a chance to consider whether they are ready to accept this important and holy work. And then on the election day the reading is to be taken from Jeremiah 7 and then the vote should be held according to custom.

4) **Nominating a new Minister—Nominating a Manager.** From now on, if someone is not elected, he may be re-elected during the next election if someone deems him suitable. The same is true for a manager, if he is not elected, he may be nominated the next time.

5) **Two Ministers on one Colony.** From now on if a colony splits, two ministers are not allowed to stay with one side unless a third minister had already been elected much earlier.

6) **Shotguns.** More seriousness should also be taken in the effort to put an end to shot guns, in keeping with the ordinance from 1956, because too many in the colonies are too loose and foolish about such things. It is appalling what is already appearing among us.

7) **Weddings—Drinking.** Steps should be taken to curb the excessive coming together that occurs for weddings, not to mention the excessive

drinking that occurs as well. What is done in the morning to honour God becomes an abomination at noon through the drinking. From now on it has been decided that one bottle of beer is allowed at lunch time, one in the afternoon, and one at supper. And no Schnapps at supper. Dear brothers and sisters, we ask you all to act as befits a people of God, and generally to be more careful about this evil addiction to drink, which gives off a tempting glow, [66] and which leads from one sin to another, namely: unfaithfulness, lies, cursing, and impure talk, which are counted among the vices in all of the Holy Scripture.

8) **Complaints.** It must also be mentioned that if complaints come before the bishop and he deems it fair to hold a hearing, then it may not be held by the colony, minister, or counsel in question. And it is still allowed that if someone feels slighted by the hearing in his own colony, or does not want to accept it, and then he may come to the bishop. This hearing, however, should remain effect until the bishop has added his own counsel as to what should be done next and all the more so if the conflict is within the leadership, if it is not unified or cannot agree. In this instance no punishment should be confirmed or acknowledged until another hearing has been held, or counsel given.

9) **Marriage.** If it should happen that two young people leave the colony and get married while in the world, then they must be remarried by the colony but must not come together according to marital custom during the period of the ban until they are married again.

10) **Discord.** If someone is living in discord, then he may not live in the house where his spouse is, or any other baptized members, rather he must be separated. The same goes for the mealtimes, namely, they should be separated in the baking house, or wherever their living quarters are. And if it is a married couple they should not come together according to marital custom if the one is in discord and the other is not.

11) **Unity.** Alas, dear Brothers and Sisters; let us all strive more toward unity and peace, especially toward the precious prize of forgiveness, especially as shepherds of our flocks. And let us, as ministers, managers, and farm bosses, come together every morning at the beginning of the day to hold counsel in trust regarding the business and welfare of the colony so that the glorious work of the community would be a pleasure garden for the Lord.

12) **Avarice and Self-Interest.** In order to combat avarice and self-interest, which is the archenemy of the community, things such as picking June berries, plucking ducks, or other such things must be stopped. Let us walk

respectably, as is fitting for children of God, lest we miss the welcome into eternal rest; that is our wish and desire for all of you.

13) **Supervision of the Young People.** More supervision should be given when the young people come together, because it is noticeable how they fall into fornication and harlotry, so that it is appalling what is appearing in the colonies. It was decided that each colony should call the brothers and sisters together in order to encourage them in this matter. Parental duty is not to be neglected when young men and women find themselves together and the evil enemy seems to have won the game. May God protect us lest we become like Sodom and Gomorrah, and our dear young people and children fall unenlightened into these vices. We also need to be alert and stand guard lest runaways try to sneak into the various colonies . . . [and behave in an inappropriate fashion]. An account will be demanded of us. Yes, let us work diligently, with earnestness, to fulfill all of these things. Dear brothers and sisters, this should be our seal and our garb, not that we try to please the world and make ourselves the same as it, [67] and thereby become God's enemies and invite his wrath and disfavour on to ourselves through worldly ways, habits, and customs. Alas, hoping for the best and trusting in God, we remain you most humble servants, Jakob Kleinsasser and Jakob Hofer.

1980

The following is a report regarding what was decided during the Ministers' and Managers' Conference, held on June 17, 1980 at the Woodland Colony in Manitoba.

1) **General Account.** As for the general account that was proposed last year, and for which a one-year period of consideration was devoted, it has been decided that we will push it back for another year or so.

2) **Colony Fire Insurance.** It was decided that general colony fire insurance would be instituted. When it is in effect three brothers from Manitoba and three brothers from South Dakota will be engaged to operate it. Their duties will be outlined in a separate document.

3) **Babysitters.** We have decided not to insure the houses because in the past years houses have so rarely been damaged. We have decided that the school children will eat lunch and supper before the adults and that a babysitter should always be at home to look after small children when the mother and father are eating. This is also a way to prevent accidents from happening because a few times fires have started because only small children were in the house alone.

If, however, it should happen that an uninsured house is damaged by fire, then all of the colonies will pay to have it replaced.

4) Acceptance. It was decided that the way in which brothers who have been removed from the brotherhood are to be reintegrated is to be discussed more at a later date.

5) Drunkenness. As for excessive drinking, it is to be considered a vice, and in addition to unfaithfulness and serious theft, it is to be punished with the ban. And such people, as well as others who broke the covenant, if they are punished by the ban, are to be released from their positions.

And in specific persistent situations some people will lose their membership and are will be justly put into separation, and this includes from their spouses.

6) People who refuse to accept discipline. Regarding the improper condition that there are brothers and also young men in the colony who are so foolhardy and who refuse to be shown the way—they should be shut out, and should be expelled from the property. And if they do not listen, they may also be expelled according to the Articles of the Association, and because they are no longer a part of us, protection may be sought from the government if it comes to that.

7) Jury or Witness Brothers. It was also decided that if a manager or someone on the leadership steps down from his post, he may still serve as a deacon or witness brother.

8) Worldly Court. It was also decided that if it arises that someone, whether a brother or a young man, for whatever reason, has to appear before a worldly court and is found guilty because of his own wantonness and impudence, and is even arrested, or goes on supervised probation, then as long as such a person is not at peace with the world he may not be vindicated in the colony, though he may be allowed to stay on the colony. But if he does not behave in an orderly way then he may be expelled from the property, or if necessary the probation officer may be notified.

But such a thing should be done in the fear of the Lord and not without the counsel of the church.

10) **Money for shoes.** The distribution of shoe money should be stopped, along any other kind of distribution of money other than the monthly allowance because it can be very damaging if it is allowed as a principle of the colony. Acts 2:45 states: "And sold their possessions and goods, and parted them to all men, as every man had need." Alas, everyone should keep to the ordinance regarding allowance.

11) **School.** The schools are to be more unified, and so that no colonies end up having problems, no school should request to be a part or be accepted by the worldly school division without the bishop's counsel.

12) **Appropriating Vehicles.** People, especially the Farm Boss, but other position holders as well, are acting as if pickups and trucks belong to them personally, even in winter when there is no farm work to be done. They are doing this so much that the colony leaders hardly has anything to say about it anymore. They are not to be parked at people's houses.

13) **Radio—C.B.** As for radios in pickups, tractors, and even in houses, these are not allowed, and it was decided that everyone who knows this and still has one is to stand up and confess and promise to get rid of it, and each one will exhort his colony brothers and sisters to get rid of such things that are not allowed among us, and that includes the C.B. [Citizens' Band radio]

14) **Cutting Fabric.** It was decided that for the year 1980 only undergarments are to be given and that everything else that was to be given is now to be pushed back for one year.

15) **Unity.** And as an encouragement dear brothers and sisters, let each one strive to walk sensibly in peace, love, and unity as is fitting for children of God, and let us carry no bitterness or anger in our hearts toward another and let no one get into disunion with another, least of all the leader of the colony. Let us daily practice forgiveness. Let us especially consider the teaching of Christ, which says that if our neighbour has something against us we are to leave our offering and go to him to seek forgiveness and to guard against all self-interest and individualism. Let us stand together in agreement through the bonds of love and peace, and then God will live among us.

In conclusion, I bid you all sincere greetings and the love, grace, and mercy of our great God and I anticipate your child-like obedience. We remain your humble fellow workers and servants,

Jakob Kleinsasser and Jakob Hofer.

[69] 1981

1) **Runaways.** If young people leave the colony, and get married while they are in the world, but then want to come back to the colony, then they must demonstrate for a period that they are penitent, and that they wish to turn from their ways, and they must go to the colony which they left and present the colony with an account of their monthly income and

expenditures, and must behave sensibly in order to show that they have the colony's interest and goals in mind.

After that they are to be dealt with in good faith, as has been the case for a long time. And if they have not been baptized they must be baptized in the colony that they left unless the minister has given counsel and something else has been advised. They are not to be accepted until they are recognized as penitent and the baptism is not to be rushed into without demonstration of Christian witness.

And for all those who return a Power of Attorney document is to be signed in order to deal with the income tax issue, and this must be done before the person can be accepted into the colony.

2) **Shunning.** Shunning should only be practiced with the greatest seriousness and according to the teachings in the gospel and of Peter Riedemann. The way things currently stand, shunning has nearly died out and interaction with those who have broken the covenant is taken lightly and entered into thoughtlessly. 1 Corinthians 5:11 states: "But now I have written unto you not to keep company, if any man that is called a brother be a fornicator, or covetous, or an idolater, or a railer, or a drunkard, or an extortioner; with such a one you are not to eat." Judge for yourselves who is bad.

Another serious abuse is happening: covenant breakers are being embraced in greeting as long as their hands are not shaken. Read about it in the writings of Peter Riedemann, on page 119, where he says that shaking hands and embracing have the same meaning, namely, that by shaking hands people demonstrate that their hearts are also bound together. The same goes for embracing, when someone draws another person into an embrace they are showing that their hearts are also drawn together. Thus, these two signs are signs of peace.

How bad does this shunning seem to certain *Leichten*? There are so many who have fallen away, so many who have broken covenants, that hardly a thought is given to shunning any more.

Where do we want to stand with this responsibility before God? Or will God judge us?

3) **Runaways.** It is a deplorable situation with the young people who have run away—the boys and the girls. They are making a spectacle and an abomination of the colony; their visits to their loved ones—whom they abandoned—in the colony bring appalling mischief into the colony: smoking, drinking, harlotry, and fornication, ill-kempt hair and clothing [70] and cars at the doors of houses as if this were the world. What is supposed to be a house of God is used for the major holidays—Christmas, Easter, and Pentecost—as a place to celebrate, which is a big distraction when one is trying to have a service on these important holidays.

It cannot go on like this for much longer; rather, from now on it is fair and right that this no longer be tolerated unless it has been permitted by the minister and the Leadership through a telephone conversation or through writing. And where parents are aware of such things, or anyone, and they do not inform the leadership, then they are liable to also be examined and punished.

4) Signing. It was also decided that all brothers and sisters should sign the addendum to the Articles of the Association, so that one has the full right to use greater earnestness against the evils, the drunkards and covenant-breakers who are already so impudent and who do not allow themselves to be corrected and so that alternative means may be sought to protect ourselves from such people.

5) Runaways as Loved Ones.[53] If it arises that young women or men who are in the world are in love with a young man or woman in the colony and it is discovered, it is not to be tolerated. And if parents turn a blind eye to it, then they are to be examined as well and are liable to punishment.

Punishing Sex outside of Marriage. Also, where it arises that young women and men trespass together [. . . ,] where it is discovered that the parents have fallen short in their parental duty and did not pay close enough attention, and have allowed such disorderly running around with their permission, and have allowed their children to get into such mischief, then such parents must apologize during the teaching and be punished.

6) Personal Mail. From now on whoever receives their own mail and refuses to remain a part of the colony mail is no longer at peace with the colony and should be punished through discord.

And each one who receives letters should try to send them back. If, however, it is a suspicious matter, the recipient should open it in the presence of the minister.

The manager should open letters pertaining to the business of the colony.

7) False Mail. Also more earnestness should be taken regarding false mail and foreign religious literature, through which so much mischief and falsehood have infiltrated the church in the past year that it was barely possible to guard against it all. Namely:

> -*One should be totally immersed during baptism*
> -*Pentecostal miracles are a sign of the true church*
> -*Foot washing, speaking in tongues, and the baptism of the Holy*
> *Spirit such as what happens to the Charismatics*

-Sick people are possessed by the devil
-Drinking grape juice during communion instead of wine
-Once saved, always saved, fasting, rapture, and the ability to pray away one's own sins, and many more things.

[71] It is appalling how Satan seeks to distract us.

Radios—Tapes—TV. Radios, tapes, and even TV have appeared among us.

Garb. There are some who are too ashamed to be recognized as a member of our community and instead dress so that one cannot tell them apart from the world; with long hair, not tied back, short dresses and more. It is nothing but a sign of how the enemy affects what is true and unfortunately we can hardly protect ourselves against it. The belief that we are a church is dying and many of your people want to live without rules or disciplines as is done in the world.

Avarice and Self-Interest—Discord—Disunity. Also regarding avarice and self-interest, discord, and disunity, there is no need for any of these things in community. People live in hypocrisy and sanctimony, deceiving themselves, boasting in their salvation and that they are children of God, when in God's eyes they are only boastful blemishes on the house of God.

8) Reporting debts. Also from now on each colony should try to accurately disclose its debts at the annual income and expenditures meeting. Where it is discovered that this has been neglected, the colony will then be fairly and properly examined.

Borrowing Money. Neither ministers nor managers have the right to borrow large sums of money without counsel.

9) Baptismal Candidates. If it arises that someone who is to be baptized is not behaving properly or has fallen into error and has not demonstrated adequately that they are prepared to stop during the probation period, then the baptism may be pushed back until Pentecost in order to give the person another probation period.

This should, however, be handled in a God-fearing way and with the counsel of the bishop.

Even if the person who is to be baptized confesses before the baptism it should only be done before appointed ministers.

Ordinance regarding the Cutting of Fabric. The ordinance regarding the cutting of fabric is to be changed so that one is no longer to cut according to the old ordinance or custom.

We charge you herewith into the care of God the heavenly father, may he give you all obedient hearts that each one would work diligently to accept the other in love, knowing that all things are done only for the welfare of the colony and the praise and honour to God, that we may remain a people of God. Sincere greetings to all with the greeting of love from us, your fellow helpers in the kingdom of Christ,

Joseph Kleinsasser and Joseph Hofer.

[72] **1982**

The following is a report regarding what was decided during the ministers' and managers' conference, held June 15-16, 1982, at the Crystal Springs Colony.

1) **The meeting.** We began with a short speech in which it was stated that we had gathered together for God's honour and for the welfare of the colony in order that we might continue to be recognized as a church of God. Therefore let each one consider with devotion and with the fear of God how he might observe the ordinances that have been brought forward.

2) **Little School** should be carried out with more enthusiasm and love. Some colonies, for various reasons, are neglecting the Little School, they excuse themselves and say that they need to use the building as a residence, and some give other excuses. A one-year period is to be given to all the colonies to which this pertains and if at the end of that time there is still no Little School then it will be examined as disobedience. Also the day will be shortened to two mealtimes, where there would normally be breakfast, lunch, and supper.

3) **Shunning.** Great earnestness should be demonstrated regarding covenant-breakers and those who have been expelled, as well as those who do not allow themselves to be corrected and continue to live in mischief and waywardness. It is noticeable that shunning is not working in this unfavourable situation, where waywardness, opposition, and disobedience are found.

4) Therefore all of the churches must take hold of this in order to purify themselves, and counsel and means must be sought whereby such things may be done away with in accordance with the Holy Scripture and the Gospel, in order that we might remain a church and a house of God. Also, there is too much interaction with those who have fallen away and with covenant-breakers.

5) **Runaways.** There is also not enough unity and agreement regarding the matter of runaways having to seek permission from the minister if they wish to come to the colony for a visit as was decided during the June 2, 1981 conference in ordinances 3-4. It was also decided that where brothers or sisters refuse to cooperate or go so far as to openly stand against the ordinance, then they will be regarded as opponents and detractors, and not as brothers and sisters who help to build and protect the colony.

6) **Impoverishment.** Because it has gotten to the point with some colonies that they have become impoverished, it was decided: if it is discovered that through an examination and through a hearing that the minister and the manager both deliberately remained silent about their continuous sinking into debt and perhaps even that they are totally sunk, so that it gets to the point of bankruptcy,[54] then both the minister and the manager are both to be declared guilty.

7) **Appointing a Manager.** In certain instances where a colony has become impoverished and as a result a manager is removed from his position, then a new manager should be appointed by the council of ministers, during a meeting at which no less than the majority of ministers from the affected area, whether it be Manitoba or South Dakota, is present.

[73] 8) **Lending Money.** It was also decided to help the Fairview Colony in North Dakota, U.S.A., to build a cow barn [Financial details are given, specifying the amounts to be contributed by each colony and the details of repayment]

9) **Insurance.** The situation of the Hutterian Mutual Fire Insurance was clarified. It is in a healthy state. The directors will remain in service for another year. Next year we will consider replacing two of them.

10) **Baptism.** It is becoming too common that those who are to be baptized as well as baptisms are not treated seriously enough. All of the ministers from colonies with baptismal candidates should come together to decide whether the candidates are fit to be baptized. If a candidate is deliberately hiding something and only confesses the sins at the baptism, and these sins—had they been confessed earlier—would have caused the baptism to be deferred or would have been punished with a serious punishment, then such a person is always to be punished with the ban if this is only exposed after the baptism.

11) **Theft.** If someone is caught in minor theft, then the person is to be put on probation for a period of time, and in serious unrepentant cases, the person should be sent away from the colony until the member admits

that he/she is ready to act for the colony's good. And then the person is to be vindicated, as was decided in Ordinance #6 from 1980.

12) **Converts.**[55] If it arises that someone from the world converts and joins the colony, especially in a situation where the language spoken is something other than German, then the person should be baptized instead of being assimilated into the church through confession. First the individual should approach the minister of the colony where the person resides and request to be baptized, and then he should go before the brotherhood and the deacons. After that the person should declare his intentions before the colony and then ask to be baptized. If the request is accepted, then the person should go around to all of the deacons on two Sunday afternoons in order to be instructed about the baptism and joining the colony.

It may also happen that on two Saturday afternoons the deacons get together in order to teach the baptismal candidate about the baptism and about joining the colony. This decision may be left up to the colony of the deacons and they may choose whichever they prefer. The baptismal candidate need not memorize anything, but if the person wishes, the candidate may read something aloud. And the questions may also be posed as they arise.

From here on the general custom for baptism may be observed.

But the question of marriage should be added to the question of baptism so that the people who are being baptized are married lest peoples' faith get shipwrecked.

Wherever it arises the bishop's and the senior minister's counsel should be sought.

Now committing these important things to God the All-powerful one and anticipating the best from him, we remain, with sincere greetings, your humble fellow helpers and servants,

Jakob Kleinsasser and Jakob Hofer.

[74] 1983

The following is a report regarding what was decided during the ministers' and managers' conference on August 25, 1983, at the Crystal Springs Colony.

First dear brothers, our gathering at this annual meeting is to seek the welfare of the colony that we might remain a people of God. May God give us his spirit and wisdom that we might accomplish that goal. There are all sorts of immodest things among us that hinder us from being approved as a people of God.

Cutting Fabric will remain the way it is for this year.

1) **Drunkenness.** Where ministers are negligent in doing something about excessive drinking, the ministers themselves are to be examined.

2) **Accounts of Money.** The colonies should be encouraged to know that whatever money is given out without an account given to the manager sows unfaithfulness over time. Whether much or little was spent, an account is to be brought by the minister to the manager, as well as by all of the other members. It was also reported that several colonies are distributing money on a monthly basis in various ways and for various things because some leave the colony less often than others. This custom should be stopped because there is an ordinance for the distribution of allowance, and each family should be given money according to it unless it is altered at an annual conference.

3) **Smuggling Schnapps.** Ministers and managers who buy schnapps from certain colonies where the schnapps has been smuggled should be challenged. They should disclose from whom they purchased it and should be earnestly examined.

4) **Shunning and Unfaithfulness.** More earnestness should also demonstrated regarding shunning, where there is not enough unity. The same applies if someone is found to be unfaithful with colony goods or money, which, according to Ordinance #6 from 1980 stipulates that the person is to be removed from his position and to be replaced, and that all who did not do anything about it are to be punished.

5) *Hulba.* Regarding getting together after the *Hulba*, and not leaving the yard until late at night, and bringing alcohol and other mischief with them, where even the young people drive vehicles without permission and disturb the colony: the only things that are missing are people staying the night and comradeship so that even the drunk and those who have fallen away might stay into the dark night. And many parents and brothers sleep quietly through it, which is also to be criticized.

From now on brides and grooms are no longer to be married until they have had their blood tested. They may go up to 30 days before the wedding to have their blood tested. So much mischief results because of current customs—these customs need to be changed.

6) **Declaration.** All baptized brothers are to take part in the declaration for remembrance.

7) Witness Brothers. There should be no fewer than two witness brothers who are nominated for the position of minister during nominations.

[75] **8) Little School.** It was asked whether the colonies are trying to hold Little School. Where it is not being held the colonies are to be punished for disobedience. It was found, however, that some colonies are only holding school for ¾ of the day and that the children are being sent home too quickly, which is a sign of resistance.

9) Personal Mail. People who receive personal mail are not being seriously punished in accordance with the long-standing ordinance that stipulates that such people are to be punished.

10) Quarrels. Quarrelling situations between leadership can no longer be tolerated, as they are an abomination and abhorrence before God and people.

11) Garb. There is much to complain about regarding garb; all sorts of worldly clothes are being worn—pants, belts, long hair—this cannot be allowed any longer, this attempt to be the same as the world. It is so bad that many are not even recognizable as Hutterite, as if it didn't matter what one wore. The goal and aspiration of such a heart is easy to see, for no light is being shone before the world but is being hidden under the table like Christ says: You are the light of the world, and the salt of the earth. Each yard that is guilty of such things should try to improve in the house and church of the Lord. Up until now no change for clothing has been mentioned and whoever is disobedient should be punished.

12) Positions.[56] Too much conflict arises when positions are occupied. Witness brothers may occupy a position for a short period, but as soon as something is decided it must be confirmed by the colony.

13) Electing Ministers. If a colony is already looking for land for a new colony, it should be requested to elect a minister if there is presently only one minister; this is something that is often neglected. Also, more diligence should be expended in trying to practice serving God.

Dear brothers and sisters; let us all strive to be obedient; nothing improper or unbearable is being requested. How good it is when things are harmonious and agreeable between God and people. Sins separate us from God. Where then will we go for eternity? Let each one walk in love and unity and peace so that the God of peace will be with us. That is what we wish for all of you as your shepherds and teachers and fellow helpers in your blessedness. Amen.

Alas, hoping for the best and trusting God, we remain your humble fellow helpers and servants of the Word,

Jakob Kleinsasser and Jakob Hofer.

[76] <u>1984</u>

The following is a report of what was decided during the ministers' and managers' conference, held June 21, 1984, at the Crystal Springs Colony in Manitoba. May the dear Lord open the ears of our hearts. Our request is that each one would take notice with the fear of God and with meekness.

1) **Tips and Drinks.** Note: Ordinance 1. August 1984: Where the ministers do not do enough to curb excessive drinking, the ministers themselves should be examined. It has been found that many colonies have not paid careful enough attention to this matter.

This drinking comes from the feed companies who give alcohol as a tip and also from various stores where money is spent on all sorts of unfaithful things. The feed companies excuse themselves by saying that they have to give out 'courtesy accommodations and tips'[57] in order to attract and maintain customers at the colonies, especially among those who urge the companies to give tips. In most colonies dealing with the leadership is of little use, because it is in the hands of the officials.

From now on no more feed may be ordered or chosen unless the deacons are all together. The officials may not act on their own authority and choose which commercial feed to use and to buy. Also in many other matters ought to be handled through the leadership.

2) **Salespeople.** Also, more attention should be paid to the feed and salespeople so that they may not sneak in with their cunning and introduce such mischief. Where the leadership is not involved, the salespeople should be cut off and no longer be permitted to do business with the colonies.

3) **Runaways.** If they wish to come back to the colony, no household appliances may be brought back with them other than what is permitted by the colony and they may not be sent ahead to the colony without first seeking permission from the colony, and this applies to members as well.

They should get rid of everything and bring the money back to the colony. Where it becomes evident that such people have kept some of the money or some of the things for themselves without permission and were baptized, they are to be sent away in order to earn it again. Everything that is not allowed should be done away with. This may not be dealt with in any other way without first consulting the Bishop.

4) **Household Appliances.** The appliances and various household goods, which are permitted by the colony, must from now on be purchased by the colony in order to more effectively guard against self-interest.

5) **Those who are to be punished.** Those who are to be punished should be called in after the church service and should remain standing by the door in order to ask for peace. Then the minister may admonish them and then extend to them the sign of peace on behalf of the colony and then those who were punished may sit down.

[77] During the singling out, those who have been separated may not live in the same house as baptized members (Ordinance #10, July, 1979).

Everyone should be in attendance at teaching and prayer when someone is to be punished. The same applies when they are to be reconciled.

A small house should be provided in front of the church where none currently stands so that those who are being punished may still come to hear the Word of God.

6) **School Teacher.** The colonies should try hard to train their own English teacher. It is noticeable in many colonies that the worldly schoolteacher is not a good example or influence on our children, especially concerning clothing.

Children not going to church services. School children who are less than 12 years old should not come to the Sunday service; rather they should all get together in the school during the teaching. All baptized brothers should alternate spending time with the children—beginning with the manager—singing with them and giving them godly instruction.

7) **Impoverishment.** It has long been observed that many of the colonies are becoming increasingly poor right before our eyes. Among them are [two colonies] in South Dakota, U.S.A. And there are many others for which things are not looking good.

Right now we have no idea how to help [these two colonies]. We will, therefore, have to stand by and watch as their colonies fall into disrepair, which is a calamity. These are the main reasons: They have sunk too deep into debt and after that fell into unfaithfulness, drinking, and disobedience, so that among most of them little faith and love is to be found and little community-mindedness.

It was reported that the church is no longer obligated to accept colonies which *ausspitzen* and have become impoverished, and where their overseers do not organize anything and the brothers are acknowledged as incompetent and without spirituality.

If it should happen that a brother or a family is innocent or comes repentantly to the church for help, or to find room with another colony, then they should be taken in but placed on probation in order to see if they may be accepted as competent members.

All brothers, ministers, managers or deacons must sit on the back bench, however, not in order to exclude them, but in order for them to start out in humility and lowliness.

They should not be seen as those who have fallen away until the church has recognized them as such.

Ministers and Managers—Officials. It was also decided that where it arises that someone on the leadership in a colony is unfit to represent his post, because of his age or even more because of other reasons, and where the spiritual and physical condition of a colony is miserable, the manager and the officials should be replaced in order to rescue the woeful situation from impoverishment. If a colony is still not improving, then counsel should be sought from the Bishop [78] and minister. It seems that we almost always wait until the colony is impoverished and it is too late.

Each colony should give its 'accountant' permission in writing to give an account of the colony's situation to the Bishop if he deems it necessary because of the colony's poor situation.

A. **Purchase Orders.** All colonies should try to use purchase orders when they buy things, or at least at such stores where too much may be purchased and easily added to the tab.

B. **Receipts for Goods Purchased.** Brothers are also to be required to provide receipts of goods purchased.

C. Better attention should be paid when **things are sold** and **taken off the colony** [a colony is cited as an example]

D. **Splitting up.** Colonies with too few people should not be allowed to split up.

Dear brothers and sisters, let us realize how serious a matter this, because when a colony becomes impoverished and loses its home and land, it does not happen without a lot of harm, misery, and loss. Woe to those who are found guilty of causing the spiritual and physical impoverishment of the colony, who have not fulfill their duty to use their talents, but instead buried them in the ground, like the useless servant (Matt. 25:30). May God save us from such a thing.

8) **Jury Duty.** If someone is called for jury duty, the person may not accept. It is a right in this country that because of religious or conscientious

reasons a person may refuse; however, it must be done as quickly as possible at the local Sheriff's office.

9) **Banking and Purchasing Fuel.** Regarding banking and purchasing fuel, all colonies should try to be more united so that as much as possible all of the colonies are doing their business at the same bank and purchasing oil from the same company, which was mentioned a long time ago.

10) **Hutterian Brethren Saving and Credit Corporation.** It was decided that a Hutterian Brethren Savings and Credit Corporation would be established. The directors are as follows:

Jacob Kleinsasser	Crystal Spring
Mike Waldner	Milltown
Sam Kleinsasser	Glenway
Fred Waldner	Sturgeon Creek
Jake Waldner	New Haven
Jake Waldner	Huron

11) **Medical Plan for American Colonies.** The state of the Medical Plan for the American Colonies was also discussed.

[79] It was also decided that children would be born only in certain hospitals which have been selected by the directors, because in some hospitals are horrendously more expensive than others.

12) **Fire Insurance.** Regarding the changing of directors of the Hutterian Mutual Fire Insurance: Jakob Waldner, of the Huron Colony in Manitoba, resigned. Johann Hofer, from the Woodland Colony, will replace him. Two helpers from South Dakota are also being sought by the Fire Insurance to help prevent fires.

13) **Church Fund.** The status of the church fund was reported

14) **Michael Wipf's Will.** All of the colonies which were in any way connected to Michael Wipf's will should sign it over to the Broad Valley Colony.

A request was also made by the [a colony in] South Dakota for alms, in whatever amount, to help it build a kitchen.

In conclusion, we would encourage everyone to pay better care, especially to Ordinance #10 from 1983. It is a shame that, even if it is read aloud, some act as if it had not been read aloud and as if it no longer applied and thus they do not obey it. In the eyes of God that is disobedience and fractiousness, which is sin, and the payment for sin is then ruined. Everything is done for the welfare of the colony and the church that we might remain a people of God. Therefore, dear brothers and sisters, we wish you all God's assistance, protection, and covering from spiritual and physical harm. In love we anticipate obedience.

Your fellow helpers in the Kingdom of God,

Jakob Kleinsasser and Jakob Hofer.

1985

Following is a report regarding what was discussed at the ministers' and managers' conference, held 26 June, 1885, at the Crystal Spring Colony. May the dear Lord open the ears of our hearts that we might hear and obey what the Spirit says to the colonies.

1) **Cutting fabric.** The cutting of fabric was discussed.

2) **Tips.** Ordinance #1, 1984. Because the problem of brothers accepting tips from feed companies occurs on an annual basis, it was decided to send another letter of warning to the companies that if it happens again and they are found guilty of giving money or improper things to brothers and not going through the leadership, then we will cease altogether doing business with them or buying feed from them. If they wish, however, they may provide a meal for us. If that happens, no brother should have the freedom to keep the money that was given for that purpose.

3) **Schnapps—Marijuana.** It looks like the purchasing Schnapps and bringing it dishonestly across the border cannot be stopped. Also, [80] 'dope'[58] or marijuana is appearing among us. Punishing with the ban does not help. Smoking dope should no longer be tolerated. We must pay closer attention and be more on guard.

Therefore any who have refused to accept a warning, according to Ordinance #3, 1983, should be sent away until through repentance they are totally free of it.

4) **Weddings.** Attention was brought to the fact that we have already discussed this 12 times, and still no solution has been found as to how we could responsibly celebrate this important celebration. Almost all of the Bishops were of the mind that it should be done in a more Christian way.

The vast majority was in favour of trying to have all of the celebrations this year without alcohol, so that no alcoholic drinks be given out at the wedding as gifts and neither on the Sunday evening nor at the appointed mealtime. The allotted amount for the bride and groom may remain the same.

5) Suspended Sentence.[59] If a brother or someone is on a suspended sentence from the world, or any other sort of conviction, then he must wait out his probation period until he can be re-accepted into the colony.

He should stay away from the colony until his time is up. If, however, it is for a minor thing, then the situation should be handled according to Ordinance #9, 1980.

6) Unmarrieds in fornication. If young, unmarried people fall into fornication, then the two are obligated to marry, so that they might come together according to the Christian ordinance. They may not marry anyone else. If however, they are cousins, the two should not be allowed to marry each other.

We are falling into great fractiousness and do not want to be corrected. Some are even leaving the colony in order to carry out their behaviour and thus make a mock marriage out of a Christian marriage. And then they want the colony to accept it, and to accept and forgive them as sorry and repentant.

And then there is the difficult issue when the girl confesses and exposes her sins but the boy lies or will not confess, which is a very difficult position. But at this point we cannot know even if the one who confessed is lying, which we can read about in Genesis 39:10 with Joseph and Potiphar's wife. The words of Potiphar were accepted until the Lord exposed them.

7) Extramarital Emission. If a married brother emits or sins for a while with anyone other than his wife, through fondling[60] or impure touching, then he should be punished with the ban because such a thing is considered adultery according to the Gospel. Matthew 5:28; 2 Peter 2:4; Colossians 3:5-6.

8) Runaways. Also the following was reminder was given regarding Ordinance #5, 1981. Where runaway boys are found as boyfriends in the colony of girls, and if the parents knew about it but did not fulfill their duty, then the parents are to be examined with great seriousness and are to be punished.

[81] **9) Self-interest.** Also colonies which are still allowing Ordinance #12, 1979—plucking goose feathers and selling them for personal profit—the leadership should put a stop to this during the teaching and should rectify its mistake.

10) Fire Insurance.[61] It was also decided to replace the directors of the Mutual Fire Insurance. The changes are as follows: Markus Momson,

Christof Arnold as deputy, David Waldner of South Dakota and Jacob Maendel of Blumengart.

11) **Splitting up and building a separate colony.** Bloomfield Colony wants permission to build a new colony on its current land, three miles east of the Bloomfield Colony. In total it owns 8000 acres.

Sunnyside Colony wants permission to build a new colony on its own land, eight miles south and two miles east. In total Sunnyside owns 6500 acres and is hoping to purchase more later.

12) **Brookdale Colony.** Brookdale Colony, South Dakota, was also mentioned because Hillside Colony has decided to help this colony and the South Dakota colonies by putting up money. A loan was also requested from the Manitoba and Woodcrest colonies, and after two years time it will be decided how Hillside Colony will pay the money back. The loan from the Manitoba and Woodcrest colonies has been deposited.

13) **Cloverleaf Colony.** It was also reported that the Cloverleaf Colony, South Dakota, will be examined again in order to see if it can be helped, to see if it can be brought into peace with the Hutterite Church.

Plainview Colony. It was also reported that things are still going very poorly for the Plainview Colony. Presently we are not ready to help them because too much fractiousness and self-interest are still evident.

In conclusion we wish for obedient hearts, voluntary children of God so that one need not use bit and bridle to lead. God desires voluntary servants. A forced oath is not what he desires. And whoever does not have the spirit of Christ does not belong to him.

Dear brothers, fear God, and hold firmly to his laws. The reward is great. It is worth the eternal joy. Let us not displace the goal, rather let us remain unmoved as we strive for the goal that is before us.

May the dear lord help us all, that we do not miss the entrance into his rest.

Dear brothers, it was discussed at the annual ministers' and managers' conference that it seems that a remarkable laziness and cooling off can be found among many. Many no longer have enthusiasm to live together in community and true serenity according to the principle of the Gospel and the teaching of Christ and the Apostles as well as our forefathers, whose descendents we are, but in whose footsteps we do not wish to walk.

During baptism it has become evident that many of our young people have no idea about the account and the history book of our forefathers, which are the articles of our faith, and because of which we are called the Hutterian Brethren. Thus, some are being baptized without recognizing [82] the basis of the Hutterian beliefs, and therefore they remain stubborn, wilful, and almost incorrigible. Therefore, it should be seen in your behaviour, before the baptism, through your obedience and surrender, that you have a new life and that you desire to be a member of the church.

Dear brothers, this is often neglected, and this step is handled far too superficially, for where the beginning was not holy, then the whole dough is unholy.

It was already discussed previously whether or not minister's counsel should be held regarding baptismal candidates. Maybe it would be nice if the young people would come beforehand to confess their sins and vices.

It cannot go on in this haphazard way for much longer. A solution needs to be found. May the dear Lord send wisdom from above.

Also let it be noted that the schools where there is not enough godly instruction are neglecting this situation. Teachers who are supposed to teach children are themselves incapable of holding Sunday School. And even where Sunday School does take place the quality of instruction about the foundations of the faith are poor.

The parents too are a poor example for their children, which is noticeable when it comes to caring for the children during the teaching, that brothers refuse to give even one hour for the children's welfare. They consider it an aberration of the forefathers' teaching, which only shows how little they actually read and know of the forefathers' teaching.

Let each one read diligently in the history book about raising children and even more in the Bible. Maybe it will open the eyes in which the error is stuck.

Also, a hired teacher teaches a significant portion of the school day. The Saviour speaks about the shepherds who are hired and how they only care about their wage and not about the welfare of the sheep. It is surely the same with the hired teachers, who are only concerned with their pay; and to them we entrust our children. How can spiritual fruit be sowed?

Also the daily view for our dear children is of the world—over time they are unknowingly looking at the spirit of the world and worldly clothing, even though we are supposed to be separate from the world.

And then we wonder why we are unable to keep ourselves more from the world and worldly clothes, such as blue jeans and wide belts with big buckles, as was mentioned above, and other abuses, with hair styles and other changes that the fractious try to push through, not only young men and women, rather also married people. And such people boast that they are brothers and sisters. It can no longer be tolerated because according to the Holy Scripture it is indecent for children of God to make themselves the same as the world (1 Cor. 13:16; Romans 12:2; 1 John 2:15). Almost no one has considered training to be an English teacher, even though we think it is necessary to train German teachers because children grow up and can no longer read or understand German. Eventually such people will be ordained as leaders of the colony. How can such people lead the colony, if they themselves have been raised as unlearned, both spiritually and physically.

Is that not reason enough, that there are so many who no longer have the desire to accept the Hutterite foundation and customs as right? The upbringing failed because of a lack of godly enthusiasm and desire to accept the duty with which the people were entrusted!

[83] It was suggested that some brothers could be appointed to examine the colonies and where they find negligence they report to the Bishop and together try to improve the situation.

Also the German teachers should speak proper German in the German school. Let each brother take more seriously the school official, for the colony has entrusted him to care for the welfare of the colony.

Dear brothers, believe us: What a person sows, he will reap. "Sow your seed in the morning and at evening let not your hands be idle, for you do not know which will succeed, whether this or that, or whether both will do equally well" (Ecclesiastes 11:6).

This newsletter should be read aloud in all of the colonies and all who have the strength and are able should try to follow this counsel, otherwise it will have to be discussed again at the 1986 conference.

We greet you in love.
Your fellow helpers in the Kingdom of Christ,

Jakob Kleinsasser and Jakob Hofer

[84] **Hutterian Brethren Statement of Assistance for Hillside Colony, South Dakota, in Canadian Funds. [A table lists the contributions of each colony]**

[85] The issue of smoking tobacco, as well as marijuana, [in a Manitoba Colony] was discussed at length by all of the Manitoba ministers and it was decided that we should earnestly fight against both.

From now on smoking should be punished with exclusion. And the person should remain shut out until he quits. If, however, he does not wish to stop smoking, then he should be sent away.

Also from now on all those who are exposed as marijuana smokers should be sent away in accordance with the conference ordinance from June 26, 1985, until such time as they can demonstrate that they are free of it.

The deacons should punish unbaptized smokers. If that does not help then they should not be tolerated.

It was presently exposed that a married brother and three young men at [a colony in Manitoba] were planting marijuana. It was decided that they should be sent away.

Otherwise all of the colonies that were tarnished by smoking should make good at the teaching, and the unbaptized smokers should be punished generally in order to be reconciled. From here on, however, tobacco smoking should be dealt with according to the ordinance from June 26, 1985.

All of those who do not quit smoking now must quit and confess it at their baptism; otherwise they are not to be baptized.

Your fellow helpers in the Kingdom of Christ,
Jakob Kleinsasser
Jakob Hofer

1986

Dear brothers,

Report from the annual ministers' and managers' conference, held June 19-20, 1986, at the Crystal Spring Colony: what was discussed regarding important business that has appeared among us but which is very inappropriate for a people of God. May the dear Lord come to our aid with wisdom and understanding.

1) **Cutting Fabric.** First the issue of cutting fabric was reported on.

2) **Fire Insurance.** David Miller Sr. and David Miller Jr. gave a report regarding the Hutterian Mutual Fire Insurance, detailing its financial situation.

It was also reported that there are still colonies that do not have any fire alarms. Why this is so difficult for some colonies to follow is difficult to understand because it is only for our own welfare. Let us strive to stand together.

Also, David Waldner, of Brightstone, Manitoba, was appointed as director of the Hutterian Fire Insurance.

[86] 3) **Raising Children.** In the newsletter from June 25, 1985, it was reported that we need to put more effort into raising our children. It has happened, however, that there are too few who accepted the encouragement to raise this treasure, our descendents, according to the model set by our forefathers, that they be protected from a young age from self-interest and stubbornness and that Christian virtues be sowed into them.

It was also reported that the worldly laws have enlightened us, and apply to us because there is too much negligence regarding our childcare. Let us read the enclosed paper about 'Child Abuse' in which it is evident that the world is very serious about the care those children receive and that they are very serious about neglect. It would be a shame if we were found to be negligent by the country's laws.

It was decided that children should be cared for during the common mealtime. Older children should be given their food either before or after the mealtime so that they can care for the [younger] children while the adults are eating.

Also, in cases where the mothers are working almost the whole day, small children should all be brought together so that an old sister and a young girl can look after them until the mother can care for them again. Child rearing is seriously lacking among us if we compare ourselves to our forefathers. Let us read and put into practice what it says in the history book of our forefathers and try harder to walk in their footsteps.

4) **Tips.** The ordinance from June 21, 1984 has still not borne fruit. Therefore it has been decided that it is no longer acceptable to take part in the big 'Hog Congress' or any other meetings where the feed companies or business people will be, and especially not meetings where there are hospitality rooms or where alcohol is served. These things do more to serve the lust of the flesh than the welfare of the colony.

Business people finance these things and then we become friends with them but they are more concerned about their own earnings than the welfare of the colony. And our brothers cannot withstand the temptation and then mischief always arises through alcohol, which we already know. And how much more is there that we don't know?

Therefore accepting invitations from feed companies or other business people is no longer allowed.

If a business wants to allow something more fair, then it should go to the colony account. If someone requests to have a meeting it should be held and put on by the colony.

And where it is necessary to research the modern developments, it should occur at the colony's expense, and should be investigated by the leadership.

5) **Dealing with Tips.** If a brother confesses that he has received tips from certain business people, as has happened a number of times, then the colony that is affected should stop doing business with this company.

6) **Brides and Grooms.** If a bride and groom leave the colony because of their license or for any other reason, two others should go along. This has been discussed several times and yet still people continue to disregard it.

7) **Garb.** Every year it is reported that the worldly garb is being pushed through forcefully and without check so much so that we can hardly resist it and dress according to Hutterite [87] custom. It was also decided that long hair would no longer be tolerated, neither will blue jeans, belts

with big buckles, and other abuses of worldly clothes. The customary suspenders should be worn.

Also among the womenfolk, the jacket or the *Mieder* are worn so short that they are almost totally unchaste. The clothes are also being stitched so tightly and the skirt is so short and see-through that such things only serve to excite and awaken fleshly lust.

Also, nearly black and even completely black headscarves are being worn, which is not fitting for virtuous sisters and young women.

Therefore it was decided that in three months it should all be improved. Where, however, through fractiousness and disobedience this is not followed, such colonies should stop holding church services until the colony is brought into order. This is being encouraged by brothers and sisters in order to bring this stain to right.

8) **Consolidating Money.** It was also decided that all of the Manitoba colonies should give $100.00 in alms for the Eden Hospital in Winkler, Manitoba. Send the money to Joseph Waldner, in Blumengart, or to Michel Waldner, in the Rosedale Colony. They will deliver it to the hospital. This hospital is only run by donations.

9) **Shunning.** Not enough shunning was shown at the funeral in the Bloomfield Colony towards those who have fallen away, because one who had fallen away was permitted to sit at the bier. All of the ministers who were there have recanted and have promised to be more careful in the future and to not be so careless.

10) **Punishing fornication.** There is too much of this mischief; young people are sinning too often through fornication, and children are being born out of wedlock. It is noticeable that every year there are more of them. And then they want to get baptized really quickly in order to get married.

We decided that that is not a repentant baptism, but only botches things up more in order to cover up a shameful thing.[62] From now on such quick baptisms should not be allowed. Such people should demonstrate that they have not given themselves to another for one year before they may be baptized. This applies to all young women and men who fall into fornication.

Also from now situations should be handled in the following way, especially when the two are from the same colony: the boy should be sent away or also the girl, and if possible the one should be sent away to a different colony in order to prevent this vice.

B. **Funerals for Children.** It was also decided that if one of these children dies, no funeral should be held, except where the parents of the child are married, then a funeral may be held.

C. **Young people sitting together.** It was also unanimously decided that in order to prevent this mischief, unbaptized young men and women who are in love should not be allowed to be alone together. When it happens it should be punished, especially when it happens in secret and in the dark. Romans 13:13 states: "Let us walk honestly, as in the day; not in rioting and drunkenness, not in chambering and wantonness, not in strife and envying. But put ye on the Lord Jesus Christ, and make not provision for the flesh, to fulfil the lusts thereof."

[88] 11) **Punishment.** It was also decided that the minister [named in the original document], who rudely criticized the senior ministers, and would not allow himself to be corrected, should be suspended from his ministerial duties for a few weeks until he humbles himself and recognizes his mistake.

Celebrating Weddings should remain as it was decided in the year 1985—no alcoholic drinks.

12) **Punishment.** [This ordinance deals with an individual case of sexual misconduct]

13) [This ordinance deals with the above issue]

14) It was also decided that the Bonhomme Colony, which was also too negligent with its youth, and runaways, should no longer hold church services until it really recognizes and understands its negligence.

15) **Runaways.** Ordinance #5, from July 2, 1981 states: The matter of a runaway appearing on the yard to visit a girl should be handled with more seriousness.

It was decided that colonies that show little concern for this evil should no longer hold church services until the matter is brought into order, at which time such colonies will be reconciled to the Hutterite church.

16) **Young people driving together.** When a whole van full of young people visit a colony, they must be gone by 11:00 to 11:30 at night because our young people do not behave reasonably and virtuously when they stay late into the night at another colony and thus it is no longer to be tolerated.

Dear brothers, why must we stand in such a battle? Surely there are men among us who are supposed to help us to protect against such garbage. Like satiated shepherds, they are more concerned with grazing themselves than with the welfare of the colony; they minister only with words and in speech but nothing is to be grasped in their deeds. This is laziness on the part of the leadership and the parents.

Let us all take better hold of our faith and our trust in God. Let not the evil enemy destroy this holy work. It sometimes seems among us that he is winning the game.

May God grant us all, brothers and sisters, more obedient hearts that we might fight for the truth, in order to conquer evil, so that what is godly might grow and take root. May God help us to accomplish this. May you be commanded by God in love.

Your fellow helpers in Christ and your Bishops,

Jakob Kleinsasser and Jakob Hofer.

[89] 1988

Dear brothers,

We would like to begin with a greeting and we wish you all the precious peace and communion with the Holy Spirit. The following is a report from the ministers' and managers' conference, held on June 28, 1988, at the Crystal Spring Colony in St. Agathe, Manitoba.

First a presentation was given about the importance of the conference—that it does not just happen because of habit and form, rather because of the welfare of the colonies and in order that we might remain a house of God and true followers of Christ.

Thereafter a general discussion occurred regarding the **Cutting of fabric.**

1) **Self-Interest and Rebates.** The matter of collecting coupons was discussed in earnest, as well as the collection of money for self-interest. Coupons are being collected out of garbage piles, and also in stores, where they are dishonestly cut out, and are being sought out in the common rooms. From whiskey bottles, antifreeze containers, and lawn mower discounts, almost $100.00 worth of coupons was torn out. $100.00 coupons for coolers, and all sorts of other kinds are taken from the newspapers, calendars, and other places. Dear brothers and sisters, have guilty consciences because of self-interest all died out? Sometimes such names have been used to sell the coupons, which is mail fraud, and is a criminal offence. Such things are vain deceits and are sinful and are abominable for colony members to take part in.

The question is, where is the leadership of the colony that knowingly permits such things and does not punish them?

2) **Distribution of Shoes.** The distribution of shoes is also not being done in accordance with the ordinance because money is still being given out so that each one may purchase shoes according to individual preference.

3) **Distribution of Money.** Also, more money is being distributed on a monthly basis than the allotted amount of allowance. This is directly contrary to the previously established ordinance and is against true community.

4) **Baptism.** The baptism is being handled too superficially. How often we have already discussed this—that this holy work is to be handled with more earnestness. Baptismal candidates are wilfully refusing to learn the assignments that are expected of them, and there are some who refused to learn the baptismal questions and answers and did not attend the sessions with the other candidates but who were baptized anyway alongside the others.

This occurred in a number of colonies and in many instances those who were not repentant and were not prepared were baptized anyway, which surely is a water baptism without fruit.

5) **Young people going together.** Young people who are in love are not allowed to go together until they are baptized because so much mischief arises as a result. It should be more earnestly prevented and punished where it has been permitted.

[90] 6) **Clothing.** As for the unchaste, tight clothing of our young people: as may be observed no improvement has occurred. The clothes that are being worn are just as tempting and unchaste. The tight and short *Miede*, the short skirt, the disreputable hairstyles, and the puffed sleeves are all a shame. And even among the boys and brothers: long hair, moustaches, sideburns, tight pants, jeans and jackets, multi-coloured jackets and shirts. It is amazing that the ministers and managers would tolerate such things.

7) **Runaways.** There are still colonies where the runaways are given too much freedom to come on to the yards, to stay overnight and to come on Sundays. The question still stands: Where is the leadership in this sort of colony and where are the obedient?

8) **Runaways coming back.** It was also decided that if runaways want to return to the colony, before they may be accepted they must produce a 'clean bill of health' which states that they do not have the disease AIDS,

which is very dangerous in the world today and from which the colonies should try to protect themselves.

9) **Ministers' Counsel.** It was decided that if the Bishops call the ministers' counsel and if at the meeting a decision is made, then it should be accepted by all of the brothers and sisters, especially if it pertains to matters of the law.

It is already so poorly accepted so that they hardly trust themselves to make any decisions and so many brothers are becoming unhappy and then they begin to blame and malign others.

10) **As for the Lakeside Deal,** shunning is still being contested, and if brothers interact with Daniel Hofer and his associates by making contact in Winnipeg or in other places, they are secret traitors and children of Judas—it is wilful sin and disobedience, rebellion, and resistance.

Alas, dear brothers and sisters, all of these points were already discussed a number of times at other conference meetings, and not only the points which have been mentioned here, but many others as well. It is noticeable that things are barely observed and are not followed As long as this is and continues to be the situation—that each one does as he pleases and as seems good to him, we will not be able to remain a people of God and a church that shines with good deeds.

Therefore, it was decided that each minister and leadership should go home and inquire if their colonies even wish to remain a part of the Hutterite church and to agree with and be obedient to and to follow the required rules, ordinances, and articles of faith. There is no point remaining a part of the Hutterite church under pressure and against one's will.

All brothers and sisters, young men and young women are to be asked where they stand, and therefore to avoid the nuisance of resistance and living in sin from day to day.

The situation should seriously be improved and such garbage should be done away with for it is possible with God's help to remain a people according to God's pleasure.

[91] We would like to hold another meeting in a short time to which all of the ministers and managers from South Dakota and Manitoba are invited, and we have set the date for August 17, 1988 at the Crystal Spring Colony in Manitoba.

Awaiting obedience, we remain, in love, your fellow helpers,

Joseph Kleinsasser, Jakob Hofer, and Joseph Wipf

August 26, 1988

Dear brothers,

First we would like to wish you all a greeting and the communion of the Holy Spirit from God.

Following is a report from the big meeting and conference at Crystal Spring Colony, on August 17, 1988.

This meeting was a continuation of the conference held June 28, 1988 at Crystal Spring Colony.

The reason for this was a serious question that was posed to all of the colonies—how many wanted to remain fully surrendered, faithful members of the true community, and to obediently follow and accept the established rules, ordinances and articles of faith without pressure or resistance, because it is as clear as sunshine that a lot of resistance has appeared and that the free spirit of Christ is no longer reigning.

1) CLAUSE 1 **Self-interest.** First a hearing was called regarding the situation regarding the accursed vices of all kinds of self-interest that are abominably being wrought among us. Contrary to the foundational belief of true community such things are being knowingly allowed.

2) **The distribution of money for shoes.** Also contrary to the ordinance money is being distributed for shoes in addition to monthly allowance, which is directly contrary to the established ordinance and the foundation of true community.

Because so many colonies were guilty of this, it was decided that all of the guilty should atone for their sins and be reconciled. The whole colony should come together, brothers and sisters, young men and young women in order to seek forgiveness. Where, however, the minister is guilty, another minister should be called to reconcile the colony in question.

Giving what is due. It was encouraged anew that it is the duty of the leadership to repay the colony such things that are permitted by the colony. Acts 2:45 states: "And sold their possessions and goods, and parted them to all men, as every man had need," not that each one provided for himself according to what his preferences were, through self-interest and stubbornness.

[92] Furthermore, **microwaves** and all high-spiritedness, such as individual earnings through tips given by feed companies and other business people, are not allowed and are not to be tolerated.

3) CLAUSE **4, from June 28, 1988 Baptism.** It was also discussed that this holy work needs to be handled more seriously. It was decided

that [a named minister] should have his ministerial duties suspended because he was found guilty in this matter. A servant of the Word has more responsibility before God and is obligated to watch over the sheep as a shepherd, especially a servant of the Word whose duties already included baptizing people according to God's pleasure, and according to the ordinance and rules of the church of Christ.

4) CLAUSE 5-6 **Clothing.** It was observed that the young people run around together and wear inappropriate clothing, and this prohibited clothing is contrary to the ordinance of the church. Many want to try to make themselves the same as the world where we are supposed to be set apart as children of God—both on the outside and the inside, and more than that we are to be a light unto the world and the salt of the earth that shines on the doings of the world.

IT WAS DECIDED that where there is still resistance and disobedience in a colony that the church services should be suspended (that is both teaching and prayers) until obedience has been demonstrated. Therefore no minister should stand for the violation of the above-mentioned points.

5) CLAUSE 7-8 **Runaways.** More seriousness needs to be demonstrated in the matter of runaways who come to the colonies rudely and feck-lessly and without permission. Note: At [a named colony] Colony where Minister [who is named in the original] was found guilty of this, it was decided that he is to be suspended from ministerial duties for one year.

And all brothers and sisters who have secretly taken in runaways without permission in the last two to three months should be punished with discord.

Where, however, this does not help, then the whole colony should be declared guilty until a solution is found to keep those who have fallen away off the yard. And if this works and the colony stands together in this matter then it may be readmitted to the church. No where in the Holy Scripture and the Word of God does it state that a holy congrega-tion, children of God may enter into community with the disobedient in the house of God, rather such people are to be shunned. And where this shunning is not practiced, then these people must be separated from the congregation.

Therefore it was decided and encouraged that if a minister and the Bishops call church counsel and a decision is made for the welfare of the colony, it should be accepted in love. And not reluctantly or openly blamed, maligned, and gossiped about, for this is a great sin that is among us so that we must fear that the dear Lord will spit us out of his mouth and will look for a new people which will shine with the light of the virtues of the spirit of God. Let us guard ourselves from the sin of maligning. He who secretly maligns his neighbour, this soul will be expelled from the people of God, says God the Lord. Brothers and sisters,

[93] this is a tool that destroys love and peace, and without love we are only a resounding gong or a clanging cymbal.

It was also reported and disclosed that the Pibroch Colony in Alberta—Dariusleut—wants to sue the Crystal Spring Colony in Manitoba—Schmiedeleut—in order to invalidate a feeder patent which was registered in Ottawa by the Crystal Spring Colony in 1985. Crystal Spring has already received a statement of claim and the Pibrock Colony's lawyer filed the matter before the federal court in Ottawa on July 26, 1988. The Pibrock Colony has already made a downpayment of $5000.00.

It was made clear that Minister Samuel Waldner of the Raleigh Colony who wrote the bad and abusive letters about Bishop Jakob Kleinsasser and the Schmiedeleut has neither been judged nor vindicated. Regardless of whether it is directly or indirectly a result of this, now that this Pibrock Colony deal is being pursued, it is no longer possible for the Schmiedenleut and Dariusleut groups to both belong to the Hutterite church unless those who are taking part in the lawsuit are put out of the church and closed out.[63]

We can see the devil's malice when we see how Satan is trying to destroy the church of our forefathers and the apostles. May God prevent that from happening.

There are many among the Dariusleut who see this thing as a great injustice—that one colony is pulling another colony before the worldly courts.

The same applies to Daniel Hofer and Paul Hofer from Lakeside who tried to amass their own followers in order to achieve their own will. For that reason they have fallen away from the Hutterite Church.

Dear brothers, let us wake up all those who are sleeping, yes from the sleep of sin, and stand up from the death of sin, so that Christ might enlighten us. We are standing in great danger. Satan is fighting with full force to destroy us. We must stand together in unity, with awe and obedience, for the more respect that is at work among you, the more love there will be for the work, says the Apostle.

We hope to challenge all of the colonies that were not at this meeting with the same question that was asked to all of the others at the August 17 conference.

Be commanded by God, who is your protection, your covering and your helper in times of trouble.

Your fellow helpers in Christ's Kingdom,

Jakob Kleinsasser
Jakob Hofer
Joseph Wipf

[94] 1989

We wish you all God's love, grace, and mercy, and the community of his Holy Spirit.

The following is a report from the annual conference, held at Crystal Spring Colony, August 24-25, 1989.

1) **Insurance.** First a report was delivered by the Millers regarding the Mutual Fire Insurance. Joerg Waldner, from the Hillside Colony in South Dakota, was appointed as director. It was also accepted that $100,000.00 should be taken from the Fire Insurance and put toward the Medical Insurance fund.

2) **Worldly Governments.** It was also discussed whether it is right or proper to turn to the worldly government, even if it leads to the worldly court, and great disunion arises as a result. Many accusations have been made against Bishop Jakob Kleinsasser. After much back and forth debate regarding the abominable behaviour of Daniel Hofer from the Lakeside Colony, which was discussed by the ministers' counsel, it was decided that because the whole church is in danger it was highly necessary to turn to the government in order to protect us from trouble.

This was already considered in the year 1980 in Ordinance #7 at the annual conference, where it was discussed how such situations should be handled:

1) Paul appealed to the high court, even to Rome, when he realized that the Jews were seriously threatening his life.

2) Our forefathers always turned to the rulers and other regents for protection, and when they found no protection they were plundered. They always took the freedom to go before the government, which was in accordance with Peter Riedeman's declaration.

3) When the forefathers moved from Sieben Buergen to Russia, they did so under the protection of General Romanzov.

4) In Russia they turned to the government to grant them freedom of conscience.

5) One time they tore down a house because of a fractious brother.

6) In the U.S.A. they sought freedom of conscience from President Grant.

7) They only turned to the government and appealed to the freedom of the country when it was the only thing left to do.

8) In the situation with Mitch Michel they protected themselves through the courts.

In the situation with Jakob Hofer at the Bonhomme Colony they protected themselves through the courts.

9) During wartime the police and sheriff did not hear or accept their call and the enemies carried away their flock of sheep.

[95] 10) In the Interlake deal they protected themselves through the court. With the Sunset, USA, situation, they turned to the worldly court, and also with the Bonhomme Colony and Jim Wainscot. Many police and sheriffs have been asked to protect us in various situations.

All of these points were considered and all brothers were challenged to declare their unity with the church. All did so, except for eight brothers, who, however, allowed themselves to be shown the right way. It was decided that these should be vindicated, and each one will seek forgiveness in his colony at the teaching.

Because the gossiping, maligning, and vilifying have become all too common, as have criticizing the court's ruling and vilifying and slandering the Bishops, whoever is found guilty of these things should be punished because it is a vice and should not be tolerated among the children of God.

> Ask "ask thy father, and he will shew thee; thy elders, and they will tell thee your elders, and they will explain to you" (Deuteronomy 32:7b).

> "Thou shalt not go up and down as a talebearer among thy people" (Leviticus 19:16a).

> "Whoso privily slandereth his neighbour, him will I cut off: him that hath an high look and a proud heart will not I suffer" (Psalm 101:5).

> "The slanderer is a fool. You shall not allow a slanderer to be among your people.

> Wherefore laying aside all malice, and all guile, and hypocrisies, and envies, and all evil speakings" (1 Peter 2:1).

> "Speak not evil one of another, brethren. He that speaketh evil of his brother, and judgeth his brother, speaketh evil of the law, and judgeth the law: but if thou judge the law, thou art not a doer of the law, but a judge" (James 4:11).

It has also been reported that all colonies should keep the teaching from Psalm 15 should all be earnestly warned that this abominable sin is not to continue. And let us keep our tongues in check. The tongue is a small member and yet it perpetrates great things. "And the tongue is a fire, a world of iniquity: so is the tongue among our members, that it defileth the whole body, and setteth on fire the course of nature; and it is set on fire of hell" (James 3:6).

3) **Colony Judgment.** If a brother or someone is unhappy with the colony's judgment and therefore turns to the Bishop or refuses counsel, then such individuals do not have the right to turn to other colonies for counsel that suits them better. And other colonies or ministers who were not instructed to take part do not have the freedom to accept these fractious individuals or to listen to them. Let us read about it in Genesis 17.

4) **Cloverleaf.** Regarding the situation with the Cloverleaf Colony no decision was reached neither was counsel given whereby it might be vindicated and resume its place with the other colonies. Therefore it remains as it was before and it has been decided that each individual should seek acceptance with a different colony where he might find acceptance.

5) **Rainbow.** Regarding Rainbow Colony it was decided to try again. Minister Elias Waldner should once again hold services at the colony but we should wait for a time to see if the colony shows itself to be obedient in the future before the whole leadership is replaced.

[96] 6) Also, at the biannual meeting, held at the Lakeside Colony in Alberta, it was reported in a displeasing report that three groups are standing in discord and that the unity of the Spirit is missing.

7) **Young People Getting together.** It was also reported the matter of young people coming together as boyfriend and girlfriend[64] before they have been baptized needs to be taken more seriously. Much mischief has arisen and continues to arise out of this. This was also discussed on June 28, 1988, in Ordinance #5,

And brothers, let us not be guilty of corrupting our children by refusing to appealing to them earnestly before it is too late, at which point we will regret it and lament.

8) It was also reported during a conference visit to Woodcrest that the brothers would like it if the ministers from Manitoba and South Dakota would try to get together as often as possible in order to get to know one another better. It was decided that on October 24, 1989 everyone should meet there.

9) The matter of [a named minister], was also discussed, because he was dismissed from his ministerial duties for one year. It was unanimously

decided that he should once again assume his ministerial duties and that his cousin [named], of the [colony named in the original] should confirm him.

10) It was reported that the Mennonite World Conference is going to be held in Winnipeg in July of 1990. They have asked that someone from the Hutterite Church be there as a representative, because there will be people there from almost everywhere in the world. It was decided that Minister Christof Arnold from Woodcrest should accept the invitation.

Dear brothers, in conclusion I would like to add some things. Let us work more conscientiously and sensitively toward what promotes love and peace. Through slander and gossip peace and love are destroyed. Our striving should be that we seek after peace and holiness, because without these two no one will see the Lord. It is a horrid plague that is spreading among us, that many hearts are burdened with falsehood and with a lack of a foundation. The evil enemy is playing a winning game among us.

Electing a Minister. It must also be reported that John Waldner of the Grand Colony is seeking a ministerial assistant, as is Jakob Waldner of the Poplar Point Colony. Both of those positions are fragile right now, therefore it is necessary that we come to their aid. We will set both of the elections for October 15, 1989. May God grant us his grace and prosperity that both might succeed for his honour and for the welfare of the colony.

It is also our wish that there would be more colonies which would seek assistance in order to think ahead to the future and in order to strengthen the situation of the colonies.

[97] **Purchasing Land.** With this writing we want to inform you that the New Elm Spring Colony has declared that it wishes to build a new yard on the old Elm Spring spot. New Elm Spring has 135 souls. Both yards together have 6000 acres and there are three turkey barns: 70 ft. × 608 ft.; 76 × 608, and 60 × 300. There is grain storage for 135,000 bushels. There is a 40 × 120 ft. utility building, and also good water supply. They would like to start building housing. They really need this and no longer want to build any more at New Elm Spring and they think that with the opportunity they will be able to buy more land.

Greetings to everyone. We would like to embrace you with the arms of our hearts.

Your Bishops and fellow helpers in Christ's kingdom.

Jakob Kleinsasser
Jakob Hofer
Joseph Wipf

1989 Fabric Cutting

	Men and Boys:	Women and Girls:	
	2 shirts	1 dress 2 pairs of pants	2
shirts			
	long underwear	summer underwear	

1990

As a greeting we wish you God's love, grace, and mercy, as well as health in body and soul. The following is a report from the minister's meeting, July 12, 1990, at the Crystal Spring Colony.

1) **Unbaptized Young Men and Women. Fornication and Children born out of wedlock.** First the matter of young men and women going around together was discussed and seriously discouraged, because fornication and children born out of wedlock appear as a result.

Such sins occur, which are not Christ-like, rather are heathen and it are even shameful to speak of them: in Manitoba four or five children were born out of wedlock, even 15 and 16 year-old boys and girls are running around and go so far that such mischief occurs. The same thing happens in South Dakota, where such horrid [behaviour] outside of marriage occurs.

And this has been discussed numerous times, in order to try to prevent such things but it does not seem to be stopping. Let us believe, however: "the children of adulterers will not come to maturity, and the offspring of an unlawful union will perish" (Wisdom of Solomon 3). It is our duty to watch and see that our children are not harmed and that they do not become pregnant—even in the house of the Lord. And Sirach 42:11: "Keep strict watch over a headstrong daughter, or she may make you a laughingstock to your enemies...and put you to shame in public gatherings."

[98] This is a shameless situation among us; it is alarming how the young people are running around together [. . .] which is shameful even to mention. Romans 13:13-14 states: "Let us walk honestly, as in the day; not in rioting and drunkenness, not in chambering and wantonness, not in strife and envying. But put ye on the Lord Jesus Christ, and make not provision for the flesh, to fulfil the lusts thereof." In English it is said: 'And not make provision for the flesh to fulfill its lusts.'

What does it help to preach annually against the work of the flesh and then like salt that has lost its saltiness to go home and to be silent on the topic while young people get together in chambers and rooms . . . .

Therefore it was also decided that young and unbaptized men and women who are in love are no longer to interact with one another.[65]

Where it does occur it should be earnestly punished and where it is found that ministers and brothers have been negligent in this matter or have even allowed it, an investigation is to be carried out and punishment to follow.

Young unbaptized men and women who are in love should no longer be allowed to sit alone together in rooms, as one says in English: 'as girlfriend and boyfriend, engaged in courting and dating' and out of which the aforementioned mischief arises.

Dear brothers and sisters, as 1 Thessalonians 5:22-23 states: "Abstain from all appearance of evil. And the very God of peace sanctify you wholly; and I pray God your whole spirit and soul and body be preserved blameless unto the coming of our Lord Jesus Christ."

2) This ordinance, not included in this translation, deals with issues of sexual misconduct and what is appropriate punishment. The point is made that for serious transgressions member could be expelled from the Hutterite Church.

3) Unfaithful Letter. It was also decided to ask who of the Schmiedeleut wrote the letter against Bishop Jakob Kleinsasser with the angry accusations about the Lake Side affair. The general counsel handled this as usual; therefore, these accusations are not only against the Bishop but against all of those who were in attendance at the time.

[99] If a minister knows something about this, he should not dare to preach because he is in discord.

All of the ministers who were assembled stood up in order to affirm that they did not know who wrote the letter. Hereafter two ministers were appointed to question all of the ministers who were not at the meeting to see if they had anything to do with it.

Jakob Gross, of the Iberville Colony, and Michel Waldner, of the Rosedale Colony in Manitoba, were both appointed to this task.

4) Requirements for Paying in. The matter of the $2.75 levy was also considered; some colonies have taken the freedom to be negligent, or have even sold their hogs somewhere else in order to avoid it. It was decided that everyone has two weeks to pay in. If that doesn't help then colonies will be punished for disobedience and unfaithfulness.

As for the Hillcrest Colony in South Dakota—a charge was laid four years ago. There are still colonies that have not complied.

In South Dakota it was decided to make a $300.00 requirement, which not everyone has paid.

Let us not come to the point where it must be collected through punishment. It is a stain that is not necessary, and should be fairly and rightly requested.

As for the Bank of Montreal, almost everything has been changed since the original 'agreement with the bank,' through which the specified amount for the church is to be collected. It is also not right that each one should act according to his discretion and short-change the church account. It was decided that another recommendation should be made later and if a different bank wants to deal with us and offers a better deal, then a different bank may be chosen.

5) **Using the Telephone.** Regarding telephone use, which was mentioned at the previous conference, it was decided that Joseph Hofer of the Cypress Colony; Jakob Hofer of Marbleridge; Chris Hofer of Interkale, and Joseph Wollman of Big Stone, through their carelessness all had too much contact with Daniel Hofer from Lakeside. They were all ordered to get rid of their telephones in order to prevent contact with Daniel Hofer of Lake Side.

With a promise to be more careful, this order was revoked and these ministers were allowed to order telephones.

6) **Rosedale, South Dakota.** It was also reported that the Bank will no longer tolerate the financial situation of [a named colony] in South Dakota and that 14 colonies undersigned a 'promissory note' for $100,000.00 US funds. And in addition to that $1,700,000.00 in debts were resolved at the Bank, for $1,100,000.00.

And now the Rosedale Colony has transferred its account to H.B. Credit. If, however, the Rosedale Colony cannot get ahead, then all of the colonies in Manitoba and South Dakota will provide counsel, but Millbrock Colony will take control. The colonies which have undersigned are as follows: Crystal Spring; Glenway; Rosedale; Milltown; Newhaven; Riverbend; James Valley; Oakridge; Baker; Greenwald; Miami; Oak Bluff; Sommerfeld, and Sunnyside.

7) **Marriage between Relatives:** The matter of marriage between relatives was also considered. Until now marriage between cousins—or siblings' children—has never been allowed. Now, however, the issue has arisen numerous times that young people are now cousins with their father-in-law or mother-in-law, or their niece or nephew, which is only half a step away from being a cousin. [100]

We must guard against marrying such close relatives. The doctors do not see a good future for such marriages, and say that in time more and more sick children will be born because of these closely related blood marriages.

Thus we will not allow any marriages closer than with a second cousin, which is already related closely enough.

Alas, may each brother and sister, young man and woman be obedient, and live alongside one another in love and peace. Let us guard against the damnable vices of slander and gossip, and false tongues, through which many people have fallen. One must complain that the Hutterites are very sick because of this plague. God alone knows whether or not there is still a cure or salve for us.

Greetings to everyone again, and let yourselves be commanded by God.

Your fellow helpers,
Jacob[66] Kleinsasser
Jacob Hofer
Joseph Wipf

September 3, 1991

We wish you all God's love and mercy as a greeting. The following is a report regarding the dealings at the ministers' and managers' conference, which was held at the Crystal Spring Colony on August 21, 1991.

First the Millers' reported on the Mutual Fire Insurance. Minister Michel Waldner, of Rosedale, Manitoba, was appointed as one of the directors.

1) **Reading the Conference Report aloud.** The reading of the conference report was discussed and it was decided that no minister has the right to not read the conference report to the colony because such meetings affect all members of the colonies.

Therefore all ministers who did not read the conference report from July 12, 1990 to their colonies should recant and should read the conference reports from both July 12, 1990 and August 21, 1991, to their colonies, and should explain things clearly so that people can understand them.

2) **Shunning and Singling Out.** It was also determined that more earnestness needs to be shown in the matter of shunning and singling out if someone has fallen away or broken a covenant or is in discord. There are always fools among us who do not heed the shunning ordinance, and who concern themselves with the judgment of which they were not a part. See Conference Report March 16, 1973, #10; July 2, 1981, #2, and June 15-16, 1982, #3.

It has also gotten to the point that when someone is under the ban and is supposed to be singled out, the wife, or the spouse who is in harmony, remains in the house, which is earnestly forbidden. That is directly contrary to the Word of God and general custom (according to July 10, 1979, #10). The Saviour says in Matthew 5:30: "And if thy right hand offend thee, cut if off, and cast it from thee: for it is profitable for thee that one of thy members should perish, and not that thy whole body should be cast into hell. Cut it off and throw it away." The Apostle says [101] in 2 Thessalonians 3:6: "Now we command you, brethren, in the name of our Lord Jesus Christ, that ye withdraw yourselves from every brother that walketh disorderly, and not after the tradition which he received of us."

If, however, it is a couple, and both are being punished, then they may remain in the house as long as no baptized members live there.

Dear brothers, as well as sisters, how often must this be repeated until it is obeyed!

It was also confirmed that if someone from a colony interacts in one way or another with someone who has fallen away or who is being punished, especially if it is without the permission of the Bishop or the minister or manager of the colony, then this person should be interrogated and punished because he is not being obedient to the teaching of Christ to avoid the fractious and disobedient. And if such people do not allow themselves to be corrected then they should be treated in the same way as those who are being punished.

3) **Marriage between Relatives.** It was confirmed that the matter of marriage between relatives should remain as it was decided during the July 12, 1990 meeting. Marriages between anyone more closely related than second cousins are no longer to be permitted.

4) **Alcoholic Beverages.** Giving out beer and schnapps at wedding celebrations is no longer allowed; it should remain as it was decided on June 26, 1985, #4 and June 19, 1986, #11. The same applies to the *Hulba*, as was decided August 25, 1983, #5. May the dear Lord help us to get rid of mischief. Many colonies are plagued late into the night trying to drive out these drunkards.

Because in so many colonies beer and schnapps are still being given out at wedding celebrations, it was decided that in all of the colonies where this is happening the minister and the manager should suspend the teaching in their colonies.

These beverages are also being found at wakes and funerals, so much so that the world must wonder what is going on because so much alcohol is being purchased.

Dear brothers, let us not pass away because of alcohol. We are coming together and we are sad and burdened because of bodily death and do not take seriously that we are also dying spiritually through this evil drink.

5) **Clothing for Young People.** It looks like the situation with young people's clothing is helpless. In some colonies it is abominable and hor-

rid—the tight and short see-through clothing that the young women are wearing. And when the young people go out they change into worldly clothes so that they are unrecognizable as Hutterites.

This was already discussed on June 19, 1986, #1 and June 28, 1988, #6. Is it true that no improvement can be expected? Woe to us, what a poor light we are! And we as ministers and managers cannot even agree on this matter.

The same goes for wedding dresses, which cover up an admirable thing with high spiritedness, pride, and arrogance. Let us watch out before it is too late that self-will does not have free reign among us. This was already discussed at length and it was decided on June 19-21, 1986, #7, that such abuses of clothing and refusal to obey should be taken seriously and no church services should be held until all of the brothers and sisters want to help to improve the situation.

[102]6) **Electing Ministers and Managers.** An encouragement regarding the election of ministers and managers: it was made clear that the election of a second minister is being put off for too long and it also seems that the minister is often doing the job of manager as well, which in our poor situation is sometimes necessary.

It has been decided, therefore, that where such a delay is necessary, it should be discussed and decided by the Bishop, so that we do not lose ourselves in this problem.

The following colonies in Manitoba are being asked to elect ministers: Grass River; Mayfair; Ridgeland; Greenwald; Newdale; Sprucewood; Maxwell; Plainview, and Sommerfeld.

For South Dakota: Hutterville; Spink; Maxwell; Riverside; Spring Prairie, and White Rock.

Discuss with your colonies and let the Bishop know.

Where the minister is fulfilling the duties of manager, he should try to put things in order. There are 15 colonies in Manitoba in this situation and we don't know how many in the U.S.

It must also be reported that there were too many ministers and managers who did not come to the conference, especially from South Dakota. Can we see this as a cooling off? It was not very praiseworthy.

There were some who had just cause but the majority should consider whether that strengthens or weakens the church. From the people in general we expect obedience and yet we, who are the leaders, show such a poor example.

Brothers! Let us stand together. The enemy rages in the light of day and seeks to destroy us.

Is there no more balm of Gilead? Is the head already drooping, and the heart sick? Who will be responsible if the shepherds will not take care of their flocks?

Therefore it is our plea that we would stand together in love so that Satan might not come between us and create disharmony among us, for a kingdom that is divided cannot stand.

Sincere greetings to everyone from us.

Your fellow helpers,
Jakob Kleinsasser and David Decker

1991 Fabric Cutting:

Men and Boys:	Women and Girls:
2 shirts	1 dress
2 pairs of pants	3 shirts
winter underwear	summer underwear

[103] **July 10, 1993**

Dear brothers.

May the precious peace of the Lord, and the community of the Holy Spirit be with you and with all of us. Amen.

The following is a report about what was decided during the ministers' and managers' meeting, held June 24, 1993, at the Willowbank Colony in North Dakota.

May the all-powerful God and Lord, the loyal, gracious, and merciful One, steer us all according to his holy pleasure to the praise and honour of his name and to the welfare of the church in these last and dangerous times. These are times of abhorrent falling away and sinking into disbelief, where in the colonies true faith is ceasing and the love in many is cooling off and more than ever before there is a need for loyal shepherds and watchmen who will stand guard and see to it that not too much mischief and evil be brought in and that the spirit of the world, with its styles, arrogance, ways, and clothes, does not gain the upper hand and drive the holy God away from his sanctuary and inheritance. That should always be our plea and our supplication to God in prayer.

May the gracious, kind, and merciful God and Father protect us from these and other evils which threaten to destroy the vineyard of the Lord.

Let us be true, watchful shepherds and watchmen, even if we must suffer because of it and if we are berated as whiners or mystics, for the reward is unspeakably great but equally great is the responsibility and punishment if the chief shepherd should appear.

Dear brothers, let us not belong to those about whom God so fiercely laments in Isaiah 56:10 when he says: "His watchmen are blind: they are all ignorant, they are all dumb dogs, they cannot bark; sleeping, lying down, loving to slumber." Then our eyes will be opened about our responsibility as shepherds and our duties.

There are still more evils and vices that are not fitting for God's people. Worldly ways are pressing upon us with force, to our decline and ruin. We should be alarmed that the forces of darkness are blinding us.

Examples: **Radios, Tapes, Ball Games, and other games** that do not belong among us, as well as skipping breakfast on Sunday. Through our permissiveness our descendents will be led astray and deceived. We have given many and various encouragements, but sad to say, with little success. And yet we are supposed to sound the trumpet.

It is also our duty to bring our prayers and evening offerings before God, something that is neglected far too often in some colonies, which is a sign of laziness or tepidity on the part of the people and the minister. Who will be responsible before God? It also seems essential to us that songs are sung during the teaching and at prayer, which is being neglected by some colonies. It was discussed and no one is to affirm this who isn't prepared to work to improve the situation.

It was also discussed and agreed upon that at a wedding no beer or other alcoholic beverages will be served in order to protect against excessive drinking in the homes and in order to relish the fear of the Lord. In 1 Corinthians 10:31 Paul says: "Whether therefore ye eat, or drink, or whatsoever ye do, do all to the glory of God."

[104]The matter of marriage between close relatives—which was forbidden in the ordinance from 1990—was also discussed. It was decided by the vast majority that all who are already baptized may marry until December 21, 1993. God alone knows the outcome.

Oakbluff members, namely Jake and Paul Mendel, talked for a number of hours and explained where they stand and how it was that they have come so far. It is impossible to grasp that such an offence and brashness could occur in the house of God and that such a thing could be done without an in-depth examination that is in accordance with the command and teaching of Christ. With the fear of the Lord they acknowledged that all baptized members should seek forgiveness during the evening prayers at a different colony in order to be reconciled and to be accepted as members again. They agreed that it was good that Minister David Waldner from Rosevalley and Minister Sam Kleinsasser be appointed as overseers.

As for the **Perverse and the Schismatics,** who concern themselves with parting or building separately, it has been decided: First, they should recognize their fault and allow themselves to be corrected by the minister's counsel, then they should repent and accept punishment, and then it will be discussed whether they should be reconciled or not.

Dear brothers, let us all do our job in accordance with sobriety and purity, as a light to the world and salt of the earth. Let us strive with godly enthusiasm against the sins of disorder that seek to destroy our community and get our descendents into trouble. The vineyard of the Lord is being destroyed and the Lord will withdraw from his people and church as it is written in Isaiah 5:14: "Therefore hell hath enlarged herself, and opened her mouth without measure: and their glory, and their multitude, and their pomp, and he that rejoiceth, shall descend into it." And what is right is being driven back and justice is being stepped on, for truth is falling by the wayside, and what is right is no longer welcome.

Dear brothers! It is our desire for all of the ministers in all of our colonies that each one would read this aloud to their congregation. For this is the only way to have a conversation with everyone. Do it for the sake of our salvation. It requires much work and many prayers, but let us not neglect to do them.

In conclusion: greetings to you from the bottom of my heart. I wish you the grace of our great God and everything good from above. I remain your most humble servant,

Joseph Wipf.

[105] **November 20, 1994**

Dear brothers,

We wish you all God's unending grace, love, and mercy and the assistance of his Holy Spirit as a greeting.

With this writing we are informing all of the colonies about what was decided during the ministers' and managers' conference on November 2, 1994, at the Spink Colony.

First a short presentation was made about how we had come together for God's glory and in order to promote the welfare of the colonies. The Holy Scripture teaches: 'Go out into the alleyways and find the old right way, and when you find it, walk in it.'

Let us uphold the holy, dear ordinances of our fathers. It pleased the Holy Spirit to establish these laws for our well-being. Whoever goes against them goes against God's order. If we read the exhortations our dear predecessors wrote in their final farewell, we will find that all of them desired that we not move the old cornerstone and in Revelation the Spirit of God bids us: 'Hold to what you have, let no one take your goal from you, and neither let them add to it nor take away from it.'[67] May the dear Lord and Father help us in this for we know that in many things we have become indifferent and that our Heavenly Father waits for us to bow down and humble ourselves before him. If we want help, strength, happiness, and blessings from God—both spiritually and physically, then let us love, praise, honour, and give glory to him.

1) **Prayer.** Laziness and tepidity in the matter of holding and going to prayers were discussed. All ministers were earnestly encouraged to try to hold prayers as often as possible, not just one or two times a week, rather they were reminded that the spiritual is supposed to be the top priority. Let us all show more concern so that we might exhort the people to come to prayers more often for we read about Israel that when they stopped giving their daily offering, they almost ceased to be God's people. Let us seek first the kingdom of God and his justice, and then the other things will be added.

Committee Members seeking assistants. All ministers who are a part of the committee, and who are often away because of church business, should seek an assistant.

Reciting Songs during teaching and prayer. An encouragement was also given to the ministers to recite the song during the teaching and prayer.

Ministers eating at home. According to the old custom the minister is to eat at home and not with the people at the common table.

After Dinner. It was also decided that there is to be an after-dinner meeting, where the manager, the cook, the two cook's assistants, the school teacher, the school mother, and the server are to eat.

[106] 2) **Raising Children.** Raising children and holding school were discussed: The German School should be held earnestly and properly and should not show evidence of laziness or idleness and the schoolteacher should not be detained by other duties, because the school is as important as prayer and teaching.

German School. It was agreed that the German School should start as follows: morning school should start October 1 and evening school should start October 10. German School should recess May 1-10.

Little School. The Little School should also be held and each colony should strive to hold Little School, which our fathers recognized as important and which is still important and essential today. It was also recognized that we must not be negligent in this matter, rather the Little School should be held at least from May 10 to October 10 from 8:15 in the morning until 5 in the afternoon.

Little School Mothers should be elected in the same manner as in the past.

Pre-school Children. The school teacher should also bring the pre-school children together in the morning and the afternoon and should teach them.

School teacher. And where it is possible the schoolteacher should also be a gardener so that he can keep the children busy in the yard and so that they do not run all around rather that they be kept in order.

Sunday School. It was also decided that Sunday School should be held as it has been until now—afternoons around 2 to 3 and not right after lunch as it is done in some colonies.

Read the account of child-raising on page 130.

3) **Clothing.** Arrogance among children and children's clothing: it was decided that more earnestness needs to be used in the matter of arrogance and English clothing worn by small children, for it has come so far that we have made our children the same as the world, and the mothers are raising them with all of the adornment of the world and are sowing in them seeds of pride and high-spiritedness, and then when they grow up they will want to continue on in that way and are ashamed of their Hutterite clothing and run around in English or worldly clothes.

The jackets of the wives and husbands should all be simple and humble, they should not be different colours or styles. Neither should they be excessively long like the worldly ones, rather they should be fitting for a brother or sister. Also, the clothes worn by the wives and the young women are far too tight and are also see-through, which is abominable and horrid. English collars are not allowed on the jackets.

Puffed sleeves and coloured shirts, lace on the wrists of brides, wristwatches, finger rings, earrings, little scarves tied in the back, improper hairstyles—all of these are evils and signs of disorder and are not allowed.

Coveralls are only to be worn in the stall and in the shops, or at work, and only simple ones in dark colours, and may not be worn around the yard or at the table. And it was decided not to allow any purchased clothes or pants, but to keep things the way they have been until now, with fabric distributed throughout the colony.

And all other evils and signs of disorder are to be done away with. Let us not make ourselves the same as the world. Pockets are allowed on the men's clothes but only those that are simple and practical but they are not allowed for children.

4) **Wheeling and Dealing.** Buying and selling on the sly should not occur in the colony, for nothing [107] good comes of it, rather many evil things result. Let us read what our account says about it: namely

by Kraemer (page 126). In Ephesians 4 Paul says that people are to do something useful with their hands so that they have something to give to those who are in need.

5) **Manager's and Minister's Accounts.** It was also decided that managers and ministers have to give an account just like all of the other brothers in the colony (see manager's Ordinance #1 from 1911).

6) **Graduation Celebration.** In some colonies the worldly practice of celebrating graduations is creeping in, where they allow their children to study at a higher level and then hold parties with 'uniforms.' Graduations with these 'uniforms' are not to be permitted.

7) **Driver's Licenses for wives** or young women are not allowed. Neither should they be allowed to operate a vehicle.

8) **Radios, tvs, Videos, vcrs, tvs in schools, Cameras, taking pictures, ball games,** playing hockey, and volleyball are not allowed. These are all signs of disorder that should be stopped in earnest, for they are only worldly evils and lures that lead and steer our children away from what is good to what is evil, especially the games. For in them the soul finds no rest, rather they are only a useless pastime. Among children it is allowed and is fair. Among adults, however, playing is not allowed because it looks hideous when they jump and hop around like silly absurd tight rope walkers. Playing does not develop anything spiritual, rather only drives good habits away because only anger, impatience, cursing, and rivalry result, and through which all godly practices are neglected. Paul teaches us in 1 Corinthians 13:11: "When I was a child...."[68] When the children of Israel were playing on Mount Sinai it was a great abhorrence in God's eyes because through it they forgot all of God's laws. Their brief period of joy was followed by a long period of sadness.

Also, all of the radios and tape players in the vehicles and machinery should not only be disconnected but should be removed altogether. Neither are any of the above-mentioned evils to be allowed in the schools.

Care should also be taken with the shotguns. None are allowed other than those that are stored at the managers' houses, for we know what great mischief can arise as a result.

9) **Hosting Barbeques and Open Houses** in the barns where feed companies bring drinks and steaks to celebrate the completion of a new building, or for any other reason, is absolutely not allowed, rather should be totally eradicated. Each pastor should question his people about drinking with the feed companies and watching videos or using vcrs. Also, too many salesmen are coming on to the yards with alcohol, which is a sin and it is a shame that the world says of us and our officials:

'look how they drink and sit where the mockers sit.' And whatever else is sought from the feed companies, whether tips or money, for each ton of feed that is purchased—it is a sin, and to the colony it is regarded as nothing except stolen, and should be earnestly investigated.

[108] 10) **Weddings, *Hulba*, and Brides and Grooms.** It was decided that it is no longer necessary to go one week before the engagement to make things right.[69]

Driving to get Marriage Licenses. Also when a bride and groom drive to pick up their marriage license, barbeques and parties are no longer to be held in parks; rather, if they want to drive to another colony they should be there for prayers and for supper.

Farewell Parties. Farewell parties are not allowed, neither parties with decorations in the dining rooms or on the vehicles, neither fantastic displays[70] if the bride and groom come on the yard. The Monday after the wedding should no longer be celebrated. Why do we try to copy the abhorrence of the world? We should think about the fact that we are children of God.

11) **Taking trips to visit friends or relatives.** Young men and women should not be allowed to go on trips to the Black Hills or to Niagara Falls or wherever else in the world to amuse themselves or to visit friends or relatives. Why should our young people drive around in the world where there is only deception and beguilement when the Apostle has already told us what is in the world in 1 John 2:15-17: "Love not the world, neither the things that are in the world. If any man loves the world, the love of the Father is not in him. For all that is in the world, the lust of the flesh, and the lust of the eyes, and the pride of life, is not of the Father, but is of the world. And the world passeth away, and the lust thereof: but he that doeth the will of God abideth for ever." What the world says about us is not commendable, indeed, of us it may be said that our reputation is not good. How can a leader—or ministers and managers—allow such things, and permit his sheep, which he is supposed to be guarding, to be fed to the world and given over to the wolves, even though we are commanded to watch over them and to keep them away from the world as much as possible. Dear brothers, we will have to give an account for how we have managed our responsibility.

Also, no one is to go along with worldly agents to the **Pork Congress** or to **Expos** unless it is useful for the colony, in which case a leader should go along and as many as possible should ride in the colony's vehicles. If, however, it is only for amusement, then as leaders we should say **no**. For what we hear about what goes on there is not good, and where is our lamp that is supposed to be on the table? One could lament a lot about it; therefore we must warn our people and try to keep them at home as much as possible.

12) **Young people going to funerals.** There are far too many young people at wakes and funerals and weddings. It was agreed upon that unbaptized men and women should no longer be allowed to drive to such events. One would think that these events would give them reason to reflect, especially if it was an accident and God called some young people home, but the actual experience is much different. Namely, a lot of mischief occurs when so many young people get together. They don't even come in to the wakes; rather they sit in the houses or on the streets or run around and drink.

Young people sitting together. Young unbaptized men and women who are in love should be earnestly prevented from going together.

Forceful steps should be taken and unbaptized young men and women should stay at home instead of coming by the van full, for who wants to be held responsible for all of the mischief and sin that arises as a result? 13) **Family Suppers** and 'love meals' should no longer be allowed, rather people are to eat at the common table all of the time, and not with their families in their homes. Also on Sunday everyone is to go to breakfast, for what an evil is creeping in that [109] there are colonies that no longer go to breakfast on Sundays, rather they lie around and sleep until the teaching, when they should be awake and praising and thanking God and studying the Holy Scripture, and the children should be at breakfast where they should be praying their little prayers. A part of true community is being torn asunder.

14) **Garage Sales, Bake Sales, and Rummage Sales** must be stopped, for they do not belong to community. Our experience shows that much selfishness is pursued at these things. Even if it initially appears to be for the community, some hold them at their own houses or at their own tables in order to earn their own money and to buy their own tin gods for their houses. And through it we allow selfishness—the greatest enemy of true community—through the door and then self-interest and mischief follow behind. Therefore let us not allow such things.

15) **Children's names.** Children's names have become too worldly, therefore each one should report to the leadership when he wants to give his child a name, so that respectable names are given, for such foreign names have appeared that cannot be said in German or cannot even be pronounced. Dear brothers and sisters, maybe it does not seem to be a lot, but why do we want to make ourselves the same as the world in all things? Whoever does not take care in the small things will fail through and through in the great things.

16) **Shunning.** Shunning should be used more frequently during wakes and funerals. Those who have fallen away or run away must sit on the side or by the door, and they should not be made a part of the congregation, for they have separated themselves from us and have left us.

How can we have community with them and even eat with them? Let us see to it that we do not contaminate ourselves because of them.

17) **The Distribution of Money.** The distribution of money for shoes or anything else is completely contrary to community and to the teaching of Christ. Therefore it is not allowed and should not occur at all, only the allotted allowance should remain in effect.

This is just as Andreas Ehrenpreis and Peter Riedemann earnestly teach us (read the note about the distribution of money that has been included below). It only brings ownership, self-will, stubbornness, and selfishness with it, and leads the soul into ruin. Where then is the teaching of the Apostle (Acts 2 and 4), when they laid all of their money at the feet of the Apostle and gave to each one according to need? Everything that is necessary should be purchased by the manager with the knowledge of the others, and should be distributed throughout the colony, and not money so that each one might buy things according to his own discretion. It is a shameful evil that is harmful to us, and through which another part of community is torn apart. Therefore let us guard against it and keep to what we have been taught. Who has the right to take the money that was laid at the Apostle's feet and to give it back to the people? (See Ordinance #10, 1981).

18) **Consolidating Money.** It was decided that each colony should pay $2000.00 to the church fund so that the expenses for the church might be paid.

19) **Consolidating Money.** Also each colony should discuss among the brothers whether they want to lend the Prairie Blossom Colony, which was expelled from its Oakbluff Colony, $5000.00 to build new housing. [110] Also, Paul Waldner from the Evergreen Colony has been appointed as overseer for them, and the money should be given to him in order to ensure that it is only used towards housing. Sam Kleinsasser of the Concord Colony has also been appointed as overseer along with Paul Waldner.

It was also agreed upon that a minister and a manager should be elected.

20) **Paying Dues.** Each colony should be encouraged to give their people their due when they get married, and also afterwards, all of the household appliances and goods that are due them when they have children, so that no money needs to be distributed. Six chairs should also be given when a couple gets married.

Driving to go visiting. It was also discussed and decided that ministers should remind their people that when they go driving to go visiting they should stay at the colony where they asked to go to, and not to go briefly to other colonies to pick up a friend and then leave and not to stay for prayers and a meal, which is very rude and evil, and often it seems that the only reason for going is for alcohol.

Leaving time. Also, the 4 or 5 o'clock trips should be stopped; rather, our people should be kept at home for prayers and if there are guests on the yard, an attempt should be made to bring them to prayers instead of sitting around in the barn or shop with them and drinking. What will our dear Father in Heaven have to say about such laziness? Remember, each one will have to give an account before God.

Dear brothers, let us pull ourselves together with God's help, strength, and assistance, and let us not start with modernization. All other ordinances remain in effect and it is also our duty before God and the church to hold to them as a standard, so that we might be protected from foolishness, garbage, evil, and from worldly horrors, practices, and ungodly ways of this world, and so that the Holy Lord will not cast us out of his inheritance and we be transformed into a horror and enemy in his eyes. For whoever wants to be friends with the world will be an enemy of God. For the world is the devil's bride.

And the saddest thing of all is when ministers and managers take the freedom to consciously and wilfully work against violate the ordinances of the colony, and thereby aggrieve many delicate consciences and confuse others.

Where should the people turn, for it is preached in Philippians 3:17: "Brethren, be followers together of me, and mark them which walk so as ye have us for an ensample." But what kind of example is that, if the leader himself is a disobedient transgressor of the ordinances?

Let us diligently seek to bring such things into order. Let us capture, bind, and crucify the Barabbas among us so that Christ will be free, and take control among us and free us from all of the evils that paralyze, bind, and weaken us, so that we might serve the living God with righteous, obedient hearts in true humility, serenity, and child-like love.

[111] Dear brothers and sisters, we mean this seriously and earnestly. It is not possible to limp on both sides: "Judgment will again be founded on righteousness, and all the upright in heart will follow it."

It is a sad and aggrieved thing to observe the increasing decline in the colony in the matters of arrogance, clothing, avarice, and selfishness. The spirit of the world, of indifference, tepidity, and the general flagging of the customs and the death of true community are all evident.

The whole church is degenerating to the point where only a disorderly cooperative without any spiritual form will be left.

We can see that our conferences will be meaningless if we follow Saul's pattern, for how can the church be maintained and built up if we work against it? If that is the case, then what is meaningful is what keeps us together.

Therefore if this fundamental evil and nuisance cannot be thoroughly fixed and abolished, then all of this conference work is an illusion and an empty shadow upon which we falsely rely, just like the Jews from the time of Jeremiah relied on vain illusions. We can read about in Isaiah 1, 5, and 6 and in Jeremiah 3, 5, and 6.

Therefore we would like all of the ministers and managers to have their eyes more open, and to stand in the gap so that not too much garbage and evil be carried in through the gates of Jerusalem, and the house and the living God be ravaged and the Lord spit us out his mouth like the lukewarm Laodiceans, or mockingly scatter us throughout the earth as salt that has lost its flavour. For our reputation already stinks before the world and besides, disobedience is a sin of sorcery and fractiousness is idolatry.

1 Samuel 15:15 and Isaiah 56:10-11 state: 'all their watchmen are blind, they all lack knowledge, they are mute dogs that will not be disciplined. They are lazy, and they lie around and sleep,'[71] etc.

May God grant that this does get any worse among us, that we like to try to decorate ourselves with feathers of a different bird, or that we try to hide behind Jakob Hutter, or just carry the name, so that he would say: these are no longer my children or my followers.

Should this not open our eyes before it is too late, for the Holy One of Israel will not be mocked. Read about it in Ezekiel 3:17 and Ezekiel 33:2-9. That is warning enough. We should also look at Ezekiel 34 to see to how many of us it applies.

Let us show more diligence when raising our children, let us apply our hearts to it like Hannah, the mother of the godly Samuel, (1 Samuel 1) who brought her son—the one for whom she had prayed—into the Lord's sanctuary from an early age, and who succeeded in raising him for the Lord, for God allows the sincere to succeed.

Dear brothers, we hope that there are still many righteous fighters among us who really try to honour God and who are concerned for the welfare of the church. Read this aloud to the colonies as is our duty in love and do not allow this encouragement to pass over them emptily, rather let it earnestly pondered. Let us all rightly consider it so that we might rejoice among one another. Let us live together in love, peace, and unity and let our effort and work be to improve the colonies and to rescue them from looming destruction, and not to remain vainly in the Lord.

[112] Should however, the Lord decide to help us with this matter, then we must stand in peace with him, or else it may be said of us: "God is

departed from me" (part of 1 Samuel 28:15). We have come into a dangerous time. If God will not open our eyes and strengthen our faith it will be
over for us. And the Lord Jesus will not make the eye of the needle any
bigger even though there are many who might like him to do so. For the
way that Christ took to Heaven and which he also showed to us is small
and there are few who find it.

Our dear Father pleads and invites all of his with the voice of a
shepherd, that we might come and find rest for our soul. We confirmed
in our baptismal covenant that God pleads and says: O that my people
would rightly acknowledge me, and would faithfully thank me for the
good things that I have done for them and that they would have faith
and trust in me in love, and that they would establish themselves on
me as on the rock, and live rightly according to my will. Their sins and
disgrace will I forgive. I will make them eternal heirs of peace in my
kingdom. Amen.

Now wishing all of you the all-powerful grace, faithfulness, love, and
mercy, and that we would stay close to God through continuous prayer,
that he might show us the means and the way by which we might keep
the church in peace and love in this time of confusion. Wishing you
all happiness, salvation, and blessings in this matter; we remain your
humble fellow servants in the Lord,

Jakob Waldner
Jakob Wipf

Note regarding the distribution of Money, taken from the sermon from
Andreas Ehrenpreiss, from the Small History Book: 'And especially, as
one hears, that through various means people concluding to themselves
and talking about 'my needs and rights,' so that each one should have
money in his own hands in case of need. To that we say "no," because
we are people and when people have money in their own hands, then in
a temptation they could needlessly give in.'

Therefore this cannot be. Because there are many godly people who
in their own strength are not strong enough to withstand temptation,
for that reason the Lord God so powerfully forbade isolation, because
of human weakness (Jeremiah 51; 2 Corinthians 15; Acts 18). According
to my consideration, it is a childish, fickle assault that has been built
on ice or sand. And above all, if one purchases everything that a people
or a community needs—like bread, salt, clothing, cattle, and whatever
is necessary for the old, the sick, for the nursing mothers and small
children—out of a common purse, then for what other reason does
one need money? It is completely unnecessary and useless, and is more
for entertainment than need. And for that there is enough for a house
or a people or a colony enough to do. See to it that you are faithful,
diligent, and frugal so that there will always be enough to care for the

above-mentioned needs. I am referring solely to the teachings of Christ and the Apostles—to the unbending foundation of truth, and have no doubts that you and of those who have understanding understand and recognize these things.

Because possessions and self-interest are so agreeable and are so loved [113] by the flesh, if one is alone, one will seek so many means and excuses that one must fear that the treasure of salvation may be thrown away. And especially that your dear young people will through this failure go after the world and will corrupt their souls; on the great Judgment Day their blood will be demanded of those who are guilty.

In the community there must be appointed servants, helpers, givers, and governors, who always have charge of the belongings and are responsible distributing to each according to need. Just as it was in Jerusalem (Acts 6:3), seven men should be appointed to the task, and to which Christ appointed Judas. It is to these officials that the Apostle Paul is writing in the twelfth chapter of Romans when he talks about using one's gifts: "Or he that exhorteth, on exhortation: he that giveth, let him do it with simplicity; he that ruleth, with diligence; he that sheweth mercy, with cheerfulness" (Romans 12:8). And to this he adds one small point: that love must be sincere, just as John also says. He writes to such brothers and officials, that they must handle themselves according to love, and must consider those who are in need, and give to each what he requires, so that when they serve they will find great joyfulness in their faith in Christ.

Now see that it was not money, but whatever was needed that was given out. What then were the needs? For the one who is hungry: food and bread; for the one who is naked: clothing. For these words were not meant for the poor who roamed from one city to another, and from one house to another, rather for those who believed and lived together in community.

You have held yourselves strongly to caring for the widows but through it you seek to overthrow the true community, but you do not even have so much as one letter of the alphabet to substantiate your argument for money. For the text does not say a word about money, rather only about daily needs, such as food, drink, clothing, and shelter for the poor. Christ the Lord himself demonstrates this through his teaching and through the example of the man who came to a friend and the friend had nothing to lay before him so the host left and went to a different friend and asked him for three loaves of bread, and not for money (Luke 11). Bread was what he needed. The general *Hausspiegel* in Sirach 29 also shows the same thing: 'The most necessary things, through which preserves one's life, are water, bread, clothing, and housing.' In the 39th chapter the same thing is discussed, and again there is no mention of money when the essentials of the needy are discussed. The Apostle in Hebrews 13 also advises and teaches about such things and says: "But to do good and to communicate forget not: for with such sacrifices God is well pleased" (Hebrews 13: 16).

And these verses, as many from the Old Testament as from the New, make no allowance for arguing about money, which is happening among you, because of your individual corruptible assertions, as if everything depended on money, even though nourishment and shelter and whatever else is necessary to survive are much better than money, and in true community no money those things would be provided and no money would be necessary.

While in Jerusalem each one received according to need, I will say it still, that no one who is educated, regardless of who it is, can honestly teach that in communities money was distributed, as some of you are saying, and are trying to convince others of with many words but without foundation. But it is according to the Scripture (Acts 6) that the money was taken out of the hands of the Apostles to buy what was needed and that each person received what was needed!

[114] December 7, 1997

Dear brothers,

May God's love, grace, and mercy be with us all, and may the blessing of the Lord hover above us, and may the community of the Holy Spirit and his protective hand hold us together in unity.

With this writing all of the colonies are being informed about what was decided during the ministers' and managers' conference, which was held on November 6, 1997, at the Spink Colony.

First a short presentation was made that we had found ourselves together in order to honour God, and in order to promote the welfare of the church, and it was asked that the gracious and all-powerful God and Father would grant us blessings and prosperity in this matter, and that this most important meeting would be for the honour, praise, and pleasure of his name, and to the improvement and edification of all of us. May the Lord God himself be our counsellor, and show us the means and the way to fight the corruption that is approaching from within and without. Our eyes should have been opened long ago to the dangers that threaten us and stand against us. Let us all be more alert and on guard against the abhorrent indifference toward what is good and the falling away from faith, and to abate arrogance and the spirit of the world, and let us walk ahead of the people as good examples for the flock, for our responsibility before God our Heavenly Father is exceedingly great.

It was decided to go through the conference letter from 1994 point by point and to ask ourselves if we have kept to the points and the encouragements.

1) **Tepidity in Prayer.** First the tepidity and laziness in the matter of prayer was discussed. All ministers who are guilty of not holding prayer often enough when they are at the colony, or of leaving the colony too often and then no prayers are held, and especially those who do not hold prayers on a certain day of the week, regardless of whether it is Monday, Tuesday, or Friday, were all challenged. These ministers were all encouraged that they should not do the Lord's work so casually, in that they unnecessarily cancel so many prayers throughout the week and through that set a bad example, as though daily services were not that important and were only a minor matter. For it says (Jeremiah 48:10a): "Cursed be he that doeth the work of the LORD deceitfully." And who is guilty of this? He who takes daily services lightly and who robs God of what is his, by neglecting to bring him the honour which is due him, and that people are not encouraged, and the daily offering for the church is not brought before God. Paul advises (Hebrews 3:13): "But exhort one another daily, while it is called To day; lest any of you be hardened through the deceitfulness of sin" and (2 Timothy 4:5) "But watch thou in all things, endure afflictions, do the work of an evangelist, make full proof of thy ministry."

There were some ministers who admitted and confessed and promised to do better. There are, however, many ministers who need to confess and to improve in this matter. Who will one day have to give an answer for this before the great God, if we dishonour him and drive him away from us? He will not be mocked and he says: 'He who honours me, I will also honour, but he who denies me, him will I deny.' It was also mentioned that some ministers have made the teaching too short; we don't want to set a time, but [115] only one hour is too short. That is a sign of tepidity and laziness, as we can read about in Ezekiel 3:17-21).

2) **Reciting Songs during the service and prayer.** During the service and prayer songs should be recited. It was decided that all ministers who are not reciting the songs should be called upon and examined and asked if they wish to follow or not and whoever does not wish to follow, should no longer be in ministry.

Ministers eating at home. According to the old custom the ministers are supposed to eat at home houses and should not eat with the people at the common table, and the two ministers should eat together as often as possible. There should also be an **After-dinner sitting** where the manager, the cook, the two cook's assistants, the school teacher, the school mother, and the server all eat.

3) **German School and Little School.** The German School should be properly and diligently held and should not begin too late in the fall, or finish too early in the spring. An encouragement was also given regarding holding Little School, and some admitted that they do not have Little

School, and so the importance and necessity of it was made clear to them, in order to properly instruct the children from a young age. It is a shame that some colonies have not held Little School for years. Also, the School Mother should try to teach the children German spiritual songs and little prayers and stories. Let us strive to conduct ourselves according to the example set by our ancestors, and let us care for our children by watching over them and guarding them.

4) Arrogance and Clothing. It was earnestly decided that more fervour needs to be used against arrogance and English clothing styles. The jackets of the men and women should not be different colours or different styles. The clothing worn by the wives and young women is far too tight and has been taken in and is see-through, and leather jackets are not allowed. Also all articles of clothing that are forbidden and which were mentioned in the 1994 conference minutes, such as English-style pants; wrist watches; finger rings; earrings; necklaces; puffed sleeves; coloured shirts; brides wearing lace on their hands; not tying one's scarf in the back; hair pins, and improper hairstyles...all these and other forbidden styles should be done away with. Only one pocket is allowed on the shirt, and it must be a simple and practical one, and is not allowed for children.

5) Wheeling and Dealing, Buying and Selling should not be tolerated; for it does not belong to community and through it self-interest is sowed. Let us follow the dear Paul (Ephesians 4:28): "Let him that stole steal no more: but rather let him labour, working with his hands the thing which is good, that he may have to give to him that needeth." And so each one may only sell to the appointed buyer in the colony and not to the people in general.

6) Graduation Celebrations with uniforms [i.e. academic regalia] and parties should not be allowed.

7) Driver's Licenses for wives and young women should not be allowed at all, and they should not drive any vehicles.

8) Radios and Tapes, Videos, vcrs, tvs in schools, Cameras and taking pictures should be earnestly done away with. The Ordinance says: The radios and tapes in [116] vehicles should not only be disconnected, but should be taken out entirely. All of the ministers and managers were questioned and those who have not kept this ordinance must make a retraction. We should be ashamed that so many were guilty of never disconnecting their radio and tape players, rather they left them freely in the machinery and the vehicles. No wonder that we all complain that there is no more faith among the young people—where are they supposed to find faith if all through the week they are listening to the radio and tapes and rarely hear prayers and then on Sunday during the teaching there is no desire for the Word of God. The head and the heart are full of worldly ways and music so that there is no room for the seed of the Word of God, and for that reason there is no good fruit, and everything is running with full speed toward vanity, the world, and the lust of the flesh.

9) **Shotguns, hunting, and fishing.** More care should be taken regarding shotguns, hunting, and fishing: our people are absolutely not allowed to drive around with shotguns and fishing rods, and yet they hang in the pickups. This belongs to the world and not to a people of God, for serious accidents could follow from this.

10) **Barbeques, Open Houses, or Appreciation Meals** where the feed companies bring steaks and drinks should no longer be allowed. Also, the feed salesmen spend too much time on the yards and bring alcohol, which is a sin and an abhorrence. Dear brothers, let's wake up! It is already too much that the people of the world say that our officials desire money or household appliances, not to mention that they sit around and drink and watch videos. It is a grave sin to take tips from the feed companies, or to unashamedly desire money for each ton of feed that is purchased. Let us encourage all of our brothers. We should not have to go to the feed companies and prohibit them from doing this, rather, our brothers in the colonies should consider their consciences and should not do it, for whoever does it assaults the good of the colony and is guilty of violating our law.

11) **Brides and Grooms, *Hulba*, and Wedding Farewell Parties.** Formalities like decorations in the dining room or on the vehicles are not allowed. This ordinance will remain just as it was decided in 1994, namely that it is not necessary to drive one week before the engagement to make things right, and if the couple is going to get a marriage license, they are not allowed to stop and have barbeques or parties at parks or anywhere else, neither may there be any sort of display like whistling or any other type of worldly abhorrence when the couple drives on to the yard. Let us all consider that we are supposed to be children of God so let us behave in keeping with our position.

12) **Letting Young men and women, or wives and families to go on trips** where they lust after the world or on 'pleasure trips' should not be allowed. How can a leader allow the sheep that he is supposed to be guarding, to be fed to the world? We should keep ourselves separate from the world as much as possible for there will still be a serious reckoning.

13) **Shunning.** It was discussed and decided that shunning ought to be used more frequently. No business should be done with covenant-breakers

or runaways, and they should not be allowed to come to work on our yards with contractors, and only those with parents, or other close relatives, should be allowed to visit, and they should not be allowed to come on holidays or Sundays, and are not allowed to come without permission from the minister. Also shunning should be more frequently used during funerals or wakes, and those who are being shunned may not eat with others, and they may not sit [117] near the dead or the casket, rather they must sit near the back or by the door. We may not have any interaction with them lest we contaminate ourselves through them.

14) **Marriage between Relatives** is not allowed, and should not be permitted, especially between cousins and first cousins once removed. Dear parents, let us help our children to resist this.

15) **Allowance.** It was decided that $3.00 allowance may be given per month but no other money should be distributed, not Christmas money or for any other reason.

16) **Child Abuse and Sexual Abuse.** Every minister should warn his congregation against child abuse and sexual abuse.

17) **Young men and women sitting together.** More earnestness should also be shown in the matter of young, unbaptized men and women sitting together who are in love—it is not allowed. And if they are together they should not be allowed to lie together in bed, or to close the door, or to turn out the light and to be together in the darkness. A forceful intervention needs to occur to prevent young unbaptized people from sitting at home or driving around in vans, for who wants to be held accountable for all of the mischief and sin that arises as a result?

We must especially ensure that young runaway boys do not come into the colonies and sit together with our girls as boyfriends.

18) **Alcoholic drinks at Funerals and Wakes.** There have also been complaints that a lot of alcohol is being consumed during funerals and wakes, which is very inappropriate for us and is a great evil. Let us seek to prevent this, for it is especially said of our young people and some brothers, and the people of the world in the cities take it seriously and say that they sell a lot of alcohol and schnapps to our people during wakes and funerals. There must be an evil spirit with these brothers, or else their consciences must be quite callous that they would not protect themselves from such abhorrence and evil.

19) **Bank Account.** Only the ministers may have personal bank accounts and no one else, rather everything should belong to the colony.

12) **Important Business.** We also wanted to encourage all of the ministers that important business must first be discussed with the deacons before it is taken before the colony brothers. Also Joseph Waelder from the Evergreen Colony was appointed as a committee minister for Manitoba because Johan Hofer from the Riverside Colony can never make it.

Dear brothers, all of the other ordinances remain in effect, and it is also our duty before God and the church to hold ourselves to them as guides, so that we might be protected from all evil and worldly abhorrence and all ungodly ways that displease God. Let us read about it in our teaching on Sirach 2:1-11, where it says that our dear forefathers, who testified to their faith with their blood, compiled our ordinances and customs from the Holy Scripture out of the garden of lust and adorned the colony with them. And the fruit of God arose as a result, which Paul names in Galatians 5. The ordinances of the church are grounded upon this and it is out of this that they grew. Moses, the faithful servant of God encourages the people of Israel to preserve them (Deuteronomy 4:6-10). So keep to them and obey them, for that will show [118] your wisdom and your understanding among all peoples, so that they will have to say: O, what wise and understanding people those are and what an admirable people! Where else is there such an admirable people who have such just customs and laws as all of these laws that I am laying before you today? Guard yourselves, and protect your soul. Dear brothers and sisters, we are living in the end times, where according to Christ's words faith will cease, and love will grow cold, and injustice, evil, and abuses—such as heavy drinking and selfishness—will take the upper hand. In their weakness the church members have become lustful and just as they did in the time of Moses and Aaron they long for harmful innovations that contradict our job and for comforts even if it means that we impoverish ourselves both spiritually and temporally. Therefore, as spiritual watchmen, we must keep our eyes open and we must mourn as Ezekiel does (in Ezekiel 9:4-11). Let us strive to uproot the weeds that are trying to take over our garden and not as short-sighted people introduce this and that according to will. The people will allow themselves to be led if we go ahead of them in self-denial and child-like obedience, and do ourselves, what we expect them to do, and do not take for ourselves false liberties. Let us all be of one mind and be proper examples for the flock. What is essential is that it may no longer be said of us: 'The ministers make the ordinances but they violate them whenever they do not find them suitable.' This is a dishonour to us and is an offence to the weaker ones.

Now in the hope that you will not toss this well-intended encouragement to the wind, but will earnestly ponder it, and take it to heart, we will pray without ceasing that our God would grant us the strength and the wisdom to walk in deeper humility and through that to honour

Christ every step. For then God will be in us, among us, and with us, in all things. May God grant that this would happen. Amen.

Herewith we commit you all to the one faithful, true God, the God of grace and the God of mercy, that he would make us all worthy, and would strengthen us in spirit. Yes, grounded on the foundation of the Apostles and the Prophets. Alas, sincere greetings to all of you and committing you to the God of all grace and wishing you peace, love, unity, and God's favour. We remain your humble fellow servants in the Lord.

Jakob Waldner
Jakob Wipf

[119] **July 15, 2002**

Dear brothers,

Greeting you with God's love and mercy.

The following is a report about what was decided during the ministers' and managers' conference that was held on July 2, 2002 at the Mayfair Colony in Manitoba.

Dear brothers, we must all admit that we have come into a bad time in which we need to stand on guard and watch, and keep ourselves close to God through prayer so that the vineyard of the Lord will not be destroyed, and that we do not give the Holy God cause to leave his sanctuary and his inheritance.

There are among vices and us evils that are very inappropriate for a people of God; worldly ways are pressing upon us with full force, which is to our detriment and about which we should be alarmed—the power of darkness is blinding us.

1) **Boys and Girls going together.** This ordinance discusses sexual behaviour and the response of the Church to certain scenarios. It urges parents to ensure that their children are properly supervised and that boys and girls who are dating are not left alone together. It reaffirms Conference Ordinance from 1990 and instructs all to read what it says in Romans 13:13-14: "Let us walk honestly, as in the day; not in rioting and drunkenness, not in chambering and wantonness, not in strife and envying. But put ye on the Lord Jesus Christ, and make not provision for the flesh, to fulfil the lusts thereof."

Unmarrieds. This Ordinance affirms the Ordinance of 1990 pertaining to sexual behaviour: In part it says: Let us read the Conference Ordinance f rom 1990. In it the law is made clear, and nothing new has been added to it here. In the old, as well as the new law, it has been left to us to decide. And where it is found that the parents did not fulfill their duty of parental supervision, then they should be examined. Sirach

42:11 states: "Keep strict watch over a headstrong daughter, or she may make you a laughingstock to your enemies...and put you to shame in public places." For clarification see Deuteronomy 22:29.

2) **The distribution of alcohol.** Much more earnestness should be shown in the matter of excessive drinking; not so much should be given out. More care should be taken, and [120] especially the young men and women should only be given a small amount or none at all, and none should be distributed to them until they are 18 years old, or whenever it is allowed by the world. Let us be an example for our children. Why must there be alcohol at every sort of job, where the young people then drink excessively and then do inappropriate things?

3) **Defiling young women.** The very dangerous matter of what to do about young men defiling young women who are underage, which is also called child abuse or rape, was also discussed. Can we be silent and not tell the world? It was decided that one should try to deal with it through the minister's counsel and through punishment from the church, and whoever runs and tells the world will be seriously examined. If, however, it suddenly comes to the world's attention then the world can deal with it.

4) **Raising Children.** Also, better care should be taken of the children, and while they are in the schoolyard they should be under the constant surveillance of the school teacher; they should not run around without being watched so that abhorrent things could take place and it would again have to go before the world. It is such a shame the things that are happening among us.

5) **Runaways coming home.** Those who left the colony and then returned must be a part of the colony for six months before they can ask to be baptized, and first they must demonstrate good evidence that a change has taken place. And they should not be allowed to bring household appliances along with them, rather everything should be done away with, and the money should be given to the colony. There are also colonies where those who have fallen away are given too many liberties, to just come on to the yard, and are even allowed to stay on holidays and Sundays. In the 1981 Ordinance #3 and in the 1982 Ordinance #5, it stands clearly that those who wish to come for a visit must do so with the permission of the minister. And where parents know that the minister doesn't know and they do not tell the minister, then the parents should be examined and punished in accordance with the 1988 Ordinance #7-8.

6) **Drunkenness.** Much more care needs to be shown in the matter of drunkenness, because the ministers and the managers are drinking too much and are far too free with the distribution of alcohol. Read about

it in the Holy Scriptures where it talks about where the heavy drinkers and the gluttons belong (Galatians 5:19-21). [72] It is counted among the vices. If one is apprehended by the world for 'D.W.I.,' or 'drinking while intoxicated,' no one should pay the person's bail, or buy him out from the world, rather, the person should sit it out and lose his license until everything is in order with the world and the person must apologize during the teaching. The minister's counsel should handle exceptional cases. And where ministers or managers are caught for drinking too much, they should be earnestly examined.

7) **Computers.** Also the computers, which have been acquired without the colony's permission, should be done away with, and DVD attachments are not to be permitted. The people of the world say that our people have 'entertainment centers,' where one can play games and videos, and can be used almost like a TV, which brings a lot of sin with it. As much as possible computers should remain in the stall or in the shops, for in the homes we should concern ourselves with our wives and children, the parents and the [121] children should not waste their time playing computer games. And for those computers that are in the houses, all of the games should be taken off.

8) **Internet.** In a short time the Internet will no longer be allowed, and those who have it will have to get rid of it—out of the houses, barns, shops, and schools. This alarming abhorrence should open our eyes. We must all help to protect our children from it for it is a great evil for a people of God. We have often experienced it that our children are not protected when they have the opportunity. The impure, heathen things that are on there should not even be mentioned. Therefore, the Internet among us in any way is not to be tolerated at all, and those who refuse to get rid of it should be examined.

9) **Engagement and *Hulba*.** Celebration of the engagement and *Hulba* is far too excessive; too many people come together and too many are invited for the engagement. Steps should be taken to ensure that only brothers and brothers-in-law are invited, and not wives or young women, and it should not be announced at prayer. People should be invited to the engagement based on the minister's approval. Dear brothers, let us not die because of high spirits in the matter of drinking and eating and unnecessary get-togethers. Let us stand together, for the enemy is rages in the light of day and is trying to destroy us both spiritually and temporally.

10) **Open Houses and Appreciation Meals.** Open houses or appreciation meals, when something is built, and where the feed companies bring steaks and drinks, must be stopped shortly. It should not be that one barn or another building needs to be christened. It stands clearly forbidden in

the conference newsletter from 1997, Ordinance #10. Dear brothers, we must wake up—the people of the world are getting away with too much. We can appear to want to make up excuses, and say that it was done for the colony's *Kuchel*, but so many people are invited that it is a sign of high spirits and a sin. From where then should the blessing come? It is for this reason that it will no longer be allowed.

11) **Rebates and Gift Certificates.** More earnestness and care should be taken regarding the rebates and gift certificates that are given out by feed companies. They should all be placed at the Apostles' feet. For all earnings and industry should be sanctified by the Lord. For God's seriousness can be seen in the examples of Achan, Gehasi, Ananias, and many others all the way up to the present day. One can give no other name than stealing.

Encouragement: In many colonies too much arrogance and high spirits are being pursued through clothing. All ministers should concern themselves with trying to quench arrogance and to resist pride in clothing. Also more care needs to be shown in the matter of head coverings and headscarves, among both men and women, and tying of the headscarves in the back should not be allowed. Paul says to the Corinthians in 11:10: "For this cause ought the woman to have power on her head because of the angels."

Dear brothers, why must we stand in such a battle? Is it not a result of laziness among parents and the leadership? Do we believe what is written in Galatians 6? What the person sows is what he will reap. Let us think often on the dear Brother Klaus Braidl's final sermon: Dear brothers, I ask you earnestly, see to it that you hold firmly to the good old ordinances of the colony, and that the old cornerstone does not move. Hold as firmly as you are able to the Christian community and protect against pride and self-interest. Let us beg and plead the dear Father in Heaven to take pity on us, and [122] grant, equip, and arm us with the strength of spirit that we might all be found to be true combatants and fighters in Jesus Christ.

We are obligated to care for the congregation, and to remember the responsibility that we have to fulfill before the great God. It is our desire that all of the ministers in all of the colonies would read this writing aloud in their colony, and also to explain anything that might not have been clearly described because this is all for the sake of our salvation and blessedness and thus such effort should be given to see to it that it would be to God's praise and honour.

We are not trying to introduce anything new with this writing, or to make any new ordinances, or to place an unbearable burden upon you. These are important points that have given us a lot of conflict. It takes a lot of work and many prayers to the Lord, so that we would not condemn the same, and also go against them, and thus be found among those who go against God's ordinances.

Dear brothers, fear God, and hold firmly to his Laws. The reward is great. It is worth the eternal joy. Let us not move away from the goal, rather hold fast and unwaveringly to it and press on toward the goal that has been set before us. May the gracious and all-powerful God help us. Amen.

Greetings once again in love, and wishing you the most precious peace of the Lord, from your fellow helpers in the Word,

Jakob Gross
John Waldner

November 8, 2003

Dear brothers,

Greeting you with God's loving grace and mercy and his precious peace.

1) **Marriage Between Relatives.** During a ministers' meeting, at the Westroc Colony, ministers from Manitoba and South Dakota once again discussed the matter of marriage between friends who are cousins once removed, which the church forbade because of the harm that we have already seen as a result of this. Our fathers were very serious when they decided to stop and completely abolish marriage between relatives, because they found that it was very detrimental and harmful to their offspring even though it was not a command from God and it was permitted by the world. But because they had been appointed to care for the welfare of the church and the offspring, they decided to take action. And in our time also, because we too can see the harmful effects, we have been persuaded to take action, even though this has often been discussed and has been forbidden by large meetings of ministers, and an ordinance has already been made forbidding it. It was unanimously decided that we will stick to the ordinance and will neither change it nor allow such marriages to take place, because the effects can be clearly seen in the children. Oftentimes there have been young people who have tried to do it anyway, but were faced with warnings and admonitions, and there have been other wilful ones who have tried to push it through with fornication and children born out of wedlock, or who have gone into the world to be married, and as baptized members broke their covenant and became perjurers, and have tried to move us through these various tactics to give in and to master the church through their own selfishness, but we simply cannot allow such harm to come upon our children. The youth lacks understanding and the flesh is blind, and runs into harm that

is often incurable, therefore we must stand together and try to uphold this long overdue ordinance.

The Ordinance is to remain in place and if there are people who try to push their wishes through and who even run away, then that is a false marriage, and they may not return to the colony as a married couple, rather if they wish to return to the colony they must mutually consent to separate and must remain apart and may not marry as long as both are living.

Therefore everyone should consider this a warning and should not think that the minister should give in to the flesh and should let the wilful ones go their own way. And the parents should show more earnestness in trying to keep their children from this, for we are holding firmly to that which was once recognized as beneficial and edifying for the church.

2) **Unmarrieds and fornication.** The matter of young men and women who go together and then go too far and fall into fornication and then virgins get pregnant and the boys abandon them and move on to another and then ask the other one enter into Christian marriage with them was also discussed. Do we do things like the world and live together for a while and then shamefully despise and forsake God's highest creation? Or defile a few and then choose whomever one pleases? Should that then be sanctified with the words of blessing, so that you can be allowed to marry like a godly married couple? Can we hope for the blessing from the God of Abraham, Isaac, and Jacob? How did Tobias and these others marry and how did they find their spouses? Fornication is a vice that has been cursed by God; it is very hated and it is sharply forbidden in his Word, and is always harshly punished. It is said that Judas the Apostle took whores [124] and took hold of another's body. What happened to Amon when he told hold of Tamar and committed this vice with her and then turned away from her in hatred? That was what God lamented in the first world—that they took whomever they pleased as wives; thousands of Israelites were extinguished when they got mixed up with Bileam. And there are many such examples where we can see how we are driving God out of his sanctuary, as can be seen among the churches in Asia and Moravia. Christ says: "Every plant that my Heavenly Father has not planted will be pulled up by the roots."[73] Therefore we must use the sword of Pinehas and try to punish such vices, to stop them, and to suppress them. We do not want to participate in the curse: Cursed is he who refrains from using the sword to shed blood. We should also consider Christ's teaching when he says: 'They have Moses and the Prophets.' Let us read what the great Prophet Moses himself has to say about God's Law (see Deuteronomy 22:28[74]).

Let us understand this properly: If a young man goes too far with a virgin and they fall into fornication, even if he has defiled others shortly thereafter, he should marry the first one with whom he fornicated. This stands clearly in God's Law and in the laws of the church, that he should marry the first one if he wishes to marry and he should not think that he can rob a virgin of her honour and then move on to the next one. From the beginning this has been God's command and the custom of all Christian and Hutterite people, so let us hold firmly to it and not let anyone move us away from it. Read the newsletter from July 15, 2002, and also the letter from July 12, 1990; August 21, 1991; July 10, 1993, and November 6, 1997. Therefore it has once again been confirmed that **he must take as a wife the first one whom he defiles and he may not look for another one.**

Proverbs 22:3 states: "A prudent man foreseeth the evil, and hideth himself: but the simple pass on, and are punished."

Also the ordinance from 1981, where it states that parents who do not fulfill their duty to supervise their children are to be examined and if they are found guilty they must apologize during the teaching, is to be renewed. We are obligated to watch that our children are not harmed, and we are not to allow unbaptized young people to sit together as boyfriend and girlfriend and to close themselves in rooms, for out of that abhorrent and shameful fornication arises. Now it is our prayer that in all things God's honour and the welfare of the church would be advanced, and also that we would be obedient, that the Bride of Christ would keep herself holy and pure.

ALAS, HOPING FOR the best and committing these things to the Heavenly Father and his all-wise counsel. Amen.

Jakob Gross
John Waldner

P.S. Please read this letter to the whole colony!

[125] **December 2, 2004**

Dear Brothers,

We wish you all God's unending grace, love, and mercy, and the assistance of his Holy Spirit.

Now we want to inform all of the colonies about what was discussed and decided at the big ministers' meeting, which was held on November 17, 2004 at the Maple River Colony. We must all confess that we have come into a bad time, in which we must be on guard and watch, and hold close to God in prayer, lest the vineyard of the Lord be destroyed.

1) **Wakes and Funerals of runaways.** The matter of runaways, who die or are killed while in the world, was discussed. Can we hold a wake or a funeral for them, and should we distinguish between those who have been baptized and those who haven't?

In the fear of God it was decided that neither wakes nor funerals should be held. Regardless of whether they are baptized or not, or young or old, they should be treated the same, because they knew what was right and wrong and if they chose to runaway they are not innocent, and they would be earnestly punished if they returned from the world.

They should be brought home from the Funeral Home and brought to the house for two hours where people may observe them in silence, that is, there is to be no singing, neither at the house nor at the grave, and then the body is to be carried to the cemetery and buried.

2) **Singing at Wakes and Funerals.** Neither is there to be any singing in the night after wakes for people who are part of the church, where the choirs stand up and sing. Nor should any English songs be sung, but only German songs about death and comfort, and there should be no singing at the house before the funeral or at the grave.

3) **Jackets at church services.** Neither should people be allowed to sit through the wake or funeral wearing a [short] jacket, rather, just as is the case during teaching and prayer, one must dress according to our Christian and Hutterite custom.

4) *Obituary Card*. From now on no *obituary cards* should be made with pictures.

5) **Runaways.** The ordinance should remain in effect that runaways must ask the minister for permission if they wish to come to visit on the yard, and they are not to be allowed to come home for holidays.

6) **Communion (Bread and Wine).** We should also stick to the Christian custom of serving communion. Starting something new is not allowed; rather, the mug is to be passed around, not small cups. The bread should be broken by the minister and then given to the brothers and sisters. Take note of this and read about it in our teaching on communion, where the breaking of bread and drinking of wine is clearly explained. We must all be of one spirit and mind during the communion, that we might all be able to drink out of a common cup. Where has the Christian love gone?

[126] 7) **Minister's Coat.** The appointed ministers should be sure to wear the minister's coat during the teaching, even if they are not preaching.

8) **Church Table.** The church table should be covered, especially during the service, for that is the Lord's command.

9) **Making Marital Arrangements.** Children should not be allowed to marry from one group [leute] to another unless it has been arranged.[75]

10) **Engagement.** Engagement should remain as it was in decided in the ordinance; it should happen after prayers and supper. Read the ordinance from July 2, 2002 regarding the engagement, in which it says who may be invited, something which has been exaggerated.

11) **Wishing Brides and Grooms luck.** Boys and girls are not allowed to drive from one colony to another during the week to wish brides and grooms luck.

12) **Computers.** All computers that were acquired without the permission of the colony must be done away with. DVD attachments should not be allowed, and as much as possible, computers should be kept in the barn or the shop, and not in the house, for while one is in the house, one's efforts should be focused on one's wife and children. Parents and children should not be wasting their time with computer games.

13) **Internet.** In short time the Internet will no longer be tolerated among us under any circumstances. Let us read the conference letter from July 2, 2002.

14) **Minister's Assistant.** Any minister that has been alone for a fairly long time should desire an assistant, and it has been decided that if it is not reported to the Bishop by the New Year, then a date will be set, for there are some who have been spoken to numerous times, and they do not listen and do not want an assistant, even though it is an explicit command of Christ.

15) **Defiling Young Women.** The matter of what to do about men or boys defiling young women who are underage—which is called child abuse or rape by the world—was also discussed. For if a 25 year-old defiles a 15 year-old, even if she was willing, it is seen by the world as rape, which is a very dangerous thing, and which carries with it very serious punishment from the world. More earnestness needs to be shown in trying to prevent it, in order that the church of God might be found pure and untainted by such a heathen way. It is an alarming shame, that we, who are supposed to be the light of the world, the city on the hill, which shines with chastity and humility in order to punish the world, would demonstrate the opposite and that through this vice we would be brought before its court and found guilty. Where we are supposed

to honour him through a pure life and community, we do the opposite, and shamefully desecrate him, just as Paul accuses the Corinthians of doing. How long will God observe such behaviour and remain with us?

The question is: Can we be silent and not notify the world? It was decided that one should try to mediate through minister's counsel and church discipline, and [127] not run to tell the world; but if it comes to the world's attention, then the world may deal with it, as was already decided during the last conference, held **July 2, 2002**.

16) **Elmendorf.** Also regarding Elmendorf, it was decided to regard them as fallen away, and to not have anything to do with them for one year, neither to drive to them, nor to allow them to drive to us. They are deviants, for they do not hold anything of our teaching or punishment. We must resist them, lest their sour dough and false teaching come to us and we be even more be misled.

Let us all be of one mind, and be proper examples for the flock, for it is essential that things get better for us. Let us pray without ceasing that God would grant us the strength and wisdom that we need, in order to walk in deeper humility, and through that to honour Christ in all things. God will then be in us, among us, and with us in all things. May God the Lord grant us all a happy Christmas season, full of grace, and hold us firmly in faith until the end. Amen.

Alas, sincere greetings to all of you and wishing you peace, love, unity, and God's favour, as we are commanded by the God of all grace. We remain your humble fellow servants in the Lord.

Jakob Gross
John Waldner

[129] **March 8, 2006**

Dear Brothers,

We wish you God's love and mercy as a greeting.
The following is a report of what was negotiated and decided at the ministers' and colony managers' conference of February 22, 2006 at the community of Evergreen, Manitoba.

Among us are evils and disturbances, which a people of God should not be subjected to; the worldly character of the world is imposing itself upon us, leading to our corruption and demise, it should make us afraid that the power of darkness is blinding us like this. We should be cognitive of more than our work, and light the world with Christian virtues and as the zealous salt of the earth and fight strongly against everything evil, ungodly and inconsistent. Our eyes should be wide open towards the dangers that await us more and more.

1) **Elmendorf and Altona.** We will consider with seriousness Elmendorf and Altona: Of Elmendorf, we know that they have fallen and are committed to being apostate, because:

* They do not follow the Christian custom of Church punishment, namely the ban or exclusion Christ ordered Peter to use. Without this, a people of God cannot exists as unclean spirits gather in the community

* They make many changes as they see fit

* They do not appreciate out teachings and do not preach them

* Anyone can get up and speak at their gatherings

* The minister allows anyone to call a gathering for prayer if he is not there

* They take women away from our communities, baptize and marry them against our beliefs

* They accept families that have gone astray in their communities without punishing them or justifying it

* They allow worldly customs and evils, such as colony managers marrying their wives in worldly ways and taking them themselves to the altar

And the Altona minister says he is with Elmendorf.

Therefore, it was decided that Elmendorf and Altona have fallen and that they should be avoided. They shall be treated as every other escapee. It must be forbidden to walk or drive with them and only children who have parents among us shall be allowed to visit once or twice a year. Also, parents who have children with us can be allowed to visit them once or twice a year. However, this can only be done with consent by the minister of this community. [130] Youth, as well as boys and girls shall not be allowed to visit them and drive with them, so that they do not cause us sorrow with their incorrect marriages. One shall not travel to them except for wakes and funerals and then only with the advice of the oldest minister. The apostle says: They are like sourdough that sours the whole dough. Thus, throw out yourselves who is evil (1 Cor. 5: 6,13)

2) Christmas concerts are allowed for schoolchildren at school and shall be simple, without *costumes* and be held without other communities. *Plays* by grown boys and girls in which we liken ourselves to the world and make the poverty of Christ born in the crib in a stable into a worldly play, shall not be allowed.

3) Weddings *(Plays)*. Plays and Acts shall also not be practiced at weddings. Our teaching strongly warn against plays that bring unholy things into comedic plays and that instead of honoring the holy God, dishonor and desecrate Him. But what good is there in reading and listening to the teachings and acting contrary to them anyways.

4) Candle-light suppers. There shall be no *candle-light supper* or family gatherings at dinner. The teachings of Isaiah 53 read: In the Christian church there are no paintings, nor candles, nor music nor other worldly things but only the detraction of one-self and the world following Christ.

5) Small school mothers. Women shall not be allowed to go around with their children and hold small schools. Instead 3 or 4 schools shall be arranged and coordinated.

6) Children's prayer. The long children's prayer shall be prayed by the children every morning and evening and shall not be shortened. The dear Savior teaches us: Pray without intermission. The dear, innocent children's prayer is well-liked by God, because they are the prayers of the just, and a just prayer will be heard if it is serious (James. 5:15).[76] Elsewhere He says: Resist the devil and he will flee from you; approach God and he will approach you (James 4:7,8).[77] What other way is there to approach God but by prayer. When we pray, we talk to him; when we hear or read His word, he speaks to us.

We shall also not be limp and dull at prayer, lay our hands on the table or into our lap as this displays laziness. Because the devil is being chased away by the prayers of those that fear God the same way a thief is chased away by loud cries.

7) Dullness at prayer. The minister shall work as much as possible to hold prayer every day and see that they do not go about the Lord's business in laziness, which shall be banned. Paul says: Rejoin yourselves every day as long as today is today (Hebrew 3:13). Because we will have to render account if we neglect the word of the Lord to the people, and take it

away from the old and sick. So this is the case even when the Lord does not receive his deserved praise and thank offering. [131]

8) **Baptisms.** Also, all communities shall reserve seven Sundays for their baptisms, as there must be consistency for this work and it must be avoided that many communities only hold it on six Sundays. Also, the godfathers shall train in the Holy Scriptures, so that they can teach the children well so that they may understand baptisms. We will not baptize unknowing children such as the child-Baptists practice already. The dear Savior teaches us: Teach all people and baptize them in the name of the Father, the Son and the Holy Spirit (Matthew 28:19).

9) **School of Tomorrow** or other so-called (*Christian Schools*) are generally not allowed in our communities. The do not belong to us and only bring with them unnecessary changes that have a false appearance of holiness. They divert our children from the rightful communal work of the Holy Spirit and they are an abuse of Christian teachings. Schoolteachers in the community shall pay special attention what English books and literature is brought into our schools, and avoid especially that unclean books are brought in and used by the children.

10) **Family Suppers** are generally not permitted and must be stopped because they are not communal. What is better is therefore to go to the communal kitchens and eat together, which will be appreciated by children and adults alike. How shall a mother cope with a large family on her own. We do not think there is anything greater than remember our fathers who have left us for the Holy Spirit; we must hold on to what we have.

11) **Garage Sales** are not allowed on the farm. It is also not allowed to drive to garage or rummage sales, because they are selfish and unjust. Why don't we stay with the teachings of the apostles: We shared everything with those in need (Apostles 2:45). They bring unfairness and mischief and unnecessary things to the community. Also many forbidden things are bough and then sold again, through which the house of God is made into a department store, which Christ calls a Den of Thieves. It took a scourge to clean the temple. We shall not be indifferent to this and think it will make no different whether we practice this or not; in short, this does not belong into the community.

12) **Meal sittings.** Girls and boys shall sit according to our Hutterite custom, namely the oldest not baptized boy shall sit by the farm manager. The oldest not-baptized girl shall sit next to her oldest sister and shall not sit wherever she wishes. We shall remain with all the customs that

were in place when the community was set up. We are not smarter than our fathers and we won't do better what they have left to us.

13) Cell Phones. *Cell phones* are being used for much mischief, but a set rule is not needed. Everyone should have enough reason, godliness and gnosis to know how to deal with it according to everyone's good conscience. [132] Also, cell phones must not be given to every family, but can be distributed by decision of the managers when needed for driving outside the colony.

14) Camera phones are not permitted and shall be prohibited.

15) Internet is generally not allowed. Many have taken the liberty to acquire it, therefore all ministers and colony managers are requested to forbid it and those that have taken this liberty must apologize and repeal this at the great gathering because they were disobedient.

Dear Brothers, it is a dishonor that we as leaders of the community consider it as if it is not important that something is forbidden, or worse that we go against it and attack the oldest ministers. Didn't we see the example of the children of Israel who wanted meat, meat and yet couldn't get it, not even for a day or a month. As it still was between their teeth, burning snakes came and led to the death of many. We must ensure that this Internet does not bring the burning snakes and the punishment of God. It is surprising that so few see the terrible aversion and the great danger of the Internet when we know the great harm and impurity in it. We also know that the young people cannot avoid this, when they have the opportunity to use it. Why don't we take a more critical stand? Many worldly people do not let this great aversion to come to their homes to protect their children from such pagan things. We should instead work against it, so that we are not also led into temptation. We shall not think that we need it to go about our business since there are communities with large economies and *manufacturing* that do not have it – it is a great evil to the people of God. We can try to filter it and *lock it out* and only allow e-mail. But whomever you talk with will tell you that before you even get to email, the pictures of exposed women already appear. The children of Israel were also captivated by pagan idolatry only because there were fleshly idols there. Therefore, let us remove it from us until further council has been sought.

Many colony managers have been ordered to examine whether it is possible to only have e-mail in communities that *manufacture*.

16) Curtains. It has also been found as good to adopt changes for when women marry, curtains for the windows shall be given and reimbursed by the community to the home into which the woman marries and ought to live in.

17) **Skirts or jackets for services.** A reminder was also issued that for teachings and prayers and at wakes and on bodies all men should wear a **Jancker**[78] and all women a **Wanick**[79] and shall not sit there in skirts or jackets but according to our community's customs.

18) **Forest River** belongs to the USA communities. [133]

19) **Elders.** Also, each community shall have two elders, besides the two ministers, community managers and farm managers.

Therefore, dear brothers, we must look the imminent danger in the eye and search in time for means and ways to counter the danger before it is too late.

This Danger and the evils cannot be cancelled out or removed only with prohibitions or commandments. We have to come to the thorough conclusion that it cannot go on like this and that we must stand together. For the honour of God and the good of the community we must given into willing obedience. With unlawful action, no community can persist in the long run, it will disintegrate or implode spiritually over time, as the sad example of Radischewa in 1819 and our Cloverleaf community prove. This example shall stand before our eyes as a warning. Because God spits out a people like this, takes all mercy, the power to do good and the resistance against evil away, and it must perish.

It is high time to open our eyes, to sound the horns and to stand against the ungodly beings, actions and things. Because we already have missed many opportunities. We ministers should, as valiant keepers and preservers of the spiritual and timely goods, each yell, preach and warn from where we are in the way God orders and implores us to do: "Cry aloud, spare not, lift up your voice like a trumpet, and shew my people their transgressions and the house Jacob their sins" (Isaiah 58:1).

Because we consider it right to wake and remind the communities how Peter wrote (2 Pet. 1:13) so that we do not burden guilt and eternal punishment on us and become lost with the sinners or that the godless' blood must be asked from our hand (Ezekiel 3: 13-19). Because our responsibilities before God are big. Let us be examples for the herd and speak with Paul: Follow me, dear brothers and look at those that are also walking and consider them as examples (Phil. 3:17). Let us do what we can in the name of God and with the strength of His spirit for the good of the communities and the honour of the great God with warnings, punishment and examples for everything good even when it seems ridiculous and useless to some, such as the sons and daughters of Lot. Because the people has to be warned and must be stopped so that it does not pursue any further the path of the flesh. We shall keep and guard that God does not leave and reject us because of the works of darkness that have emerged and established themselves to our demise.

From his vineyard the Lord demands the fine grapes and not the bitter wild grapes. He demands from his people and his community the godly vineyard, the guilty thankfulness, the childlike obedience, true faith and loyalty and most of all, godly love. He also seeks the fruit of the mind for his fatherly love, mercy, caring and loyal protection that we still enjoy. But it can easily be taken away from us if we do not stand up again and better ourselves.

Now we wish everyone God's almighty grace, loyalty, love and mercy, that we may keep close to God with continuing prayer asking that his holy name, honour and worship be for the spiritual and timely good of his community. Amen.

[134] We remain yours as loyal servants of the Lord

Jakob Gross
John Waldner

Note. One shall also note the people from Fort Pitt in Sask. These people have been isolated from the Dariusleut and their ministers have been removed. They were also forbidden to visit the Dariusleut or to drive to them. So it is with us, too, we must avoid them and have nothing to do with them. One shall not drive to them and they shall not come here. These people are under the influence of false teachings and wrong beliefs. They take people and families from other communities to them without punishment or justification but a little sourdough sours the whole dough. The end.

[135] **Dec. 28, 2007**

Dear Brothers

We wish you God's love and mercy as a greeting.

The following is a report of what was discussed and recognized at the ministers' and colony managers' conference of December 5, 2007 at Maple River colony.

Dear brothers, we all have to recognize that we have come to an evil time in which we must be careful and stand on guard, and keep to prayer to God, so that the vineyard of the Lord is not being destroyed and that we do not give the Lord a reason to flee his kingdom and inheritance. Among us are evils and vice that are unsuitable to people of God, the worldly nature is encroaching on us leading to our decay and perdition, it should scare us that the power of darkness blinds us like this. Therefore, we will consider and evaluate our spiritual and timely condition; to determine what state we are in. With God's help, advice power and godly wisdom and in light of the Holy Scripture, we will better ourselves by keeping to God though continued and renewed prayer that He enlighten and show us how to remove and clean like feces, and counter in the best and most effective ways, the vice among us, so that we do not we do not take the path of the <u>worldly spirit, the grizzly pride and the temptation to become like the world</u> that would lead us and the communities into corruption. It was asked whether it makes sense to gather and concern ourselves with the evils among us when we just go home afterwards and choose not to apply the improvements, and our people are right when they say: The ministers make the rules, but they also overstep them, where they don't agree with them. This is a dishonour to us and through that a nuisance to the weak.

1) **Asking for a girl's hand in marriage**. It was agreed that no changes should be made to courting and marriages. It shall stay at the old, Christian and fatherly custom to ask permission to marry after prayer, to then assemble the wedding party and only then to go into the common eating quarters and celebrate *Hulba*. It shall not be allowed that sisters or women who are to marry, travel to another community and stay there for a while, as if they would keep our sisters as foreign wives and condition them according to their customs, they shall stay home until the wedding. The ministers ought to endeavor to tell the children in time that we will not accept how unchristian-like they are treated by others with their independent thinking so that children and parents cannot come together.

Also, the minister of the originating community shall give a courting brother a letter. It shall not be allowed to wish luck for the courting trips, because too much drink is being used in such cases, [136] and we must starkly limit how much drink and alcohol is given out because it looks pagan, it is therefore recognized that <u>only four one litre bottles can be given to the marrying couple</u>.

2) **Handing out drinks.** <u>We must be stricter and use more common sense when considering drink and drinking</u>, and young boys and girls shall only receive limited quantities if any. Dear brothers, let us not indulge in such mischief in food and drink and unnecessary gatherings, but be an example and role model to our children while the enemy rages and seeks to destroy us spiritually and timely as it happens often that when the young people gather, they drink too much and do unseemly things.

3) **Theft, spirit contraband, *gambling*.** We must take large and gross theft, spirit contraband and gambling more seriously, as those who steal from the community and ruin their body and soul and health through drinking and cost the community unspeakable amounts of money shall be sent away from the community to where they can pursue their worldly life and earn their own money they steal, drink or *gamble* AWAY. This should however be dealt with by the Church council.

4) **Computers.** The computers must also be done away with. They shall only be allowed in the houses of the colony manager and farm manager and where it is permitted by the council of the eldest and the church. Those that are being used by the Amtsleut[80] shall be in the barn and not be used with games, video and DVD *attachments,* as they bring great sin with it. In our homes we shall engage our wives and children and not take the liberty to acquire a computer, because parents and children can then play on the computer and waste time. Where nobody listens to this or obeys this, the matter shall be investigated and punished.

5) **Open House – appreciation meals.** Open house, appreciation or walkthrough doings and ribbon cutting events when something has been built shall generally not be allowed, it cannot be that a barn or other building needs to be christened when it is clearly forbidden according to the conference report in 1997 #10. Dear brothers, wake up, it is already too much that is being done by the worldly people, and we can always look for excuses and think it is communal in the communities to invite so many people, it is however mischief and sin. Where shall the blessing come from then, therefore it shall never be allowed.

6) **Conventions.** Conventions or appreciation doings are being attended too much, yet in hindsight they shall not be allowed except where they benefit the community; As a result, our people find themselves on such playgrounds such as the Blue Bomber Stadium in Winnipeg, where they play with uncovered and half-naked women and hug the cheerleaders, all the brothers that have hugged or held foreign women shall be punished with Unfrieden[81] and all those that have taken part and did not report it shall ask for forgiveness in prayer. And if someone stays at a hotel and goes to the swimming pools where there are women, he shall be investigated and punished. [137]

7) **Dress.** Much mischief and arrogance is being done with the dress, therefore all ministers shall seriously consider the matter and limit and fight the arrogance with the dress-code as well as with the head coverings and head scarves, and not allow that the headscarves are bound at the back. Paul said in, 1 **Cor.** 11, **5**-10: Therefore the wife shall have a cover on her head for the angels' sake, and carry the hair right as it is expected of a brother or sister with a beautiful head, and not cut it short, wear puffed sleeves, the collar on the **Jancker** wide open, the dresses of women not short or long and nicely dark, and grown women shall not wear white **Linder** dresses (that are too *light coloured*). The men shall also wear their beard right and not cut it like warriors with a moustaches or what they call *goatees.* And if someone should get noticed by the minister for not carrying himself correctly, how it is expected of a

brother, he shall not remain **aufgesetzt**. Arrogance makes a devil out of an angel and will lead to our downfall, which must be bitterly cried about

8) Drawings – Door prizes. At weddings or other Hutterite gatherings (*school meetings & Christmas concerts*) door prizes or other draws are forbidden and no things shall be given away that do not belong to the community.

9) Nach-Es table. The colony manager shall not eat with the people but at the Nach-Es table according to our old Hutterite custom and we shall not thing we are smarter than the elders before us that have left us thing for good reason, and as head of the community we shall not counter such order. We demand obeisance from the people and we shall lead them in obeisance.

10) Internet. The internet was also discussed and there was not found a right to allow it, and to preserve the order it is not permitted, and whoever takes the freedom to allow it oversteps God's order and the success of this vice will be to our detriment, destroy our children and shall remain forbidden while it continues to be discussed.

11) Pleasure trips. Those that allow to many freedoms with trucks full of people that go on trips, although it has often been forbidden, shall be investigated and punished. The mischief with *cell phones* that leads to much sin among young people, as well as radios and tape shall be treated more seriously and eliminated completely.

Dear brothers, why do we have to stand in such battle? Is it not laziness by the leaders and parents? We believe what it says in Chapter 6 of Galatians, what men sow, men reap.

Shortly before his end Moses spoke to the people of Israel: See, I have shown you today the good and the life and the evil and death, they shall choose. He gave them the choice: accept or deny; he did not force them. Sirah says in Sir 15, 14: He created man from the beginning and gave him the choice.[82] If you are willing, [138] you will keep the commandments. Christ teaches and speaks: If someone follows me, he shall show clearly that the God does not force anyone by force but leave everyone their free will. I consider this to be the case, because the great joy and glory is too great, too dear and too wonderful that God must burden the people by force. Men shall choose eternal joy from his own drive and free will and his own wise actions. If man is however foolish and has no desire for the heavenly spirit, he shall also receive the fruit of his choice.

Let us often think of the dear Klaus Braidl's and other elders reminders to think of the community order. Dear brothers, I implore you that you be careful against disunity, because you can think for yourself what terrible grief this would lead too, and you can think for yourself how many widows and orphans would be led into grief. See that you hold tight to the good, old order of the community, that you do not move the old boundary stones, hold tight to the Christian community and counter the selfishness as hard you can and want.

Hans Kräl said: Dear brothers, hold earnestly to the Christian community and the order of the community that you shall not give up on.

Andreas Ehrenpreis said: We shall forever stay with good, old order so that the community remains righteous and preserved in good peace, which has been guarded and sealed and founded by the blood of many heroes, this shall not be doubted. If we look at the result our faithful predecessors have produced, we will not be lead to shame.

We must pray and implore that the dear father in heaven have mercy on us, equips and arms us with the strength of the spirit so that we may be recognized as rightly fighters of Jesus Christ and that we receive a godly drive against all sin and unrighteousness.

We are required to care for the community and to think of our responsibility that we have before the great God. It is also our desire that all ministers in all community read this writ to the communities, explain it to the people point by point, do not read it over as if it had no importance, but remember that it is written for the preservation of the community even to our all good and God's honour and worship.

Christ said: Plants that my heavenly father did not plant must be destroyed.

With this writ, we do not wish to start anything new or make new orders or create great burdens that make us struggle, cost a lot of work and prayers to the Lord. So let us not ignore this or go against it, so that we are not looked upon as those that counter God's order.

Dear brothers, fear God and hold on tight to his rights. The reward is great. Eternal joy is worth it. Do not let the goal fade, but remain focused on the given goal.

To this help us the merciful and almighty God, Amen.

[139] Be again greeted in love, and wishing you the noble peace of the Lord, your helpers in the holy word.

Jakob Gross
John Waldner

[140] [141] **September 15, 2008**

We wish you God's love and mercy as a greeting.

The following is a report of what was discussed and recognized and the great assembly of the ministers and colony managers on August 5, 2008 in the community of Oaklane.

Our eldest and leaders warn and encourage us with seriousness that we must make a bigger effort and be more serious against all the evils that are coming down on us, and that are being permitted too much by us as leaders, because the decay awaits everywhere. We are responsible for preserving the holy work of the Holy Spirit, and to keep it pure and clean without spot or pleats from all worldly and fleshly ideas. We shall not drive God away from his kingdom so that the terrible calamity, namely the decay of the community and the punishment of God does not come over our children. We must try even harder to be a good example to our children in a true community and to prevent them from running with the world: the communal life is the Cross of Christ that we must carry and follow it like Christ. Luke 13, v24 said: Struggle for a way to walk through the narrow gate.

1) **Married couples rules:** Ministers and parents were encourage to tell all young married couples at the wedding that they shall hold to the Christian matrimony the way the Lord created men and be pure in their standing. [Ministers are enjoined to council against unconventional sexual behaviours]

2) **Internet.** *Internet* was discussed at many lengths to see whether it is possible to conduct our business without it and it was recognized by everyone that it brings much vice and great danger with it to allow it in communities. But the communities with manufacturing claim that they cannot work without it. It was recognized by the great majority that it can be allowed in communities with manufacturing, but nowhere else, not by the ministers and colony managers, not in schools and not in homes. And all communities that think they must have it for manufacturing must get permission from the elders and ministers' council, they shall make an *application* with the eldest before they can use it, and not everyone can go and use it without permission and there shall be records of who has it and who uses it.

All ministers and colony managers that took the liberty to use it in their homes or allowed in school had to stand up and repent. <u>It is generally not allowed in schools and in the homes or offices of ministers and colony managers</u>, and all that in the future take the liberty to have it at home or in their communities without permission shall be seriously punished. Therefore dear brothers, let us be an example of submission and obeisance to the people, as otherwise this laxity will be detrimental and harmful, because it isn't right and who will be responsible for it? We have been pushed [142] to allow it contrary to our findings, have allowed it to weaken our spiritual stand and face the question of how many have already sinned with the internet? Because the unclean, pagan character with unchaste pictures that you can find on it is an opportunity for the young people to sin and err with the unclean spirit of this world.

3) **Punishment and discipline.** No minister who has not been confirmed and ordained can discipline brothers and sisters, except for asking

brothers to repent, but where a higher punishment is justified, such as Unfrieden or expulsion, he must be confirmed.

4) **Purchasing land.** When purchasing land for a future farm, one must according to our custom first ask permission and not first buy the land and then ask or not ask at all.

5) **Return of escapees.** Escapees that wish to return with debt or wish to pay off their debt at home or pay back their debt away from the community were discussed: Escapees that come back must pay off and finish their debt and other worldly things and come back free from such debt and worldly things, and it these happen to occur after their return, they must go into the world and finish their business, and they shall be investigated in detail, to see if they have a criminal record or have otherwise committed a sin in the world.

6) **Escapees as lovers.** It shall not be allowed for escapees to sit with boys and girls of the community as lovers and when baptized people sit with escapees, they shall be punished with temporary excommunication, while non-baptized people shall attend teachings. It shall generally not be allowed because much vice is brought into the community this way, and parents that allow it shall be seriously investigated.

7) **Garage sales.** To go to rummage or garage sales is generally not permitted for a long time already, and who has allowed it must repent, and who is guilty in this must notify the elders. Bake sales have also long been forbidden as the orders of 1994 clearly indicate, and the experience shows that much selfishness is being done at that many worldly people and escapees come to our farms at such events, which is very dangerous.

8) **Beard.** There is not enough success in people wearing a right beard, but rather a trimmed one, and all should wear a beard worthy of a brother and goatees are not permitted.

9) **Wedding invitations.** Too many invitations are made to weddings and courting contrary to our community customs, and everything shall stay as it has [143] been permitted. The community from which the bride originates and the community with which we parted from last time shall be allowed to be invited to the weddings.

For asking for a girl's hand in marriage, the order of July 2, 2002 shall remain in place. And if the other side does not let itself be invited, such a community shall seek out one of our communities and convene that they would now meet, but never take the freedom to invite two or three or more communities according to their own will and against the order.

More Christian songs shall be sung, and we shall not let the worldly choir's songs to take over that are only pleasant for the sound and the flesh. One only needs to read our justification in the text, of the singing, to see how we can sin against God.

10) **Music instruments.** And especially music with instrument shall not be allowed at any time, and all ministers and colony managers that have allowed it and took part in it must repent.

11) **Pictures.** The taking of pictures is also being practiced as if it was permitted, and it is being practiced without thought or shyness, although God has strictly forbidden it, and all those that overstep this, overstep God's order and cannot escape unscathed.

12) **Draws and door prizes.** Draws and door prizes shall not be allowed at any time.

13) **Nomination of ministers.** Many brothers that have been elected as ministers are among us that cannot read and cannot preach for very long. Those responsible shall take better care in seeing who is being nominated and ensure that our schools teach our children how to read properly, because it is otherwise a dishonour and shows laziness and complacency towards the most important office of the community.

It was also recognized that two men of the Heartland community in Manitoba that come and go and have been recognized as escapees, shall not be allowed to live with their wives anymore but must avoid them and not have anything to do with them.

Also, the wonderful work of the community is going downhill at a fast pace. And aren't the ministers and colony managers responsible for this? Those that see too much through their fingers and do not stand steadfast against the many evils, take such liberties as putting up pictures in houses or making music. It is complete disobedience and idolatry and we must think of how Saul fared because of it. Let us step against the decay so that God does not grow tired of having mercy on us and let us decay completely and spread into the world and allow our children to run into the decaying world and that we are found guilty before God as those that carried out the Lord's work inadequately and that spilled the blood of our innocent children. Let us hold on to God in prayer that he may sent his wisdom down from above, that we have counsel to counter the terrible hardship. That we even have a godly drive to fight all evil and wrong. As Amaleck went out to fight against Israel, let us stand with Moses against it through prayer, by raising our hands to heaven, and to counter Amaleck so that Israel may win.

Andreas Ehrenpreis said: we shall always remain with the old order so that the community be maintained in its rightly way and in good peace, while many heroes have insured and sealed it with their blood as a foundation for us not doubting it. If we follow the results of all our faithful predecessors nobody will be harmed.

Dear brothers, fear God and hold on to his laws. The reward is great. The eternal joy is worth it. Let us not lose sight of the goal, but stretch out for the set goal.

In this help us the merciful and almighty God, Amen.

Be greeted again in love and wishing you the noble peace of the Lord, we remain your help in the word.

Jakob Gross
John Waldner

[145] **May 8, 2009**

Dear brothers

God's endless mercy, love and charity to greet you, that the God of peace and the order may keep us together like a shepherd takes care of his sheep.

With this we would like to inform all communities of what was discussed and decided at the great assembly of ministers and colony managers at Mayfair community on April 28, 2009.

1) **Camrose.** It was discussed how we can help the five families at Camrose that have left Waldheim, as they have often asked for help and that they may be accepted into a community. They have long been advised to ask a community to be accepted, which they have tried hard to do by visiting, calling and writing communities without success. Also, the old ministers have tried to travel with more ministers to five or six communities to support them and much effort was made at communities that are short in help and need the help of more men, women and children. They were also not able to stay at Waldheim. Everything seems to have been in vain. So it is our spiritual duty to help these people that have been coming and asking us for years, the way Christ sent his disciples to the lost sheep of the house of Israel.

This was discussed at length and it was decided that we will help and that communities must help them. Ten communities were asked if they would take it upon them to help them, but none would. After a long discussion, it was decided that we will suggest five communities that will take one family each and we will send ministers to talk to these communities and they must try to take in one family. These communities are Spring Valley, Hillside, Deerboine, Twilight and Huron. The ministers of these communities accepted our decision. We are confident in God's blessing and growth all our efforts and work will bring for the help we provide these poor people in the misery they have been struck by. The promises are many and great, as long as we do this with our hearts and for our

Christian duty. Let us not rue the effort. What has been recognized as good by the conference of ministers and colony managers shall not be stopped or reversed by any community brother. Please accept it with love.

2) Harlotry – unmarried. It was also agreed that when boys and girls get too close to each other and fall to harlotry, they can never marry anyone else. This is according to the Holy Writings and to our rules and it must remain this way. Where a part of this has turned to the worldly world or run away, making it not bound to the community any longer, it is accepted and the other can marry someone else in the community, provided the council of elders allows it.[146]

Let us however recognize that for those that are too closely related, the order of the conference of July 2, 2002 and of the 1990 conference continues to stand, and it cannot be allowed.

3) Games. All those that were guilty for allowing *skating rinks* and not countering them, which to our surprise many were guilty of, must all repent at the great assembly and they must remove this vice and evil and never allow it again in the future. In many of our teaching it clearly says that where Jesus has come, one shall not go onto ice or other game or ball places; it is allowed for children and appropriate, but it is not allowed for adults because it looks ugly when the jump and hop like simple, absurd tightrope artists. Playing does not lead to anything spiritual, but goes against all good conventions, as anger, impatience, cursing and competitiveness comes to light while godly exercises are being neglected.

4) Boys and girls as lovers. It shall also not be allowed that girls and boys sit as lovers in dark homes, lock themselves in and be together disgracefully, uncovered, naked so that terrible, great sin and vice occur. (note: for the ministers. This does not need to be read. Boys and girls that lay together uncovered or naked is harlotry and shall be punishable by banishment.) And boys, regardless of whether they are baptized shall generally not stay overnight in the same house or with the family of a girl, it is not appropriate and shall not be allowed; they shall also not be able to walk the farm together freely and take each other by the hand without shyness. Everything is already being done too commonly and without shyness, and many great moabitian vice and evils are coming upon us. We shall believe in this, that God has an aversion towards this and has punished this terribly since forever so it shall not go without punishment among us.

5) Dress. It is often being reported that the worldly and English habit and dress are being enforced and that we almost cannot continue to dress according to Hutterite customs. It was recognized that we can no longer accept the unauthorized dressing contrary to the order of the community, such as pants with different pockets at the back and with buckles on the side, and other such worldly fashion and abuses, such as long skirts and different skirts that do not belong to our Hutterite dress and order and shall be done away with because we are children of God and cannot allow any deviations, and be outside and inside a beacon of light to the world and a salt to the earth that goes against the way and the grain of the world, therefore no minister and servant of the Bible shall allow these points and disorders any longer.

6) **Entertainment devises[sic].** Radios, *tapes* and all musical instruments must be destroyed in all *vehicles* and other *machinery*, as much stupidity, foolishness, worldly vice, unclean, ungodly spirits of this world are being brought into the community this way, and the worst is that ministers and colony managers [147] and leaders aren't working against it but rather overstep the order and tarnish our conscience and confuse or anger others. Dear brothers, we shall not delay since it is sad and depressing to observe the decay of the community through arrogance, overdressing, worldly spirit, laxity and the death of a sense of community.

7) **Internet.** Internet was discussed again and it is difficult to admit that it is a great evil and brings great evil; We all know it and who shall be responsible for it, when we are being pressured to give in, and thereby weaken our spiritual stand by bringing it into the community and give the people the opportunity to see and sin against the unclean ways of this world. It was recognized that Internet cannot be in homes, including the homes of ministers and colony managers, and where it is found that the Internet is being used for *manufacturing* without means to block it so that only email is accessible and someone commits a sin through it, he shall be punished with shunning, regardless of whether it is a minister or colony manager. Because the order clearly states that it shall not be put into houses, which has been punished before, and that who sins with such an unclean spirit must be punished with shunning. It is and remains a great ruse of Satan to catch us into his net; it shall also not be used without consent from the council of elders.

8) **Fort Pitt.** On March 14, 2006 we already circulated a letter regarding Fort Pitt in Saskatchewan. These people have severed themselves from the people of Darius and their ministers have been removed. These people in Fort Pitt have asked themselves to be removed from the Dariusleut and the constitution, and their ministers have been removed from Vital Statistics and they cannot marry anyone. It was also decided that we should avoid them and not have anything to do with them, visit them, and they shall not visit us. These people with their wrong teachings and ill thoughts have fallen astray so much that they decided two men would now be ministers, as they fall from one evil and aversion into another, and who has contact with them shall be investigated.

9) **Runaways – death.** It was also discussed at the *pre-meeting* how to proceed with runaways who die in the world, and things shall remain as they were proclaimed on December 2, 2004. There cannot be a wake or funeral, the dead shall be kept two hours in the home in silence and without song, and he shall not be carried into the church, a school or another building but be taken from the home straight to the cemetery. It was however considered and allowed that ministers can go to church with the people and sing many songs as long as the dead remains at home.

It is also happening too much that we go to runaways' funerals in the world or in other communities, and each minister shall ensure that this does not happen so often.

[148] Dear brothers, let us hold on to the humility, lowliness and simplicity of Christ. Because the darkness is sneaking in like a pest that represses and suffocates the godly, the faith and the sense of the holy Spirit of our forefathers, while the weeds grow next to it and God rejects his Kingdom as he does not enjoy it anymore.

Already, great evils and aversions are happening among us, so what will happen when the Lord begins to winnow his wheat? Then we will have pauper peasants,[83] as the small history book of Radischewa illustrates. We ministers must do our shepherding duty; keep the Lord's vineyard free of all evil and prove ourselves worthy workers. The responsibility before God will be great. One shall read thoughtfully what has been decided here, and we ask God that he leads and steers everything to the good of the community and that he awakens and strengthens those men who help build the community, who carry the secret of the faith according to 1 Tim 3:9, who are completely aware of their duty of guardians and shepherds and not just carry it by name.

It is our greatest wish, that God does not abandon us until the end, which He will do, as long as we don't deny him our allegiance, let us think about the duty, when the work of the Lord isn't being done wholeheartedly and of the great reward for eternity if we use our greatest efforts to teach the children the obeisance, respect and honouring towards God, upon which follows the good of the whole community as every link in the chain is fulfilling its duty. The Lord may give us strength and endurance for this.

Serving the merciful, great and gracious God. We remain as your servants at the word....

Jakob Gross
John Waldner

<u>P.S. All ministers are encouraged to read this protocol to the community and to explain it so that the people may know what is right and to be more on guard.</u>

[149] **February 16, 2011**

An encouragement in regards to excessive drinking and other evils

Concerning addiction to drinking, Ministers and colony managers (Haushaltern) must exercise greater control in regard to alcohol purchases, particularly where they themselves are deeply involved or the board does not do enough about uncontrolled drinking.

Also there is excessive drinking during wakes and funerals, so that the world becomes concerned with this happening especially because on such a day so much alcohol is purchased.

Dear brothers, let us not die because of drinking; we come together to grieve about a death but do not let it seem we are also dying spiritually.

The matter of excessive drinking has been discussed many times, and has been recognized to be a burden that leads to unfaithfulness and robbery, and causes duty to be neglected, and rather creates an ungodly, disorderly people, wasting the money of the widows, orphans, and the sick who donated it to the church. These people have unfaithful ways and allow themselves to be led by the evil spirit, which causes them to become spiritually abandoned and shunned. And they fall into other harmful wickedness that cannot be tolerated by others. Let us save ourselves from these bonds that the devil entraps us, and instead heed our calling at all times, in sobriety, continence, and self-control, that we may be a light to this world, and salt to this earth.

Christ himself mentions these vices in particular and says: "But take heed to yourselves, lest your hearts be weighed down with carousing, drunkenness, and cares of this life, and that day will come on you unexpectedly. For it will come as a snare on all those who dwell on the face of the whole earth. Watch therefore, and pray always that you may be counted worthy to escape all these things that will come to pass and to stand before the Son of Man."

Interpreting Christ's speech: "If you love me, keep my commandments," says the Holy Spirit in John 14, 15–31: where do you find those, whose hearts and souls do not complain about such messiness, are not deceitful, secretive, and untidy, and geared towards eating and drinking. That means that Christ is greatly dissatisfied with gluttony and excessive drinking but harks back to his meekness. Also concerning nourishment, it is gluttony when one is obsessed by such things, especially a desire to have things in excess. One should be content with nourishment alone.

Also in our chronicle and history one will find trusty witnesses that have fought against such wickedness, and were unable to leave the drinking, which caused them to leave their lives behind. As we heard from Jeronimus Käls and his wife, that they just went to eat in a bar at night, but many people tried to convince them to drink alcohol.

There they showed those people, that they do not want to take part in such activities, because they have been baptized, are new-born, and are recognized (by heaven), through sacrificing their earthly life. <u>What kind of witnesses are we today to this world against those vices? Our praise is not enough!</u>

Let us be eager but with a godly eagerness, and especially we ministers and bosses. Let us stand firm to fight against these vices, blowing our trombones [150] against this 'heaven screaming' sin, that is practiced to such extent, that the duties of the church are neglected, and dominates many other churches, one after the other, making it difficult to find proper advice about this issue.

<u>Especially ministers and the board:</u> we must unanimously stand against these vices, and find advice in order to withstand such mischief. And find advice with God's help and assistance in order to bring it to Christian-like orderliness, because excessive drinking has become like a cancer that leads to sad episodes that will be trying, as well as difficult to avoid. Let us not become part of this foreign problem, drinking to excess and justifying it as acceptable, which causes nations to become addicted to alcohol.

Both we and our descendants will be afflicted with impoverishment and immorality, which we will have to answer for, if we don't do anything against it, but let the nations run wild and let the 'drinking devil' out.

It is time that great seriousness is applied in regards to the topic of constant drinking, because both ministers and colony managers allow themselves the freedom to buy alcohol when they drive out (somewhere), and drink excessively at their destination and while en route. Also too much freedom exists in distributing alcohol to different places which then are tarnished and become impoverished.

Let us read in the Holy Scripture where drinkers and devourers belong. (Galatians 5, 19–21). Where one drinks significantly, one will also eat a lot; both are vices that are not part of the kingdom of heaven. Let us be an example to our children. Why must work involve drinking alcohol; where then the young people drink excessively, it leads to improper behaviour and sexual activity, of which the world becomes aware. It is already a significant shame that such things as excessive drinking occur within us.

Barbequing and Hunting, which are not allowed, are also practiced to a great extent, the shot gun is used a lot, and great memories are made, but the duties of the church are neglected and impoverished.

Also when a building has been completed, many people inaugurate it with an **open house or an appreciation meal** in which steaks and alcoholic beverages such as beer and brandy are served. After people have been drinking, they start to sing, which is prideful and sinful. Although they feast on the meat, the grace and blessing of God flees from this place. **That all shows the indolence of the ministers and the board.**

From we ministers who are like shepherds, if we do not complete our work within our congregation we must answer in front of God. May God bless us and give us strength.

Song: Come you peoples' children: Verses 10 & 11

1. They daily drank here,
Encountered each other,
On some easy places,
There they will tear each
    other apart,
Yes like the dogs bite,

11. Those on good days, with riding,
    driving, hunting,
Made it quite funny,
They must sit and cry,
Soon to be freezing and soon to be
    sweating,
Because there no fun is thought
about

Song: Oh blind world wake up

15. All you drinkers and devourers, all you should
Be consciously scared,
What Christ says about the rich men
That only wanted to taste the best
Which sits only a little while beside him
It only costs a drop of his pain
Just as the trunk will taste[84]

[151]

In regard to **Hockey Rings**,[85] they should not be tolerated. How much mischief arises from this pride? The German school is also neglected. **Radios and tapes** should also be removed from vehicles and farm machinery.

We shall also keep and continue to wear our traditional Hutterite dresses, and diligently keep all the regulations that govern Hutterite communities. Also more seriousness should be applied in regards to the **forbidden pants** with various pockets that are located on the sides and at the back. Also **puffy sleeves** on dresses, as well as **light colored dresses** that are only suited for little children should not be permitted

Remarks

Dear Brothers:

It is high time, that we, the shepherds and provosts, should do our duty. For we see that the old master, the evil enemy, the devil, has a tactic, and a master plan. He has donned his armor, and is aiming his poisoned arrows at the community, the shepherds, and provosts, in the hope that when he has destroyed the body, the herd will be well scattered. One can clearly see this during the time when Christ was crucified and buried, and his disciples decided to pursue paths of their own choice, causing them to scatter. This is why the shepherds must remain on constant guard, because it is clearly predictable what will occur when the body will be damaged, the herd will be easily drawn into the ways of the devil. This means that when the Shepard will be caught up in drinking, and keeps quiet about the situation, it will soon be proven true that only a small piece of sourdough will ruin the entire dough.

These writings shall be read to the church.

We greet you all in the name of the Father in all his grace, peace, love, which we wish you all. All you helpers of the Lord remain in him.

Jacob Gross

John Waldner

[152] **November 20th, 2011**

Dear brothers,

We wish you all God's unending grace, love and mercy and the presence of the Holy Spirit.

We would like to inform all of the churches and provide you with a report, as to what was discussed and decided at the ministers' and colony managers' conference on **October 19, 2011 at the Oak Lane Colony.** We must recognize that we live in an evil time that we must remain on constant guard, and remain in prayer to God, so that the vineyards of the Lord will not be destroyed.

1) **Necessities for married couples.** We have discussed and decided what a married couple shall receive from the church on the day of their marriage. (**more details on page 156**)

2) **Wedding presents.** No money shall be given for wedding presents

3) **Trips to the zoo.** It should not be allowed for girls and boys to go to the zoo, or on any other trips, or to stay overnight in the city. *All those that have allowed this, have caused problems.*

4) **Lost persons [Verloffene]**[86] **that die.** It was discussed whether or not we can hold a funeral for runaways who die in the world, and whether we can make a distinction between a person that has been baptized or not. It was recognized in fear to God, that it shall remain as it was previously recognized in the **2004 Regulation #1**, which states that—no funeral/ burial shall be provided to the lost persons regardless of how young or old they are, or whether they are baptized or not; all of those persons shall be treated equally, because they can distinguish between what is right and wrong, and will not remain innocent when they run away. Also no funeral ceremony will be provided in a funeral home.

After the corpse was kept in a funeral home it must be brought home, and remain there for two hours, and shall be viewed under complete silence. There shall be no singing in the house nor by the burial site, nor when carried to the cemetery. There must be a difference in burial between those that are considered a part of the church and the ones that are considered lost persons. Because Christ says: <u>Let the dead bury the dead. One question remains whether or not a lost person shall be buried in the church cemetery???</u> Especially those that are in the world, and have a wife and bear children in the world, and do not want to know anything about the community, yet still request to be buried in the church cemetery.

5) **Singing at a funeral.** Also when persons die who are members of the church, the night following the burial no singing shall occur, meaning that no choirs should wake up and sing. Also no English songs shall be sung in front of the corpse while in the house or at the burial site, but only German songs that explore themes of death and consolation. Also it shall not be permitted to sit **in front of the corpse with skirts nor jackets,** but be dressed as one would during the lesson or prayer, which is according to the Christian and Hutterite rules governing the dress code. Also no picture shall appear on an **Obituary Card.**

[153]

6) **Gifts for the bereaved.** It is also greatly exaggerated with giving gifts and flowers when someone dies, which looks like a time of happiness, when it really is a time of sorrow and meditation. And that defeats the purpose of our church ritual, because our morbidity and decrepitude that are part of our devotions should be respected, but instead it becomes a time of gift giving. Such hubris that is being practiced shall be discontinued, and no longer be allowed nor continued.

7) **'The lost' (runaway former members of the community) taking a walk.** As the Regulations state, the lost must ask the Minister if they would like to take a walk on our property. Also it shall not be permitted for them to come home on holidays. This is according to **Regulation #5 established on December 2, 2004.**

8) **Youth going on trips.** In order to be allowed to go onto any trips persons must be baptized, and all other girls and boys that are not baptized shall not be permitted to go.

9) **Group discussions.** On weddings and group discussions too many people are being invited, which is against the rules of our church; also it shall not be permitted to take along women on such group discus-

sions, so they must stay behind as it clearly states in the **Regulation #9** established on **July 2, 2009** which was rewritten and reconfirmed as a valid rule on **December 28, 2007 #1.** It shall remain according to the Christian and fatherly manual.

10) **To be married to someone from another group.** Also it shall not be permitted that our sisters become wedded with a man from another group without being matched together. **Group discussions shall proceed as it states in our rule book, and will occur after prayer and supper.** Also it shall not be permitted that women attend a different church before marriage, because it seems such groups see our women as foreign persons and go according to their rules and conditions. Our women shall remain in our communities until marriage.

And the preachers should make an effort to explain this to the children that we will not permit this process to occur in a different way, especially in a way that is ungodly. Please read **Regulation #9 established July 2, 2002 in our group discussion.** Again this will be discussed during our discussion period as it is over exaggerated.

11) **Garage and room sales.** Garage sales are not permitted on the property, as well as to bring panels to garage and room sales. This all impels self-interest and inequality. Why do we not stick to the teachings of the Apostles: you distribute according to one's needs (Acts 2, 45). This is such cockiness; things are sold that are not permitted in the first place. Briefly, it does not belong to our community, and it is us that must give account for such doings.

12) **Cell phones.** With the usage of cellphones plentiful cockiness and sin is being practiced. It is certainly not allowed to give a cell phone to boys and girls. Every board should have enough fear of God and understanding, how to handle this matter. A cell phone should not be owned by every family, but should only be used through consultation and when necessary. Because we [154] can clearly see with our eyes that a horrid, impure, and sinful being is what follows such doings. Also **radios and tapes** are not permitted in vehicles and farm machinery.

13) **Clothing.** More seriousness should be applied towards **pride and worldly clothing,** because we should rather be simple and humble, instead of becoming part of a worldly fashion style. Especially those **long see-through smocks,** which are abominably, horrid, and not chaste. There should be a clemency, that the **head covers** of the women should not be tied at the back (1. Corinthians 11, 5-10). **Smocks should be dark,** and grown up girls should not wear children's clothes (*it is not too lightly colored*). Also too many worldly decorations are allowed, such as

finger rings, earrings, necklaces, and clothes that are see-through, or **sandals** that are worn to bible study.

Also **picture taking** is excessive in general and especially of the bride and groom during weddings. For most, taking pictures is not seen as a sin, and many persons have them standing and hanging in their houses, which is a form of worshipping idols. It is, and will remain a sin in the eyes of God; it's an abomination and aversion. This is the cause through which holiness escapes.

It is often said that the desires of the English people and this world, and their fashions for see-through robes and long smocks are unstoppable. It is nearly impossible to fight against these things, and they shall no longer be tolerated. Wearing such forbidden gear is contrary to the Regulations of the Hutterite community.

We as the children of God should preserve our identity, and should be a light in the world and salt to this earth with our outer and inner appearance. By so doing we shall speak against the ways of this world and show an example. No Minister or servant of the Lord shall ignore the above mentioned points and they should ensure there is no disobedience.

14) **Alcohol.** Alcohol addiction should be treated very seriously. It should not be widely distributed, especially not to young boys and girls. It should not be freely taken when it's already in excess. With this problem almost the entire colony becomes stained. It occurs many times, that young people come together and drink a lot, which results in doings that are improper and not chaste. Read in the scriptures as to where the drinkers and devourers belong (Galatians 5, 19-21). It is a burden and great evil within us. Also where Ministers and colony administrators engage in excessive drinking, or distribute too much alcohol easily, a serious investigation shall be made.

Dear Brothers, let us not die because of such hubris in eating, drinking, and unnecessary consumption. Let us be an example to our children. The enemy rages and searches to destroy spirituality and time. And those who celebrate earthly pleasures and find happiness and bravado in them, and live as if there is no existence of God, will be judged by him, as if there is no new day that they are able to escape the trial. As if there is no judge over the living and the dead.

As Job says:" They rejoice with clapping and harps, and eat and drink, and are happy with fear, but the end of happiness is crying and screaming in eternity."

Read the round reading from February 16th, 2010 on page 149 [155]

Therefore, dear brothers, these evil doings can't be broken or eliminated through naked rules or through simply not permitting it. We must come to a thorough understanding that this cannot continue, that we must stand together, willingly being obedient in order see wealth within our congregation and remain in honesty to God. With unjust doings a congregation is unable to exist in the long run, both spiritually and in time, it will fall apart or a separation will occur. A sad example is the fallen Raditschewa community in 1819. Such example should confirm to our eyes and serve as a warning, why we must remain in such a battle. Is it not a languishment from the board and parents? Do we believe what is written in Galatians chapter 6, whatever man plants that he will harvest? Right before his death Moses said to the people of Israel: See, I have set before you today life and good, death and evil. They shall choose because he gave them the choice; to accept or to throw away; he did not force them. Sirach 15, 14 if you want, keep the commandments. Christ teaches: if someone wants to follow me, come and follow me. He shows clearly, that the Lord does not force anybody with violence, but he gives everyone free will. I urge that it is because the great happiness and glory is way too big, way too expensive and exquisite, that God the Lord would force man to follow him. A human should decide from his own motive and free will to think and act smartly, and choose eternal happiness. But if a human is foolish and has no interest in the heavenly being, he/she will at once receive the fear that accompanies his/her choice.

Let us remember the dear Klaus Braidls and all the elders and their admonitions in regards to the church rules. As they said, one should always stick to the good old rules, in order for the Church to remain upright and conserved in good peace. That is because it is sealed with the blood of heroes which laid a strong solid ground, which does not need to be doubted. If we will observe and follow the steps of all the Godly and our forefathers, it will not become a disgrace to us.

Let us all be like-minded and proper paragons to the herd. With help, it shall become better with us. Let's pray without demanding, and may God give us strength and wisdom to accomplish that, in order for us to walk in deepest humbleness, so we can spread the teachings of Christ into many areas. God will then be in us and with us in all things. God the Lord wants to keep our faith stalwart and strong until the end. Amen
Now, in all hope, that all this may be fulfilled with appreciation. We greet you all; and the God of grace, peace, love, we wish you all. All you helpers of the Lord remain in him.

[156] A married couple should receive on their wedding:

For boys: The Church shall provide the following to where the groom resides

    6 Chairs and a Table

    Wall Clock

    Toaster or Toaster oven

    Coffee Maker

    Coffee Pot or Thermos

    Single Range (Efela) or Skillet

For Girls: the Church shall provide the following to where the bride resides

    8 Bath towels, 8 Hand towels, and 8 Wash Cloths

    Iron and Ironing board

    6 Laundry Baskets and 1 Pail

    6 Storage Totes (Tuckers)

    Waste basket and Scissors

    8 pc. Dinning Ware and Silver Ware

    3 pc. Stainless Steel Cookware

    300 Clothes Pins

[157] August 1st, 2012

Dear Brothers,

We greet and wish you god's love and his mercy:

The following is a report as to what was discussed and decided during the major Ministers' conference on **July 19, 2012** in the **Sturgeon Creek Church.**

Our elders and provosts seriously urged that more seriousness of purpose and enthusiasm is needed, which must be applied against the many evil doings that emerge amongst us. Too many things are being approved by us provosts; meanwhile decadence is threatening all around. We are in debt by the holy works and Holy Spirit that we search and receive. Yes, it is pure and unpolluted, without stains and wrinkles, which are from the fleshly being.

1) **Getting married to the other group.**[87] There was a lengthy negotiation as to what to do with the unChristian work written by Jakob K[88] on June 28, 2012, that is not fearful towards God. They want to take away our sisters without obeying the old fatherly—

Christian manual, which was created by the good spirit of our enlightened Ministers of our congregation. This was created on the basis of the Holy Scripture, which was established and left behind to us and practiced for over 120 Years. That they want to take away our sisters to get married to them, without proper discussion and matching, and then make them become part of another congregation. Then they want to impregnate them before marriage, which destroys the Christian baptism.

We do not want to take part in such unchristian and emotionless works, which shall also not be permitted. This mischief, they have tried to bring into the Delta [Group Two Colony] church on July 15, 2012, because they have not brought a letter, but only the writings of Jacob K. which were not accepted. It was clearly explained to them, that nothing else will happen nor be done, as only according to the community's and Christian manual. That is, to bring a letter, which is asked of them, in order to doubt with the brother and talk to the parents. If the parents then agree for the marriage to occur in a godly manner, the couple will be wedded in front of the church. The reasons were read to them from the Holy Scripture and from the old fatherly discussion book, and it was told to them, why it must be done, and that we will not change anything from it. But those six persons did not agree to these old rules. Several hours were spent with them, in order to rebuke them, but it was all for nothing, and they went home without having achieved anything. This all was observed for a lengthy period of time, and then a writing was imposed, which was read to the congregation, and also accepted by them, as follows:

If it can go according to the advice given and the approval of the parents and the congregation, and they are wedded according to Christian standards and our community manual, we will allow them to be wedded until January 1, 2013.

And then there should never be marriages between the two groups. Because we cannot find anywhere in the Holy Scripture that it should occur any different than it already states in the books written by our ancestors. Also all the [158] ministers and the great congregation were in agreement, because we do not want to take part in nor be fouled by the many evil doings and transgressions.

It shall be told to all our children and parents that **they must be matched together,** because it is the rule of God, and we cannot change anything from it. This is because when the couple is matched together they are first put openly in front of the congregation, in order for the congregation to bear witness for the fact that they are seriously being matched together. This is because it cannot be differently in a Christian marriage. And we will let nothing dissuade us from this. Let us read the revelation of John 22, 18-21, as it says: nothing shall be added nor be removed from the book that the spirit of God has imposed, but God's command is: hold what you have, that no one may steal your crown.

2) Bride and groom clothing. It was also decided in regards to the prideful, insolent, and haughty dress of the bride, who is already covered with such happiness and brilliance, and is so precious. Also the smocks and sleeves are cut out; it is almost impossible to describe it in words how inappropriate this is. And when the day comes, it is adorned with such fashion, which is against the Christian and congregational rules, and far from the true humbleness and Christian virtues. The kinds of insolent dresses some appear in is already too astonishing. The question arises: where are the parents that are the head of the house? It shouldn't go so far, that the ministers and even the old ministers must have such great worry and battle against this.

And then there are almost **white dresses (Light colored)** that are see-through, as well as long smocks, which were already previously mentioned; these are not compliant and appropriate for God's people. They should be allowed less frequently, and there must be shown more seriousness and eagerness from the ministers against those things. And soon they shall not be allowed, because it is already too much for the 'world's people' when boys and girls dress themselves with such see-through and suggestive whorish clothes. It is a shame for us that we as guardians and watchers shall be in the house of God.

It was recognized that the forbidden clothes must be put away, and the bride must show her wedding dress to the Minister, before it is completed, to avoid a big disturbance. Also a sample must be brought to the minister, so that it cannot be changed, and there is no uproar on the wedding day. Let us remember the 4th verse in the song: come you peoples children: *you look for pretty dresses and clean jewelry, how unfortunate! Your smell is full of muck, thousands of flames are colliding together, right above you, and you stay naked just as you are.* And the song #325, verses 11 & 12: *humans often show off their clothes, and are blown up in vanity; but how we receive them, not understanding and not contemplating; clothes show the sin, which we have done in Adam; we shall when we applied them, still the great case to be pondering. Christ's crimson shall alone be an emblazonment to my soul.* Verse 12: *don't you see revenge waving; that tinges from the word of God, that with trappings, with shine and make up, you that scoff the creators wisdom, and with such slight hope of magnificence make yourself hated by God?* Let us remember the devil's list, he searches with all his power to uncover, what God has covered with his mercy (his clothes), and the poor people divest themselves with such whorish clothing.

[159]

3) **Wedding invitations.** Also unbaptized boys and girls shall not be allowed to go to weddings or drive to the "Hulba" (only brothers and sisters of the married couple), which is according to the congregational rules and the Conference Regulations. Great evil doing and unbalance arises through forbidden trips, which should not be countenanced as they lead to great mischief.

4) **Pictures.** There was great debate about picture taking, which is causing much shame. But many do not think it wrong. The walls of the homes are filled with such things, and <u>family pictures</u> taken with the ministers standing freely around. Also pictures are being taken freely and insolently at weddings, which is done without fear as if no God exists in heaven. This is an abomination. It clearly states in the Ten Commandments that it is strictly forbidden to worship images of idols. We have every right to loudly complain about such principles, and to earnestly condemn these things. These are Moabite epidemics and evil doings, and that is why God the Lord gave the children of Israel to the pagans to rob them, and then God disgorged and cockled them. Also **Musical Instruments** are being permitted, as if they are allowed, which all a misunderstanding and an evil doing, which brings a worldly element into the church. And this pollutes God's holiness and causes God's love to drift from us. Where do we want to go then, and what will happen to our children, and who will carry the burden, when God takes his hand away from us and spreads us throughout the world.

Let us read Ezekiel 16, 49-52, where the prophet exclaims: "Behold, this was the iniquity of thy sister Sodom: pride, fullness of bread, and abundance of idleness was in her and her daughters; neither did she strengthen the hand of the poor and the needy. And they were haughty and committed abomination before me; therefore I took them away as I saw good."[89]

5) **Field trips for children.** Also field trips for children should never be allowed. Let us think about it, into what kind of danger do we place our children. We have left from the world, and now we lead children back into the world, busload wise, knowing how dangerous it is in the world. They can be stolen or harmed, or an accident can happen. We already stand in great danger when we leave them at home, and have the duty to check up on them frequently. At home, on our property, a small coming together can occur between children and parents, by which we can abide with our children and have a picnic together, and then we must not lead them away from the congregation.

6) **Songs by teaching and prayer before the preaching.** It was also reminded that by the teachings and prayer a song must be announced. It shall also **not be allowed to preach in English,** but it shall remain by our German language, and no one should allow themselves to take

the freedom, and act according to their will. And despite the warnings, some still continue to do so, and to think that one is wiser and smarter than their predecessors. All those that do not want to follow, shall be interrogated with great seriousness.

7) **The lost [Verloffene] and Funerals.** Also the lost shall not be allowed to come onto the property in general, nor during funerals without the permission of the Minister. Also the unbaptized [160] should not sit by the coffin, but on the right side beside the door. They must be dressed appropriately, and if they cannot behave themselves from head to toes, they should stay away.

And do not make God drift away from his holiness, so that the awful infelicity, which is the fall of the congregation that may come upon us and our children through God's punishment. More seriousness should be applied for our children to proceed in a true community. We must keep away from running with the world, and learn: "that a life with the community is Christ's cross, which we have to take upon us," and follow as Christ says in Luke 13, 24: Strive to enter through a narrow gate.

Therefore, dear brothers, let us be an example of obedience and subservience to the people, because such indulgence will already create enough discord and mischief.

So the work of the congregation goes downhill with increasing speed. Is not the colony manager [Haushalter] and minister at fault? Those that let things slip through their fingers, see mischief as not being bitter, and are party to laxity. Those that participate with music, take pictures, and have pictures standing around in homes show complete disobedience and idol worshipping, and let's thinks why Saul had such a particular ending.

Let us bring about justice in order to defend against corruption, so that God the Lord may not become tired by taking pity over us, and let us become addled; Scattering us in the world, so that our poor, innocent children run towards the evil of this world, and are seen as guilty in front of God because they have casually impeded the Lord's work. Then the innocent blood of our children is asked of us.

Let us remain in prayer to God the Lord that he may send his wisdom from above, that we have the appropriate advice and deeds to defend against horrible misery; yes, to have a Godly driving force to fight against all sin and unjustness. Even though Amaleck looked strong, and ready to fight against Israel, let us walk with Moses, and remain in prayer, and lift our hands to the lord in heaven. So must Amaleck be subdued, and then Israel will win.[90]

Andreas Ehrenpreis writes: One should always stick to the good old rules, in order for the Church to remain upright and conserved in good peace. That is because it is sealed with the blood of heroes who laid a strong solid ground, which does not need to be doubted. If we will observe and follow the steps of all the Godly and our forefathers, it will not become a disgrace to us.

Dear Brothers, fear God and hold steadfast to his cause. The reward is great. It is eternal happiness. Let us not change the goal, but let us reach for the furthest.

Let us again be greeted in love and the peace of the Lord. We wish all you servants to remain in the word.

Jacob Gross

John Waldner

Notes

1. Notduerftige.
2. The bread cutter would also be expected to serve and to keep order in the dining room.
3. *Einverleibt*, which refers to the act of being integrated into the community, similar to confirmation or baptism without water.
4. Kinderwagelen is written. Based on context it seems that the reference is to "Kinderwagen."
5. Hurerei, which literally means harlotry but refers to all extramarital sex.
6. "Schnur und Tochtermann."
7. Schindeln, lit. shingles.
8. *Fleckenschuhe* are a type of shoe with toecap ornamentation.
9. Also used as a bench seat.
10. Refers to those who serve the food and alcohol at weddings.
11. Dirne: this is an obsolete German word used to refer to a harlot, but is used in the Hutterite dialect to refer to young women generally.
12. Engagement celebration, (from the Ukrainian hul'nya – to make merry or carouse?) and also a celebration the night before the wedding; it seems similar to the *Poltera-bend* which is still celebrated in Germany.
13. Barrchens.
14. Zehrgeld.
15. The word for this is Teppich, which means "carpet" or "rug" in German but here means linoleum. The German word for linoleum is "Lino" or simply "Linoleum." (R.S.)
16. This statement was already written in English.
17. The wrong reference was cited for this verse. It was cited as 2. Phil. 2:12-13.
18. Lit. "Run the colony to seed." (R.S)
19. The correct citation for this passage is Luke 2, 9.
20. Aufgestreifelt.
21. Horn-Haar.
22. Moabitisch.
23. Osterlehr.
24. An allusion to Revelation 3:16.
25. This is an allusion to Mt. 7:13-14: "Enter through the narrow gate. For wide is the gate and broad is the road that leads to destruction, and many enter through it. But small is the gate and narrow the road that leads to life, and only a few find it."
26. Philippians 4:9.
27. Nursing mother.
28. Zimmetrinden.
29. Abgespanntes Kind.

30. Leadership, lit. "the board."
31. This heading is written in English in the original.
32. There are two paragraph headings numbered for in the original.
33. Einschuettung.
34. "rosige." I'm not sure if this means pink or floral, or even bright.
35. Psalm 37:21 states: "The wicked borrow and do not repay but the righteous give generously."
36. This is the King James Version. A direct translation of what is written in the text is more like: "It seemed good to the Holy Ghost and to us to make such ordinances."
37. The English terms are used in the original.
38. 1 Corinthians 5:6-7a.
39. 1 Timothy 2:9a.
40. Acts 15:28.
41. 1 Corinthians 11:5-6, 10, 13. In the German it is all depicted as one seamless passage.
42. Jeremiah 8:21-22.
43. Leadership, lit. "the board."
44. Vetter (Uncle) is an affectionate honorific term applied to respected elders.
45. There is no Ordnance #9.
46. Ziegelten
47. Raditschewa was a colony in Ukraine that fell apart spiritually and discontinued community of goods.
48. Jeremiah 8:21-22.
49. Isaiah 48:18.
50. Only Jeremiah 13:15 is actually quoted.
51. Romans 12:2.
52. Matt. 28:19.
53. In a romantic way, ie lovers.
54. Ausspitzen.
55. The English word is used in the original document.
56. Amt—could also refer to offices or agencies.
57. This phrase is rendered in English in the original manuscript.
58. The English word is used in the original document.
59. The English words are used in the original document.
60. This could also be translated as cuddling.
61. The English words are used in the original.
62. Literally: to cover a shameful thing with flowers.
63. This marks the beginning of the schism in the Schmiedeleut. For a full account see Alvin Esau, *The Courts and the Colonies*.
64. Or as two who are in love.
65. Verker mit einander zu haben.
66. Jakob is now spelled with a "c" —a sign of increasing Anglicization.
67. Allusion to Revelation 22:18-19.
68. "When I was a child, I spake as a child, I understood as a child, I thought as a child: but when I became a man, I put away childish things."
69. Zu recht machen.
70. "Pfantasei" literally translates as fantasy.
71. Paraphrase of Isaiah 56:10-11, 1 Samuel 15:15 is totally different, and appears to be an error.
72. This passage does not actually mention gluttons but it does mention drunkards.
73. Matthew 15:13.
74. "If a man happens to meet a virgin who is not pledged to be married and he rapes her and they are discovered, he shall pay the girl's father fifty shekels of silver. He must marry the girl, for he has violated her. He can never divorce her as long as he lives."
75. Kinder zusammen stellen.

76. And the prayer of faith shall save the sick, and the Lord shall raise him up; and if he have committed sins, they shall be forgiven him.
77. In the King James Version of the Bible, James 4:7 is: Submit yourselves therefore to God. Resist the devil, and he will flee from you. 4:8 Draw nigh to God, and he will draw nigh to you. Cleanse your hands, ye sinners; and purify your hearts, ye double minded.
78. A *janker* is a man's light jacket.
79. A Wanick is a woman's light jacket without a collar. It is used when attending church.
80. The people who work in a specific location, such as the pig barn, dairy or repair shop
81. Unfrieden, "not in peace with the community." It is the most severe sanction short of excommunication and expulsion from the colony.
82. Sirah is one of the books of the Apocrypha. It does not appear in all editions of the *Holy Bible.*
83. Pöbelvolk.
84. These songs are translated literally, word for word. [DF]
85. The words "Hockey Rings" are in English in the original document. It seems that the term "Hockey Rinks" was intended.
86. "Verloffene" is used for those who leave the colony and are lost to the community and to God. This word does not exist in the High German language, but is used in Low German, a variant of the High German word: *"Verlaufene,"* which has the meaning of 'being lost.' [DF]
87. This clearly refers to marriage between members of Group One and Group Two Schmiedeleut colonies, not to marriages between the Schmiedeleut and the Darius and Lehrerleut.
88. Jacob Kliensasser, minister of Crystal Spring Colony, Manitoba, the leader of the Group One colonies.
89. The text actually cites only verses 49–50 KJV.
90. See Exodus 17:8–16 KJV.

References

Bar-Lembach, Ruth. 1992. *A Member of the Community: Childhood and Adolescence in a Hutterite Colony and a Bruderhof Settlement in North America.* Ramat Efal: Yad Tabenkin.

Bennett, John W. 1967. *Hutterian Brethren: The Agricultural Economy and Social Organization of a Communal People.* Stanford, CA: Stanford University Press.

Boldt, Edward D. 1978. "Structural Tightness, Autonomy, and Observability: An Analysis of Hutterite Conformity and Orderliness," *Canadian Journal of Sociology,* 3 no. 3: 349–63.

——. 1989. "The Hutterites: Current Developments and Future Prospects." In James S. Frideres (ed.), *Multiculturalism and Intergroup Relations.* New York and London.

Brumann, Christof. 1998. *Die Kunst des Teilens: Eine vergleichende Untersuchung zu den Überlebensbedingungen kommunitärer Gruppen.* Hamburg: LIT.

Cash, Martin. 2013. "Hutterites Not Afraid of Change: Colonies Turn to Non-Ag Industries as Province's Hog Market Slumps." *Winnipeg Free Press,* May 29.

Chronicle of the Hutterian Brethren, The, Vol. I. 2003 (originally published in 1987). Elie, MB: Hutterian Education Committee.

——, Vol. II. 1998. Ste. Agathe, MB: Crystal Spring Colony.

Currie, Buzz. 1997. *A Red Sea Rising: The Flood of the Century.* Winnipeg: Winnipeg Free Press, 1997.

Eaton, J.W. 1952. "Controlled Acculturation: A Survival Technique of the Hutterites," *American Sociological Review* 17: 331–40.

Esau, Alvin J. 2004. *The Courts and the Colonies: The Litigation of Hutterite Church Disputes.* Vancouver: UBC Press.

Evans, Simon. 1974. "Spatial Bias in the Incidence of Nativism-Opposition to Hutterite Expansion in Alberta," *Canadian Ethnic Studies* 6: 1–16.

——. 2010. "Alberta Hutterite Colonies: An Exploration of Past, Present and Future Settlement Patterns," *Communal Societies* 30, no. 2: 27–63.

Evans, Simon M. 2013. "Some Factors Shaping the Expansion of Hutterite Colonies in Alberta since the Repeal of the Communal Properties Act in 1973." *Canadian Ethnic Studies* 45 (1–2): 203–236.

Everitt, John. 1980. "Social Space and Group Life-styles in Rural Manitoba." *Canadian Geographer* 24: 237–54.

Frideres, James S. 1972. "The Death of Hutterite Culture," *Phylon* 33, no.3: 260–65.

Freedman, Samuel, and Cameron Harvey. 1983. *Chief Justice Samuel Freedman: A Great Canadian Judge: A Collection of the Reasons for Judgment of the Honourable Samuel Freedman, Justice of the Court of Queen's Bench of Manitoba (1952-60), Justice of the Court of Appeal of Manitoba (1960-83), and Chief Justice of Manitoba (1971-83).* Winnipeg: Law Society of Manitoba.

Friedmann, Robert. 1961. *Hutterite Studies.* Goshen, IN: Mennonite Historical Society.

Gackle, Paul and Sarah Kearney. 2008. "A Day on the Colony," *Winnipeg Free Press,* September 14, B 1–3.

Garvey, John. 2013. "Reining in Religious Freedom: A Hostile Government Chips Away at the Faith-based Life." *Washington Times,* July 1.

Gross, David. 2013. *Schmiedeleut Family Record*. High Bluff, Manitoba: Sommerfeld Digital Printing Centre.

Gross, Leonard. 1998. *The Golden Years of the Hutterites*. Kitchener, ON: Pandora Press.

Gross, Paul. 1965. *The Hutterite Way: The Inside Story of the Life, Customs, Religion and Traditions of the Hutterites*. Saskatoon, SK: Freeman Publishing Company.

Harrison, Wes. 1992. "The Role of Women in Anna Baptist Thought and Practice: The Hutterite Experience of the Sixteenth and Seventeenth Centuries," *Sixteenth Century Journal* 23, no. 1: 49–57.

Hartse, Caroline. 1995. "Social and Religious Change among Contemporary Hutterites," *Folk* 36: 109–28.

Hebrew Encyclopedia. 1968. "Anabaptists." Jerusalem and Tel Aviv, Vol. 4: 298–299.

——. 1969. "Jacob Hutter." Vol. 13: 679–680.

——. 1974. "Christianity." Vol. 25: 350–354.

Hitchen, Ian. 2008. "Ex-members Slam Hutterite Colonies' Rule," *Winnipeg Free Press*, June 14.

Hofer, John. 2004. *The History of the Hutterites*. Elie, MB: James Valley Book Centre.

Hofer, Joshua. 1985. *Japanische Hutterer, Ein Besuch bei der Owa Gemeinde* [Japanese Hutterites, A Visit to the Owa Community]. Elie, MB: James Valley Book Centre.

Hofer, Rebecca. 2009. *Removing the Hutterite Kerchief*. Kelowna, BC: Collegium.

Hofer, Samuel. 1998. *The Hutterites: Lives and Images of Communal People*. Saskatoon, SK: Hofer Publishers.

Holzach, Michael. 1993. *The Forgotten People: A Year Among the Hutterites*. Sioux Falls, SD: Ex Machina Books.

Horsch, John. 1985. *The Hutterian Brethren 1528–1931*. Cayley: Macmillan Colony.

Hostetler, John A. 1974. *Hutterite Society*. Baltimore and London: Johns Hopkins University Press.

Huffman, Tammy. 2014. "First Hutterite Colony in Missouri Moves Here," *The North Missourian*, January 22.

Ingoldsby, Bron B. 2001. "The Hutterite Family in Transition." *Journal of Comparative Family Studies* 32 (3): 377–392.

Ingoldsby, Bron B., and Suzanne R. Smith. 2001. "Public School Teachers Perspectives on the Contemporary Hutterite Family," *Journal of Comparative Family Studies* 36 (2): 249–265.

Janke, Dwayne and Alan Hood. 2008. "They're Here," *Word Alive* 26, no. 3: 4–13.

Janzen, Rod A. 1999. *The Prairie People: Forgotten Anabaptists*. Hanover, NH: University Press of New England.

Janzen, Rod, and Max Stanton. 2010. *The Hutterites in North America*. Baltimore, MD: Johns Hopkins University Press.

Janzen, William. 1990. *Limits to Liberty: The Experience of Mennonite, Hutterite and Doukhobor Communities in Canada*. Toronto: University of Toronto Press.

Katz, Yossi. 1996. *The Religious Kibbutz during the Mandate Period*. Ramat Gan: Bar Ilan University Press.

Katz, Yossi and John C. Lehr. 1999. *The Last Best West: Essays on the Historical Geography of the Canadian Prairies*. Jerusalem: N.p.

Kirkby, Mary-Ann. 2007. *I am Hutterite.* Saskatoon, SK: Polka Dot Press.

Kleinsasser, Jennifer. 2006. "Graduation Address at the Oak River High School Graduation," *Preservings* 26: 89.

Koranda, Jeaninne. 2003. "Part of Ritzville Hutterite Group Is Moving to Oregon," *Seattle Times,* March 8.

Kraybill, Donald B. and Carl F. Bowman. 2001. *On the Backroad to Heaven: Old Order Hutterites, Mennonites, Amish and Brethren.* Baltimore and London: Johns Hopkins University Press.

Laatsch, William G. 1971. "Hutterite Colonization in Alberta," *Journal of Geography* 10: 347–59.

Landshut, Zigfried. 2000. *The Kvuza* (a facsimile edition of the book published in 1944). Ramat Efal: Yad Tabenkin.

Laslett, Peter. 1980. "Introduction" in Peter Laslett, Karla Osterveen and Richard M. Smith (eds.), *Bastardy and Its Comparative History.* Cambridge, MA: Harvard University Press.

Lehr, John C. 2010. "Owa: A Dariusleut Hutterite Colony in Japan," *Prairie Perspectives: Geographical Essays* 13: 30–38.

Lehr, John C., Brian McGregor and Weldon Hiebert. 2006. "Mapping Hutterite Colony Diffusion in North America," *Manitoba History* 53 (October): 29–31.

Maendel, Dora. 2006. "Hutterite Christmas Traditions," *Preservings* 26: 87.

Maendel, Liss and Ruth Maendel. 1969. "Hutterites' Reply: 'Glad to Walk His Narrow Path'," *Winnipeg Tribune* (January 9).

McGarry, Mike. 1968. "Sam Made It—On the Tough Outside," *Winnipeg Tribune* (December 28).

Meged, Aharon. 1947. "A Christian Commune in Canada," *Mibifnim*: 543–53.

Miller, Timothy. 1993. "Stress and Conflict in an International Religious Movement: The Case of the Bruderhof." Paper prepared for the CESNUR/INFORM/ISAR Conference, London, UK (March). http://www.perfound.org/tm_arch.html

Niv, Amitai. "The Residue of a Social Novelty," *Hakibbutz* 6–7 (1979): 115–30.

Oved, Yaacov. 1988. *Two Hundred Years of American Communes* New Brunswick, NJ: Transaction Books.

——. 1993. *Distant Brothers: The History of Relations Between the Bruderhof and the Kibbutz.* Ramat Efal: Yad Tabenkin.

——. 1996. *Witness of the Brethren: A History of the Bruderhof.* New Brunswick, NJ: Transaction Books.

——. 2009. *Communes and Intentional Communities in Second Half of the 20th Century.* Ramat Efal: Yad Tabenkin.

Penner, Drew A. 2013. "Brand New Colony: Hutterites Build on Soaring Metal Sales by Planning New Home," *Mountain View Gazette,* May 7.

Peter, Karl, Edward D. Boldt, Ian Whitaker and Lance W. Roberts. 1982. "The Dynamics of Religious Defection among Hutterites," *Journal for the Scientific Study of Religion* 21, no. 4: 327–37.

Peters, Victor. 1965. *All Things Common: The Hutterian Way of Life.* Minneapolis: University of Minnesota Press.

Picard, André. 2011. "When ignorance is not bliss," *Globe and Mail,* June 9, L6.

Pitzer, Donald E. 1997. *America's Communal Utopias.* Chapel Hill: University of North Carolina Press.

Preston, B. 1992. "Jacob's Ladder," *Saturday Night* 107, no.3 (April): 30–38, 76–80.

Redecopp, Bill. 2009. "Fire Trucks: Hutterite Style," *Winnipeg Free Press*, April 1.

——. 2012. "Internet No Longer an un-Hutterite Thing," *Winnipeg Free Press*, December 12.

Riedemann, Peter. 1970. *Confession of Faith* [originally published in 1545 as Rechenschaft unserer Religion]. Rifton, NY: Plough Publishers.

Rozen, Frieda Schoenberg. 1985. "The Role of Women in Communal Societies: The Kibbutz and the Hutterite Colony." In Yosef Gorni, Yaacov Oved and Idit Paz (eds.), *Communal Life: An International Perspective*. Yad Tabenkin: Transaction Books.

Ryan, John. 1977. *The Agricultural Economy of Manitoba Hutterite Colonies*. Toronto: McClelland and Stewart.

——. 1985. "Hutterites," *Horizon Canada* 2, no. 21: 494–99.

Schmiedeleut Family Record. 2003. James Valley Colony.

Schroeder, William. 2001. *Hutterite Migrations in Europe*. Winnipeg: the Author.

Shadmi, Menachem. 1985. *Communes in the World and the Kibbutz*. Tel Aviv: Sifriat Poalim.

Shalman, Shlomo. 1996. *The Niderkaufungen Community*. Ramat Efal: Yad Tabenkin.

Shealtiel, Shlomo. 1997. "The Zadaroga and the Circumstances of Its Disintegration," *Shorashim*.

Smith, Suzanne R. and Bron B. Ingoldsby. 2005. "Courtship and Moral Reasoning of Hutterian Youth," *Communal Societies* 25: 113–26.

Stahl, Solomon. 2001. *The History of Bonne Homme Colony, Manitoba*. Fordville, MB: Forest River Colony.

Stahl, Lisa M. 2003. *My Hutterite Life*. Great Falls: Farcountry Press.

The Nine. 2013. *Hutterites: Our Story to Freedom*. Kearney, NE: Risen Son Publishing.

Von Schlacta, Astrid. 2004. "Struggle for Identity and Confession. The Hutterian Brethren in the Molochna Colony, South Russia, 1842–74," *Preservings* 24 (December): 38–40.

Ward, R., J. Lehr and B. McGregor. 2007. "Graven Images of a Closed Society: The Huron Hutterite Colony, 1920s," *Manitoba History* 54: 45–50.

Worm, Shalom. 1968. *Communes and Their Way of Life*. Tel Aviv: Ayanot.

INDEX

Page numbers in **bold** refer to maps and graphs. *Plates* are located between pages 216 and 217.

C

cameras. *See* photography

Canada, Hutterites in
about, 27
demographics, 23–24, **24–26**, 27
history of, 22–23, 30, 150–51
land restrictions, 63, 151–56, 203
See also specific provinces and colonies

Carinthian German. *See* German language

cars. *See* vehicles

Cartier municipality, Manitoba, 53, 134

Castor Colony, Alberta, 55, 65*n*2, 117, 171

CD players, 22, 135–36, 211

celebrations. *See* holidays and celebrations

cell phones, 137–38, 143, 148*n*9, 211, 218, 258, 407, 412, 426
See also telephones

childbirth. *See* birth rates; pregnancy and childbirth

children
about terminology for, 251*n*2
allowances and distributions, 278, 285, 309
caregiver from birth, 169–70
demographics: family size, 27–28, 92, 169, **246**; percentage of colony, **248**
dining customs, 59, 133–34
discipline of, 98, 126, 131–32, 135, 332
family bonds, 78, 126–27, 133, 135, 166, 168–69, 207
field trips, 424, 432
funeral attendance, 270, 382, 433
gardening, 61, 135
hairstyles, 302, 317
illegitimate children, 358
in Old World settlements, 16
leisure activities, 131, *plates*

names of, 382
prayers, 77, 125, 298, 405
religious beliefs on, 92, 121
sleeping arrangements, 283, 284, 298, 330
supervision of, 110–11, 335, 356, 395
work, 111, 133, 135; for side-money, 113–14
worship attendance, 76, 197–98, 347
See also birth rates; clothing, children's; education; infants and toddlers

Christianity
status of women, 164
See also Bible; evangelical Christianity; Hutterian Brethren Church; Protestants; Roman Catholics

Christmas celebrations
about, 78–79
Christmas concerts, 280, 287, 405
Christmas trees, 79, 270
gifts, 270
special services, 77

The Chronicle of the Hutterian Brethren, 15

Church, Hutterian Brethren. *See* Hutterian Brethren Church

church buildings, 58, *plates*

Church of God, 40–45

church services. *See* worship services

citizens band radios, 321, 329, 332, 337

Clark, Bertha W., 124

Clearview Colony, Manitoba, 103

clothing
about, 67–72, 172, *plates*
approval of gifts, 272
buttons on, 68, 281
defectors' clothing, 264, 268
distinctiveness by leut, 67, 71–72

W

wakes. *See* funerals and wakes
Waldheim Colony, Manitoba, 63, 417
Waldner, Julie, 117
Waldner, Michael, 20
Waldner, Peter, 117
Walter, Darius, 20
war. *See* First World War; Second World War; pacifism
Washington, Hutterites in
 demographics, 23–24, **24–26**, 27
 history of, 152
 list of colonies by parent, year and leut, 23, 243
watches. *See* jewelry and adornment
weapons
 prohibition on, 4, 11
 punishment, 96
 shotguns for hunting, 288–89, 333, 380, 422
weddings
 alcohol use at, 145, 265, 271, 333–34, 350, 358, 373
 bride's clothing after wedding, 273
 clothing at, 303, 325–26
 gifts of alcohol, 274, 297, 308, 350, 410
 at groom's colony, 172
 guests at, 145, 212, 273, 282, 321, 382, 415, 432
 money gifts, prohibition, 424
 photos, 258, 318–19, 427, 432
 same in Canada and U.S., 282
 special features, 303; decorated cakes, 271; decorated vehicles, 391; drawings and door prizes, 412, 416; farewell parties, 381, 391; music, 198, 273; plays, 405
 wedding dresses, 172, 374, 379, 390, 431

 See also engagement and courtship; engagement party (Hulba); marriage; newlyweds
weggelufene, wecchglufne and *weccklufna,* terminology, 50*n*14
 See also defectors
Weinzedel. See farm boss/*Weinzedel*
Wellwood Colony, Manitoba, **244**
Westroc Colony, Manitoba, 59, 62, 65*n*12, 133
Whiteshell Colony, Manitoba, 103
widows and orphans, 32, 49, 264, 299
 See also death
wife, minister's, 171, 258–59, *plates*
Willow Creek Colony, Alberta, 200
Willowbank Colony, North Dakota, 103
Wilson Siding Colony, Alberta, 99*n*9
wine. *See* alcohol
Wipf, Jakob, 20
Wipf, John, 200
Wipf, Joseph, 198
Wipf, Michael, 349
Wolf Creek Colony, South Dakota, 21
women
 about roles, 160–61, *plates*
 cultural change and, 173–74
 defectors, 182, 185, 188
 diversity in, 174
 future trends, 173–74, 207
 group discussion prohibition, 425–26
 group loyalty, 166, 170
 hairstyles, 71, 293
 higher education, 128–29, 136–37, 168, 173, 195
 history of gender roles, 131, 161–65
 influence of: education, 167; elections, 164–65; generally, 164–68; kinship relations, 170;

Y

About the Authors

YOSSI KATZ IS a full professor in Geography at Bar-Ilan University, Israel. He holds the Chair for the Study of the History and Activities of the Jewish National Fund. He specializes in the modern history of Israel, Zionism, the process of Jewish settlement in Israel, and the Hutterite colonies' settlement process in North America. He has published 23 books including: *The Business of Settlement: Private Entrepreneurship in the Jewish Settlement of Palestine, 1900–1914* (1994); *Partner to Partition: The Jewish Agency's Partition Plan in the Mandate Era* (1998); *Between Jerusalem and Hebron: Jewish Settlement in the Pre-State Period* (1999, 2nd printing, 2003); *The Last Best West: Essays on the Historical Geography of the Canadian Prairies* (with J.L. Lehr, 1999); *The Religious Kibbutz Movement in the Land of Israel* (1999, 2nd printing 2003); *The Battle for the Land: The History of the Jewish National Fund* (2005); *Forgotten Property: What Became of the Assets in Israel of Holocaust Victims* (Hebrew, 2002); *The Forsaken: Israel, the Reparations Agreement and the Question of Compensation and Restitutions for the Holocaust Survivors* (Hebrew 2009).

JOHN LEHR IS a professor in the Geography Department at the University of Winnipeg. His research interests focus on the historical geography of agricultural settlement in western Canada. He is particularly interested in frontier settlement and in the processes of migration, cultural transfer and community formation by ethnic and religious groups in newly settled regions. He is author of *Community and Frontier: A Ukrainian Settlement in the Canadian Parkland*; co-author (with David McDowell) of *Trailblazers: The Lives and Times of Michael and Muriel (Smith) Ewanchuk*; and co-author (with Yossi Katz) of *The Last Best West: Essays on the Historical Geography of the Canadian Prairies*.